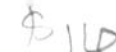

GOLDEN HOURS

The Paintings of Arthur J. Elsley
1860-1952

Dedicated to the memory of
Marjorie Wheatley (1903-1997)
whose dream it was to have this book
published in testament to her father

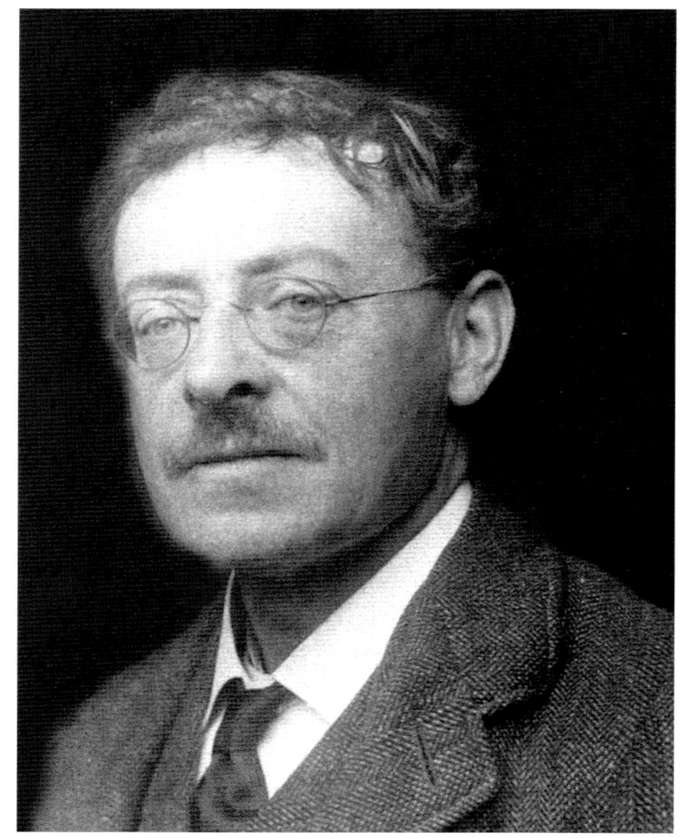

Arthur J. Elsley, c.1900.

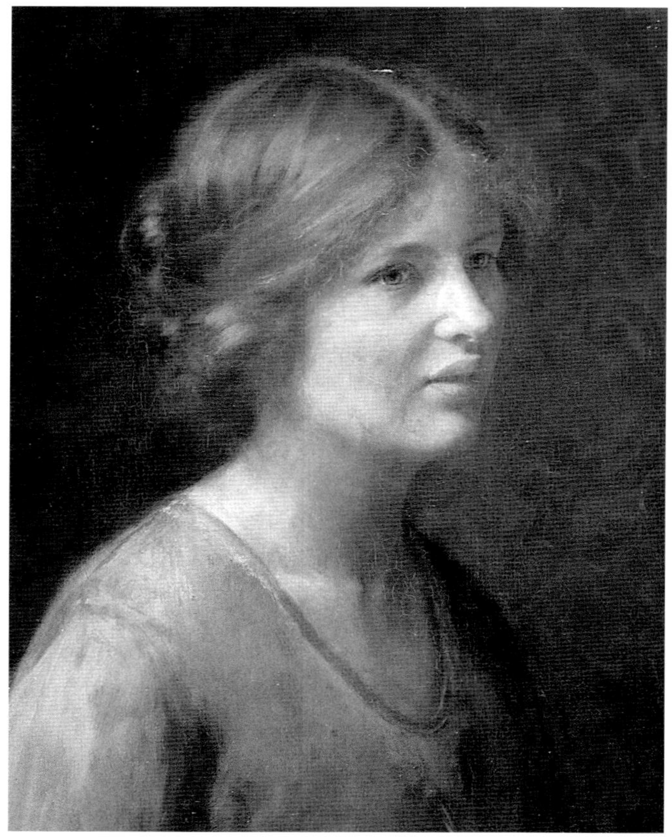

Marjorie Elsley, 1923, painted by her father. **See page 131**.

GOLDEN HOURS

The Paintings of Arthur J. Elsley 1860-1952

Terry Parker

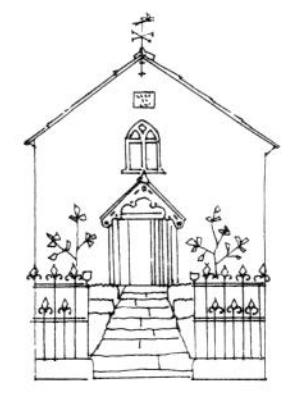

RICHARD DENNIS
1998

ACKNOWLEDGEMENTS

My gratitude to Kate Sims, a close friend and companion of the late Marjorie Wheatley née Elsley, for her invaluable assistance and to Marjorie herself whose generous help has made this book possible.

I would like to thank the following individuals for their help in the compilation of this book: Celia Bailey; Andrew Barlow, Royal Pavilion Art Gallery and Museum, Brighton; Lesley Barnes; Melanie Barrett; David Beevers, Preston Manor, Brighton; Martin Beisley and the staff of Christie's, London; Edward Bentley; Stuart Biellik; Mark Bills, Russell-Cotes Art Gallery and Museum, Bournemouth; Jenni Bissett; Susan Chapman, Head of Administration, The Royal Liverpool Children's Hospital; Jan Clark; Gary Collins, Unilever Historical Archives; Dorothea Conti; Simon Edsor, The Fine Art Society; Elizabeth Farrow, Dodo Designs; Constantinas Francos, Christie's Inc., New York; Dr. Catherine Gordon, Director of the Witt Computer Index; Sandra Gore; Veronique Gunner, Sotheby's, London; Karen and Steve Heney; Jane Holland, formerly of Christie's, London; Jo and Nigel Jackson; Elizabeth Law, Hartlepool Museum Services; Nick Lee, University of Bristol Library; Robin MacDougall; Bettie McKenzie, Project Director, The People's Art Project, Red Oak Public Library; Ross Milne; Sophie Money, Phillips, London; Edward Morris, Walker Art Gallery, Liverpool; Joan O'Brien; Robert Opie, The Museum of Advertising and Packaging, Gloucester; Lesley Owen-Edwards, Unilever Historical Archives; Jeremy Rex-Parks, Archivist, Christie's, London; David Roe, Felix Rosenstiel's Widow & Son Ltd; Joseph Sharples, Walker Art Gallery, Liverpool; Lyn Siddle; Dr. Alan Smith, Fine Art of Oakham; John and Cherry Stephens; Jeanette Strickland, Unilever Historical Archivist; Clive Watson; Vince White; Ruth Wood; Zahd Zaqub.

I am indebted to the staff of the following libraries, auction houses, companies and institutions: J. Bibby & Sons; Bonhams, London; The British Library; The British Library Periodicals Division, Colindale; The Courtauld Library; Croydon Reference Library; The Fine Art Society; The National Art Library; Nottingham Reference Library; The Royal Academy Library; St. Bride's Printing Library; The Art and Design Library, Westminster; The Witt Library.

I would like to thank the following for their help and the use of their photographs and images: Robert Barham; The Bridgeman Art Library, courtesy of the Russell-Cotes Art Gallery and Museum; Eileen and Steve Burton; Mr. and Mrs. Alexander Chiger; Christie's, London; Christie's Inc., New York; Hartlepool Museum Services; Martin Ham; Tony Haynes, Haynes Fine Art; Dave Kay; Ian Lynch; Mrs. Meath-Baker, The Medici Society; John Noott Gallery; Wallace Nutbrown, Thomas Ross and Co; Shirley and Jan Pesik; Phillips, London; Howard Rehs, The Rehs Gallery, New York; Dr. Alan Smith, Fine Art of Oakham; Pat and Tim Smith; Kath and Mick Smith; Sotheby's, London; Sotheby's Inc., New York; Sotheby's Sussex; Odon Wagner Gallery, Toronto.

Edited by Sue Evans

Print, design and reproduction by Flaydemouse, Yeovil, Somerset

Production by Wendy Wort

Published by Richard Dennis, The Old Chapel, Shepton Beauchamp, Somerset TA19 OLE, England

ISBN 0 903685 57 4

British Library Cataloguing-in-Publication Data. A catalogue record for this book is available from the British Library.

CONTENTS

GLOSSARY OF TERMS

R.A:	Member of the Royal Academy.
Chromolithograph:	Most of the colour prints were chromolithographs, popularly known as chromos. Up to twenty-two separate plates were used to achieve the richness of colours.
Photogravures:	The other popular form of high-quality reproduction, also known as mezzogravures. A photograph was taken of the painting through a fine mesh and this image was transferred to the printing plate leaving fine dots. Usually printed in sepia ink but sometimes in black.
Photolithograph:	Modern printing process which replaced chromolithography. First used to reproduce Elsley's work in about 1902.
Crystoleum:	A photographic image is stuck onto the inside of a piece of convex glass and coloured by back painting. These are now highly collectable.
Studio Sale:	In 1989 Elsley's daughter, Marjorie Wheatley, decided to sell his remaining works. On 1st October 1989, thirty-seven years after his death, a Studio Sale of 71 paintings, in 23 Lots, was held at Sotheby's, Sussex.
Print sizes:	The sizes given are for the image only.
Titles:	All 'adopted' titles are in square brackets.

FOREWORD

My interest in Arthur Elsley's work began in 1989 when I attended his Studio Sale which was held thirty-seven years after his death. Later, in July 1993, I had the good fortune to acquire his own collection of prints. Elsley is now known as a *chocolate box* artist – a dismissive term for those painters whose work, in the opinion of their critics, is merely commercial. However, at the time they were painted, Elsley's pictures were not used to decorate confectionery boxes but hung at the Royal Academy alongside those of his illustrious contemporaries. In 1933, Cadbury's Chocolate commissioned paintings from many famous artists including Dame Laura Knight, Mark Gertler, Ernest Proctor, Arthur Rackham, Edmund Dulac, Dod Proctor, C.R.W. Nevison, Philip Conrad, G. Sherringham and Arthur Watts. Many of these were, like Elsley, also scoffed at in later days.

Elsley's paintings are highly sentimental, idealised depictions of everyday Victorian life – a far cry from the harsh realities of the lives of many – but those who ignore his work are missing its social insights. His works were incredibly popular. Prints produced from his paintings had runs of up to half a million and were more familiar to the average late-Victorian and Edwardian family than any other painter's work of the period. During his lifetime, his pictures were reproduced as prints, crystoleums, calendars, advertising show-cards, postcards and in numerous books and magazines – very much the mass media of their day. The prints were considered ephemeral and, as the cost of framing was high, many were simply fixed to the wall with drawing pins then torn down and discarded when the following year's print or calendar was acquired.

Many late-nineteenth century painters used photography – a far more common practice than is generally realised as it saved the extra expense of models sitting day after day – and, in Elsley's case, this provided the realism and captured 'the moment' he was looking for. He then glamorised the setting by substituting the dirt floor or the wooden plinth with a middle-class interior or the grounds of a stately home.

The locations of the original artwork for many of his popular works are unknown. Where possible I have used a photograph of the original painting but most are reproduced from the artist's personal collection of prints. I have included all the paintings and prints I know of, but have excluded exhibits that I cannot, as yet, identify. Elsley's ouput was so prolific that it is impossible to produce a fully comprehensive list of all his works.

Arthur Elsley's daughter, Marjorie Wheatley née Elsley, was his principal model and lived with him for much of her life. I spent many happy days with Marjorie and am indebted to her for her invaluable and generous help in researching this book. Her reminiscences brought his work to life, and access to numerous photographs of his studio and models, together with other, related material, provided me with a rare and privileged insight into the life and work of this important artist.

Sadly, Marjorie died on the 2nd August 1997. It had long been her ambition to find a publisher for her beloved father's work and I am delighted that the wealth of information she shared with me has now made this possible.

T. P

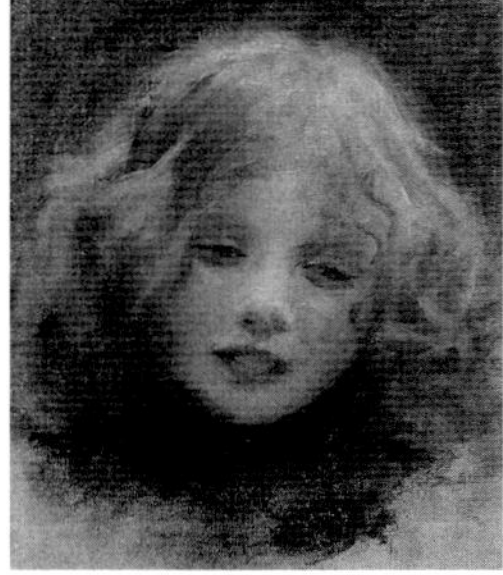 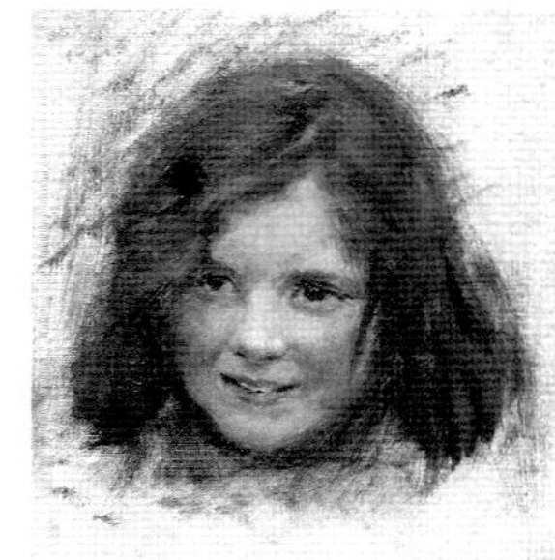 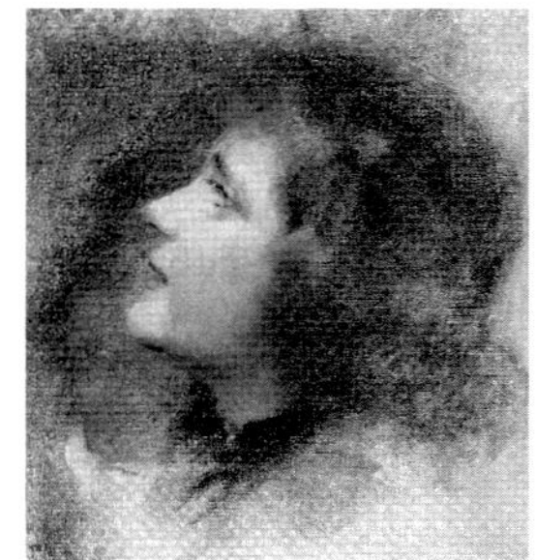

Small oil sketches sold at Elsley's Studio Sale.

INTRODUCTION

Arthur John Elsley was born on the 20th November, 1860 at 10 Derby Street, just off Curzon Street between Hyde Park and Green Park, Mayfair. He was the son of John Elsley, a coachman, and Emily née Freer, and the fifth of six children, (three sisters and two brothers). His father, was an amateur artist who had exhibited an oil painting entitled *A Group of Horses* at the British Institution Exhibition, 1845. The onset of fibroid phthisis in about 1872 led John Elsley to retire as a coachman and take up a post as resident caretaker to a firm of stockbrokers at 12 Angel Court, London, opposite the Bank of England and the London Stock Exchange.

Young Elsley's earliest surviving work is a very proficient pencil sketch of *Vic*, a cairn terrier drawn in 1871 when Arthur was eleven years old. In 1874 he visited the Zoological Gardens in Regents Park, as had many

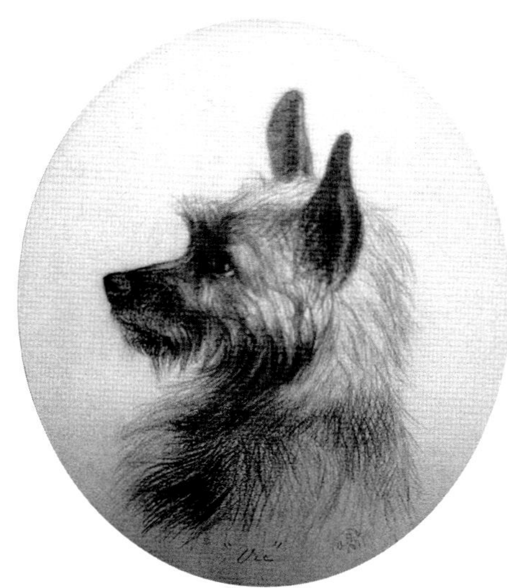

Vic, 1871.

artists before him, and made excellent pencil sketches of a chimpanzee, a giraffe and an arctic wolf. These drawings, together with similar ones of farm animals, are likely to have formed part of the portfolio he submitted, when he was fourteen, to gain entry to the South Kensington School of Art, later to become the Royal College of Art. *Pearson's Magazine*, April 1898, p.347, writes that "his father was a talented amateur, so that much sympathy and no opposition was offered to his choice of career". It was at this time that Arthur contracted measles which permanently damaged his eyesight.

In December 1876 he became a probationer at the Royal Academy Schools where his tutors were Frederick Pickersgill (1820-1900, Keeper of the Royal Academy

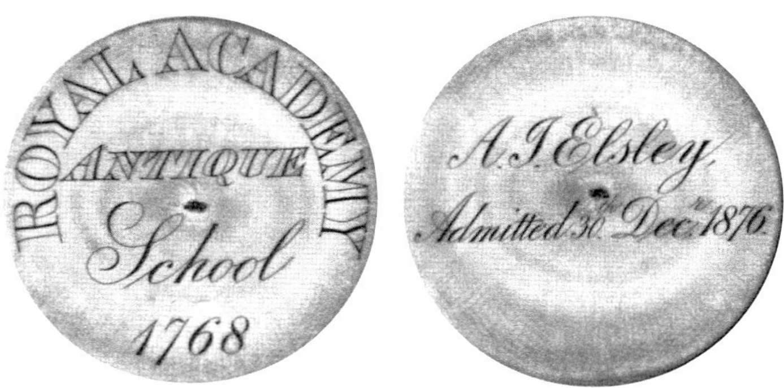

Elsley's Royal Academy bone.

1873-1887); Edward Armitage (1817-1896, Professor of Painting 1875-1882); John Marshall (d.1896, Professor of Anatomy 1873-1890); and Henry Bowler (1824-1903, Professor of Perspective 1861-1899). Sir Francis Grant was President of the Royal Academy until his death in 1878 and was succeeded by Frederick Leighton, later Lord Leighton.

Each student was issued with a cross section of animal bone engraved with their name and used as an entry pass to the school. Elsley's classical Royal Academy schooling is very evident in the diagonal compositions of his paintings. In his first year he copied J.F. Herring Senior's *Three Horses Watering* which then hung in the National Gallery. A later interview in *Pearson's Magazine*, April 1898, p.347, recorded "the discovery of an early effort of his, faked to the appearance of an old master; but this he declares is by no means an uncommon experience with artists."

Elsley's first Royal Academy exhibit in 1878 was entitled *Portrait Of An Old Pony* (No.600) and this was the only exhibit seen by his father as he died less than a month

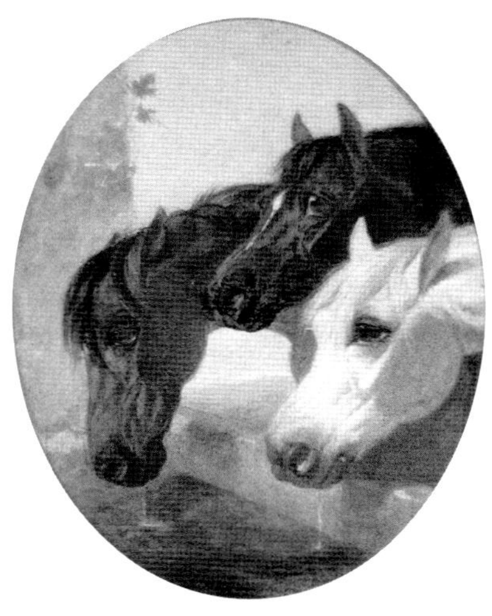

Elsley's copy of J.F. Herring Senior's *Three Horses Watering*, 1877.

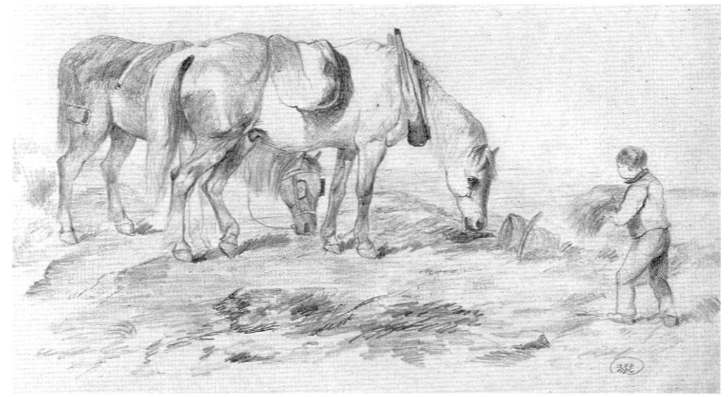

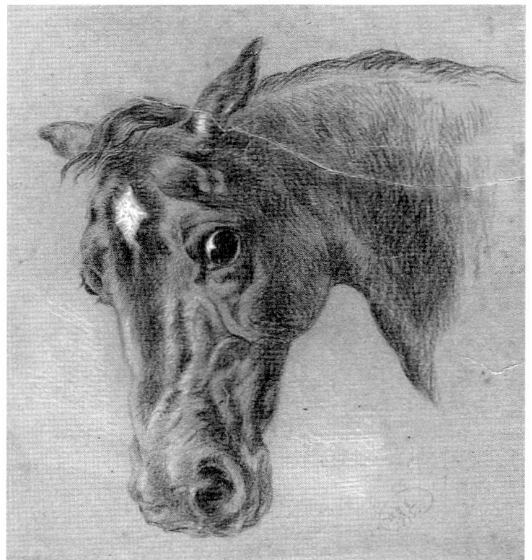

Pencil sketches, 1871.

later. At seventeen and as the eldest son, Arthur took over as head of the household.

Elsley was a keen cyclist and his daughter writes of his sketching expeditions "imagine him on his penny farthing bicycle setting off on a fine spring morning...to breathe the clean fresh air of the countryside", "Arthur J. Elsley The Children's Artist" by Marjorie Wheatley, *This England*, Winter 1981, p.15. While at the Academy Schools he joined a group of his fellow students, most likely including his friends Solomon Joseph Solomon (1860-1927) and George Grenville Manton (1855-1932) for a tour of Belgium and Northern France around Rouen.

In 1880 his second Royal Academy exhibits *Spring* and *Autumn* (No.631) were hung high above Val Prinsep's *The Imperial Assemblage at Delhi* which took up nearly the whole of the east wall of Gallery VII. After leaving the Royal Academy Schools in 1881/2 Elsley earned his living from portrait commissions of children, horses and dogs. One of his canine portraits was entitled *Punch And Carlo*, 1885, oil on canvas, 36ins x 28ins (91.5cm x 71.5cm).

His early exhibits were primarily domestic equestrian. Other works were commissioned by the Benett-Stanford family who lived at Preston Manor, near Brighton, Sussex. The first, a portrait of their dog *Jim*, was painted in 1880 while Elsley was still a student. *Ellen Benett-Stanford On Her Horse Congress* was painted in 1885, and one of her husband, *Vere Benett-Stanford*, was exhibited at the Royal Academy in 1886, followed by another of him in 1888. Elsley continued to paint canine portraits for the family throughout his career, including *Pickle* 1893, *Kylin* 1917, and *Chu-Ki* 1927. Many of these works are still exhibited in Preston Manor which is open to the public.

Arthur was twenty-four years old when his first known published work was printed in the boy's magazine *Young England*, No.43, April 1885. This was a black and white line engraving, $16^{1}/_{2}$ins x 9ins (42cm x 23cm), entitled *April Floods In The Eastern Counties* – the inscription reads "drawn by" indicating the original was either a black and white pen and ink drawing or a water-colour. Floods regularly featured in magazine articles and illustrations of this period.

By 1887, Elsley was sharing a studio at 151 Gloucester Road, Kensington, with fellow, former Royal Academy student George Grenville Manton who made his living from portrait painting and had exhibited at the Academy since 1880. Manton's most popular work, *The House That Jack Built*, was reproduced as a colour chromolithograph by *Black and White Magazine* in 1898. He also painted *The Royal Academy Conversazione 1891* which still hangs at the Academy.

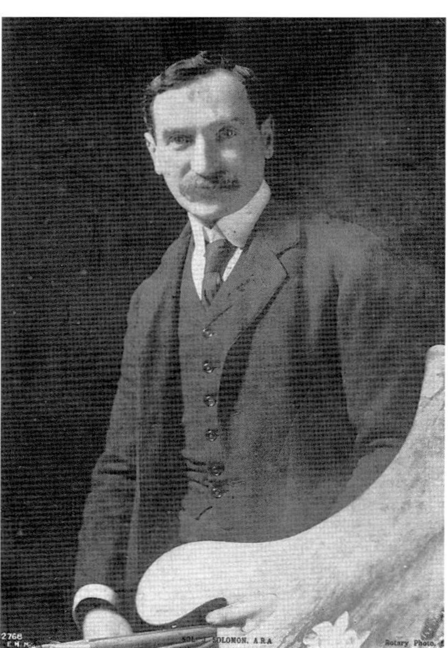

Solomon J. Solomon (1860-1927).

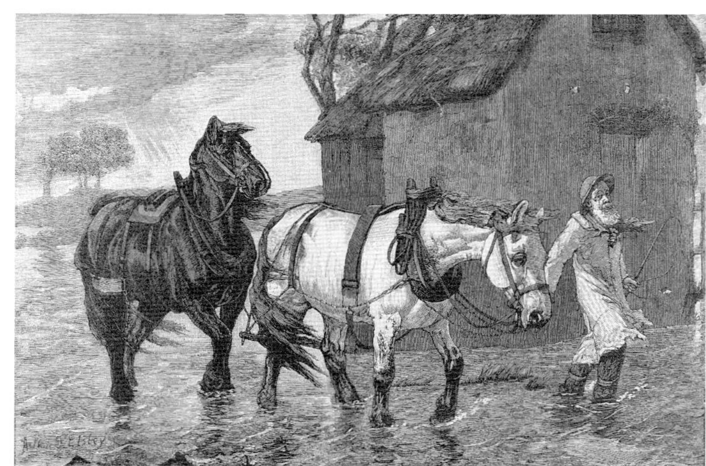

April Floods In The Eastern Counties, 1885.

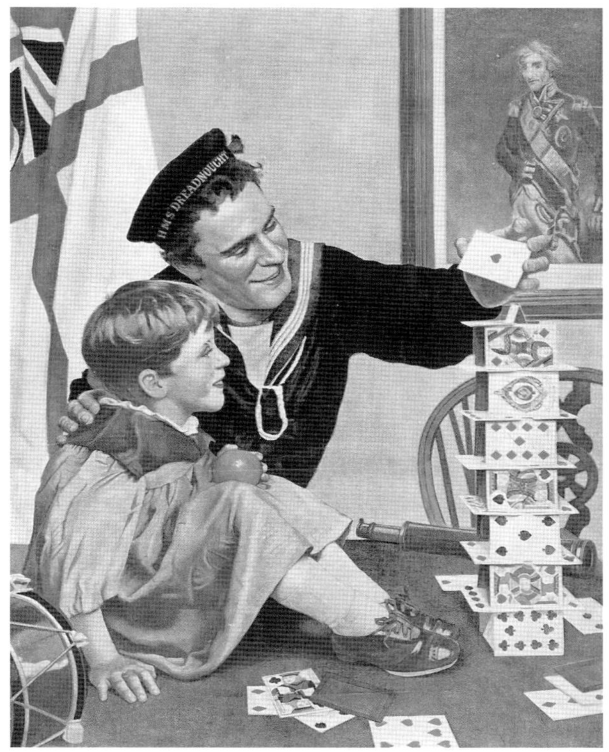

The House That Jack Built by George Grenville Manton.

Manton introduced Elsley to the artist Fred Morgan (1847-1927) and, when Manton decided to quit the studio in 1889, Elsley shared Morgan's studio in the grounds of 7 North Bank, St. John's Wood while continuing to live with his mother and siblings in Angel Court. Morgan's career was in a state of flux following the scandal of his divorce from the artist Alice Havers (1850-1890), together with the only partial success of the change in subject matter of his paintings. Sharing the studio proved mutually advantageous. Morgan, already a successful artist, had a problem painting animals and in the past had collaborated with Allen Sealey (1850-1927) a specialist in canine portraits – a role now fulfilled by Elsley.

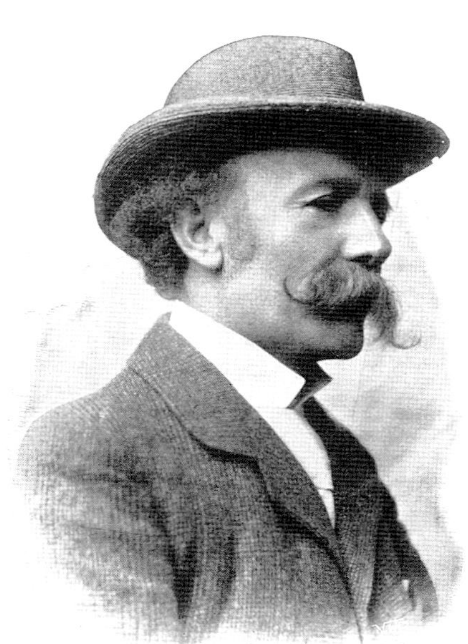

Fred Morgan (1847-1927).

In the Crystal Palace Exhibition of 1891 Elsley won a silver medal for *The Baliff's (sic) Daughter of Islington* a 40ins x 50ins (102cm x 128cm) oil painting which he had exhibited in the previous year's Royal Academy Exhibition (No.563). The success of the print *I'se Biggest*, 1892, which was so popular that it had to be re-engraved, and the prestigious *The Illustrated London News'* choice of *Grandfather's Pet* as their Christmas print, meant he was able to afford to marry his second cousin Emily (Emm) Fusedale in November 1893. She was ten years his junior and the eldest of three, her sisters were Amy and Rose. Like John Elsley, her father, George, was a coachman. She and Amy had modelled for Arthur for at least ten years – the latter was the girl in *Castles in the Air*, Royal Academy 1888 and *A Good Samaritan*, Institute of Painters in Oil 1889.

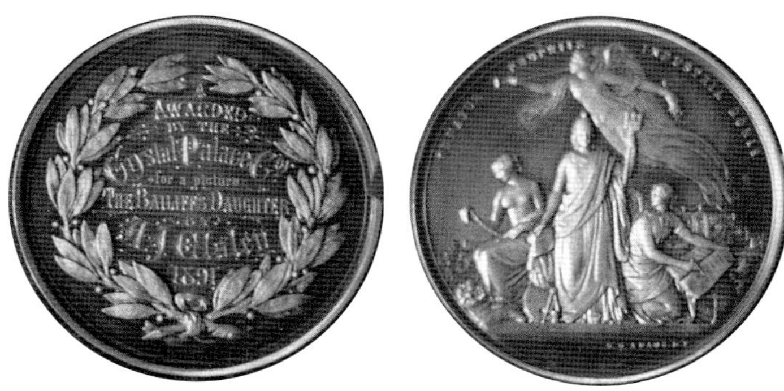

Crystal Palace medal, 1891.

Emm and Arthur were married on the 11th November 1983, at St. Thomas's Parish Church, Portman Square, London W.1., and rented a home at 28 Finchley Road, St. John's Wood. Elsley now had a studio to himself. Despite the move, the interplay of ideas and compositions, together with the use of the same models, indicates a continued co-operation with Morgan.

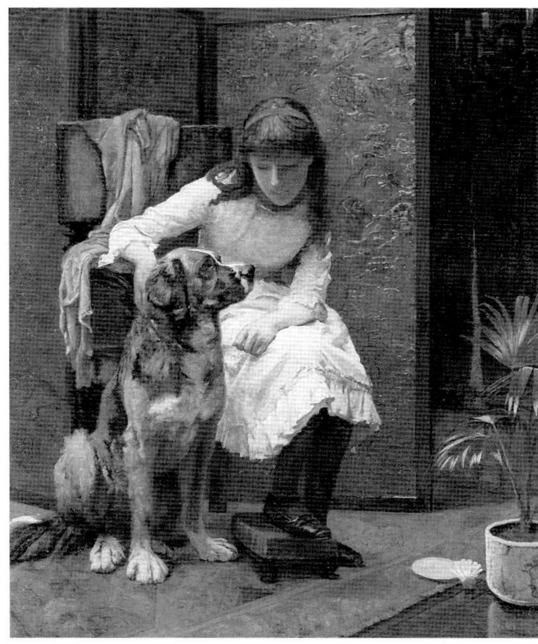

Private And Confidential, Royal Academy, 1885. Oil on canvas, 30ins x 25ins (76cm x 63.5cm). One of the Fusedale sisters was the model.

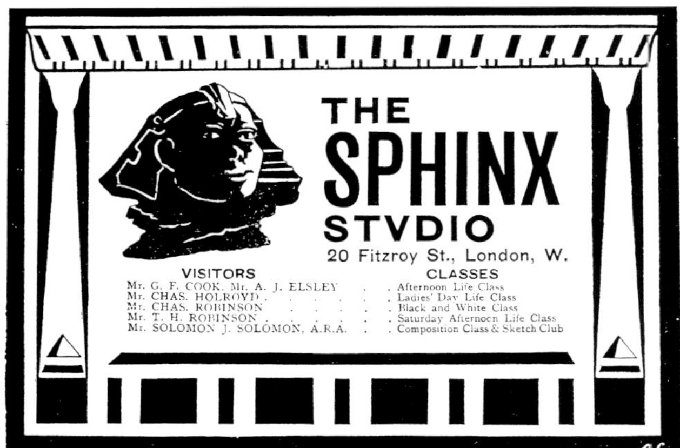

Advertisement in *The Studio*, 1898.

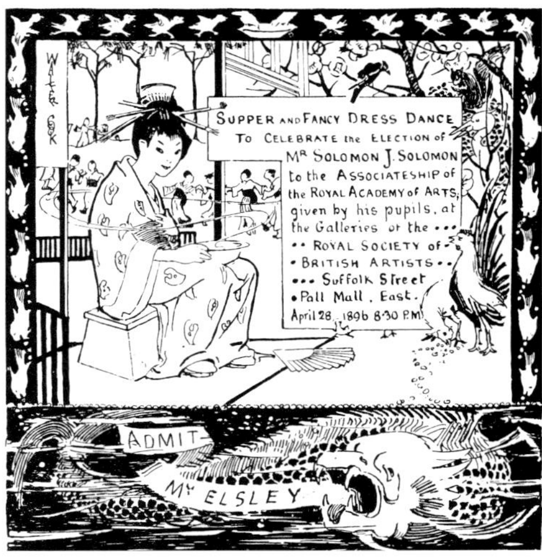

Elsley's invitation to Solomon J. Solomon's party.

In 1894 half of the villas in North Bank were demolished to make way for the Central Electric Light Company's generator which was needed to power the new railway and station at Marylebone. Number 7 remained, but the area around was a huge building site which even disrupted the nearby Lords cricket ground. Both artists continued to use the studio in the garden but neither lived there. Morgan remarried in July 1890 and moved to Blenheim Gardens, Willesden Green. The house was then rented to York Stephens, the actor and theatre manager.

When the artist Charles Burton Barber died in 1894, Elsley took over his mantle as the foremost exponent of paintings featuring children and pets. Barber had spent much of his later career painting for Queen Victoria at Osborne House, her summer home on the Isle of Wight. *The Illustrated London News*, 25th January 1896, p.120, observed:

"Mr. Elsley appears more distinctly as a follower, though not an imitator, of Mr. Burton Barber, differing from him by allowing his children more than one pet at a time, and going beyond the limitations of a fox-terrier or a collie. He has a keen sense of humour, especially in his treatment of puppies' backs, which, as students of dog-life well know, are their most expressive features."

Solomon Joseph Solomon, with whom he had become friendly at the Royal Academy Schools, was elected an Associate Member of the Royal Academy in 1896 and Elsley was a guest at his celebratory fancy dress party given by his pupils at the Royal Society of British Artists, Suffolk Street on the 28th April. Two-and-a-half years later,

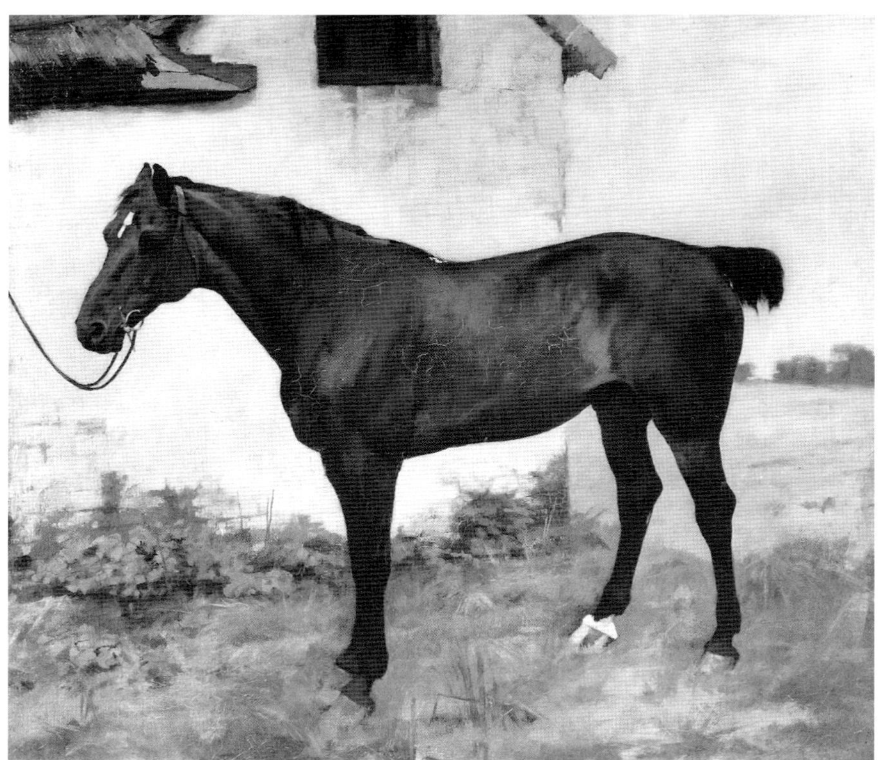

Early equestrian oil painting.

Solomon opened his studio at 20 Fitzroy Square, Bloomsbury as The Sphinx Art School. Arthur and George Frederick Cook (exhibited 1879-1898), Charles Holroyd (1861-1917), Charles Robinson (1870-1937) and Thomas Heath Robinson (1869-1937) were asked to act as visiting tutors. The school was advertised in *The Studio* magazine but was a short-lived venture.

Those who influenced Elsley's art include George Stubbs, Sir David Wilkie, John and Fred Morgan, Emile Munier, Briton Riviere, Charles Burton Barber, James Yates Carrington, George F. Cook and the publisher Charles William Faulkner. Elsley was a great admirer of Constable's landscapes, Rembrandt's use of light and shade, and the work of Graham Petrie (1859-1940).

Amongst the many artists influenced by Elsley were: Isaac Snowman (1874-c.1919), George Sheridan Knowles (1863-1931), Davidson Knowles (exhibited 1879-1902), Arthur Drummond (1871-1951), William Henry Gore (1880-1920), Walter Hunt (1861-1941), Fannie Moody (1861-c.1940), Ernest Walbourn (exhibited from 1890, d.1927), Leyton Brook, William Edward Frank Britten (1848-1916), Bernard Fuguod, and Emile Vernon (1872-1920).

At the turn of the century Fred Morgan's family moved from Willesden Green to Upper Norwood in South London, which was too far to commute to North Bank and the studio was vacated. Meanwhile Arthur and Emm leased 26 Queen's Road (now Queen's Grove) in St. John's Wood. It was likely to have been around this time that Morgan accused Elsley of using one of his ideas and the two men became permanently estranged.

Arthur set about more adventurous, multi-figured works on a grander scale. He built these up like a jigsaw, using oil sketches and photographs together with the child and canine models in the studio who sat individually, and were not in the studio at the same time. For pleasure he loved to paint landscapes but these were rarely exhibited. Some of these were incorporated into the outdoor works, while other settings were taken from photographs of gardens in his collection of bound volumes of *Country Life* magazine. Works were composed and painted in the studio and this accounts for some of Elsley's problems with perspective, not helped by his short-sightedness which sometimes caused him to use opera glasses in order to see his models!

Arthur and Emm's only child, Marjorie, was born on the 24th August 1903. Photographs, together with Elsley's paintings of her, show that she bore an uncanny resemblance to a model he had used a few years earlier who might possibly have been the child of one of his siblings or, perhaps, one of Emm's sisters. Marjorie's birth saw the start of a golden period of highly successful paintings featuring his daughter in a variety of situations and settings.

The Great War was to have a dramatic effect on his output of paintings. Extract from "Arthur J. Elsley The Children's Artist" by Marjorie Wheatley, *This England*, Winter 1981, p.15:

> "During the First World War he worked part-time at munitions and, because of his skill in being able to file accurately to a thousandth of an inch, he was given the exacting task of filing the jigs used to test gun-sights in the making."

His short-sightedness was ideal for such work but it put additional strain on his eyes and made it difficult for him to paint. He produced just three commercial works in 1915, none in 1916, and his only Royal Academy exhibit in 1917 was a portrait of Marjorie which was not for sale.

Elsley continued to enjoy painting for pleasure despite his failing eyesight and even exhibited at the Royal Academy as late as 1927. This work, *An Italian Garden, Casa Leoni, Bergamo* (No.384) was painted in 1926. Elsley organised a holiday-exchange of his London home with a villa in Italy and painted at least six other oils on this trip.

In 1928/1929 the family took holidays in Royal Tunbridge Wells, staying in Calverly Park Crescent, and in 1930 Elsley purchased 28 Madeira Park, a large three-storied Victorian house. His last known painting was a local landscape *Path Through Wood, Frant To Eridge Road*, signed and dated 1931. Following this, his eyesight became so poor that he contented himself with woodwork, metalwork and gardening.

Arthur Elsley died at his home in Tunbridge Wells on 19th February 1952, aged ninety-one. He was cremated at Brighton Crematorium and his ashes scattered in the Garden of Remembrance. Emm lived for a further eight years and died on the 3rd February 1960, aged eighty-eight. Thirty seven years after his death a Studio Sale of 71 paintings (in 23 Lots) was held at Sotheby's, Sussex, on 1st October 1989.

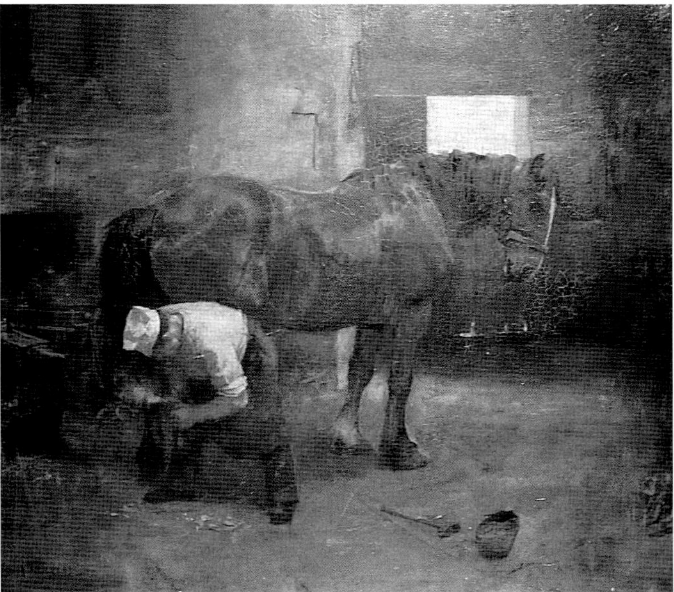

A Smithy, Institute of Painters in Oil Colours, winter 1887, 30ins x 33.5ins (76cm x 85cm).

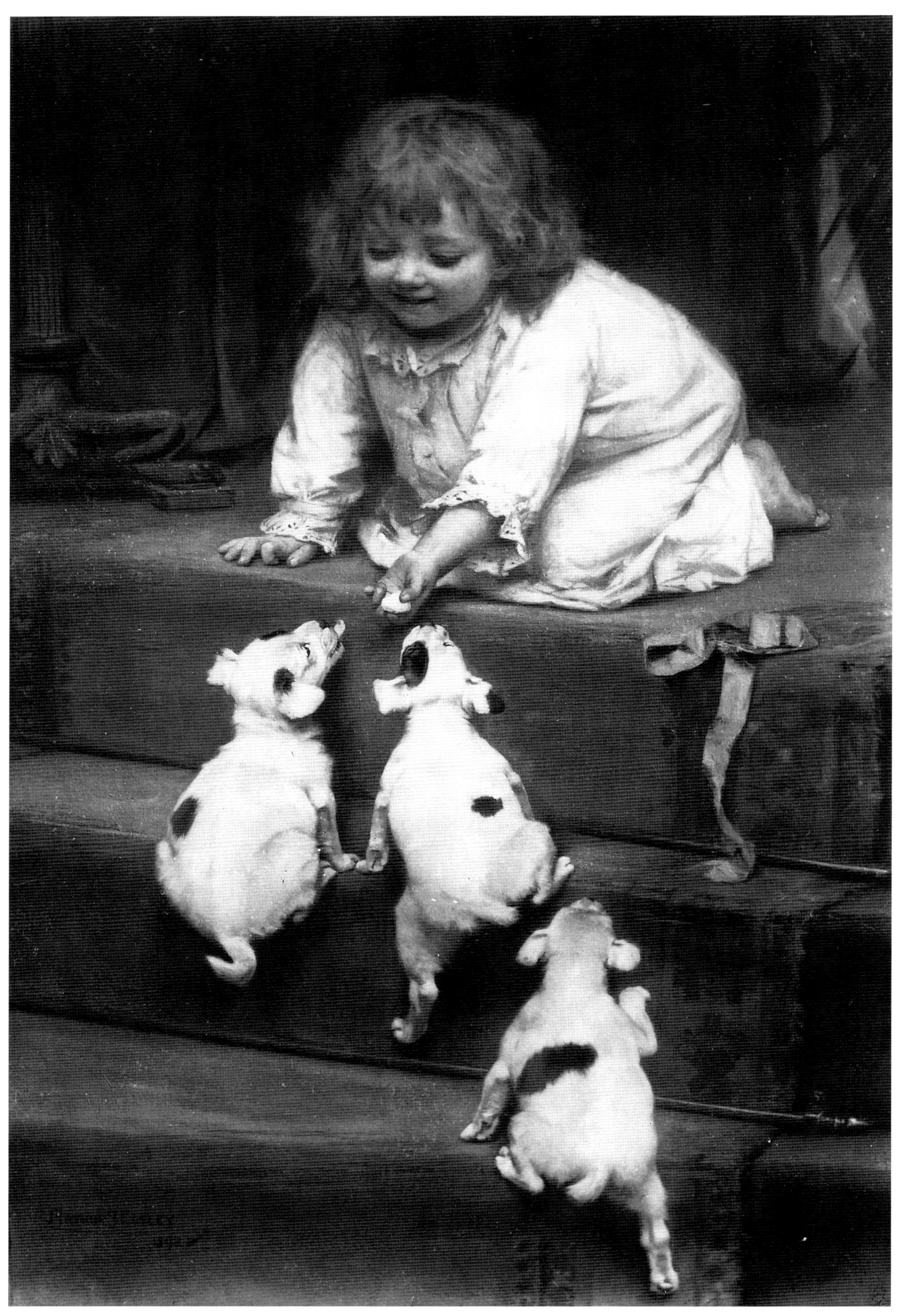

A Dead Heat. **See page 21.**

THE PAINTINGS & PRINTS

Assisted Education *circa 1889*

Details of original painting unknown.

The style of this painting is fairly crude and the cats are poorly drawn in comparison to the excellent feline studies in later works. In 1887 George Grenville Manton introduced Elsley to his friend, Fred Morgan. Morgan was thirteen years Elsley's senior, and a very successful artist. A brilliant child portraitist but a poor painter of animals, Morgan was working on his Royal Academy exhibit of that year entitled *Playmates* and Elsley offered to paint the kittens in this work.

The same ginger-haired girl and kitten appear in Morgan's *Come Under The Mistletoe* colour chromolithograph presented with *The Penny Illustrated Paper*, Christmas 1888.

Reproduced as a colour chromolithograph presented with the *Pictorial World*, Christmas 1887. Colour chromolithograph, 17¾ins x 25½ins (46cm x 65.5cm), presented with *Pictorial World*, 31st October 1891.

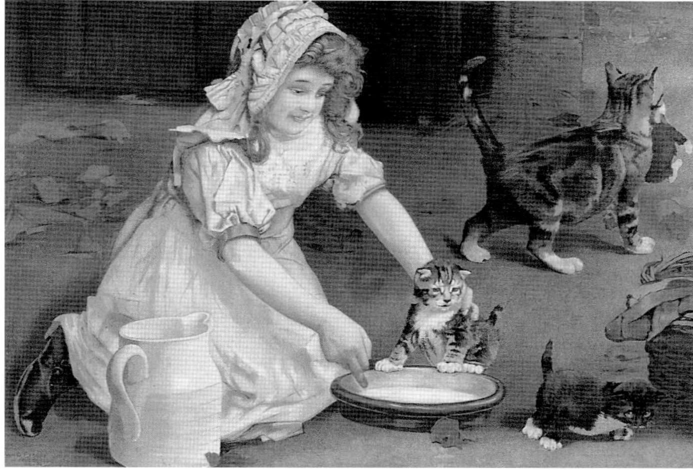

Assisted Education

Ruff Play *circa 1889*

Fred Morgan and Arthur J. Elsley

Oil on canvas, 26ins x 36ins (66.5cm x 91.5cm), signed by Morgan and Elsley. Once owned by Rehs Galleries, New York, who called it *Ruff Play*.

In this work Morgan painted the girl (who featured in many of his canvases c.1888/9 and Elsley's previous work) and Elsley the two terriers, which he also painted in Morgan's work of a girl on a tree seat eating strawberries with an attentive boy dressed as a sailor. This painting is influenced by John Morgan's (Fred's father) last Royal Academy painting *The Order Of The Blue Ribbon* which was posthumously exhibited in 1886.

Unrecorded as a print. **See page 54**.

A Tug Of War *signed and dated 1889*

Details of original painting unknown.

In 1889 George Granville Manton gave up the studio he shared with Elsley and it was agreed that Elsley would move into Morgan's studio in the grounds of 7 North Bank, St. John's Wood – the artist's quarter of London. This proved to be a turning point in Elsley's career and advantageous to Morgan who was going through a personal crisis over the divorce from his first wife, the artist Alice Havers. Elsley often cycled on his penny farthing to Mitcham, Surrey, an area famous for its lavender fields and this work was possibly painted there.

Published as a colour chromolithograph frontispiece in *The Child's Companion*, January 1891 and 1915 and also used for the cover of the same publication in 1909.

Unrecorded as a print

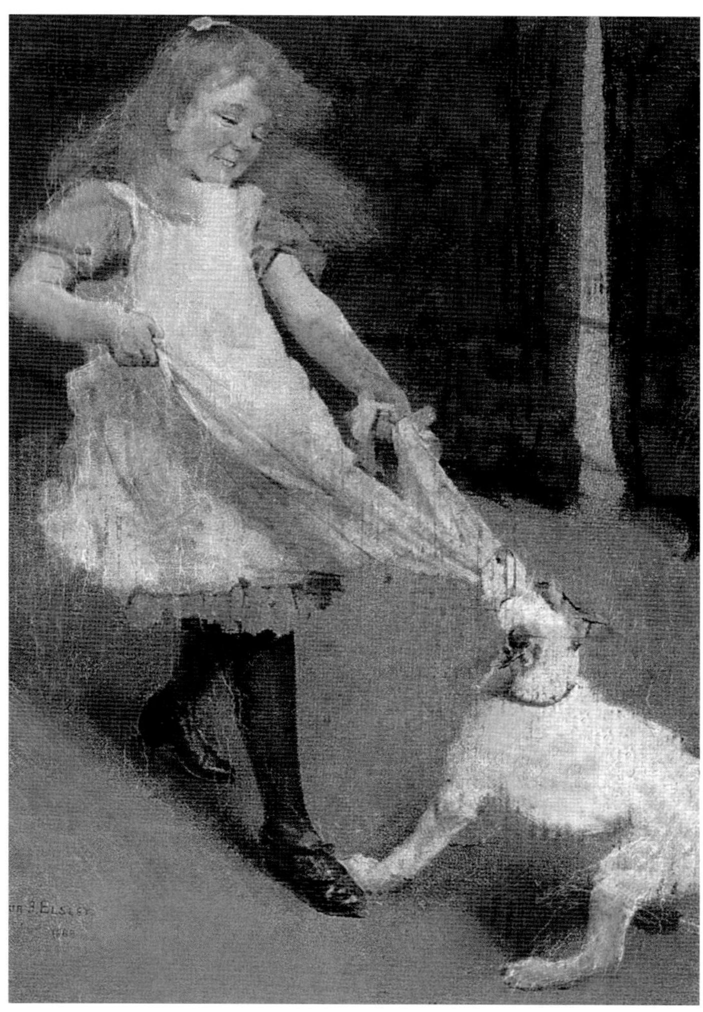

A Tug Of War

Hold Tight *circa 1890*

Fred Morgan

Oil on canvas, 50½ins x 38¼ ins (129cm x 97cm). This was Fred Morgan's 1891 Royal Academy exhibit (No.541), priced at £300. It either sold before the exhibition or was unsold. The same title was exhibited at the Corporation of Manchester Gallery in 1890 (No.292).

Elsley was originally a highly skilled equestrian painter and his talent is evident in his painting of the horse. Morgan had seen Elsley's work, *A Siesta*, featuring the same old grey mare, exhibited at the Institute of Painters in Oil Colours in 1889 (No.515). In 1883 Morgan was a founder member of this institution which was to become the Royal Institute of Oil Painters in 1909. Elsley's oil painting, 29½ins x 24½ins (75cm x 62.5), was auctioned at his Studio Sale (Lot 26).

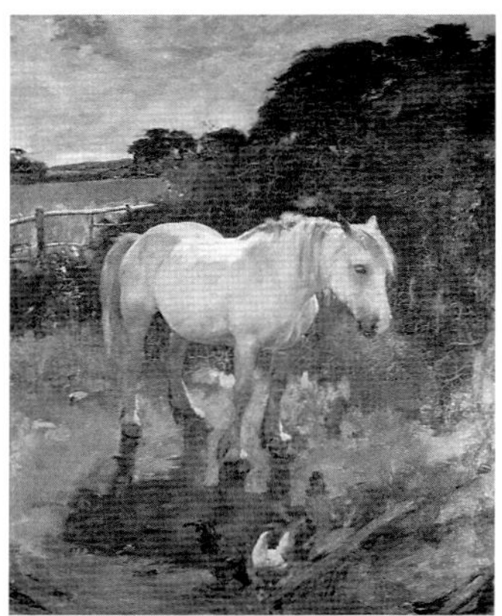

A Siesta

First reproduced as a medium size photogravure (publisher unknown), then in 1908/9 as a sepia photogravure, 13¼ins x 9ins (33.5cm x 23cm), obtained by collecting six coupons issued weekly with *Mother and Home or Home Chat Magazine*.

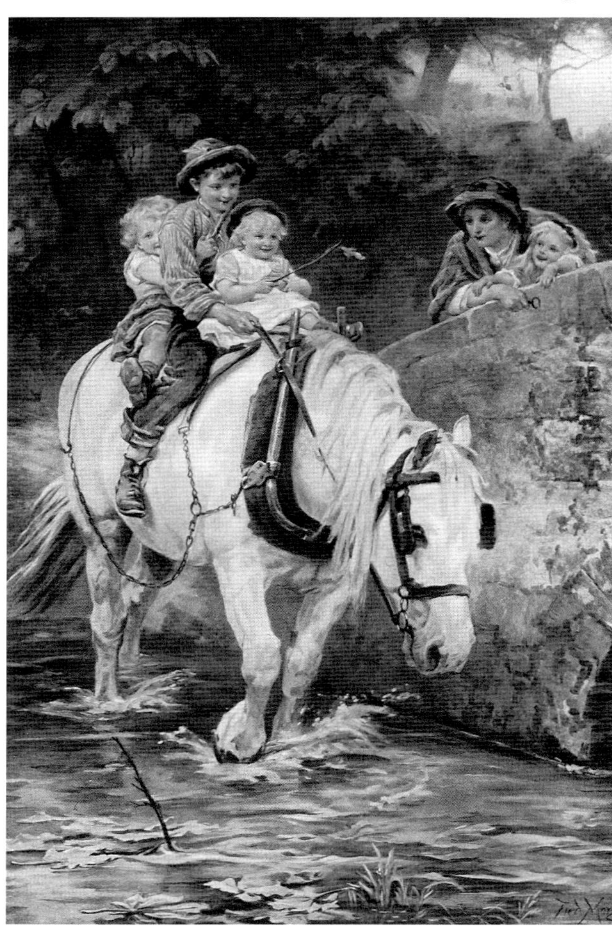

Hold Tight by Fred Morgan.

An Unwilling Partner *signed and dated 1890*

Oil on canvas, 30ins x 25ins (76.5cm x 64cm). Exhibited at the Royal Academy in 1890 (No.1043) and sold for £150.

Elsley was influenced by the popular canine artist and Royal Academician, Briton Riviere whose earlier painting, *Victims*, also shows a girl dancing with a terrier. Extract from "Pictures of Children" by Fred Dolman, *The Lady's Magazine*, September 1901, p.218:

> "It was as an equestrian portrait painter that he began his professional career twenty years ago. Then he happened to paint *An Unwilling Partner* – a little girl dancing with a big dog – and the unexpected and extraordinary success of this picture sealed his fate".

Extract from "The Children's Season" by Rudolph De Cordova, *The London Magazine*, December 1904, p.626:

> "Why shouldn't I join together the children, horses and dogs? thought Mr. Elsley one day. He did; and the outcome was the first subject-picture from his brush, *An Unwilling Partner*, representing a little girl dancing with a puppy. It was sent to the Royal Academy Exhibition. It was accepted. It was hung. On the private-view day it was bought. On the opening day the lucky purchaser sold the picture for considerably more than he had paid for it.
>
> That picture determined Mr. Elsley's career as a painter of child-life; and a career for which he was particularly suited, for he has an intense love for children. He has often been heard to say it would be impossible to paint children if the artist did not love them."

Either these articles are inaccurate because he painted *A Tug Of War* in 1889, or he started this work in 1889 and didn't complete it until the following year. This was Elsley's most successful work to date and the first to sell for a three figure sum. It was also described in *Royal Academy Notes*, 1890, p.123 as "A little girl teaching a dog to dance".

Sepia photogravure produced by J.T. Grover & Co., Nottingham. Colour chromolithograph presented with *The Penny Illustrated Paper*, Christmas 1891. *The Illustrated London News* "Notes on the Christmas Numbers", 5th December 1891, p.726, says of this print "A formidable rival in the affection of the children is the coloured plate of the *Penny Illustrated Paper* – Arthur G. (*sic*) Elsley's *Unwilling Partner*." Black and white photograph in *Royal Academy Notes*, 1890, p.123 and *Royal Academy Illustrated*, 1890, p.116. Black and white sketch in *The Illustrated London News*, 10th May 1890, p.593. Colour chromolithograph frontispiece, *Our Little Dots*, Vol.14, 1900, incorrectly titled *Come And Have A Game*, copyright J.T. Grover, Nottingham.

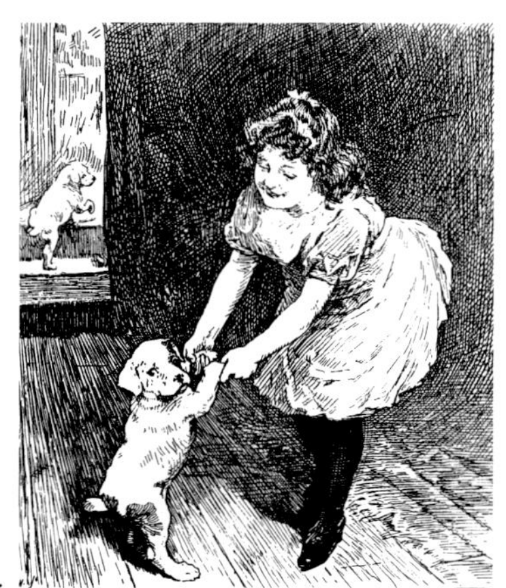

Sketch for *An Unwilling Partner*.

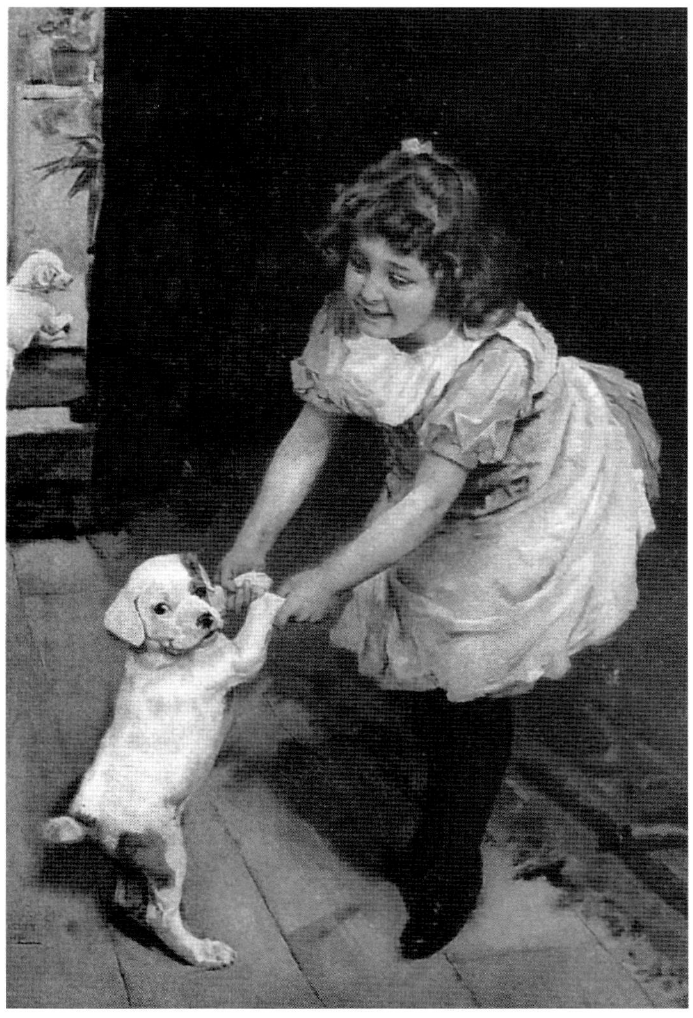

An Unwilling Partner

More Frightened Than Hurt *signed and dated 1890*
Oil on canvas, 30ins x 20 ins (76.5cm x 51cm). Exhibited at the Institute of Painters in Oil Colours, 1890 (No.559). Elsley exhibited two works at this exhibition whilst Morgan only showed *Don't Tumble* (No.480).

The puppy is the same as in *An Unwilling Partner*, 1890. Many years later Elsley told his daughter how the noise of the parrot house had driven him mad! This painting is not to be confused with *Just In Time*, c.1897-9 which was retitled *More Frightened Than Hurt* when published in *The Child's Companion*, 1905, and as a calendar in 1913.

Unrecorded as a print. **See page 60**.

Early Risers *signed and dated 1890*
Oil on canvas, 25ins x 29½ins (64cm x 75cm). Exhibited at the Institute of Painters in Oil Colours, 1890 (No.661). Also exhibited at the Bath Victoria Gallery's Autumn Exhibition, 1900 (No.83). It was loaned by George Woodiwiss, the leading force in founding the Gallery and Chairman of its Committee. He was a Justice of the Peace, Liberal Councillor and Mayor of Bath in 1897. His fortune was made as an engineer, and he acquired a very large art collection. Woodiwiss died in October 1906.

Elsley would have been familiar with the popular print of John Everett Millais' *Awake*, Royal Academy, 1867, which also features a young girl sitting up in bed. Elsley's reworking of this painting entitled *Surprised*, c.1893, was published as a Pears print in 1915 and renamed *The Invaders*. **See page 49.**

The picture was reproduced as a colour chromolithograph page in *The Child's Companion*, 1892 (opposite p.102).

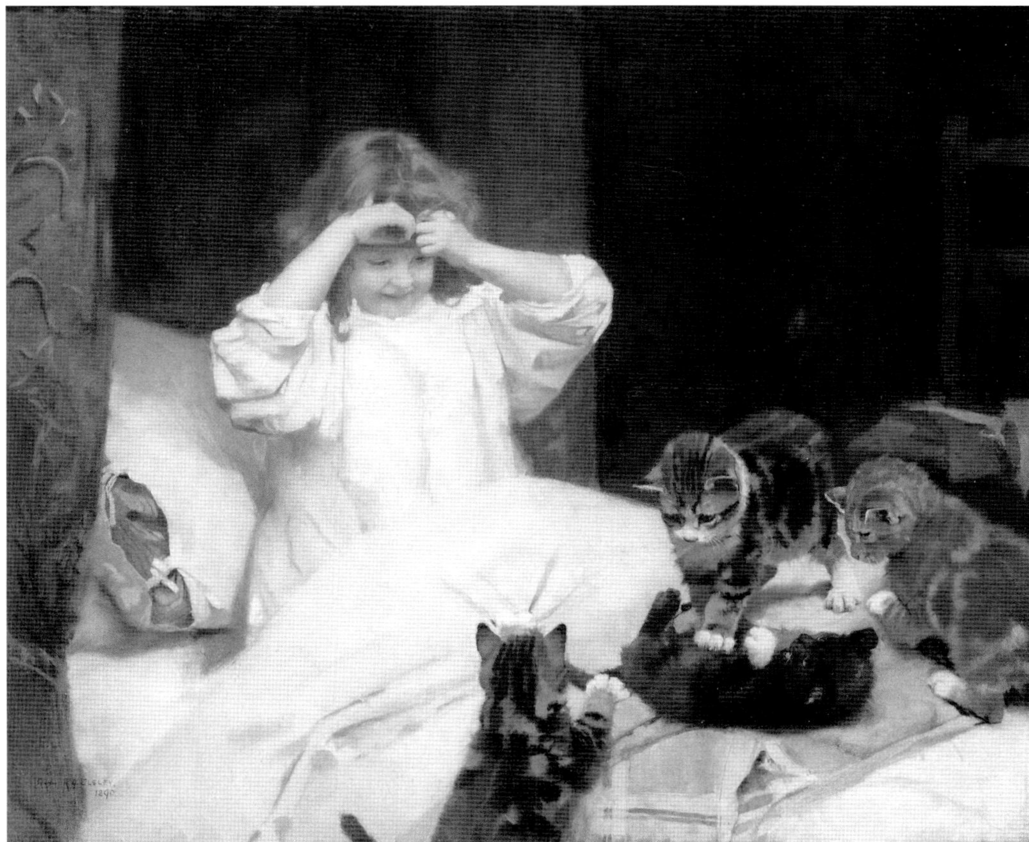

Early Risers

Victims *circa 1891*

Oil on canvas, 37ins x 44ins (94.5cm x 112cm). Exhibited at the Royal Academy, 1891 (No.1156), priced £250 but was unsold.

Elsley, yet to perfect the skill to paint kittens, used the theme of Briton Riviere's work, *Victims*, Royal Academy, 1889, to develop *An Unwilling Partner* and he adopted the same title for this picture.

The Illustrated London News, 23rd May 1891: "Mr. Arthur J. Elsley's *Victims* (1156) – not altogether to be pitied." Black and white photograph in *Royal Academy Notes*, 1891, p.134 and *Royal Academy Pictures*, 1891, p.115. Black and white line drawing reproduced in *The Illustrated London News*, 23rd May 1891, p.683. *Royal Academy Sketches*, 1891, p.88.

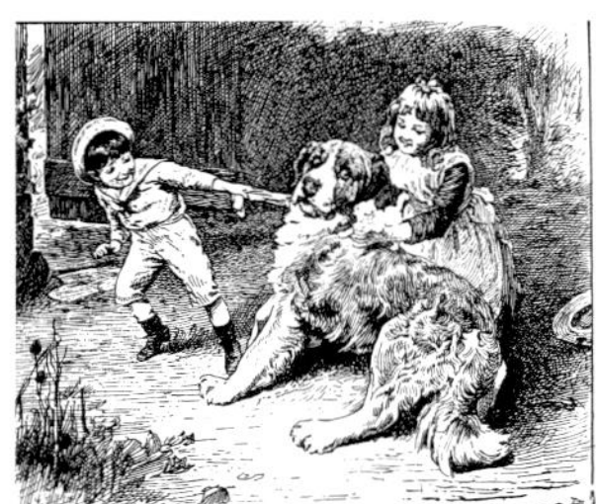

Sepia photogravure, copyright J.T. Grover & Co, Nottingham. **See page 49**.

Happy Days / The See-Saw *signed and dated 1891*

Oil on canvas, 34¾ins x 28¾ins (88.5cm x 73.5cm).

The subject of this work is a timeless children's pastime and is featured in numerous paintings throughout the centuries.

Colour chromolithograph, 21¾ins x 17¾ins (56cm x 46cm), entitled *Happy Days* presented with *The Penny Illustrated Paper*, Christmas 1893. **See page 50.**

Go Away, Sir! *signed and dated 1891*

Oil on canvas, measuring 28ins x 23½ins (71.5cm x 60.5cm). Owned by the Odon Wagner Gallery, Toronto, in August 1996.

This is the only Elsley work to feature a pug. Not to be confused with an *Ivy Soap Advertisement* painted in 1897, or *Before the Bath*, 1900.

Colour chromolithograph, 17ins x 13¼ins (43cm x 33.5cm) presented with *The Ludgate Monthly*. In the print a copy of the magazine has been superimposed top right on a pillar. **See page 60**.

The Garden Of Eden *circa 1891*

Fred Morgan

Oil on canvas, 29ins x 18½ins (74cm x 47.5cm), bought by the printer and publisher J.T. Grover & Co., of the Eagle Works, David Street, Carlton Road, Nottingham. Thomas Barratt the proprietor of Pears, and Joseph Grego the editor of the soon to be published *Pears Annual* were looking for suitable paintings to reproduce in their maiden issue. In October 1891 Grover sold it to Pears for £94 (including £35 copyright). Pears sold it in 1909/10 but the purchaser is unknown. The painting was likely to have been exhibited at the Institute of Painters in Oil Colours, Winter 1890 (No.480) entitled *Don't Tumble!* and again at the Corporation of Manchester Gallery, 1891 (No.296) where its catalogue price was £80. Grover probably bought it at the latter exhibition for reproduction as a print, but sold it to Pears in return for the contract to produce the same. The profit from such a large printing contract (about 300,000 copies) was as great as publishing the print itself.

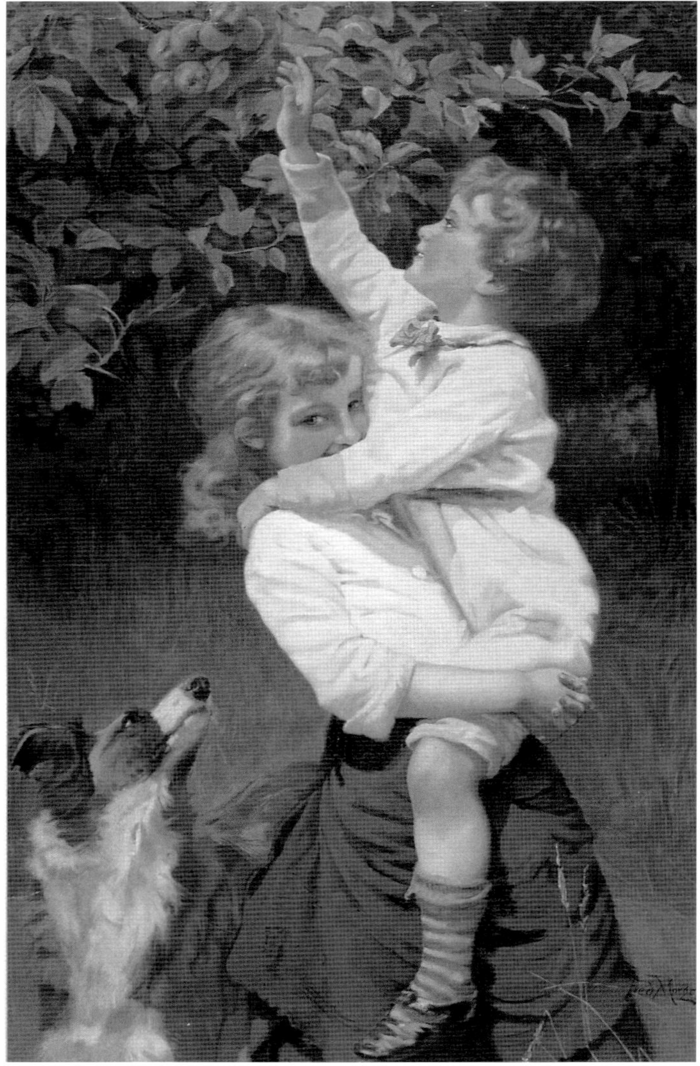

The Garden Of Eden by Fred Morgan.

In this Morgan work Elsley painted the collie, his pet dog, which also featured in his own works *Don't Tell* and *Grandfather's Pet*, both painted in 1892.

Colour chromolithograph, 28ins x 17½ins (71.5cm x 45cm), was presented with the first *Pears Annual 1891*.

The Captain and His Crew *circa 1890*

Fred Morgan

Details of original painting unknown.

Elsley painted the dogs. This painting gives the view from the opposite end of the boat to Morgan's Royal Academy 1891 exhibit, *A Willing Hand* (No.442).

Colour photolithograph, 9¼ins x 6¾ins (23.5cm x 17cm), *Horner's Penny Stories*, 4th April 1914, copyright unknown.

Now For The Baby Dogs *circa 1891*

Fred Morgan

Details of original painting unknown.

The same puppies as in the previous work were again painted by Elsley.

Large sepia photogravure produced by Birn Brothers Fine Art Publishers, London. Colour chromolithograph presented with *Father Christmas*, 1891 (an annual children's magazine from *The Illustrated London News* stable). This issue of the magazine was so popular that all three print runs were sold out by mid-December. Sepia photogravure, 17ins x 11ins (43cm x 28cm), copyright *The Illustrated London News*. Proof prints @ 1 guinea, advertised in *The Sketch*, 1901.

The Bath – His Turn Next! *circa 1891*

Fred Morgan

Oil on canvas, 34½ins x 24½ins (88cm x 62.5cm). Pears bought the work from J.T. Grover & Co., in May 1892 for £150 and it now hangs in The Lady Lever Art Gallery, Port Sunlight, Liverpool.

Another dog painted by Elsley. The bar of soap is actually painted directly onto this picture, unlike most works where the printer added the advertising onto the printing plates.

Black and white line engravings of this work appeared in magazines c.1895 and were reproduced in colour in various publications including the back cover of *The Gentlewoman*, and *Pears Annual 1915*. Also produced as a show-card illustrated in *Modern Advertising*, 2 Vols, Pitman, 1926, p.541.

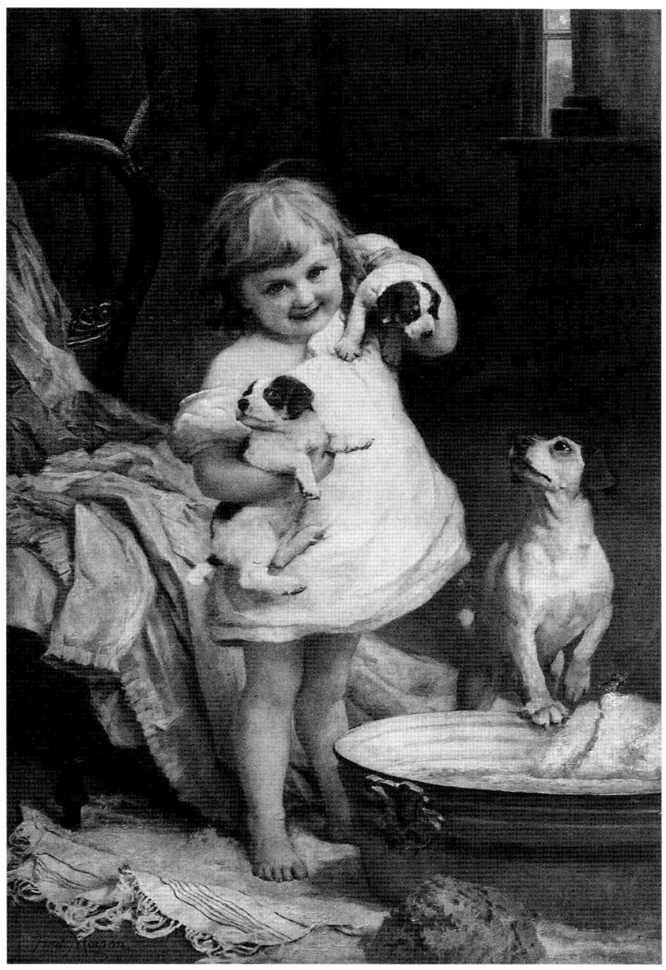

Now For The Baby Dogs by Fred Morgan.

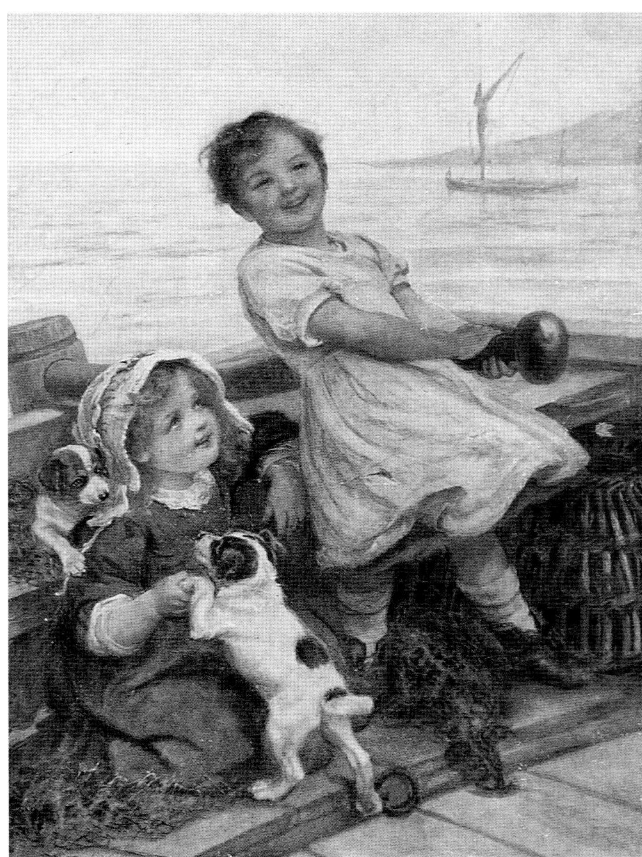

The Captain And His Crew by Fred Morgan.

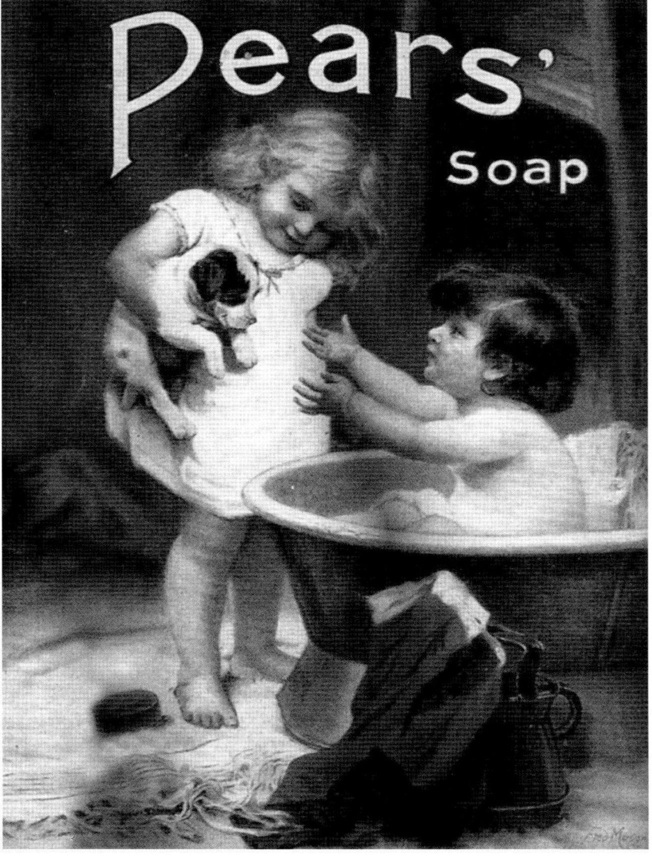

The Bath – His Turn Next! by Fred Morgan.

Doubtful Kindness *circa 1891*

Details of original painting unknown.

Colour chromolithograph page, 9ins x 6¾ins (23cm x 17cm), in *Boys* magazine, Vol.1 No.2, 1982. **See page 51.**

Shake Hands! / In Children's Happy Hour *circa 1890*

Details of original painting unknown.

The composition is very like Morgan's *Wild Roses*, Royal Academy, 1889 (No.137).

Colour chromolithograph book page, 10ins x 7½ins (25.5cm x 19cm), image 8ins x 6ins (20.5cm x 15cm), called *Shake Hands! A New Year's Greeting*. Possibly titled *In Children's Happy Hour* when reproduced as a print in the U.S.A. **See page 54**.

Don't Tell *signed and dated 1892*

Oil on canvas, 32ins x 24ins (81.5cm x 61.5cm). Exhibited at Royal Academy, 1982 (No.135), priced £120 but unsold. Auctioned as *Conspirators* by Sotheby's, London, in 1974.

This painting features Elsley's own dog. It illustrates an article from *Children's Annual* entitled "Bobbie and Laddie" with a black and white trimmed version, date and signature removed, reads "From a Drawing by Arthur J. Elsley. By permission of Messrs. E.W. Savory, Ltd":

> "Most little boys and girls have brothers and sisters to play with. But Bobbie had only Laddie. Bobbie was quite little and Laddie was extremely big, – but such a kind dog! One day when Bobbie and Laddie were playing together, Bobbie broke a plate he had been told not to touch. First Bobbie cried, with his face buried in Laddie's hair, – because he was so frightened. Then he began to wonder how he could explain to his mother. And at last he said, 'Laddie! I shall say you did it!' Laddie looked at him with large sad eyes. 'Yes,' continued Bobbie, 'so you did. Just as much as me, anyhow. I daresay it was *all* your fault. Naughty dog!' Laddie sighed gently. And then in came mother. 'I heard a crash,' she exclaimed. 'Surely you haven't broken my plate?' Laddie hung his head and looked very guilty and miserable. He seemed just as if he were saying, 'Yes, I broke it, and I expect a beating. Don't blame Bobbie. It's all my doing.' And Bobbie began to say, 'It's Laddie's fault!' But he never got that far. He suddenly turned and flung his arms round Laddie and said, 'Dear old dog! it wasn't your fault at all!' Then Laddie licked his arm: and Bobbie sat down on the floor and told his mother. 'You'd better send me to bed!' But she kissed them both. She said, 'I had rather see friends keep true to each other than have all the plates in the world!"

Poor-quality black and white photolithograph, 21½ins x 16ins (55cm x 40.5cm), calendar signed and dated 1892, copyright Berlin Photographic, and printed by Maclure, MacDonald & Co., Glasgow, with a poem entitled *Be Sure and Don't Tell*. Poor-quality colour chromolithograph, 23¾ins x 17¼ins (59.5cm x 44.5cm), presented with *Yuletide* magazine, 1893, copyright Cassell & Co. Black and white photolithograph, 8ins x 6ins (20.5cm x 15cm), printed 1901, now copyright Raphael Tuck.

Be Sure and Don't Tell

Dear doggie, console me, see what we have done!
Perhaps you and I will both pay for our fun;
And look at the pieces! why were we so rash?
How the whole thing came down – what a terrible smash!
Do you know of a doctor who mends dishes well?
When mother awakens – be sure and don't tell!

How happy we were, you and I doggie dear,
While we played in the garden with nothing to fear!
There were no broken dishes to cause us such pain;
I wish we were both in the garden again!
Do you hear, doggie, somebody ringing the bell?
Perhaps it's police – be sure and don't tell!

The men at dear father's can join things with lime;
How would that do could we both find the time?
Have you heard of a glue, or something like that?
Just feel how my heart goes all pit-ity pat!
Did you notice how quickly the whole affair fell?
Don't tell, darling doggie – be sure and don't tell!

Have you got any money? perhaps it could do
Some wonderful things for me and for you;
I have sixpence upstairs, but that's nothing at all
To mend all those pieces we've broken so small.
Dear doggie, our trouble is coming pell-mell;
But, doggie, my darling, be sure and don't tell!
There's mother at last! oh what shall we try?
It can do us no good if we sit down and cry.
Dear mother is gentle, and patient, and good;
You and I couldn't help it – we couldn't be rude!
If she kisses the pieces they're sure to get well;
So cheer up, dear doggie, I'm going to tell!

Postcard published by *Cassell's Saturday Journal* (date unknown). Modern card printed by The Medici Society.

Colour photolithograph frontispiece to *Bo Peep, A Treasury For The Little Ones*, Cassell & Co., 1896. Colour chromolithograph frontispiece to *Our Little Dots*, Vol.20, 1906 (date now removed below signature). **See page 52.**

I'se Biggest *both signed and dated 1892*

Version 1

Oil on canvas, 32ins x 24ins (81.5cm x 61.5cm), signed and dated 1892. Exhibited Royal Academy, 1892 (No.1008), sold for £150. Auctioned at Christie's, London, 28th April 1894 (Lot 69), and was bought by Vokins for £111.6s. It is now owned by Haussner's Restaurant, Eastern Avenue at Clinton St., Baltimore, Maryland 21224, U.S.A.

This version has a shuttlecock bottom right – a popular game with the Elsley family – and this decorative shape features eleven times in his paintings. Extract from "The Children's Season" by Rudolph Cordova, *The London Magazine*, December 1904, p.626:

> "*An Unwilling Partner* was followed by *I'se Biggest*. This was an adaptation of a real incident Mr. Elsley once saw – a little girl measuring two dogs. The St. Bernard in the

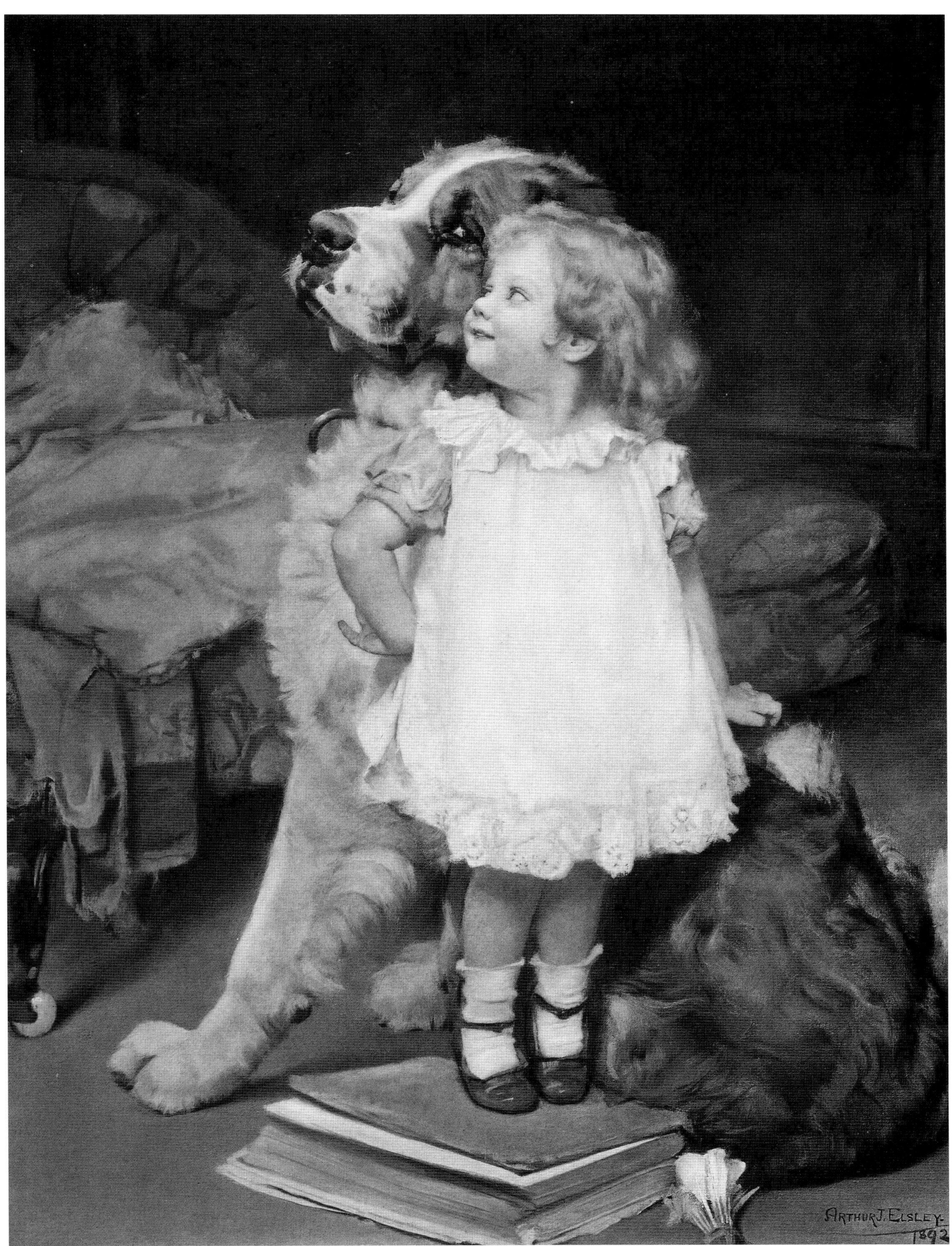

I'se Biggest. Version I.

picture belonged to a Mr. Winter, of Wardour Street, who was the proprietor of a large antique furniture warehouse. Mr. Elsley did not know him at the time that he first saw the dog. He was walking down the street, lost in wonder as to where he would find a model suitable for the picture which he had in mind, when he saw a man coming towards him leading the very animal for his purpose. He asked whose it was, and, when he was told, called on the owner. He found that the St. Bernard, which answered to the name of Rollo, was to a certain extent a public character, for it was performing at the Lyric Theatre; and at a given cue it used to get up, bark, and walk off the stage during its performance with the precision and accuracy of a human being."

Extract from "Certain Small People" by G.W. Wood, *The Sunday Magazine*, 1892, p.536:

"What could be more charming in its way than Mr. Arthur Elsley's *I'se Biggest*, an arch, innocent little rogue, in pink frock and white pinafore, measuring her height against a big, good natured St. Bernard? The small mortal, in spite of the thick book she is standing on, still falls short of being biggest by a couple of inches, and the dog turns his soft brown eyes towards her with a look of amused tolerance and gentleness, as if he thoroughly understood her, but was too wise and responsible to take part in any foolery of the kind. The sense of humour comes out more strongly in this pretty scene than in any of the other canvases I noticed. "

Extract from *St. James Budget* magazine, 10th November 1893:

"Not the least charming and popular of the pictures at Burlington House last year was *I'se Biggest* by Mr. Arthur J. Elsley of which we give herewith a miniature reproduction. It is not often that people begin to demand artist's proofs of a picture even if it has been decided to reproduce it, but that is what happened in this case. The reproduction has now been made by the hands of Messrs. Frost & Reed of Bristol who have just published a very fine photogravure of the picture. *I'se Biggest* is one of those simple and unaffected pictures which readily lend themselves to reproduction and has so much nature and so admirable a touch of humour in it that no doubt great numbers of those who admire it at Burlington House will be delighted to have an opportunity of hanging a version of it upon their own walls."

Black and white photograph in *Royal Academy Pictures*, 1892, p.18; and *The Illustrated London News*, 7th May 1982, in the photo review of the Royal Academy Exhibition.

Sepia photogravure, 23ins x 17$^{1}/_{4}$ ins (59cm x 44.5cm), copyright Frost and Reed, lst August 1893. 250 Artist's proofs @ 4 guineas, 25 presentation prints, 50 lettered proofs @ 1$^{1}/_{2}$ guineas, India prints @ 1 guinea. All sold except for India prints in May 1908 and January 1913 catalogues. This print was so popular that the printing plate had to be re-engraved.

Version II

Oil on canvas, 32ins x 24$^{1}/_{2}$ins (81.5cm x 62.5cm), signed and dated May 20th 1892 – a skipping rope replaces the shuttlecock on the floor, bottom right.

These paintings were inspired by Charles Burton Barber's *Trust*, Royal Academy, 1888 (No.387), and *Don't Ee Tipty Toe* (No.433), by John Morgan, Royal Academy, 1885, which shows two children being measured by their elder sister. Extract from "When Landseer Joked in Paint" by Sydney Carter, *Everybody's Magazine*, 19th September 1953:

"A boy was walking through the streets of London when he saw a man servant leading an enormous St. Bernard dog. The boy, fascinated, followed them home; he then knocked upon the door and asked if he might make a drawing of the dog.

The boy was Edwin Landseer; his age thirteen. In 1817 – two years later – the drawing appeared in an exhibition. In 1820 the dog featured in a more ambitious work, *Alpine Mastiffs Reanimating a Distressed Traveller*. With this picture, Landseer established himself as 'the foremost painter of animals then living.'"

Landseer's painting of *Princess Mary Of Cambridge (Duchess Of Teck) As A Child*, features a St. Bernard and was exhibited at The Victorian Exhibition, 1891. This in turn led to it being reproduced on the front page of *The Illustrated London News*, 19th December 1891. Elsley would certainly have seen the engraving.

Colour chromolithograph, 26$^{1}/_{2}$ins x 17$^{1}/_{2}$ins (68cm x 45cm), not signed and dated, was presented with *Father Christmas Magazine*, 1983. This followed a success with Elsley's *Our Christmas Goose* the previous year. **See page 53.**

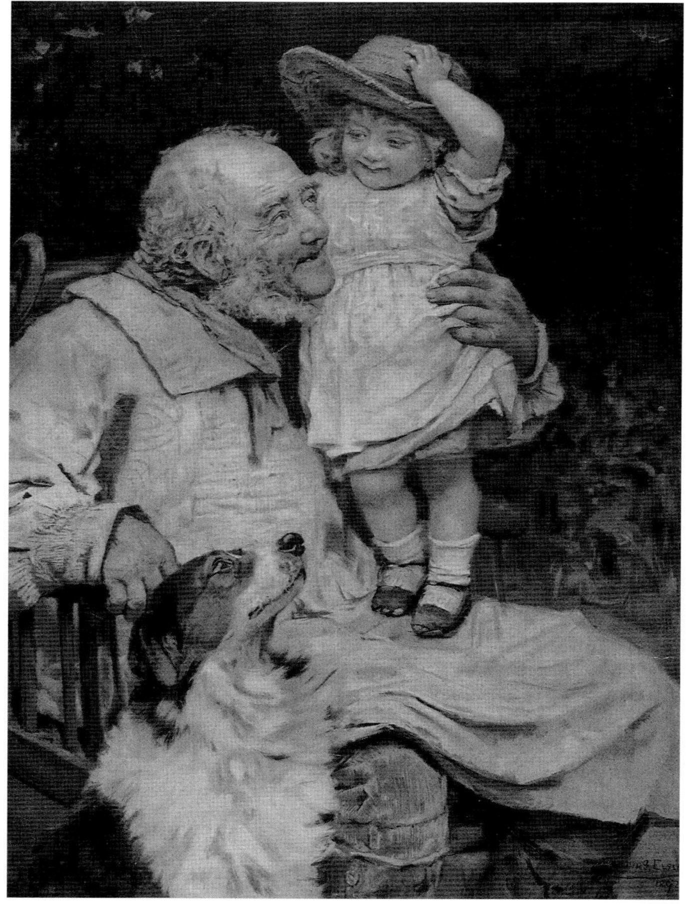

Grandfather's Pet

Grandfather's Pet *signed and dated 1892*

Details of original painting unknown.

Colour chromolithograph, $23\frac{1}{4}$ins x $17\frac{1}{2}$ins (59.5cm x 45cm), presented with *The Illustrated London News*, Christmas 1983. *The Illustrated London News* was the pinnacle of popular weekly publishing and a children's artist "had arrived" when their work was reproduced as the Christmas presentation print. Elsley followed in the footsteps of John Everett Millais, James Sant, Frank Holl, Philip Richard Morris, Charles Burton Barber, and his landlord, Fred Morgan.

Our Christmas Goose *signed and dated 1892*

Details of original painting unknown. Exhibited at the Walker Art Gallery, Liverpool, Autumn 1892 (No.1047) entitled *The Christmas Goose*.

Elsley was quick to see the commercial possibilities and popularity of Christmas themes. This was the first of his Christmas paintings which were produced annually for the next ten years and then less frequently.

Colour chromolitho-graph, $25\frac{1}{2}$ins x $17\frac{1}{2}$ins (65.6cm x 45cm), presented with *Father Christmas Magazine*, 1892. Unfortunately the quality of the engraving with the crude reproduction of the children's faces does little justice to the original painting. **See page 60.**

Source photograph for *Our Christmas Goose*.

Surprised / The Invaders *circa 1893*

Oil on canvas, 24ins x 30ins (61.5cm x 76.5cm). Pears bought this painting originally entitled *Surprised* from Joseph Grego, the editor of the *Pears Annual*, for £30 including copyright in May 1893. Lever Brothers the manufacturers of Sunlight Soap acquired Pears in 1915, and following the death of the founder, Lord Leverhulme, on 7th May 1925, it was auctioned at Knight, Frank & Rutley, Horwich, Lancashire in November 1925 (Lot 1085).

This painting was a reworking of *Early Risers* 1890. The model (who appears in *A Dead Heat*, 1893) is different, and her eyes are now looking up. The bed-curtains are a different colour, and one of the kittens has been replaced by the doll. When Lever Brothers took over Pears in 1915 they found this work in stock and decided to reproduce it as one of the five prints presented with the *Pears Annual 1915* (twenty-two years after it was purchased). The title change to *The Invaders* probably alluded to the Great War.

Thomas Barratt, the owner of Pears and mastermind of their publicity, died in 1914 the year before Elsley, one of the most popular artists in the Pears style, was to have his only painting reproduced by them. Seven of Morgan's works, from 1891 to 1910. were bought for reproduction as Pears prints together with another for advertising purposes.

Colour chromolithograph, $13\frac{1}{2}$ins x 18ins (34.5cm x 46.5cm), printed in twelve colours. **See page 49.**

A Dead Heat *signed and dated 1893*

Oil on canvas, 38ins x 24ins (97cm x 61.5cm). Exhibited at the Royal Academy, 1893 (No.516), priced £150 but unsold.

In James Yates Carrington's *Such Agetting Down Stairs*, painted pre-1892, the puppies are falling down the stairs not climbing up.

The painting was plagiarised as a political cartoon by J.A.S. (James Affleck Shepherd) for the 1894 Liberal leadership campaign. The faces of the three contestants – from left to right, Lord Rosebery, Sir William Harcourt and Earl Spencer – were superimposed on the faces of the puppies! Elsley earned enough money from the royalties of this work to marry Emily Fusedale on the 11th November 1893, at St.Thomas Parish Church, Portman Square, Marylebone.

Extract from "The Children's Season", Rudolph De Cordova *The London Magazine*, December 1904, p.627:

> "Perhaps of all Mr Elsley's works, A *Dead Heat* was the most tiring and troublesome to paint. The reason was the difficulty in the getting the puppies to stand in the position he wanted. As a preliminary, the stairs were made and taken to the studio. With a piece of meat in his hand, Mr Elsley would endeavour to entice the puppies to the top; and he would study the various positions in

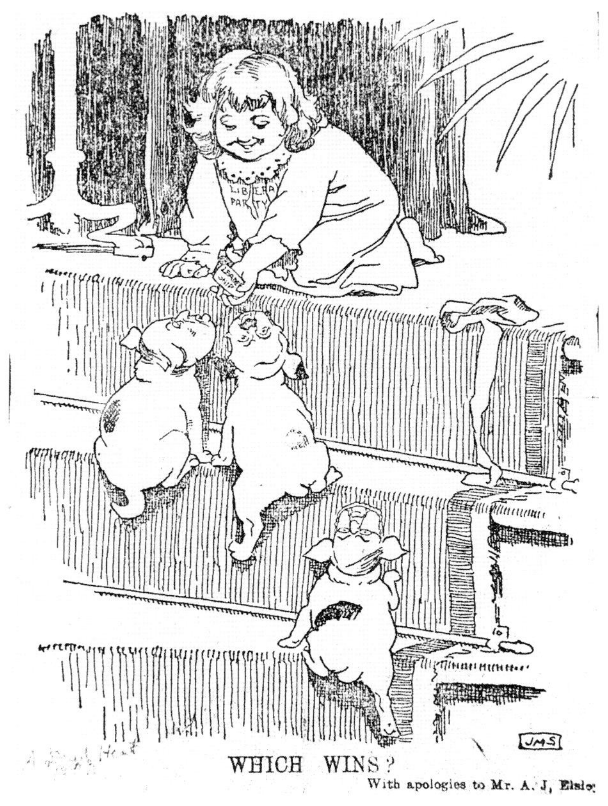

which they scrambled up until he had discovered those which suited his purpose best. Having determined the positions, the difficulty was to get the animals to keep them. Of course, only one dog could be painted at a time, so the difficulty of the problem was reduced, at all events, to a certain extent. In the earlier stages of the proceedings, however, there was an unexpected difficulty. The puppy would not remain on the steps unless it was supported or held there; and Mr Elsley found that as soon as he turned his back to go to the easel the little animal would scamper down the steps. When Mr Elsley attempted to catch it, it would run off round the studio, evidently thinking he was playing a game with it. The humour of this, however amusing to the dog, got monotonous and fatiguing to the painter, to say nothing of the way in which it interfered with the progress of the picture."

How to keep the dog quiet and not have to chase it every five minutes was the problem. It was solved by the aid of a leather bag. Mr Elsley put the dog as nearly as possible in the position in which he wanted it, watched it carefully until he could remember no more, then picked it up, popped it into the bag, went back to the easel, and painted until he had finished all he had seen. Then he would open the bag, put the dog back into position, watch it a little more, and repeat the operation. After this had gone on a few times the little beast used to improve the period of rest by calmly going to sleep in the bag. The feet and legs of all the dogs were painted from the same animal. In time it became so trained in the process that it would actually go to sleep in the position in which Mr. Elsley placed it, and so became an ideal sitter."

Extract from "Pictures of English Child-Life", *Cassells Family Magazine*, May 1896, pp.461-468:

"This artist thinks dogs are even more interesting sitters than children; they are so full of character. Puppies and kittens are, of course, like children – very difficult to deal with. They are either very fidgety or very somnolent. The pups in the picture were induced to scramble up the stairs – built up in the studio – by the attraction of a piece of meat at the top."

Black and white photograph in *Academy Notes*, 1893, p.100, opposite Fred Morgan's *Roses And Thorns* (No.526). Both works were copyright Berlin Photographic. It is likely that a representative visited their studio and chose both for reproduction. Black and white photograph in *The Harmsworth Magazine*, Vol.I No.2, August 1898, and *Munsey's Magazine* (U.S.A.), date unknown.

Engraving, 20ins x 13¼ins (51cm x 33.5cm), *The Graphic*, 22nd September 1900, pp.428-9, copyright Berlin Photographic. This was the first Elsley work published by Berlin Photographic and marked the start of a long association which lasted until the Great War.

Large sepia photogravure published by Berlin Photographic in 1893. Medium size black and white photolithograph calendar print for Central Stores, Ealing Road, Wembley, 1909, copyright Berlin Photographic, and printed by Maclure, MacDonald & Son, Glasgow. This version includes a poem. **See page 12**

[Play Time] *signed and dated 1893*

Oil on canvas, 30ins x 22¼ins (76.5cm x 57cm).

The model for the mother in this and *As Happy as a King* is probably Mary, Fred Morgan's second wife. A similar white kitten appeared in *Victims*, 1891. Modern colour print produced by Stephen Selby Pictures.

Unrecorded as an old print. **See page 56.**

Peep Bo! / As Happy As A King *circa 1893*

Details of original painting unknown. Exhibited at the Institute of Painters in Oil Colours, 1893 (No.424), entitled *Peep Bo!*

The print was renamed *As Happy As A King*. This was a popular title used by, amongst others, John and Fred Morgan, but the best known is William Collins' Royal Academy exhibit 1836 (No.194), which now hangs in the Tate Gallery.

Black and white photograph in Institute of Painters in Oil Colours, 1893 catalogue, p.53. Elsley also used the windswept hair look in *Youthful Patriots*, c.1892-4 and *Heave Ho!*, 1896.

Sepia photogravure, copyright T. Seymour Meade of Manchester. The only Elsley to be reproduced by Meade.

Youthful Patriots *circa 1893*

Details of original painting unknown.

Elsley took a photograph of the unfinished work. The model for the old seafarer was W.D. Anderson. From Elsley's address book he lived at 28 Wharton Street, Lloyd

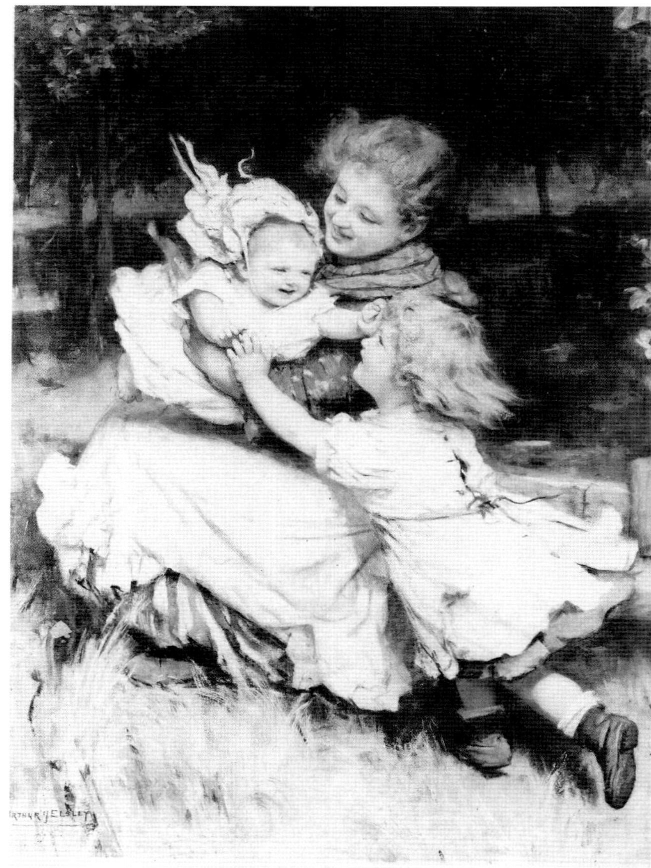

Peep Bo! / As Happy As A King

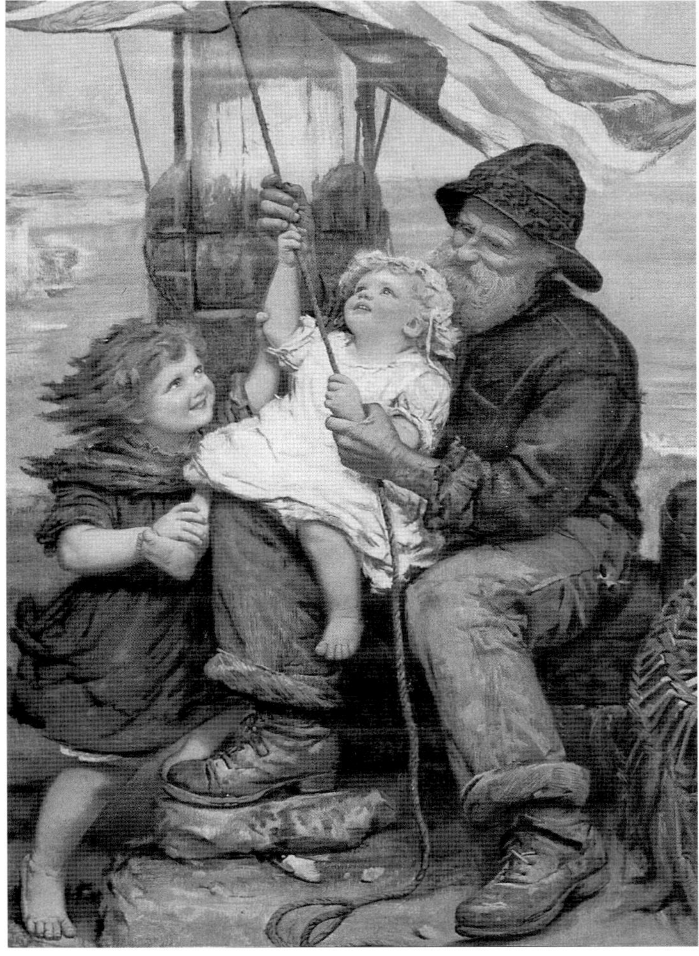

Youthful Patriots

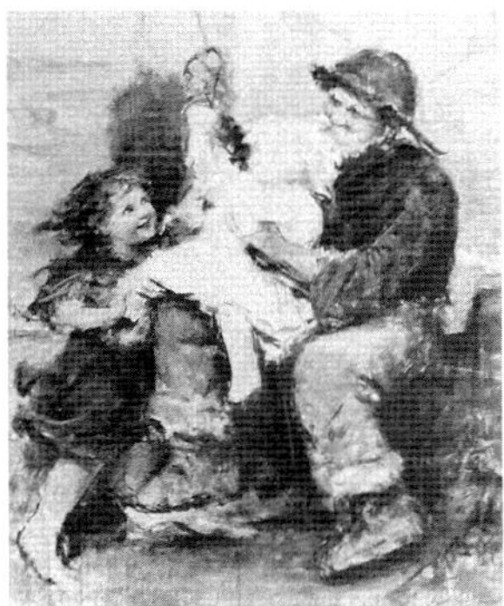

Photograph of unfinished *Youthful Patriots*.

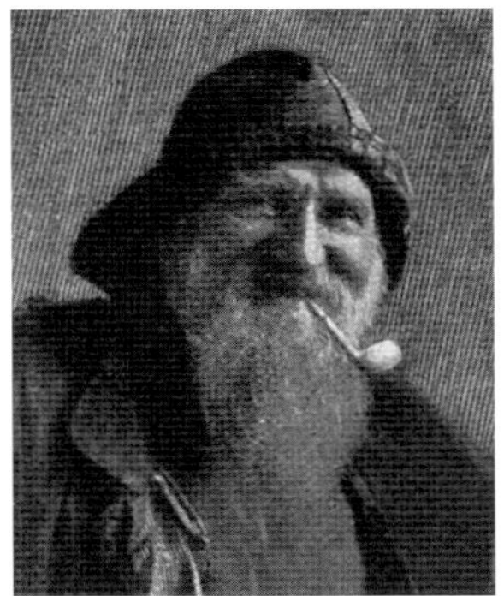

Photograph of Mr. W.D. Anderson.

Square, London W.C.1., and is described as having costumes for "innkeeper, fisherman and countryman's dress". Extract from "A Man of Many Poses" by Lenore Van Der Veer, *The Royal Magazine*, December 1901:

> "Mr Anderson has had the distinction of posing for almost all the great artists of today, and his features have appeared in many academy pictures. ...It is now more than thirty years ago since (he) sat for his first pose. ...He...followed a seafaring life in the Royal Navy. His physique is still that of a powerful man, though his hair and beard are now a silver grey.
>
> In private studios 1/- an hour is the tariff. ...Really good models are always in request, and are often paid retaining fees in slack times by the more prosperous artists. Also they command a better price per hour than the rank and file.
>
> Models frequently attend exhibitions and find it amusing to stand near enough to some picture in which they figure conspicuously to overhear the remarks made by the visitors. Half the people who attend picture galleries have little acquaintance with art, and know nothing of what goes on behind the scenes. The artist's model enjoys their blunders."

This painting is very like Fred Morgan's *Who Do You Love?*, Royal Academy, 1894, which also features Mr Anderson.

Sepia photogravure, details unknown.

Plucking His Feathers *circa 1893*

Details of original painting unknown.

Is this the result of the turkey attack in *Just In Time*, c.1893-9? **See page 40**. Extract from "Models", *Pearson's Magazine*, September 1901, p.243:

> "When artists wish to paint an old lady, an ideal grandma, they send for Mrs. Knight. She has been sitting in the studios for year and years, and has seen the lights and shadows of eighty-four summers come and go. Her nerves are far more steady than those of the average schoolgirl of to-day, and the artists tell me wonderful things of her endurance in keeping a pose – no easy thing to do, by the way, as one quickly finds out by trying...

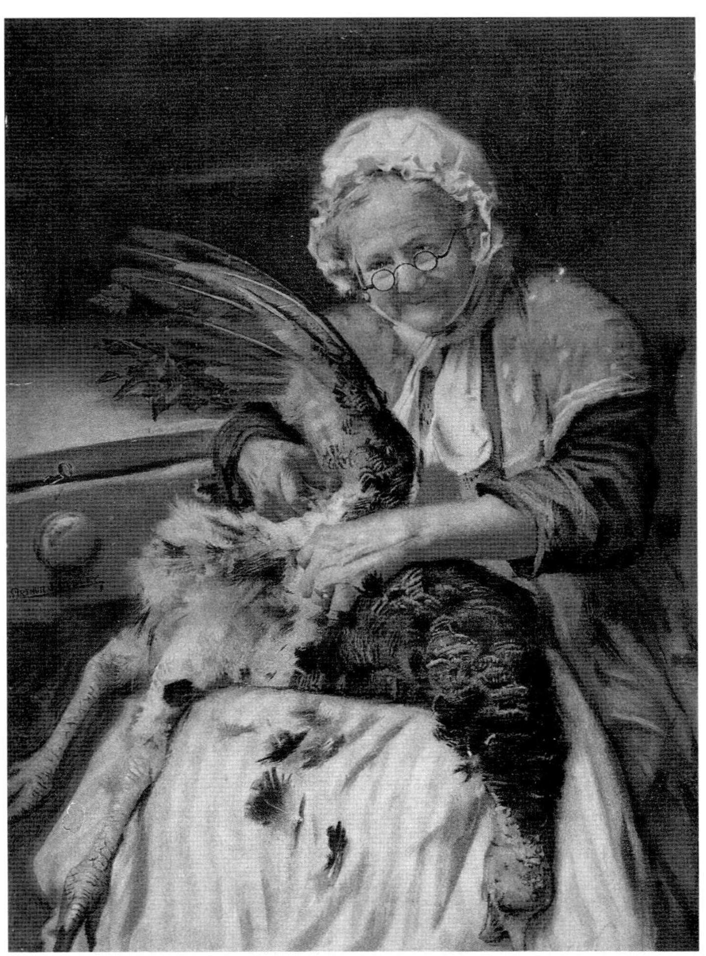

Plucking His Feathers

...An Academy picture of more than ordinary interest from the brush of A.J. Elsley shows this old lady plucking a goose...". (This painting is not listed as being exhibited at the Royal Academy!)

Mrs Knight sat for many other artists including Charles E. Wilson's *A Quiet Afternoon*, (Royal Academy, 1897).

Colour chromolithograph, 17ins x 11¾ins (43cm x 30cm), signed but not dated, possibly for one of the Weldon's publications.

Besieged *signed and dated 1893*

Oil on canvas, 36ins x 26ins (91.5cm x 66.5cm), which now hangs in the Lady Lever Art Gallery, Port Sunlight, Liverpool. It was presented by Lever Brothers in 1983 (Accession No. LL 3417).

Fred Morgan painted a picture with the same title in 1884 and, ironically, three of Fred Morgan's works had already been used by Sunlight's rivals, Pears. The model for the old lady is Mrs. May Knight, who lived at 149 Cleveland Street, London W.1.

The painting was reproduced as a full-page Sunlight advert in *Pears Annual 1916* (Lever Brothers now owned Pears). On this version a bar and box of Sunlight Soap were superimposed. Information label for exhibit at Lady Lever Art Gallery reads:

"Humorous subjects were one of Elsley's specialisms and humour has an obvious appeal to the advertiser. In the painting of 1893 washing is portrayed as a quaint and amusing old custom or pastime, as a splendid occasion for family games and merriment; no doubt Lever hoped this would make it more appealing to his customers."

Described and reproduced in *Victorian and Edwardian Paintings in the Lady Lever Art Gallery*, Vol.1, p.31, by Edward Morris (H.M.S.O. 1994):

"This painting was presumably bought by Lever for advertising purposes. Two different undated advertisements for Sunlight Soap reproducing LL 3417 and giving it the title *Besieged* are in the Port Sunlight Heritage Centre".

It was reproduced as a colour chromolithograph advertising show-card for Sunlight. **See page 61.**

Wait a Minute / Plum Pudding

signed and dated 1893

Oil on canvas, 33ins x 25ins (84cm x 64cm). Exhibited at the Royal Academy, 1894 (No.911), and sold for £150.

This was Elsley's first work after marrying Emm. Prior to this he used to pick up a puppy, study it, put it back in the basket and then paint it from memory. Now, in Emm, he had a keen assistant to hold the puppy and she was also very good with children, holding their arms in the required positions. A German bisque figure of the girl and puppy now in a high chair was produced, as was *Goodbye*, 1894.

Black and white photograph in *Royal Academy Pictures*, 1894, p.62; *Royal Academy Notes*, 1894, p.138; *Royal Academy Sketches*, 1894, p.36 and *The Leisure Hour* in early 1896, p.274. Also reproduced as *Wait a Minute* in *The Harmsworth Magazine*, Vol.1 No.3, September 1898, p.330. Called *Manners At Table*, in *Pearson's Magazine*, Vol.XVIII No.10, August 1904, illustrating Rudolph Cordova's article "Laughter in Art".

Sepia photogravure, 20¾ins x 15ins (53cm x 38cm), copyright Berlin Photographic, 1894. Colour chromolithograph, 23¼ins x 17½ins (59.5cm x 45cm), entitled *Plum Pudding*, issued with *Father Christmas Magazine*, 1894. Small sepia photogravure, 12½ins x 8¾ins (32cm x 22cm), entitled *Wait A Minute*, presented with *Weldon's Bazaar of Children's Fashions*, Christmas 1905, (on this version the date below his signature is removed). A badly doctored version of this work with the pudding crudely replaced by a pair of tea cups was produced as a colour chromolithograph print, 18½ins x 16ins (47.5cm x 40.5cm). Entitled *Tea For Two - Don't Be In A Hurry* it was probably produced as a calendar. It is cropped top and bottom thus removing Elsley's signature. **See page 54.**

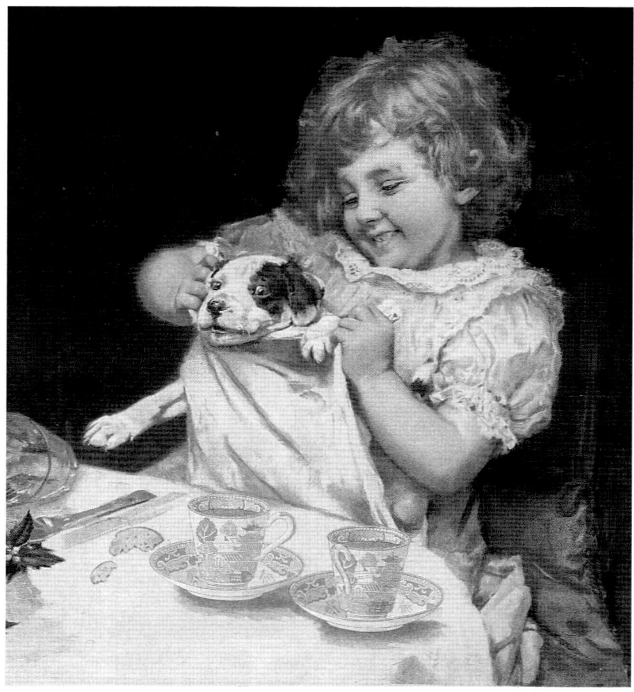

Tea For Two / Don't Be In A Hurry

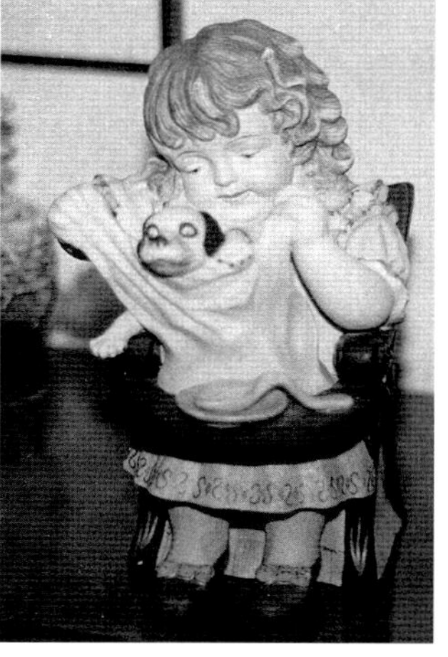

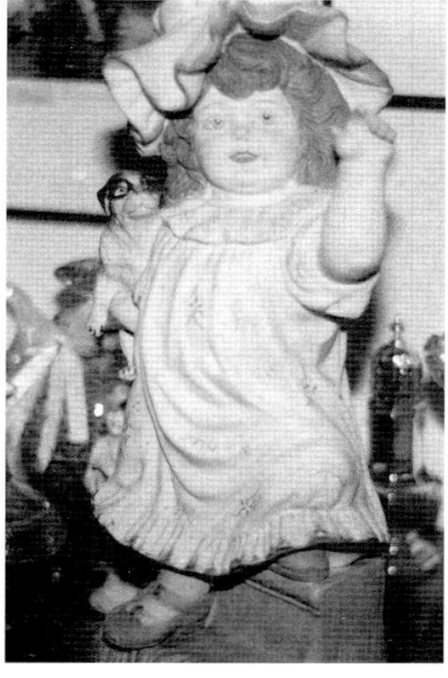

Left, German bisque figure of *Wait A Minute*.
Right, German bisque figure of *Good-bye*, **see page 25.**

Which Hand Will You Have? / You Can Trust Me *circa 1893*

Details of original painting unknown. Exhibited at Glasgow, 1894 (No.239), and at the Walker Art Gallery Liverpool, Autumn 1894 (No.289), both times entitled *Which Hand Will You Have?* and priced £130 (copyright reserved at Liverpool). Signed above the shuttlecock on the stairs.

Colour chromolithograph, 23¾ins x 16¾ins (61cm x 42.5cm), not signed or dated. Also black and white photolithograph calendar, printed by Maclure, MacDonald & Co. **See page 55.**

Favourites All *circa 1893*

Details of original painting unknown.

Colour photolithograph, 8ins x 6ins (20.5cm x 15cm), presented with *Horner's Penny Stories*, date unknown. The print is not signed or dated and Marjorie Wheatley disputes that this is her father's work.

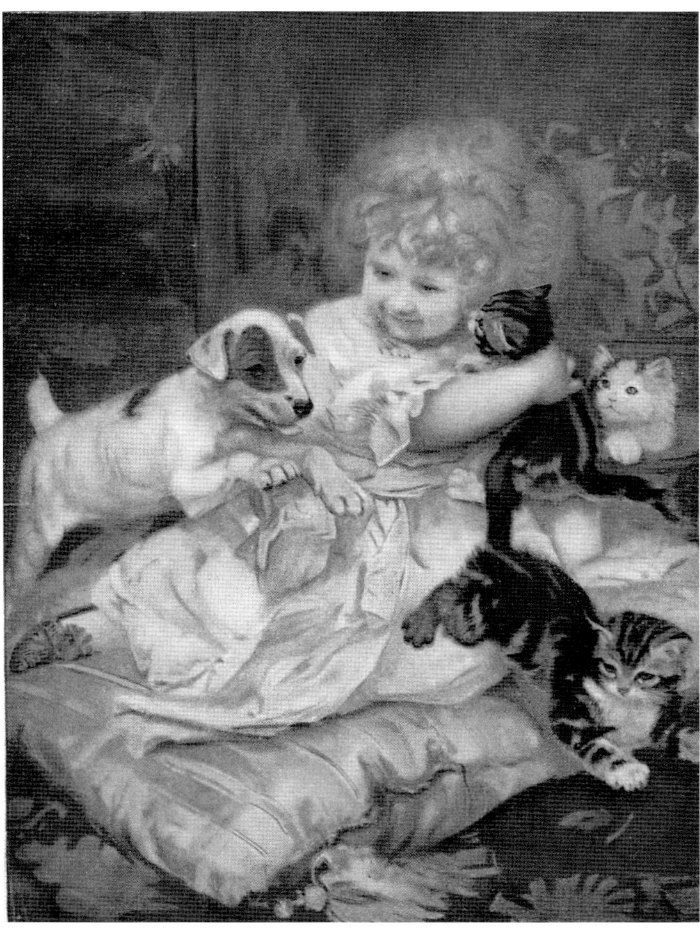

Favourites All

Good-Bye *signed and dated 1894*

Details of original painting unknown.

Extract from *The Illustrated London News*, 25th January 1896, p.120:

"In two recently published etchings, *Good-Bye* and *A Dead Heat* (Messrs. Frost & Reed, Clifton) Mr. Elsley appears more distinctly as a follower, though not an imitator, of Mr. Burton Barber, differing from him by allowing his children more than one pet at a time, and going beyond the limitations of a fox-terrier or a collie. He has a keen sense of humour, especially in his treatment of puppies' backs, which, as students of dog-life well know, are their most expressive features."

Extract from "The Children's Season" by Rudolph De Cordova, *The London Magazine*, December 1904, p.630:

"The fox-terrier puppy the little girl is carrying in *Good-bye* was quite a remarkable animal. It knew nothing of fear, and its intelligence was such that if Mr. Elsley put it on the top of a chest over six feet high in his studio, and said 'Jump!' the little animal would jump into his arms quite fearlessly.

Fox-terriers, Mr. Elsley has always found to be the best sitters. He once had one which would sit for three-quarters of an hour in an easy position. If the studio-bell rang all he would have to say was 'Stay there, Topsy'; and though he might be gone five or ten minutes, yet, when he returned, the position had been maintained with the utmost care."

Good-Bye, a black and white photograph in *Munsey's Magazine* (U.S.A.) date unknown, illustrating an article "Artists and Their Work"; and *The Harmsworth Magazine*, Vol.1 No.1, July 1898, p.110, retitled *The Favourite*. Detail reproduced in *Our Darlings*, 1902, captioned *Good-bye Daddy! Good-bye Mother!* Colour chromolithograph frontispiece of *Our Little Dots*, Vol.19, 1905, date removed and now called *Ta-Ta!* Sepia book plate *The Wonder Book*, a picture annual for boys and girls, 1916, captioned *Good-Bye!* Also sold as 10ins x 8ins (25.5cm x 20.5cm) photograph of original painting. A German bisque figure of the waving girl with the terrier under her arm was produced, as was *Wait A Minute*, 1893.

Sepia photogravure, 21ins x 15ins (54cm x 38cm), copyright Berlin Photographic Co., 1894. Later reproduced as a sepia photogravure, 15½ins x 10¾ins (39.5cm x 27.5cm), presented with *Weldon's Ladies' Journal*, Christmas 1903 (date below signature blotted out), copyright 1894 Photographische Gesellschaft (Berlin Photographic). It was produced as a pair with the *Myra's Journal* print of *Pets* (1896) also issued in December 1903. Also sold as 10ins x 8ins (25.5cm x 20.5cm) photograph of original painting. **See next page.**

So Tired! *signed and dated 1894*

Oil on canvas, 36½ins x 27½ins (93cm x 70.5cm). Now owned by Hartlepool Museum Service, formerly the Gray Art Gallery. It was part of the Gallery's original collection presented by Sir William Creswell Gray in 1919, and had been given the title *Her First Love* by the time it was catalogued in 1920.

Extract from *The Illustrated London News*, December 22nd 1894, p.798:

"Messrs. Frost and Reed (Bristol) are not long in following up the success which attended the production of Mr. A.J. Elsley's picture, *I'se Biggest*; and the new

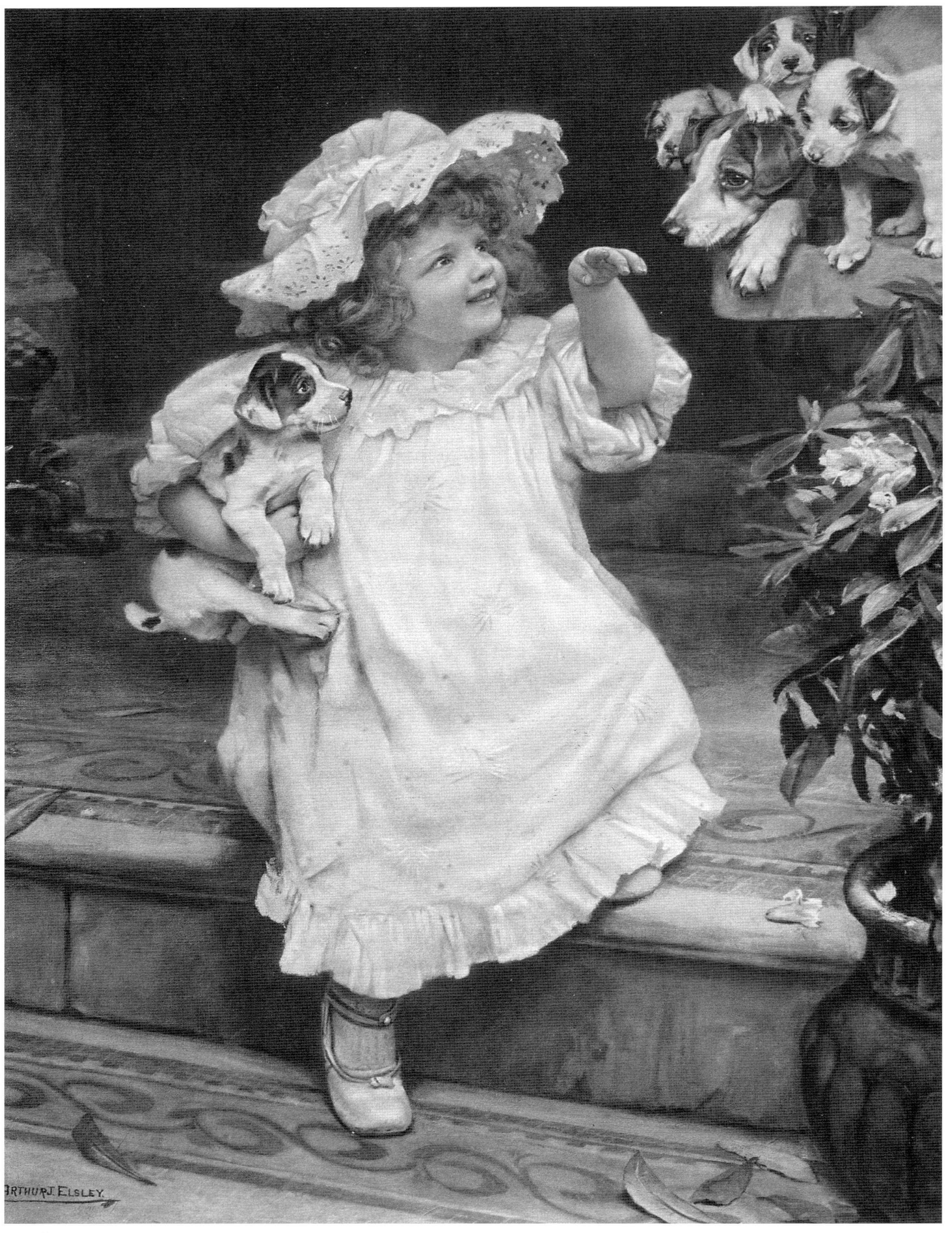

Good-Bye

episode of child-life, *So Tired*, which has just been published, makes an excellent companion work. It is evident that the romps of the small child and her large companion – a fine St. Bernard dog – have reached their inevitable climax, and the mixture of real triumph on the part of the child and the admirably simulated exhaustion of her playfellow are quite in keeping with truth – as those who have ever watched playmates of this kind can abundantly testify."

Extract from "The Children's Season" by Rudolph De Cordova, *The London Magazine*, December 1904, pp.626-628:

"Rollo was an extraordinarily intelligent dog; and was the model Mr Elsley used in *So Tired*, in which the dog is represented asleep on a sofa, with its great head reposing in the lap of a little girl. Only in the earlier stages of the sittings is it Mr Elsley's custom to have the children and the animals together. The reason for this is that when they are brought together the children invariably begin to play with the animals, and it is impossible to get anything like a satisfactory result from the sitting. Rollo's head used, therefore, to be placed on a cushion of the exact height of the little girl's lap. While the sittings for *I'se Biggest* were going on, Rollo, when he arrived at the studio (to which he was taken by a boy), used always to lie down and rest after his walk from Wardour Street to St John's Wood, where Mr Elsley lived. When, however, he found that he was to sit on the sofa, which was softer and therefore far more comfortable than the ground, he never would lie down, but would wait patiently until the sofa was pulled out and put into its place, when he would get on it, place his head on the cushion, and go to sleep. Once or twice the cushion was found not to be quite right, and Rollo had to be awakened in order that it might be properly adjusted. After that had happened a couple of times, he always waited to make quite sure that the cushion was exactly right before he went to sleep. So he would lie for hours, proving as fine a model as the heart of an artist could desire.

At four o'clock he used to be fetched. A few minutes before that hour he would wake and raise his head from the cushion, from which nothing could move him earlier in the day. Then he would get off the sofa and begin to grow uneasy. There was a grandfather's clock in the studio; and as soon as it struck four he would begin to bark, as much as to say, "Time's up, and I'm not going to sit any more." If his master was a little late in fetching him, no persuasion could induce Rollo to get back on to the sofa, and it was useless to attempt to use force; for when the great animal once took his stand it required much more than a man of ordinary strength to move him against his will."

So Tired was not the immediate successor to *I'se Biggest*, for at least two pictures came between them. These were *A Dead Heat* (1892), and *Good-bye* (1894).

Sepia photogravure, 17½ins x 22¾ins (45cm x 58.5cm), engraved by Hanfstaengl and published by Frost & Reed in 1894. 250 Artist's proofs @ 4 guineas, lettered proofs @ 1½ guineas, and prints @ 1 guinea. (Artist's and lettered proofs still available in Frost & Reed's May 1908 catalogue, but were no longer available in January 1913.)

The Years Art, 1895, lists the print as a companion to *I'se Biggest*. **See page 57**.

[Play Time] *signed and dated 1894*

Oil on canvas, 40ins x 29ins (102cm x 74cm). Auctioned in 1996 at Christie's, London, who gave it the title *Play Time*, (not to be confused with the 1893 painting of the same title).

This work is a follow up to *Besieged*, 1893, again with Mrs. Knight with the three children.

Unrecorded as a contemporary print.

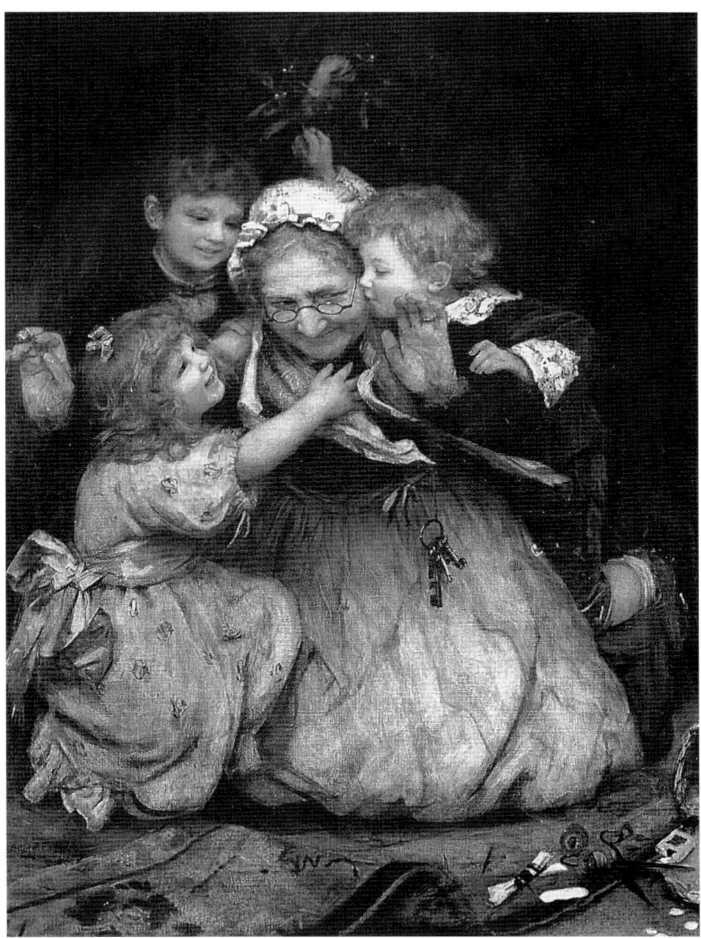

[Play Time]

Tally Ho! *signed and dated 1894*

Oil on canvas, 36ins x 26ins (91.5cm x 66.5cm). Auctioned at Christie's, London, in 1934, the property of Sir John Child and bought by Packe for 14 guineas. Recently owned by Rehs Galleries, New York, who called it *The Young Huntress*.

Colour chromolithograph, 19ins x 14¾ins (49cm x 37.5cm), copyright Grover & Co., Nottingham. Also reproduced as a colour chromolithograph colour advertising show-card, 18¾ins x 14¾ins (48cm x 37.5cm), for Old Calabar Dog & Puppy Biscuits. **See page 61**.

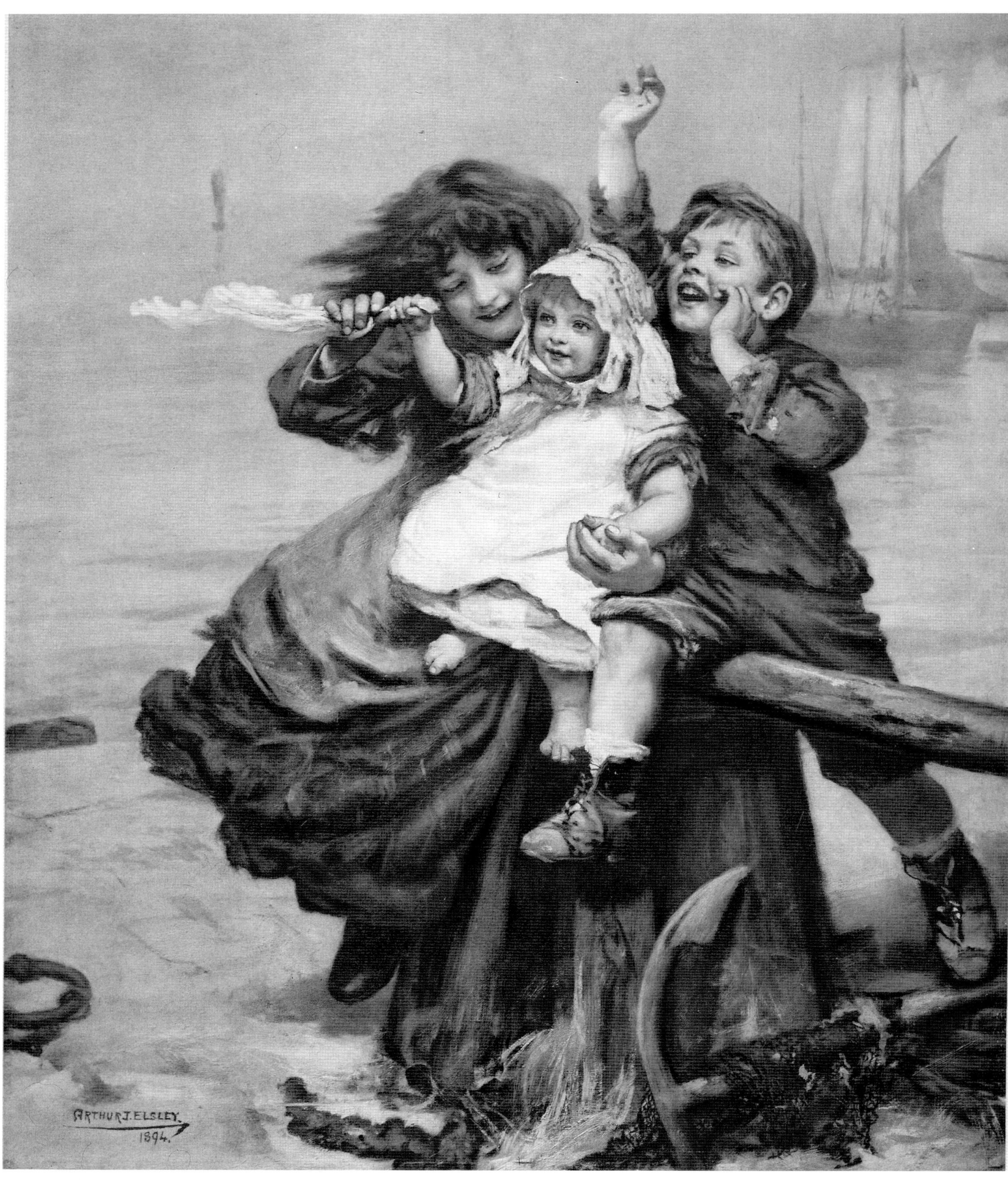

Here's Father!

Here's Father! *signed and dated 1894*

Details of original painting unknown. Exhibited at the Institute of Painters in Oil Colours, Winter 1894 (No.224). This appears to be Dover beach.

Illustrated in 1894 Institute of Painters in Oil Colours catalogue, p.50.

Sepia photogravure, 23ins x 19ins (59cm x 49cm), copyright S. Hildersheimer 1898.

Second Thoughts *circa 1894*

Details of original painting unknown.

Colour chromolithograph, 26¼ins x 17½ins (67cm x 45cm), possibly a calendar.

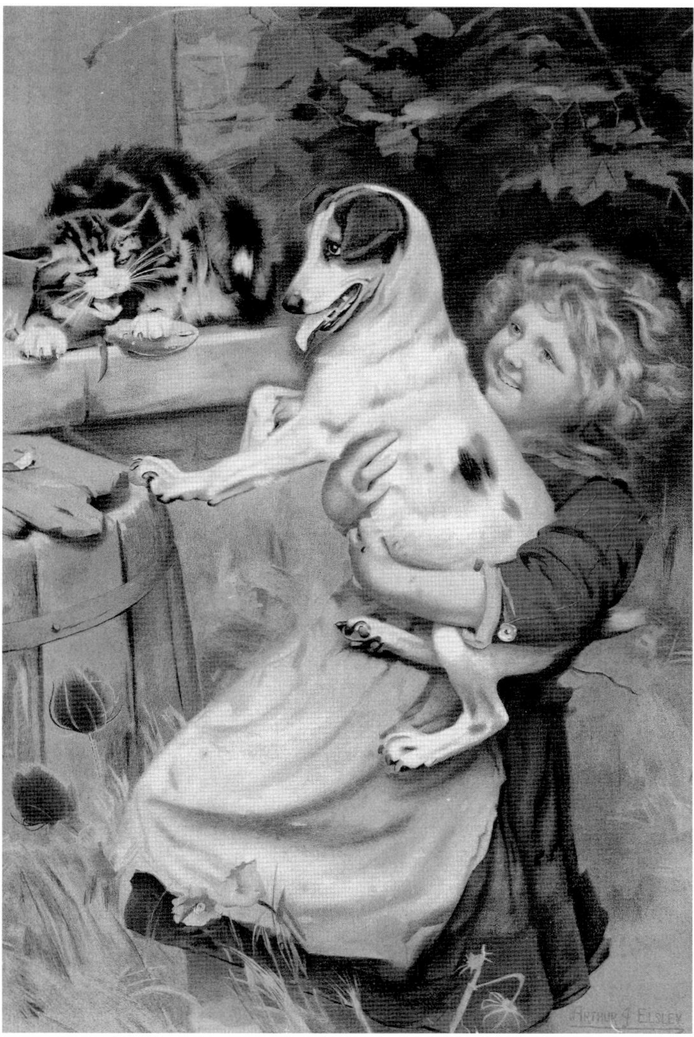

Second Thoughts

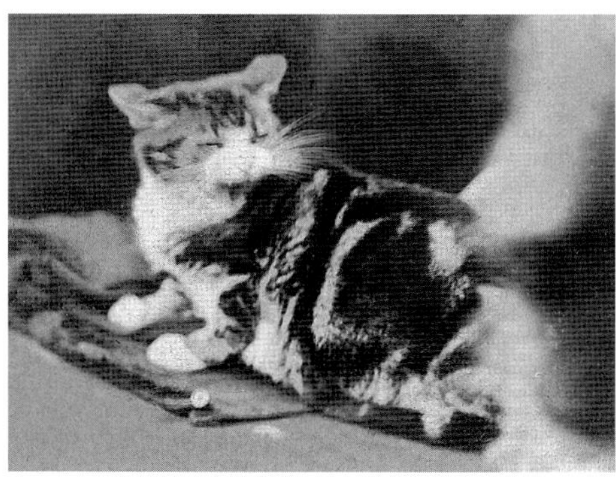

Source photograph for *Second Thoughts.*

[Mischief] *signed and dated 1894*

Oil on canvas, 33ins x 24ins (84cm x 61.5cm).

The same girl and dog appear in this unpublished work. It was sold as *Mischief* at auction in 1986, and again as *Caught In The Act* in 1993.

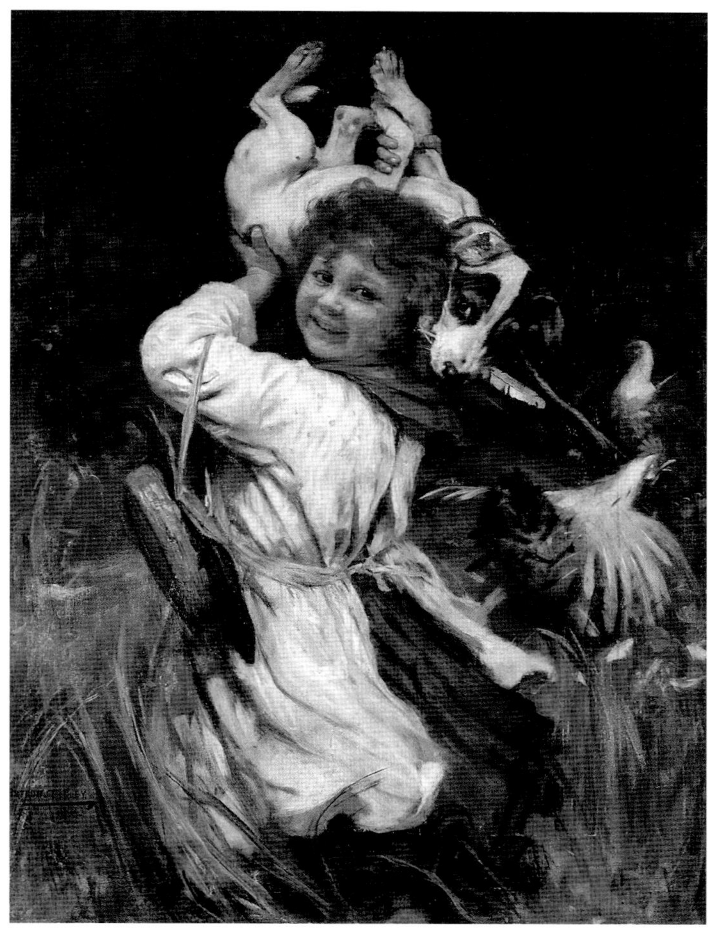

[Mischief]

A Tight Fit *signed and dated 1894*

Details of original painting unknown. Exhibited at the Institute of Painters in Oil Colours, Winter 1895 (No.355), no price given though other exhibits were priced.

It featured the same old man as in *Grandfather's Favourites*, 1895. Extract from *The Illustrated London News*, 25th January 1896, p.120:

> "The place left vacant by Mr. Burton Barber, as painter-in-ordinary of dogs and children, has soon found a worthy occupant in Mr. A.J. Elsley. His picture, *A Tight Fit*, which is reproduced on the present page, tells its own story, and need only here be mentioned as an excellent instance of the painter's power."

Black and white photograph *The Illustrated London News*, 25th January 1896, p.120; *Pearson's Magazine*, Vol.1 No.2, February 1896, p.123; and *Black and White Magazine*, February 1896.

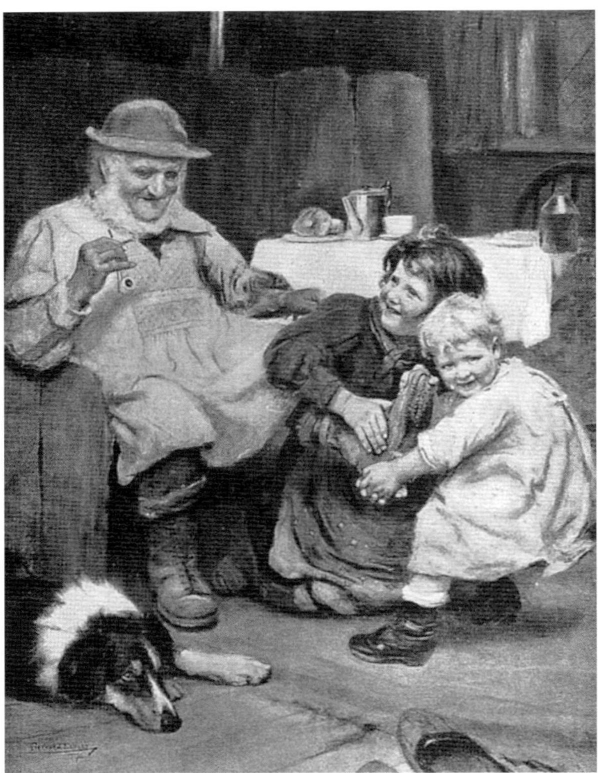

A Tight Fit

Sepia photogravure entitled *A Tight Fit* published by Messrs. Forman, the Nottingham printers, publishers of calendars, the *Nottingham Guardian* and *Evening Post*. Thomas Forman must have been running a high profile publicity campaign for their print in early 1896 as it was reproduced in at least three of the most popular magazines.

A False Alarm / Christmas Morning

signed and dated 1894

Details of original painting unknown.

Robert Barr wrote a tongue in cheek piece for *The Idler*, Vol.VI, November 1894, pp.520-534, entitled "The Christmas Picture" describing how his fictional hero:

> "...went back to his studio to plan his picture, throwing his heart and soul into the work. He knew the kind of thing *The Sphinx* wanted: a pretty child with a dog or a cat. This represented the standard of art at the end of the century, attained by the great British public. It must be done in flaming colours, and would, as the editor had written, be printed on fifteen lithographic stones".

Ironically The Sphinx Studio was to become the name of Solomon J. Solomon's short-lived Art School at which Elsley was to teach in late 1898 and early 1899.

Black and white photograph, *The Harmsworth Magazine*, Vol.5, December 1900, p.480, entitled *Christmas Morning*. American colour calendar manufactured by Thos. D. Murphy Co., 1904, the first of many to be used in America, which eventually led to special commissions for American use only.

Sepia photogravure, 24$^{3}/_{4}$ins x 18ins (63.5cm x 46.5cm), entitled *A False Alarm*, published in 1895 by Siegmund Hildersheimer & Co., London, 150 Artist's proofs @ 3 guineas, prints @ 1 guinea. Also reproduced as a small sepia photogravure maybe for one of the Weldon's publications. Hildersheimer published Fred Morgan's *The Ferry* at the same time as the earlier print.

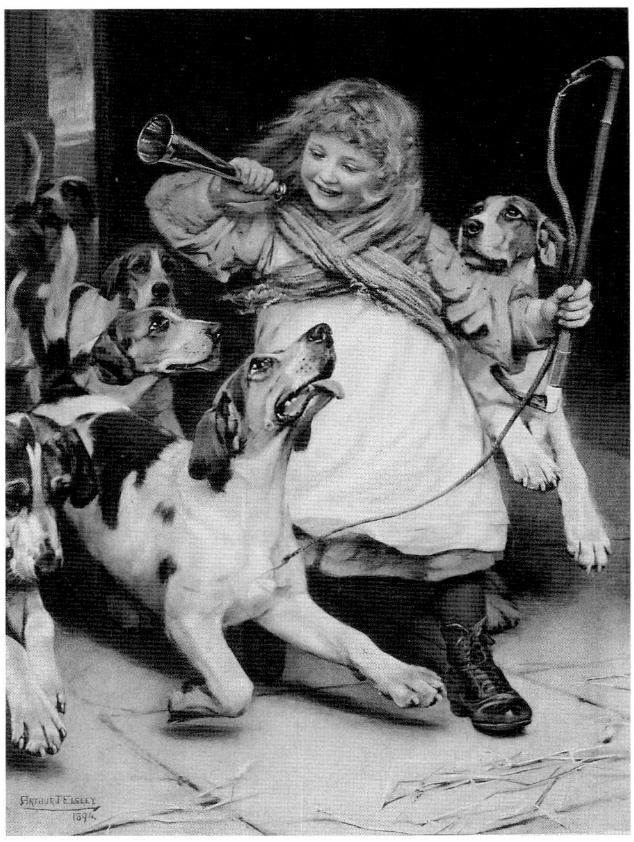

A False Alarm / Christmas Morning

Snapdragon *circa 1894*

Details of original painting unknown. Exhibited at the Royal Academy, 1895 (No.484), priced £180 but unsold.

Snapdragon was a game played at Christmas involving picking raisins from a dish of burning brandy and eating them while they were still alight! A poem illustrated by Fred Morgan's first wife, Alice Havers, was published in *Little Folks* 1888:

> The winter day is almost done,
> And back from the ice the children run,
> And round a flaming dish they throng,
> While "Hurrah for Snap-Dragon!" is their song.
> Ah, you are a wondrous game,
> With your leaping fire and tongues of flame,
> For you call up visions of ages dim,
> Of castles owned by giants grim,
> Of fiery dragons in darksome caves,
> Of sweet princesses held as slaves,
> Of knights in armour of gleaming gold,
> Of gallant rescues by heroes bold:
> Visions in truth most strange to see,
> Of the brave old days of Chivalry.

Colour chromolithograph calendar, 14ins x 19$^{3}/_{4}$ins (35.5cm x 50.5cm), signed not dated (possibly reproduced later and the date removed). **See page 59.**

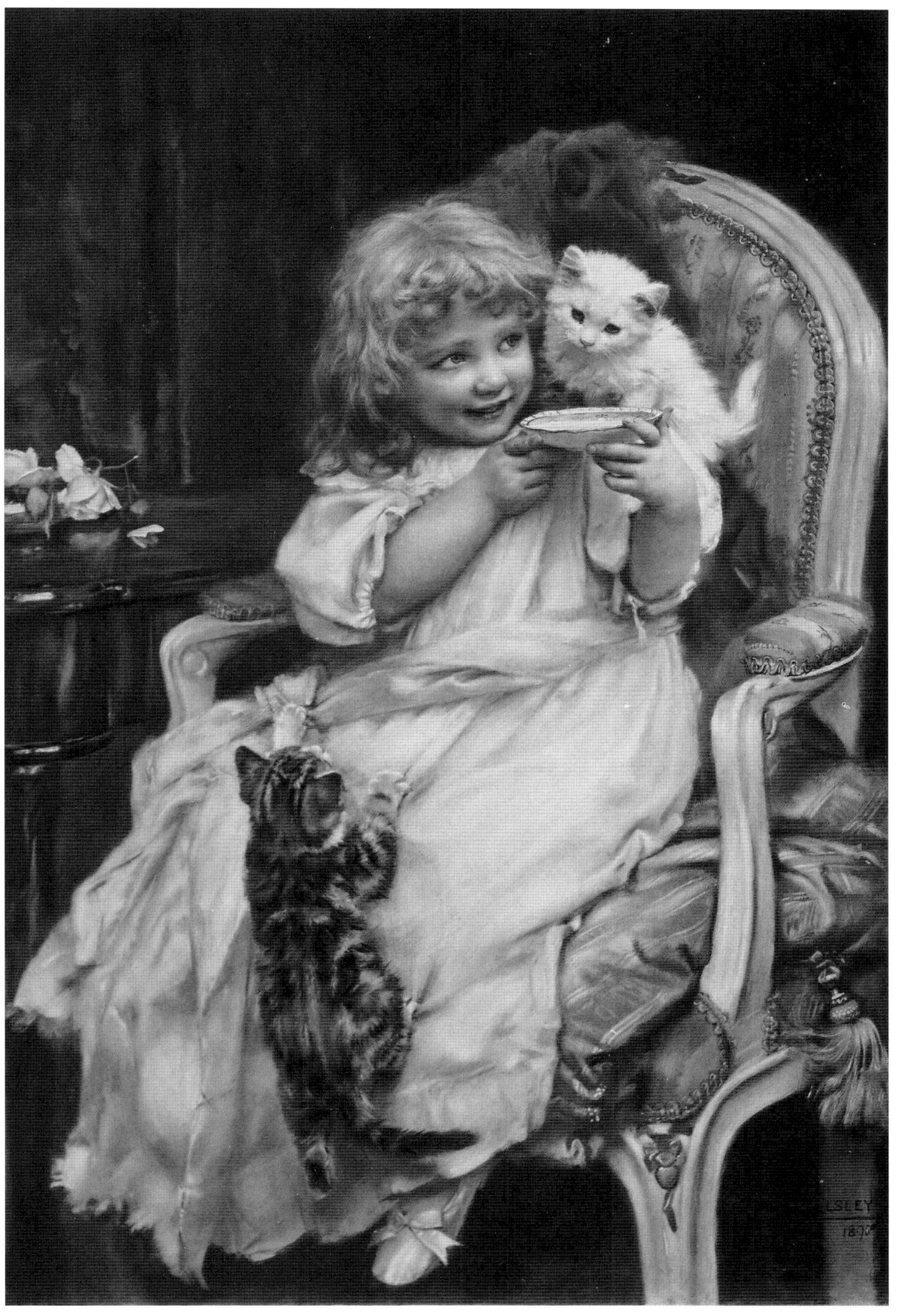

Make Haste. **See next page.**

Make Haste *signed and dated 1895*
Oil on canvas, 34ins x 24ins (86.5cm x 61.5cm). Exhibited at the Royal Academy, 1895 (No.325) in Gallery IV, and sold for £150.

The Ludgate Magazine, Vol.I, New Series No.4, February 1896, pp.277-8, asked popular artists "to state which of your works is your favourite...Mr. A.J. Elsley writes: I am inclined to prefer my picture in this year's Academy, *Make Haste*."

Emm was photographed in the studio with a kitten on her shoulder. This painting inspired the French artist Emile Vernon's (1872-1920) *Playing With The Kittens* signed and dated Paris, 1919.

Black and white photograph in *Royal Academy Pictures*, 1895, p.95, and *Pearson's Magazine*, April 1898. Sepia photogravure, 22ins x $14\frac{1}{2}$ins (56.5cm x 37cm), engraved by Hanfstaengl and published by Frost & Reed, 4th November 1895. 200 Artist's proofs @ 3 guineas, 25 presentation India proofs @ 1 guinea. (Artist's proofs nearly all sold in May 1908 catalogue, and no longer available in January 1913 catalogue.) Later sepia photogravure presented with *The Ladies Pictorial*, 21st November 1914, now copyright Hildersheimer. **See previous page**.

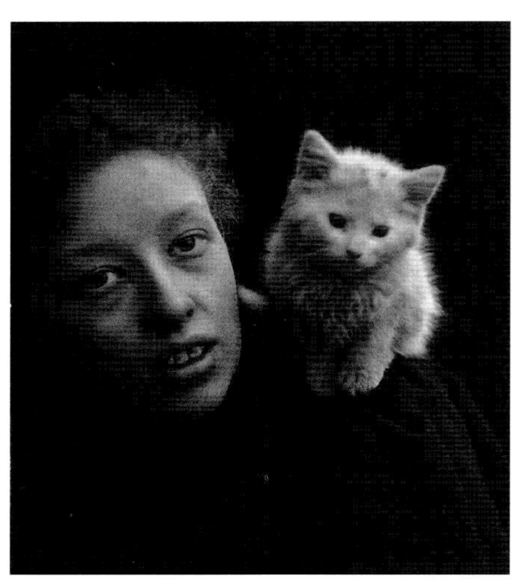

Source photograph of Emm Elsley with kitten for *Make Haste*.

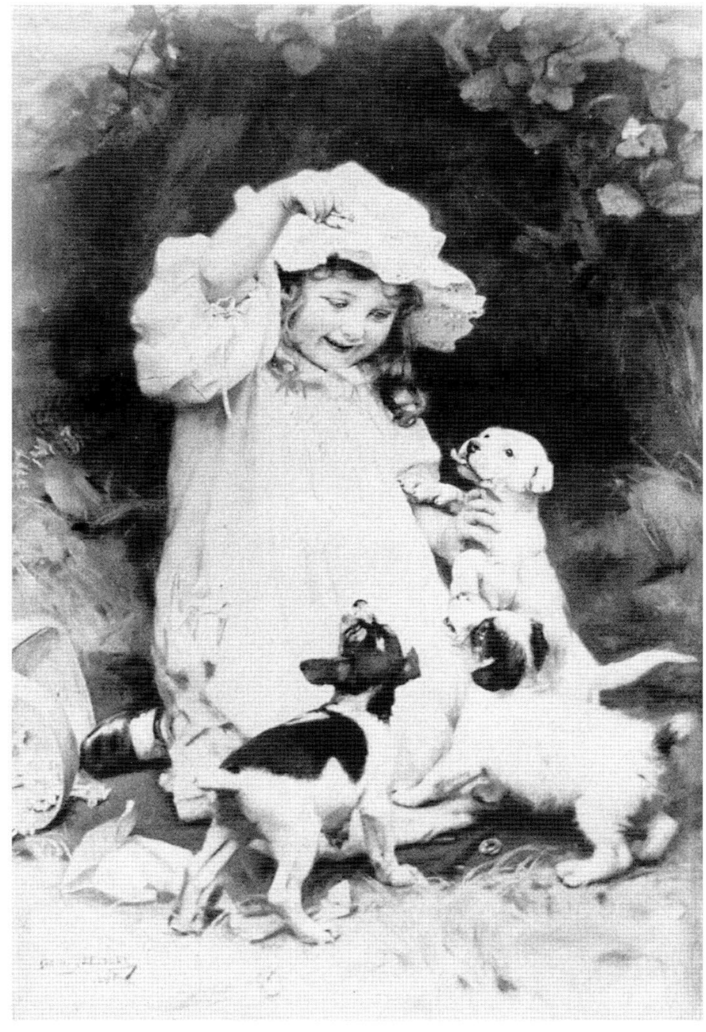

Who Speaks First?

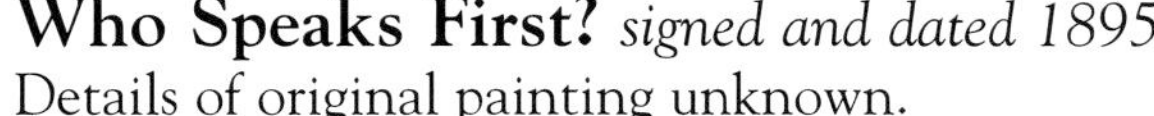

Who Speaks First? *signed and dated 1895*
Details of original painting unknown.

Not to be confused with American calendar manufactured by Thos. D. Murphy Co., 1922. Black and white photograph, *Pearson's Magazine*, Vol.VI No.33, September 1898, p.237.

Reproduced as a photogravure, $14\frac{1}{4}$ins x $21\frac{1}{2}$ins (37cm x 55cm), engraved by Hanfstaengl, and published by Frost & Reed, 4th November 1895. 200 Artist's proofs @ 3 guineas, 50 lettered proofs @ 2 guineas, 25 presentation proofs, unlimited India prints @ 1 guinea. Artist's proofs and India prints still available in May 1908 catalogue, but not in January 1913 catalogue.

Breaking Them In *signed and dated 1895*
Oil on canvas, $34\frac{1}{2}$ins x $24\frac{1}{2}$ins (88cm x 62.5cm).

There are echoes of Sir Joshua Reynolds' painting of *Puck*, and Messonier's popular painting of Baccus astride a barrel.

Colour postcards by Hildersheimer, c.1903.

Small sepia photogravure, signed and dated 1895, approximately 8ins x 6ins (20.5cm x 15cm), published as a pair with Fred Morgan's *Happy Times*, Royal Academy, 1888. Sepia photogravure, 15ins x 10ins (38cm x 25.5cm), presented with *Weldon's Ladies' Journal*, Christmas 1902. Sepia photogravure, $20\frac{1}{4}$ins x $13\frac{3}{4}$ (51.5cm x 35cm), published by *The Illustrated London News*, 1913, copyright S. Hildersheimer & Co. Ltd., (date under signature removed). The image was used again because Elsley couldn't produce enough new works to keep up with the demand and the owners of copyright could gain more royalties. Used as a colour chromolithograph calendar by various companies, including Scales & Sons, Burton-on-Trent (date below signature removed).

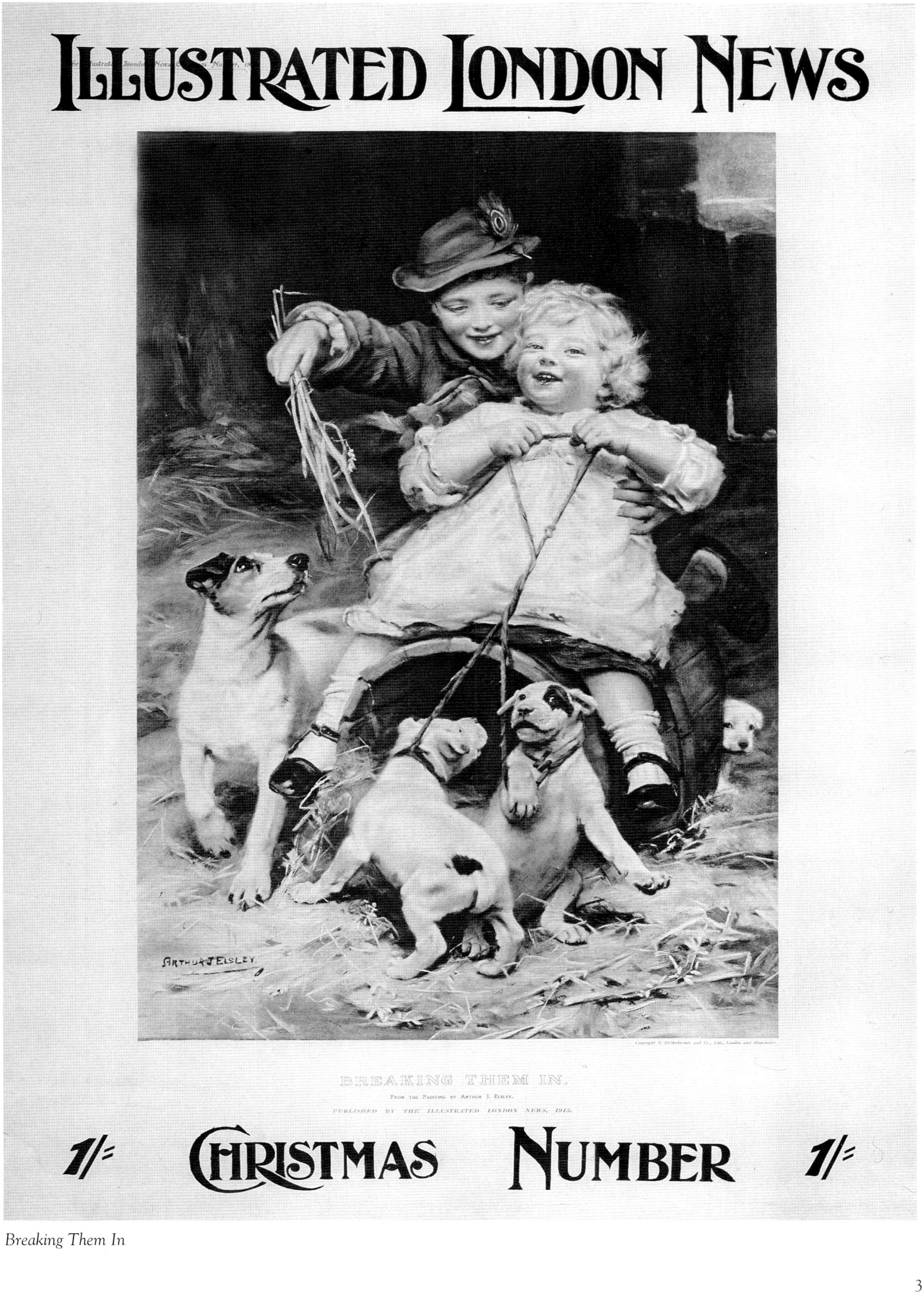

ILLUSTRATED LONDON NEWS

ARTHUR J ELSLEY

Copyright S. Hildesheimer and Co., Ltd., London and Manchester.

BREAKING THEM IN.

FROM THE PAINTING BY ARTHUR J. ELSLEY.

PUBLISHED BY THE ILLUSTRATED LONDON NEWS, 1913.

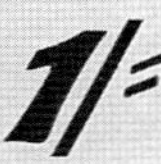

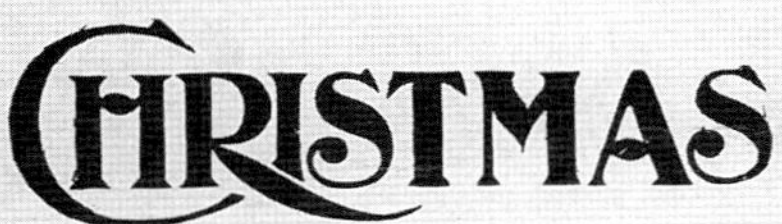

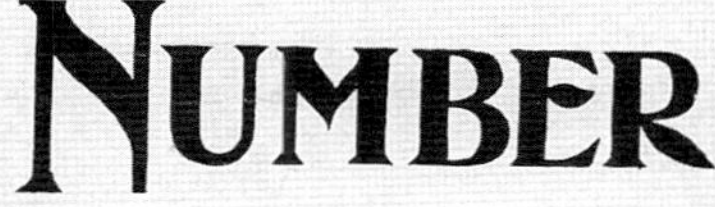

1/-

Breaking Them In

A Young Briton *signed and dated 1895*

Details of original painting unknown.

The old soldier is wearing the uniform of a Chelsea Pensioner, and his hat is on the back of the chair. He is showing the young boy his sword, although Chelsea Pensioners don't normally carry them. The pensioner's legs appear to be too long! The featured newspaper, *The Broad Arrow Naval And Military Gazette*, was published from 1868-1917. The Elsley print features in a Cecil Aldin cartoon, *A Christmas Party*, used to illustrate the article "Christmas in Pictureland" by John Oldcastle in *The Windsor Magazine*, December 1898, p.14.

Colour chromolithograph $23^{1}/_{2}$ins x $17^{1}/_{4}$ins (60.5cm x 44.5cm), signed not dated, presented with *The Illustrated London News*, Christmas 1895. A poor-quality photolithograph version, 18ins x $13^{1}/_{4}$ins (46.5cm x 33.5cm), appeared later, possibly as a calendar, now entitled *Britons Never Shall Be Slaves* (a line from the patriotic anthem *Rule Britannia*) and the title of the newspaper has been altered. **See page 62**.

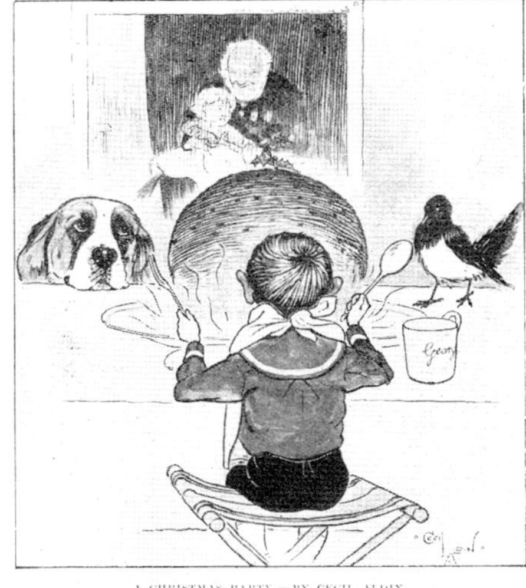

Cecil Aldin cartoon.

Motherly Care / The Foster Mother

signed and dated 1895

Version I

Oil on canvas, 38ins x 25ins (97cm x 64cm). Exhibited at Royal Academy, 1896 (No.607), called *Motherly Care*, priced £150 but unsold. In this version the woman is wearing a hat.

Extract from "Artists and Their Work", *Pearson's Magazine*, April 1898, p.348:

> "A picture that he is now finishing, called *The Foster Mother*, was a source of much trouble. The subject is a peasant girl feeding some lambs from a bottle. The lambs were very timorous at first, and he could make no progress, but after a while they became so tame that he never had more obedient sitters."

Black and white postcard produced by Hildersheimer c.1903 entitled *The Foster Mother*, signed and dated 1895. Photograph, *Royal Academy Pictures*, 1896, p.170.

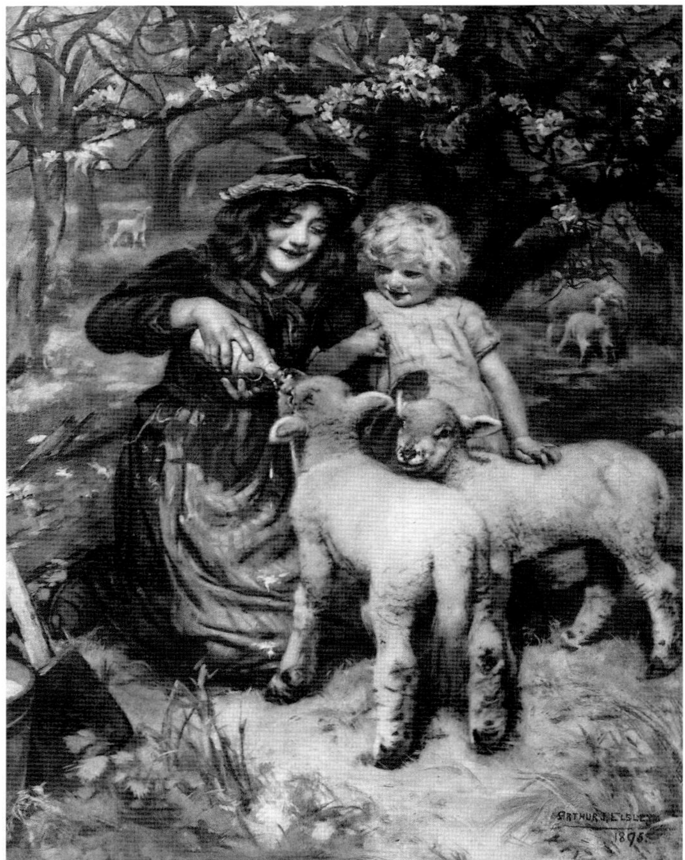

Motherly Care / The Foster Mother. Version I.

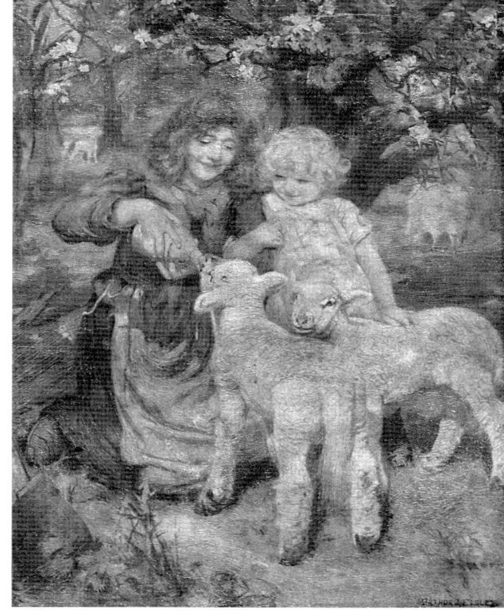

Motherly Care / The Foster Mother. Version II.

Sepia photogravure, 23ins x $17^{1}/_{4}$ins (59cm x 44.5cm), copyright Hildersheimer.

Version II

This version is called *The Foster Mother* but the woman is not wearing a hat. It looks like a doctored version of the original and is signed but not dated.

Version II was reproduced as a colour postcard by Hildersheimer. One of the versions was used as the colour chromolithograph frontispiece of *The Child's Companion*, 1903, and now called *Feeding The Lambs*.

Poor-quality colour print on canvas, $17^{3}/_{4}$ins x $13^{3}/_{4}$ins (46cm x 35cm), called *The Foster Mother,* presented with *The Queen Magazine*, 20th November 1915. *The Queen* is printed bottom left on the image.

[An Uninvited Guest] *signed and dated 1895*

Oil on canvas, 30ins x 20ins (76.5cm x 51cm). Auctioned in 1985.

This is the only known title but is unlikely to have been the original. cf. *Safe Quarters*, c.1895, the same girl and dog are featured. The first of his works to include strawberries – a popular prop in paintings of children.

Recently owned by Schillay & Rehs Gallery, New York, who called it *All Mine*.

Reproduced as a show-card, $20^{1}/_{2}$ins x $15^{1}/_{2}$ins (52cm x 39.5cm), for Brook's Sewing Cotton, c.1896. **See page 61**.

Safe Quarters *circa 1895*

Details of original painting unknown.

Elsley, like most artists, kept a costume basket and his young models were often draped with pieces of material when a whole outfit was not available. cf. *An Uninvited Guest*, signed and dated 1895, in which the same girl and dog are featured.

Colour photolithograph printed on textured paper, 12ins x 9ins (30.5cm x 23cm), presented with *Weldon's Bazaar of Children's Fashion*, Christmas 1911, copyright Alfred Vivian Mansell & Co., London.

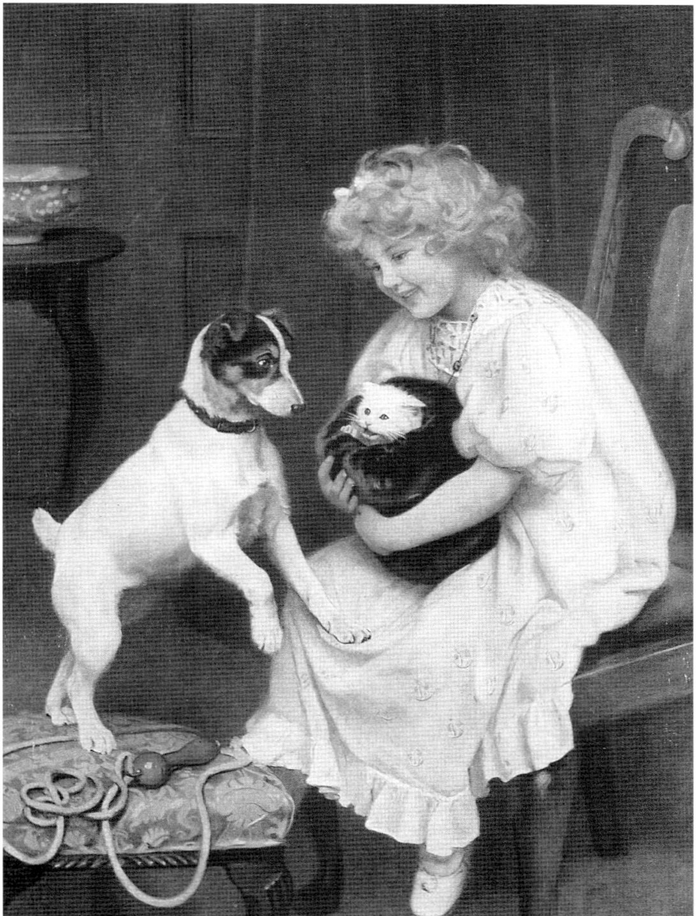

Safe Quarters

Who Is It? *signed and dated 1895*

Version I

Details of original painting unknown.

Dog with front legs apart, signed and dated 1895, copyright Frost & Reed, Bristol. Black and white photograph from *Black and White Magazine*, May 1896, p.698.

Version II

Dog with front legs together. Black and white photograph in *Black and White Magazine*, May 1896, p.698. Reproduced as photogravure, not signed or dated, 23ins x

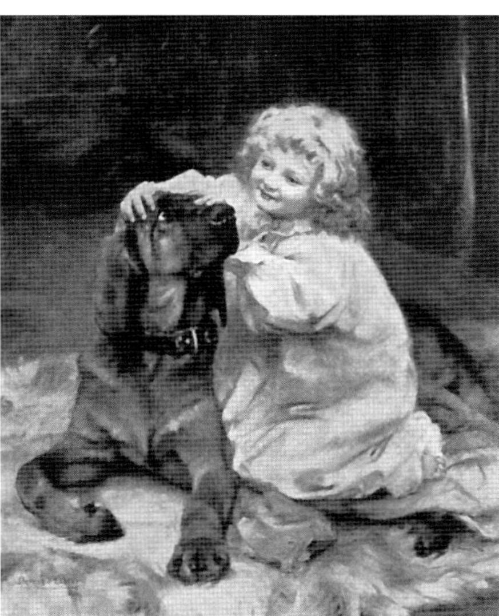

Who Is It? Version I.

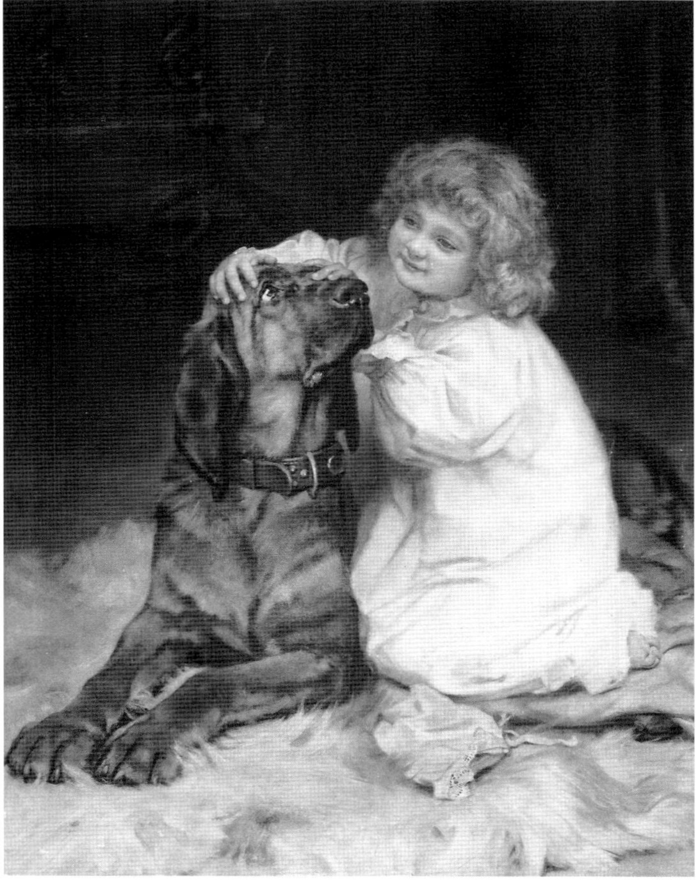

Who Is It? Version II.

17¾ins (59cm x 46cm), engraved by B. Pratt and published by Frost & Reed, Bristol, 4th November 1895. Not to be confused with *Who Speaks First?*, 1895, which was also published by Frost & Reed.

This version is probably Version 1 overpainted. It was common practice for print publishers to request artists to amend their works and Elsley, disgruntled at being asked to do this, may have scrubbed out his signature and date. 200 Artist's proofs @ 3 guineas, 50 lettered proofs @ 2 guineas, 25 presentation proofs, unlimited India prints @ 1 guinea. (Lettered proofs all sold, but India Prints still available in May 1908 catalogue were all sold by January 1913.)

Adverse Winds *signed and dated 1895*

Oil on canvas, 37ins x 28ins (94.5cm x 71.5cm).

Steps or stairs are a recurring theme in Elsley s work, whether as a major element or purely as background.

Colour chromolithograph 18¾ins x 13½ins (48cm x 34.5cm). **See page 58.**

[A Birthday Cracker] *signed and dated 1896*

Oil on canvas, 34½ins x 24½ins (88cm x 62.5cm), auctioned at Sotheby's, London, in 1973 entitled *A Birthday Cracker*. It features the same little girl as the previous painting, with a different old man.

Elsley incorporated an oil sketch, 18ins x 10¼ins (46.5cm x 26cm), of cottage steps which was sold at the Studio Sale (part of Lot 4), now in the author's collection.

Soft Persuasion *signed and dated 1896*

Details of original painting unknown. Exhibited at the Royal Academy, 1896 (No.8), unsold at £150, but the copyright had already been reserved.

Extract from *The London Magazine*:

"The dog that sat for *Soft Persuasion* was a remarkable creature in more ways than one. Instead of wagging its tail from side to side, like an ordinary dog, it used to wag it up and down over its back. Whenever it came indoors it always wiped its feet on the mat, to an accompaniment of many growls, as if to call attention to its carefulness;

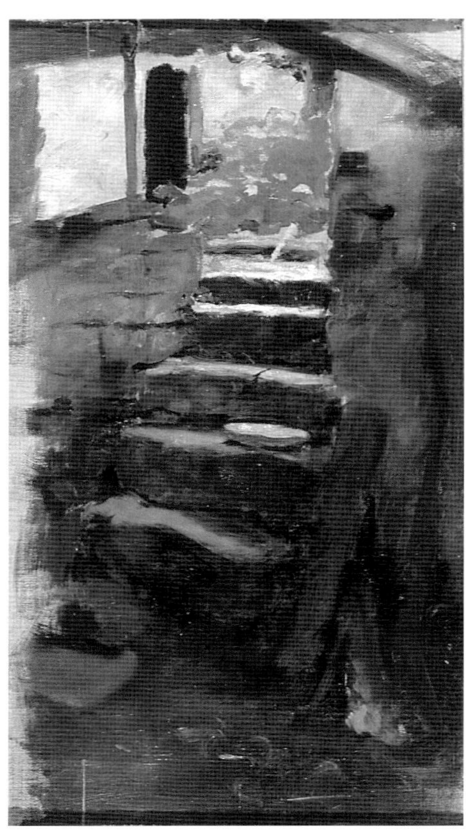

Unsigned oil sketch of steps.

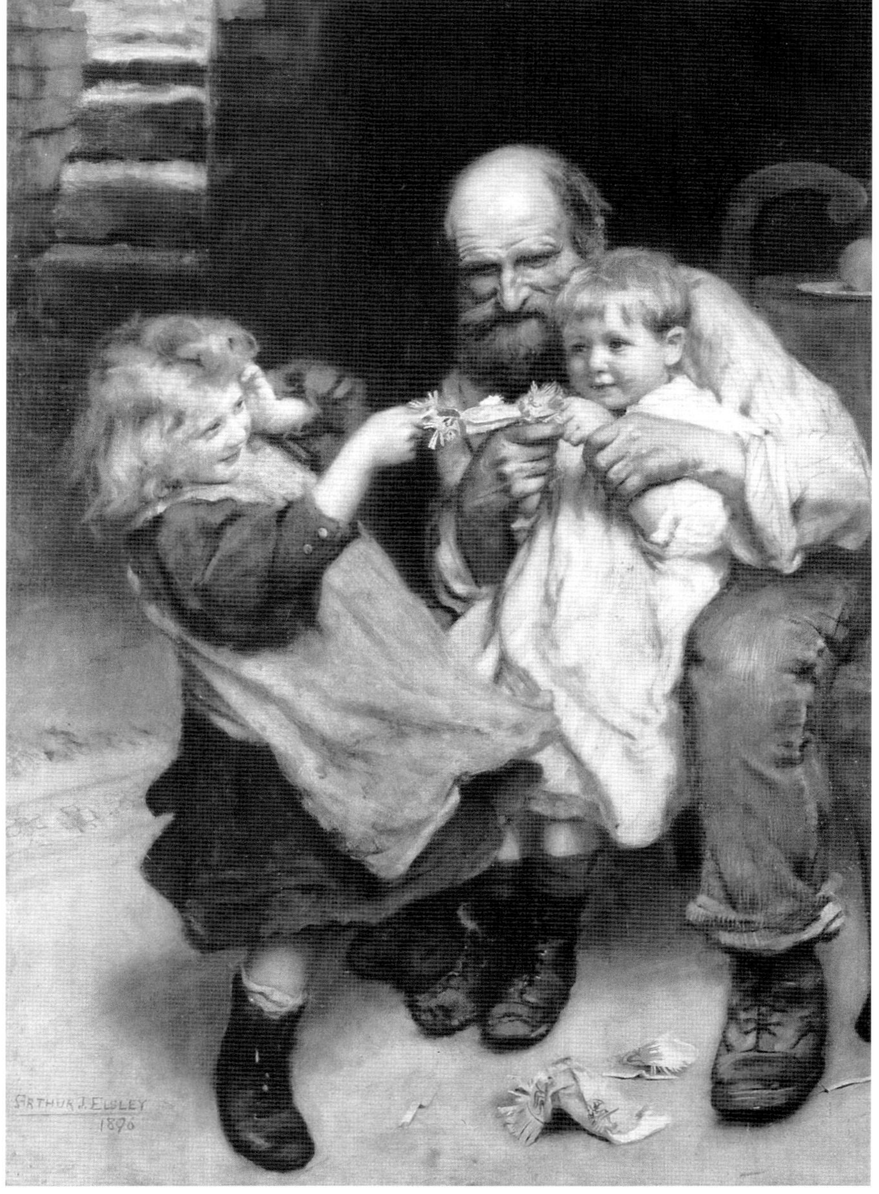

[A Birthday Cracker]

while its delight was to play 'hide-and-seek', in which game it had been carefully trained by its master. 'Now, Grizzle', the owner would say, 'we'll have hot boiled beans.' Grizzle would get up, wag its tail, and go to the door to be shut out, after it had been shown what was to be hidden, and would come in and search, if necessary for an hour, in order to discover the article."

Royal Academy Notes, 1896: "Child in pink dress offering a biscuit to a fox-terrier" (not illustrated).

Another artist copied *Soft Persuasion* and renamed it *Coaxing*. The copied painting (not signed or dated) appeared as a poor-quality colour chromolithograph frontispiece in *Our Little Dots*, 1916, and again in *Little Folks*, 1917. Black and white photograph, *The Leisure Hour*, 1897; *Pearson's Magazine*, Vol.5 No.25, January 1898; and *The Harmsworth Magazine*, Vol.3 No.13, August 1899; and again in *The Sunday Magazine*, 1899.

Sepia photogravure, copyright Berlin Photographic 1896. Sepia photogravure, $15^{1}/_{4}$ins x 11ins (39cm x 28cm), presented with *Weldon's Ladies' Journal*, Christmas 1904.

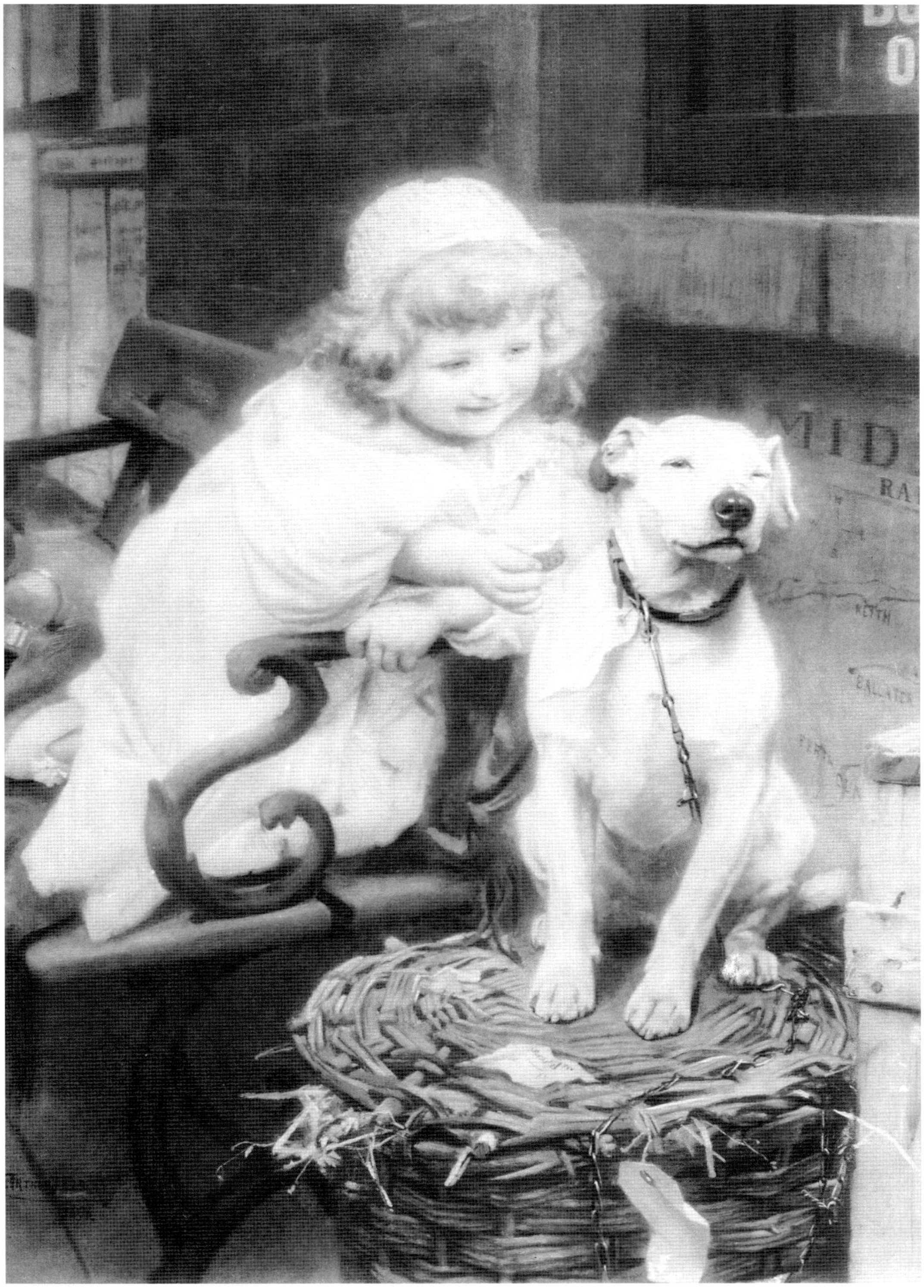

Soft Persuasion

Source photograph for *Soft Persuasion* and *More Haste Less Speed*. **See page 65**.

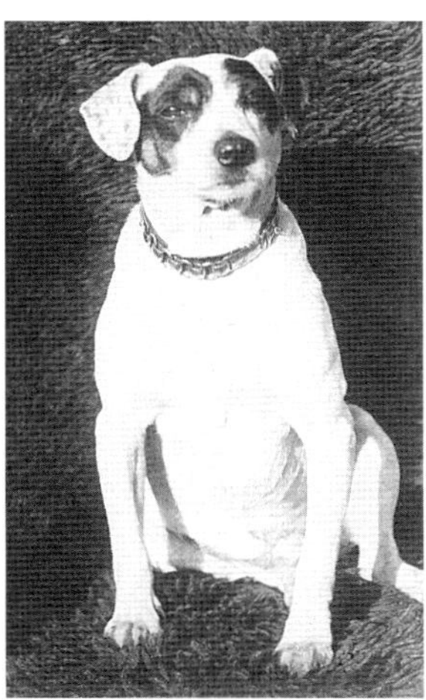

Pets / Doves *signed and dated 1896*

Oil on canvas, 22ins x 17ins (56.5cm x 43cm). Exhibited at the Royal Academy, 1896 (No.698), entitled *Pets*, unsold at £160, but the copyright had already been reserved. Oil on canvas, 25½ins x 15½ins (65.5cm x 39.5cm), auctioned at Christie's, London, 1925, but *Royal Academy Pictures*, 1896, p.191, describes it as 22ins x 17ins (56.5cm x 43cm). There may have been two versions.

The model appears to be Fred Morgan's youngest son, Courtney, who was born on the 4th June 1894. He is in a very similar pose in *Out of Reach*, Morgan's 1897 Royal Academy exhibit (No.693). Both works are inspired by Sir Joshua Reynolds' *Portrait Of Master Hare*.

Black and white photograph in *Royal Academy Pictures*, 1896, p.191. Black and white postcard published by S. Hildersheimer c.1903, copyright S. Hildersheimer.

Sepia photogravure, 19½ins x 12½ins (50cm x 32cm), called *Doves* presented with *Lady's Pictorial*, Christmas 1899, signed, not dated on print. Sepia photogravure, 15ins x 10½ins (38cm x 26.5cm), entitled *Pets* presented with *Myra's Journal*, 1st December 1903, signed not dated on print. Reproduced as a pair with *Good-Bye*, 1894, presented with *Weldon's Ladies' Journal*, December 1903.

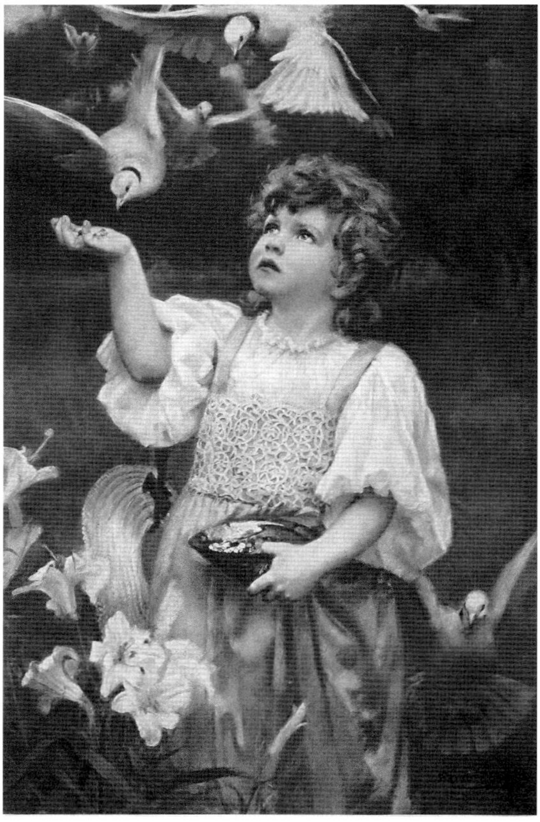

Pets / Doves

[Heave Ho!] *signed and dated 1896*

Oil on canvas, 24ins x 33ins (61.5cm x 84cm). Exhibited at The Royal Society of British Artists, London, Spring 1898 (No.183), no price given.

It is possible that a water-colour version of this painting was sold at Christie's, London, in 1941.

Possibly painted at Winterton-on-Sea in Norfolk or the Isle of Wight. Fred Morgan had produced a popular series of paintings with a beach theme since *A Willing Hand*, Royal Academy, 1891 (No.442). **See page 59**.

Breakers Ahead *signed and dated 1896*

Oil on canvas, 29ins x 38ins (74cm x 97cm). Exhibited at the Royal Academy, 1898 (No.891), unsold at £200, but the copyright had already been reserved. A version of this picture, 30ins x 42ins (76.5cm x 107cm) described as *Children On A Donkey On Beach* was sold at Sotheby's, New York, 12th March 1979 for $7,500.

At about this time it appears Elsley also painted the same donkey in Fred Morgan's *Whoa!* (reproduced as a colour chromolithograph, *Sketchy Bits*, Summer Number 1897). Black and white photograph in *Royal Academy Pictures*, 1898, p.98.

Copyright Messrs. Eyre and Spottiswoode, Fetter Lane, London E.C.

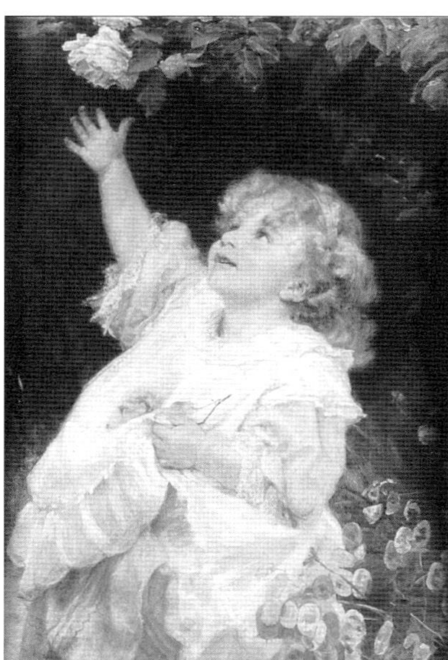

Out Of Reach by Fred Morgan.

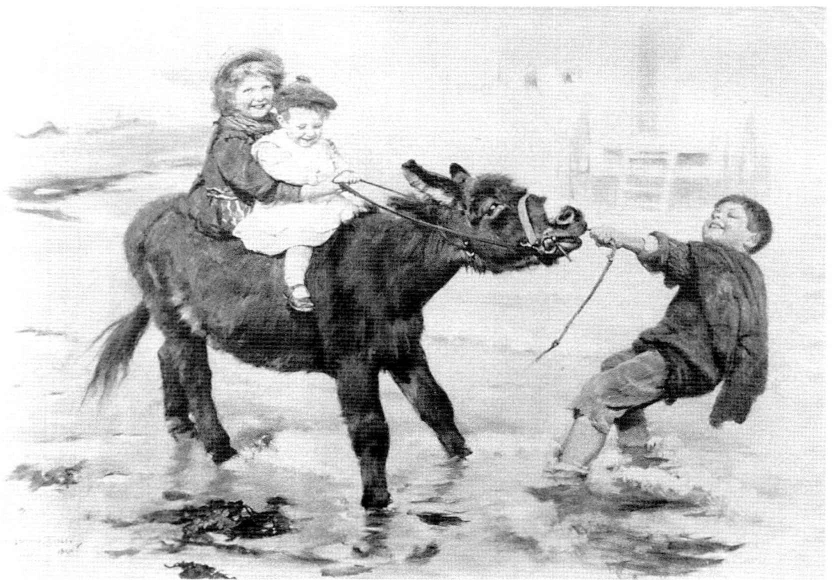

Breakers Ahead

Are You There? *circa 1896*

Oil on canvas, 29ins x 21ins (74cm x 54cm), not signed and dated and likely to have been painted by Elsley, was auctioned at Sotheby's, London, 22nd March 1989 (Lot 180). Now entitled *A Conversation* it sold for £3,100.

Elsley did not own a telephone as he wanted to avoid the annoyance of being disturbed when he was working. On the rare occasions he needed to use one he went to the nearby tobacconist's.

It was reproduced as a colour advertising show-card for Peek, Frean & Co., Biscuits & Cakes, c.1897. **See page 61**.

A Tempting Slide / Temptation *signed and dated 1897*

Oil on canvas, 30¼ins x 22½ins (77cm x 57.5). Exhibited at the Royal Academy, 1897 (No.1046), unsold at £160, but the copyright had already been reserved.

Black and White Handbook to the Royal Academy and New Gallery, 1897, names this work *Temptation*. The catalogue was produced well in advance of the exhibition and Elsley may have changed the title for clarity. Auctioned as *On the Screen*, signed and dated 1897, at Christie's, London, 21st April 1933 (Lot 119). Vendor N. Mitchell, bought by Le Roy for 10 guineas.

Elsley's paintings are more humorous than Morgan's. This work is the follow-up to *Are You There* on the comical theme of dogs confused by modern technology. Like most artists Elsley and Morgan were keen amateur photographers, and the Elsley family owned a lantern slide. Sir David Wilkie R.A., before the advent of photography, painted *The Rabbit On The Wall* showing a father making animal shadow-shapes with his hands on a wall.

Black and white photograph in *Royal Academy Notes*, 1897, p.27; *Royal Academy Illustrated*, 1897, p.89, and *Harmsworth's London Magazine*, Vol.7, September 1901, p.98, now called *Too Realistic! – The Magic Lantern*. Colour chromolithograph page, 7ins x 5ins (18cm x 12.5cm) in *Child's Own Magazine*, Vol.69, 1902, called *The Magic Lantern* (date below signature removed).

Sepia photogravure, 21¼ins x 15ins (54.5cm x 38cm), copyright Hansstaengh, Munich.

Chicks *circa 1897*

Details of original painting unknown. Exhibited at the Royal Academy, 1897 (No.705). It was described as "three children fondling a chicken" in *Royal Academy Notes*, 1897, p.22, but was not illustrated.

Sepia page *Sunday at Home*, 1898, p.480. Black and white photograph *Pearson's Magazine*, Vol.VI No.31, July 1898, p.9, *Hamsworth's London Magazine*, September 1901, p.189, and *Munsey's Magazine* (U.S.A.), date unknown, illustrating article "Artists and Their Work".

Sepia photogravure, 19½ins x 14¼ins (50cm x 36cm), copyright Berlin Photographic, not signed and dated on print.

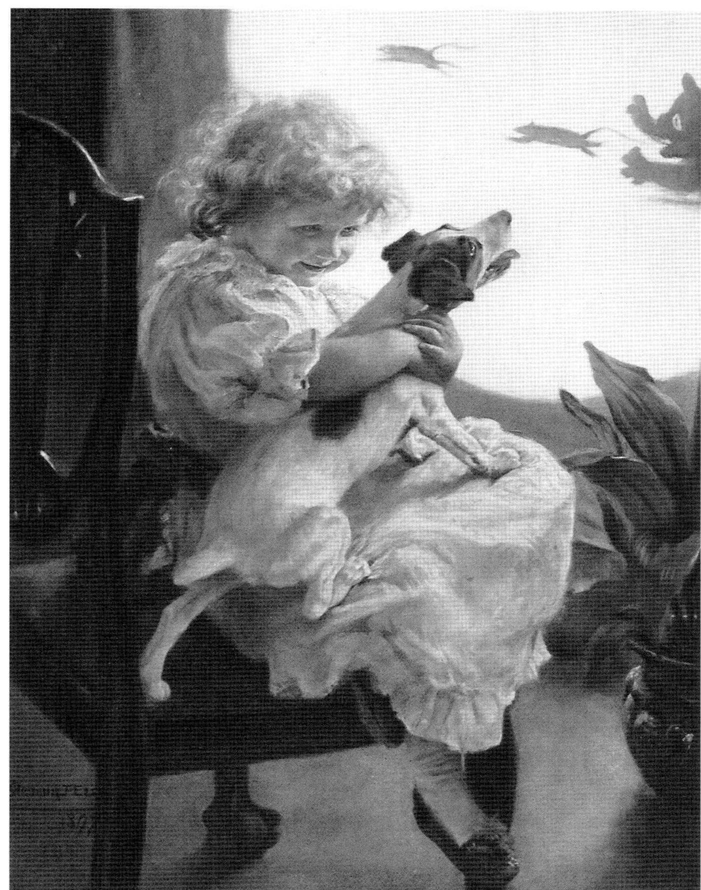

A Tempting Slide / Temptation

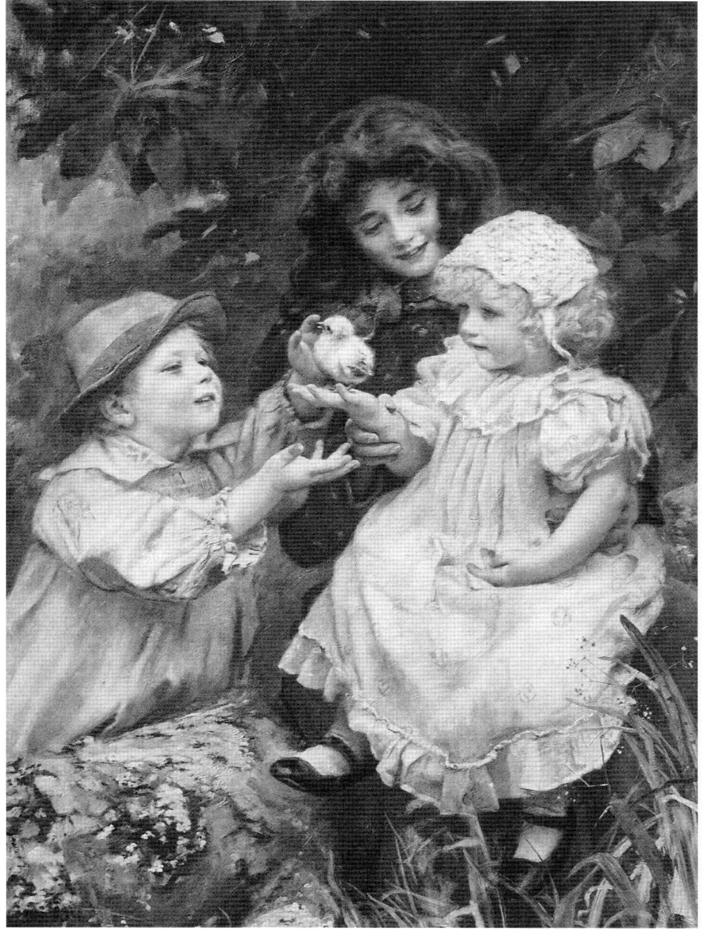

Chicks

Homeward Bound *circa 1897*

Oil on canvas, 29ins x 20½ins (74cm x 52cm), signed not dated.

The models are Mrs. Knight and an unknown man. He also sat for *Caught Napping*, 1899. They are presumably reading about their son's return from the Navy.

Unrecorded as a print. **See page 62**.

Their First Swim *circa 1897*

Oil on canvas, 35ins x 25½ins (89cm x 65.5cm). Recently owned by Rehs Galleries, New York, who called it *Learning to Swim*.

The hen is foster-mother to the ducklings and is looking shocked at their being able to swim!

Colour chromolithograph calendar, 23ins x 17ins (59cm x 43cm), copyright Faulkner, printed by Alf Cooke Printing Company, 1905. Small colour photolithograph, presented with *Horner's Penny Stories*, 30th November 1911. Title possibly *Their First Dip*. **See page 68**.

Just In Time *circa 1893*

Details of original painting unknown. It is difficult to date this painting as it appears to be the companion work to *Our Christmas Goose*, 1892, but features the same boy as Fred Morgan's *Whoa!*, c.1896, and his *A Lively Haul*, Royal Academy, 1897, and Elsley's *Full Inside*, 1899. Frontispiece in *The Child's Companion*, 1905 (retitled *More Frightened Than Hurt*).

Sepia photogravure, 20ins x 12½ins (51cm x 32cm), publisher unknown. Colour chromolithograph calendar for 1913, approximately 21ins x 14¾ins (54cm x 37.5cm), retitled *More Frightened Than Hurt* (the title of another painting from 1890). Entered at Stationery Hall, no copyright given, signature and date cut off image.

[A Clean Getaway] / Ivy Soap Advertisement *signed and dated 1897*

Details of original painting unknown. Possibly sold either as *The Baby's Bath*, oil, 39½ins x 27ins (100.5cm x 69cm), Christie's (Art Sales Index 1931/2), bought by Nicol for 7 guineas; or *The Order Of The Bath*, auctioned at Christie's, London, 11th February 1916, (Lot 70) oil, 31½ins x 21½ins (79.5cm x 55cm), bought by Mitchell for 19 guineas.

Not to be confused with *Go Away Sir!*, 1891, or *Before The Bath*, 1900.

Ivy Soap changed the scrubbing brush in the original painting to a bar of soap when it was used as an advertising insert. These were colour advertisements printed on high-quality paper, unlike the newsprint paper of the magazine into which they were inserted. Modern postcard, Robert Opie Museum of Advertising and Packaging, showing Ivy Soap advertising insert.

Reproduced as a high-quality colour chromolithograph, details unknown. **See page 69**.

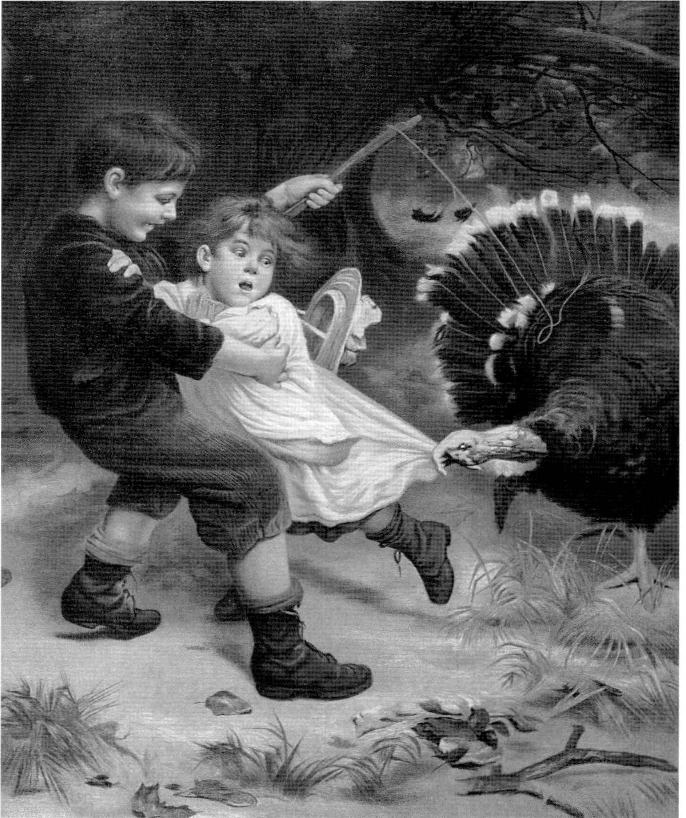

Just In Time

Any Room For Me? *signed and dated 1897*

Details of original painting unknown.

Cleverly constructed scene bringing together snow and using the umbrella as a prop. The old man also appears in Fred Morgan's *Grandfather's Birthday? / Children's Children Are The Glory Of Old Men*, 1897.

Colour chromolithograph, 18¾ins x 13½ins (48cm x 34.5cm), presented with *Weldon's Ladies' Journal*, Christmas 1897. **See page 64**.

Under The Mistletoe *signed and dated 1897*

Details of original painting unknown.

This girl and dogs appear in many of Elsley's works of this period, and the skipping rope is used again!

Colour chromolithograph, 20ins x 15ins (51cm x 38cm), presented with *St. James Budget* magazine, Christmas 1898, (printed by L. Van Leer & Co., Holland). **See page 68**.

You Mustn't Touch *circa 1897*

Details of original painting unknown.

A *Children's Annual* article entitled "You Mustn't Touch" is illustrated with a black and white trimmed version, date and signature removed, which says "From a Drawing by Arthur J. Elsley. By permission of Messrs. E.W. Savory, Ltd". This would indicate the original was not an oil painting. Not to be confused with *You Mustn't Pull*, 1901.

Colour photolithograph, 8ins x 6ins (20.5cm x 15cm), presented with *Horner's Penny Stories* the popular story paper. The image has been trimmed to exclude the girl's leg and the print is not signed and dated.

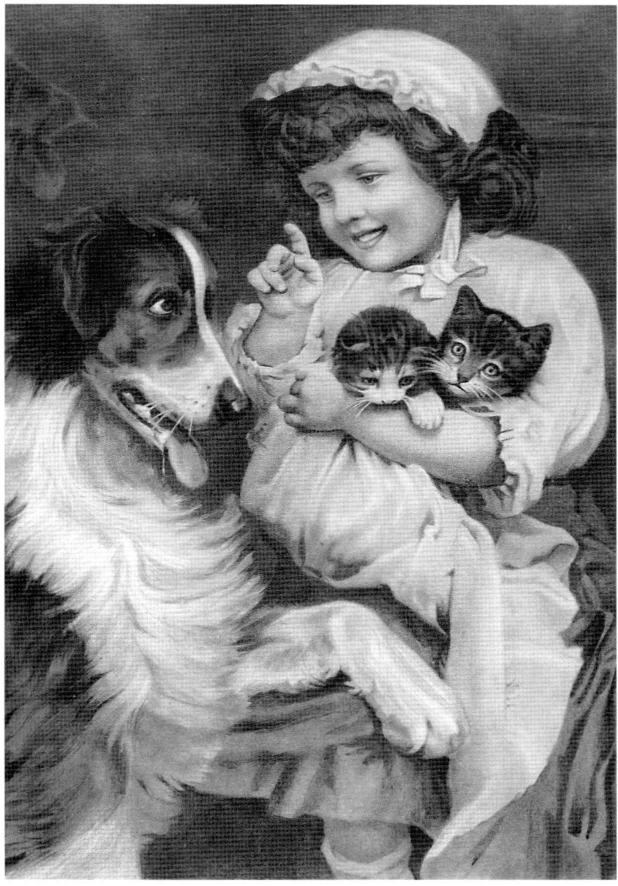

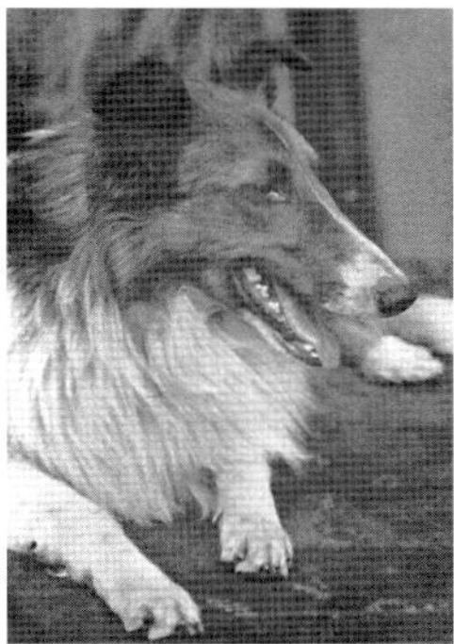

Above, *You Mustn't Touch.*

Left, source photograph of Elsley's pet collie.

Weatherbound *signed and dated 1898*

Details of original painting unknown.

This is a return to the use of a barrel as a prop as in *Breaking Them In*, 1895. Sepia page, 7¼ins x 5½ins (18.5cm x 14cm), in *Partridge's Children's Annual*, 1909, and now known as *Our Friend Rufus*.

Colour chromolithograph, 29¼ins x 22¼ins (74.5 x 57cm). **See page 64**.

Hard Pressed / Time To Get Up *signed and dated 1898*

Oil on canvas, 34ins x 26ins (86.5cm x 66.5cm) entitled *Hard Pressed*. Exhibited at the Royal Academy, 1898 (No.468). This work appears to have been auctioned many times with different titles.

Oil on canvas, 33½ins x 25ins (85.5cm x 64cm), called *Time To Get Up* (signed and dated 1898) was auctioned by Christie's, London 11th February 1916 (Lot 69), and bought for £23.9s. by Mitchell. Oil on canvas, 33½ins x 25ins (85.5cm x 64cm), entitled *Good Morning* (signed and dated 1898), sold at Christie's, London 14th July 1933 and bought for 12 guineas, again by Mitchell.

Oil on canvas, 33ins x 24¾ins (84cm x 63.5cm), entitled *Morning Visitors* (signed and dated 1898), was sold at Christie's on 20th December 1934. Vendor Sir John Child and bought by R. MacConnal for £12.1s 6d. Oil on canvas, 33¼ins x 25ins (85.5cm x 64cm), entitled *Good Morning* (signed and dated 1898), was sold at Christie's 15th July 1938. Vendor R. MacConnal and bought by Lewis for 8 guineas.

Owned by Haynes Fine Art in May 1994. Extract from *Haynes Fine Art Exhibition Catalogue*:

> "The combination of children with domestic animals is, for most collectors, an irresistible recipe. In the words of George Elliot, it is 'a beauty with which you can never be angry, but that you feel ready to crush for inability to comprehend the state of mind into which it throws you'. There are no words which can describe the admiration I have for this extremely important canvas. I only hope you will not miss the opportunity of seeing such a rare and beautiful work of art."

Black and White Handbook to the Royal Academy and New Gallery illustrate *Time To Get Up*, but Royal Academy listings give this exhibit the title *Hard Pressed*. Sepia photogravure called *Time to Get Up*, 23ins x 17¼ins (59cm x 44.5cm), engraved by Hanfstaengl and published by Frost & Reed 1st October 1898. 100 Artist's proofs @ 3 guineas, 25 presentation India prints (no price given), India prints @ 1 guinea. **See page 60**.

Any Port In A Storm / Late For School

signed and dated 1898

An oil version may be called *Hard Pressed*.

A photograph of the studio shows a small painting of this subject on the easel (this could be a water-colour). A water-colour described as "After Elsley" was exhibited at The Cork International Exhibition of 1902 (No.477), lent by *The Illustrated London News*.

The model for the old school mistress was Mrs. Knight. Elsley appears to have been influenced by Thomas Blinks' *The End of the Tail* (engraved in *The Illustrated London News*, 13th March 1886), but that work concentrates on the dogs capturing the fox and is far more violent. In British art there is a long tradition of schoolhouse themes, and Elsley was innovative in combining this with the subject of the hunt. This was one of his series of hunt paintings.

Colour chromolithograph, 28¼ins x 19ins (72.5cm x 49cm), presented with *The Illustrated London News*, Christmas 1899, called *Late For School*. Advert for *The Illustrated London News* in *Pears Annual 1899*, calls this print *Any Port in a Storm*, which was likely to have been its original working title, but *The Illustrated London News* advertisement of the 11th November 1899 calls it *Late For School*. Also a limited edition proof prints *The Illustrated London News* photogravure, 17ins x 12½ins (43cm x 32cm), price 10s 6d (advertisement in 1902 does not state whether black and white or colour). **See page 63**.

Divided Attention *circa 1898*

An oil sketch on board, 16¼ins x 12¼ins (41.5cm x 31cm), for this work was sold at Sotheby's, London, in 1992 with the title *A Playful Cat*. Elsley signed the original oil painting on the footstool. The final work has a kitten on the floor which is not in the sketch.

Pearson's Magazine, September 1901, p.243, in an article entitled "Models" writes of the model Mrs. Knight:

"...she is seen again, painted by this artist, as a delightful grandma telling stories to a sunny haired lassie at her knee".

Colour chromolithograph, 18¾ins x 13½ins (48cm x 34.5cm), *Weldon's Ladies' Journal*, First Supplement, Christmas 1898. The book in the painting reads "D for dog". The original oil painting was in the possession of the publishers at this date. Published again as a sepia photogravure, 12½ins x 8¾ins (32cm x 22cm), in *Weldon's Bazaar of Children's Fashions*, Christmas 1904. No one is credited with copyright on either version. In a colour chromolithograph the title of the painting has been changed to *Don't Look Back*, and the book within the painting is now titled "*Young Soldier* No.1504, Volume XI, Saturday...". **See page 62**.

Caught Napping *signed and dated 1899*

Details of original painting unknown. A picture with this title was exhibited in Birmingham, Autumn 1897 (No.194), priced £130.

The same old man also sat for *Adverse Winds*, 1895 and *Homeward Bound*, 1857.

Colour chromolithograph, 23ins x 16¼ins (59cm x 41.5cm), probably a calendar, signed and dated 1899. **See page 62**.

At Bay / Pay Toll *signed and dated 1898*

Oil on canvas entitled *At Bay*. Exhibited at the Royal Academy, 1899 (No.579), Gallery VII, and sold for £120. Probably the oil painting measuring 33½ins x 24½ins (85.5cm x 62.5cm), entitled *Mistletoe* (signed and dated 1898) which was auctioned at Christie's, London, on 15th June 1925, and bought by Mason for 55 guineas.

Not to be confused with *Under The Mistletoe*, c.1897.

Black and white photograph, *Black and White Handbook to the Royal Academy and New Gallery in 1899*.

Poor-quality colour chromolithograph called *Fay Toll*, copyright unknown. **See page 64**.

Divided Affection *signed and dated 1899*

Details of original painting unknown. Exhibited at Royal Academy, 1899 (No.743), and sold for £150.

The collie was the family pet named Old Bruce. He also appears in *Bath Time*, 1900. A head and shoulders oil sketch of the girl, 9¾ins x 8ins (24.5cm x 20.5cm), was sold at the Studio Sale (Lot 24). Extract from *Illustrated Interviews*, XLVI, "Mr. Briton Riviere, R.A." by Harry How, *The Strand* Vol.XI, January 1896, p.5:

"The Royal Academician, Briton Riviere, observed: 'The most restless sitters are the collie and the deerhound. Still not withstanding their restlessness, I am very fond of both, and have frequently painted them.' "

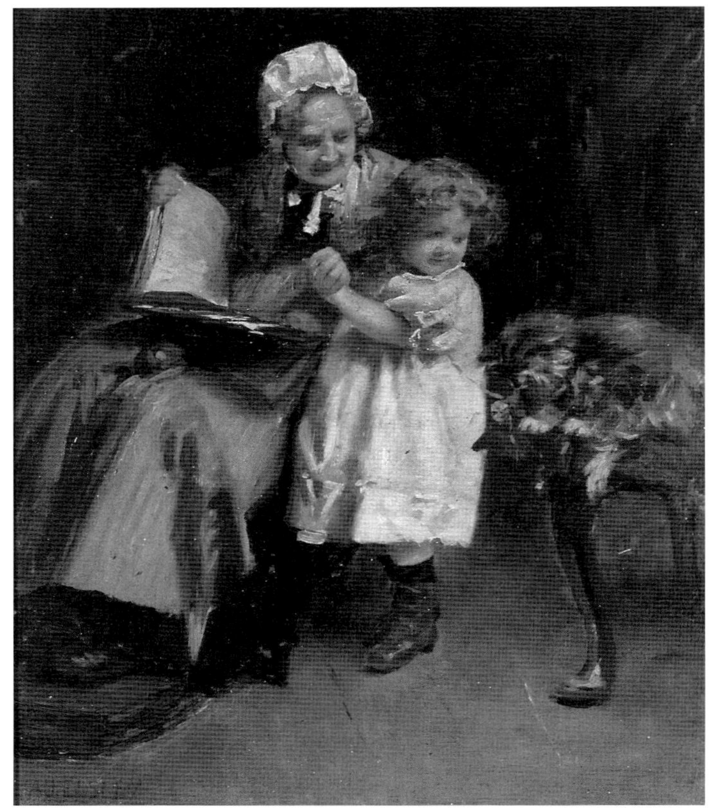

A Playful Cat

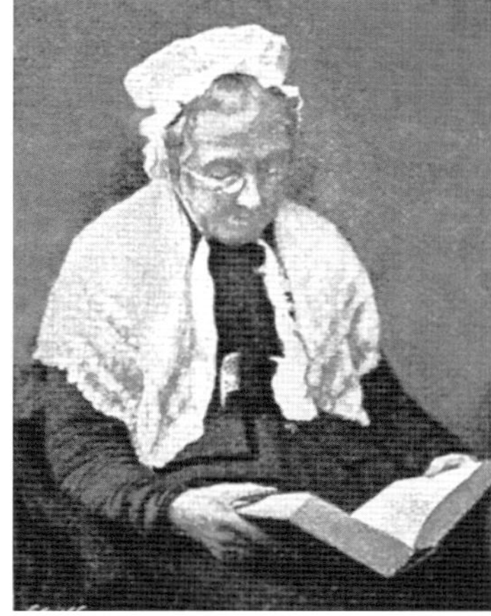

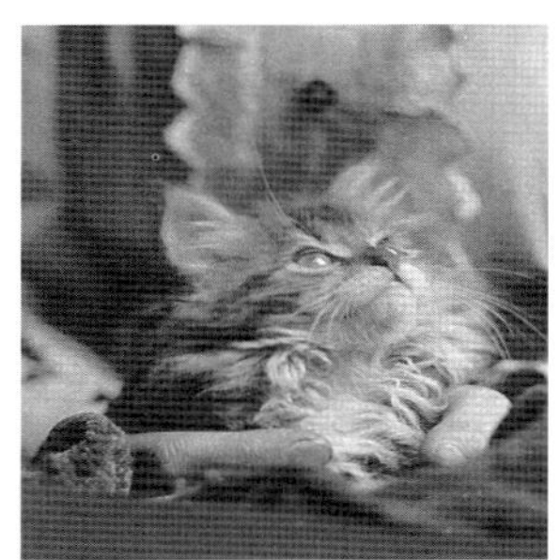

Above, source photograph for *Divided Attention*.

Left, photograph of Mrs. May Knight.

Reproduced as a black and white page in *The Windsor Magazine*, November 1905.

Sepia photogravure, 21ins x 15¼ins (54cm x 39cm), copyright Berlin Photographic. Later reproduced as a black and white photolithograph, 21ins x 15ins (54cm x 38cm), probably a calendar. Berlin Photographic were one of the largest print companies prior to the First World War and reproduced works as prints, crystoleums, and as 10ins x 8ins (25.5cm x 20.5cm) photographs.

Full Inside *signed and dated 1899*

Details of original painting unknown. Elsley photographed the unfinished and unsigned painting. There are a number

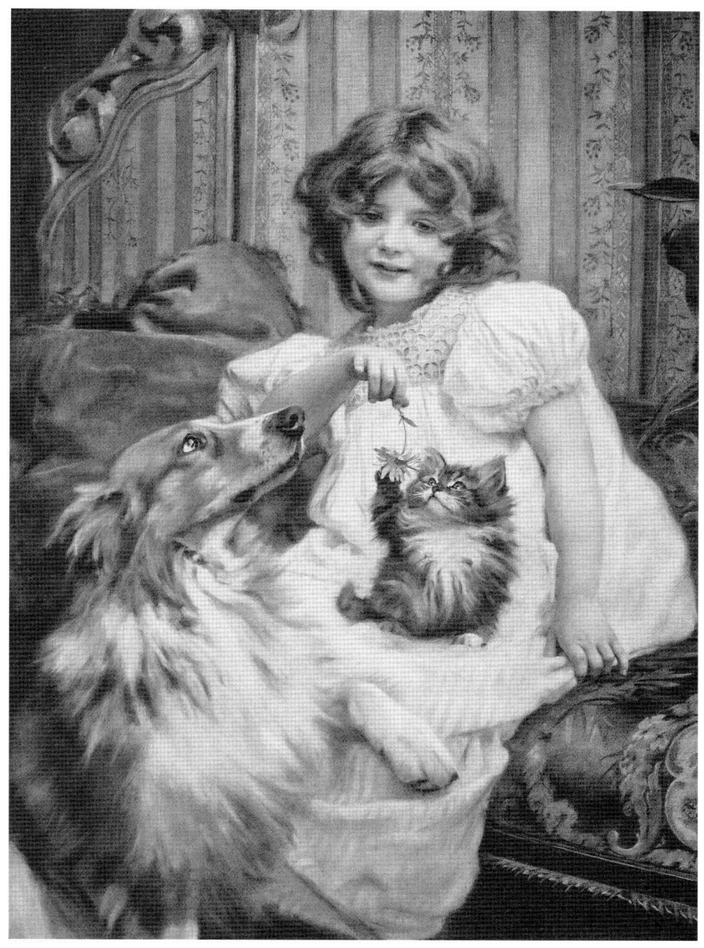

Divided Affection

of variations: much heavier rain, no background top right, sketchy wall behind the umbrella, the boy is not wearing a hat, chickens are not running for cover, and there isn't a hole in the side of the barrel.

Both *Weatherbound*, 1898, and *Breaking Them In*, 1895, use barrels in their composition. The genre artist, Charles Hunt (1803-1877), also used an empty barrel turned on its side. He painted children playing in it outside a grocer's shop.

Elsley was a master of humorously-faced dogs, much in the Landseer tradition. Extract from "The Children's Season" by Rudolph De Cordova, *The London Magazine*, December 1904:

> "*Full Inside*, which depicts two merry little children in a barrel into which several dogs are trying to force an entrance, was suggested to Mr. Elsley one sunny morning as he walked through a street and saw an empty barrel lying on its side on the pavement. At once his fancy pictured it with its two merry occupants, and he translated the sunshine into rain, not only because it offered a distinct and definitive reason for the children being in the barrel, but because the dogs would appear much more miserable, and would therefore afford a higher and more dramatic contrast with the laughter of the little ones, while the wet pavement, reflecting the shadows, would give a much more effective foreground."

Sepia photogravure, 23ins x 18ins (59cm x 46.5cm), engraved by F. Hanfstaengl, copyright Frost & Reed 1900. 250 Artist's proofs @ 4 guineas, 100 Lettered proofs @ 2 guineas, India prints @ 1 guinea. Artist's proofs nearly all sold in Frost & Reed's January 1913 catalogue. This was the first work by Frost & Reed since *Time To Get Up* in 1898. Small sepia photogravure presented with *Weldon's Illustrated Dressmaker,* Christmas 1910 (as a companion to "A Broken Melody", 1909, *Weldon's Bazaar of Children's Fashion* of the same date).

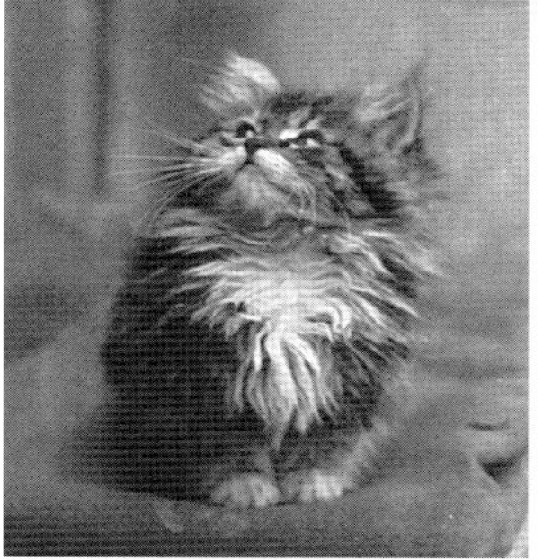

Source photograph for *Divided Affection.*

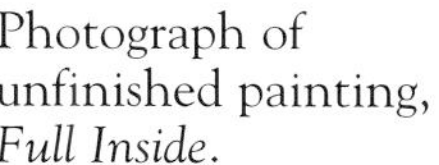

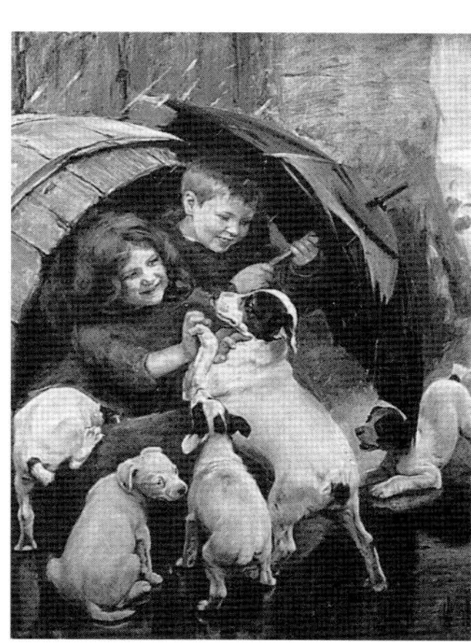

Photograph of unfinished painting, *Full Inside.*

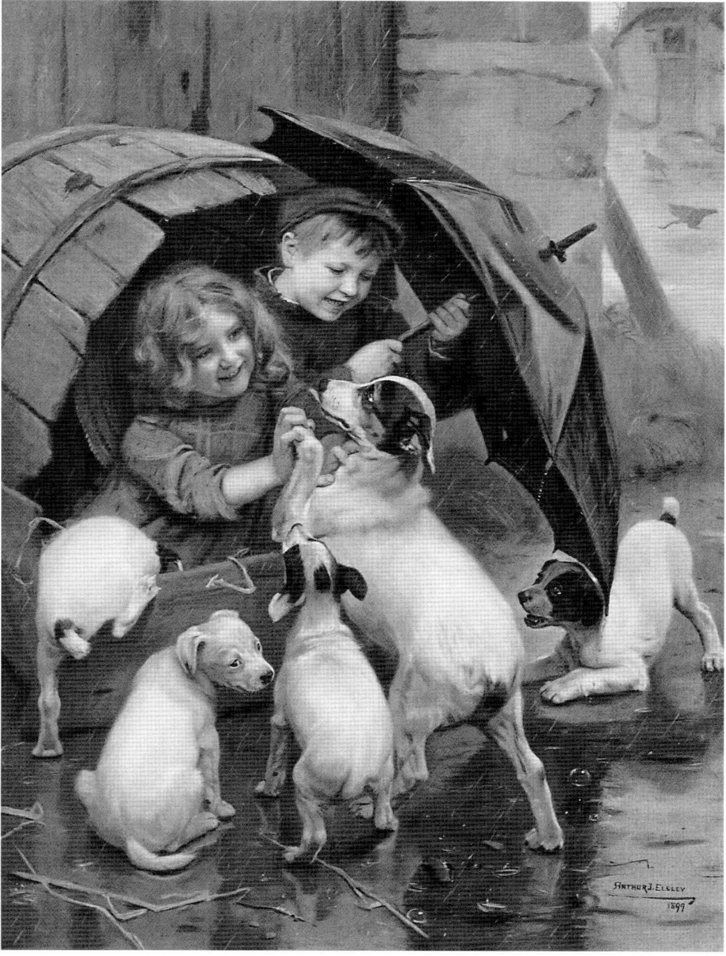

Full Inside

More Haste Less Speed *signed and dated 1899*
Oil on canvas, 37ins x 33¼ins (94.5cm x 86cm). Owned by Fine Art of Oakham in 1992, and was owned by the same family for the previous thirty years

Set on a railway station, with a steam engine preparing to depart. In the foreground a red-faced and flustered woman, four children and a dog in tow, struggles to stop the sack of apples she is holding from disgorging its contents over the platform. This is one of three paintings featuring railways. cf. *Soft Persuasion*, 1896 (Midland railway, girl on platform bench, with the same dog), and *The Home Coming*, 1900. The boy who is catching the apples also modelled for *Their First Swim* c.1900, and the nonchalant terrier appears in *Soft Persuasion*, 1896.

Medium size colour chromolithograph presented with *Weldon's Ladies' Journal*, Christmas 1899, copyright unknown. **See page 65**.

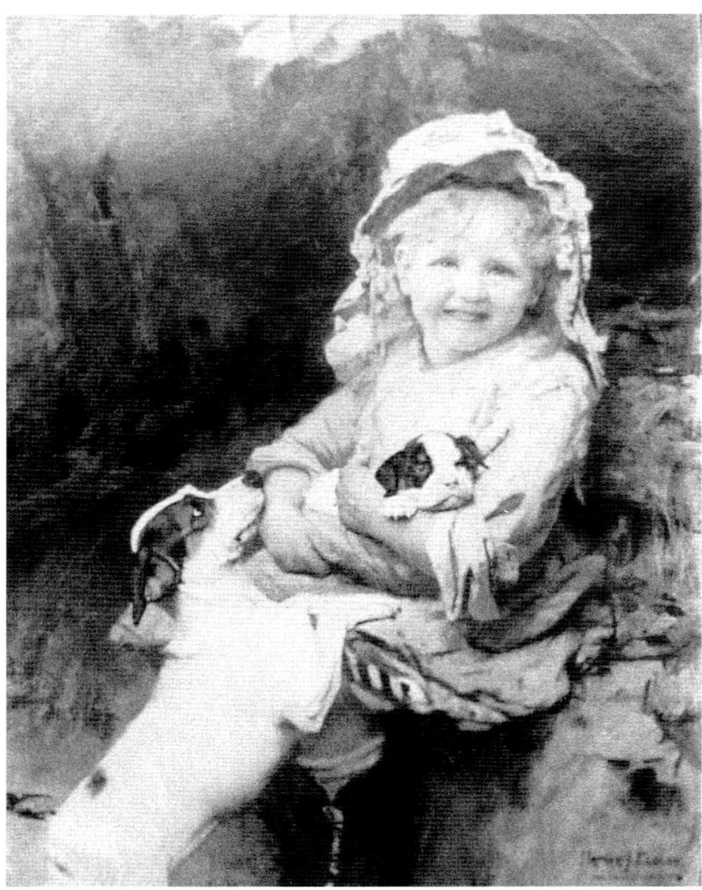

[Title Unknown]

[Title Unknown] *circa 1899*
Details of original painting unknown.

Girl with a puppy on her lap and terrier at her feet. The same dogs appear in *Full Inside*, 1899.

Forbidden Ground *signed and dated 1899*
Oil on canvas measuring 48ins x 39ins (122.5cm x 99.5cm).

This is part of a series of pictures featuring the hunt. cf. *Late for School / Any Port in a Storm*, 1898; *A Touch of Nature*, 1902; and *[Tally Ho]*, 1904). A continuation of the humorous paintings of monks by Henry Stacy Marks (1829-1898). The theme of mirthful monks was not a new one. Pears had great success with two prints; Torrini's *A Good Joke* in 1891 and Sani's *Macaroni* in 1893. Elsley added another dimension by the inclusion of the hunt. The group of three monks are very well-painted with excellent facial detail and great humour.

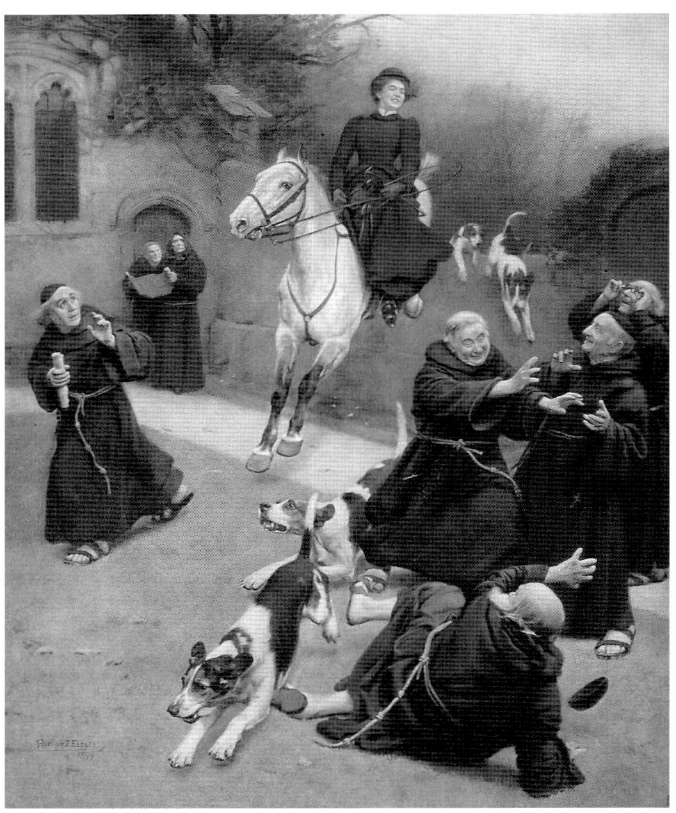

Forbidden Ground

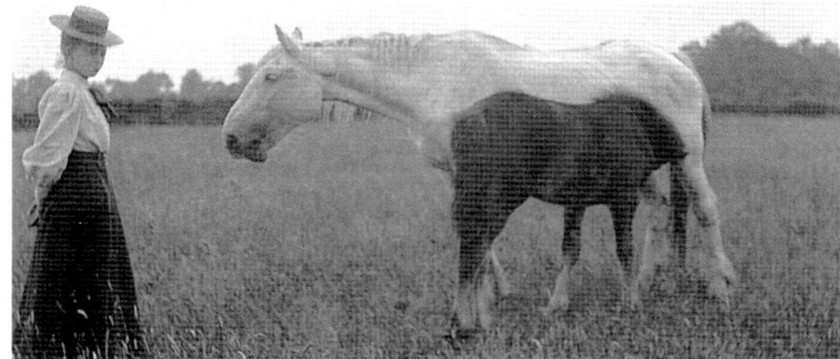

Source photograph of Emm with horses.

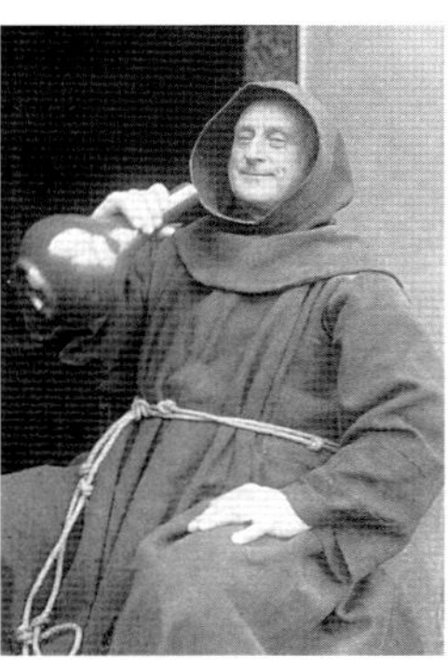

Source photograph of a monk.

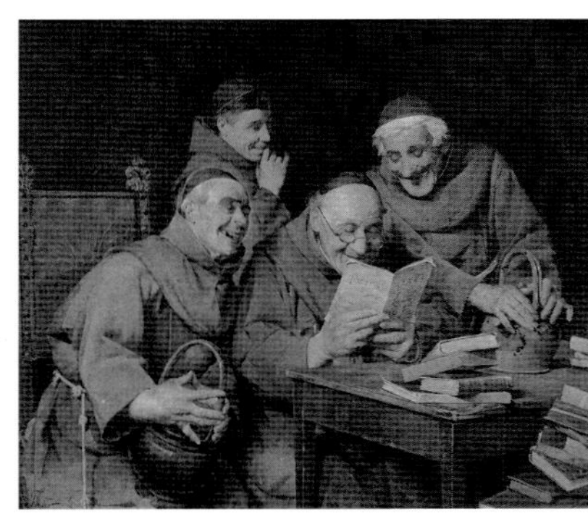

Pietro Torrini's *A Good Joke*, Pears print, 1891.

Sepia photogravure, 24ins x 19.5ins (61.5cm x 50cm), copyright Raphael Tuck, London 1902, entitled *Forbidden Ground*. The Tuck print was also made into a wooden jigsaw by J.C. Vickers, Regent Street, London as part of their New Art Series.

There He Goes *circa 1900*

Oil on canvas, 39ins x 28ins (99.5cm x 71.5cm), signed not dated.

The Lady's Magazine, September 1901, interviewed Morgan and Elsley. Morgan states that his:

> "...happiest faces have been taken from children who have had no experience of studios."
> The artist's memory, Mr. Morgan continued, 'is perhaps his best friend; both attitudes and expressions can be retained in the memory for years in much the same way as landscape painters can remember transient colours and effects in sky and distance'.
>
> Mr. Arthur J. Elsley largely shares Mr Morgan's views with regard to professional models. He often picks up a model among children in the street, the mother – when she is discovered – as a rule, readily bringing the little one to the studio.
>
> Mr. Elsley has sometimes got a pretty face, too, as well as a pretty background by means of his cycle, which has made him familiar with the country for many miles around London. Mr. Elsley is fond of bringing domestic animals as well as rural surroundings into his pictures."

Colour chromolithograph, 24¼ins x 18ins (62cm x 46.5cm). Colour page in unknown magazine.

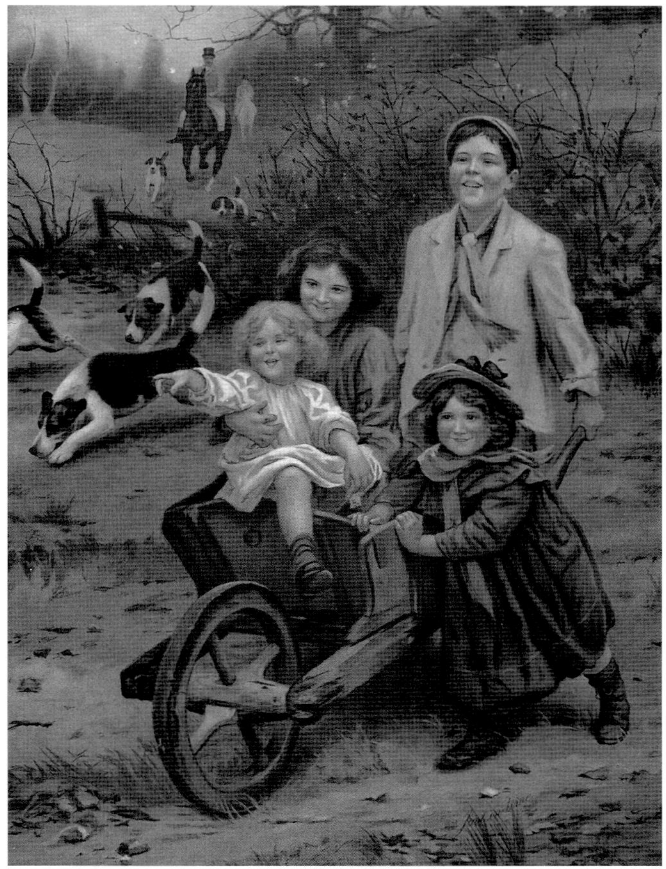

There He Goes

Little Bo-Peep *signed and dated 1900*

Oil on canvas, 31ins x 22ins (79cm x 56.5cm). Exhibited Liverpool, Autumn 1900 (No.209), price 100 guineas.

This was the first of four paintings bought by Joseph Bibby, the proprietor of Bibby's Animal Foods based in Liverpool. His company published *Bibby's Quarterly* and *Bibby's Annual*. Like Barratt at Pears and Joseph Beecham, founder of the pharmaceutical company, he wanted to share his love of art with the masses, but he combined this with his own quasi-religious message.

Colour cover, 14¼ins x 9ins (36cm x 23cm), image 10ins x 7ins (25.5cm x 23cm), *Bibby's Quarterly* - Literary Supplement, Vol.4 No 1, Spring 1901. Commentary on cover reproduction on p.28. **See page 66**.

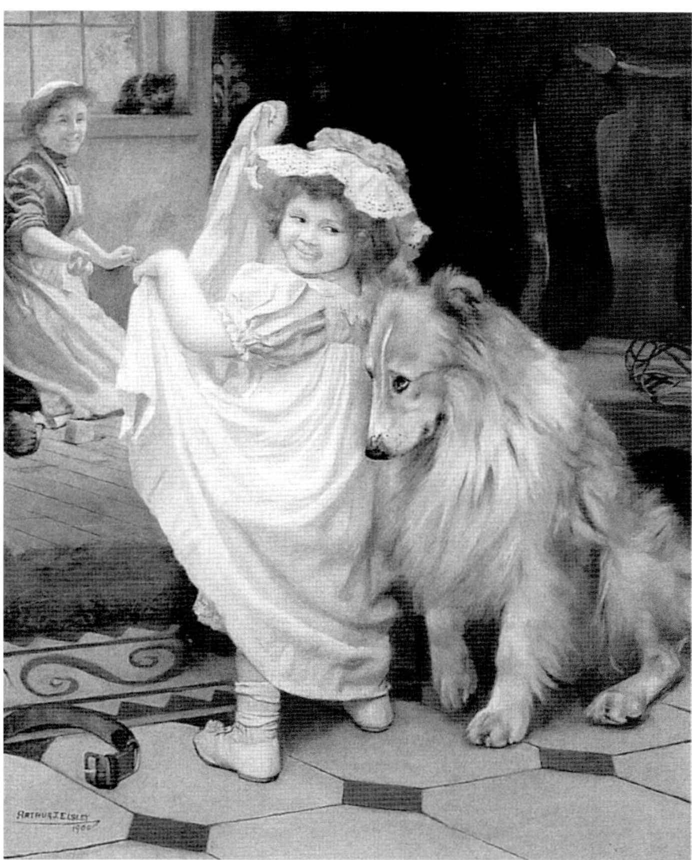

[Before The Bath]

[Before The Bath] *signed and dated 1900*

Oil on canvas, 34½ins x 27ins (88cm x 69cm). Owned by John Noott Gallery in 1989.

Possibly sold as *The Baby's Bath*, oil painting 39½ins x 27ins (100.5cm x 69cm), Christie's, London (Art Sales Index 1931/2), bought by Nicol for 7 guineas. Not to be confused with *Go Away Sir!*, 1891, 28ins x 23½ins (71.5cm x 60.5cm), or the *Ivy Soap Advertisement* of 1900.

Reproduced as a sepia photogravure.

Home Again *circa 1900*

Details of original painting unknown.

The painting shows four children waving to a train of triumphant soldiers returning from their victory in South Africa at the Relief of Mafeking, May 1900. This is reminiscent of Edith Nesbit's classic children's story *The Railway Children*, which was published five years later in *The London Magazine*, January 1905, p.729.

From the late 1890s until 1901-2 the Elsleys took their holidays in a cottage in West Milton a few miles inland from Bridport on the Dorset coast. They were joined on holiday by Elsley's great friends George Cook and his brother the artist Walter Cook (who had also worked as a tutor at the ill-fated Sphinx Studios). This work was probably conceived on one of these vacations. Not to be confused with *Home Again*, 1910.

Large sepia photogravure engraved by F. Hanfstaengl and published by Thomas McLean, 1900, entitled *Home Again*, 200 Artist's proofs @ 4 guineas, India prints @ 1 guinea. There is no record of McLean exhibiting the original painting at his London Gallery. Colour chromo lithograph calendar for Blue Cross Tea, (The British & Bennington Tea Trading Association). The soldiers waving from the train windows have been changed to a mother and four children, and a Blue Cross Tea label is attached to the fence. **See page 69**.

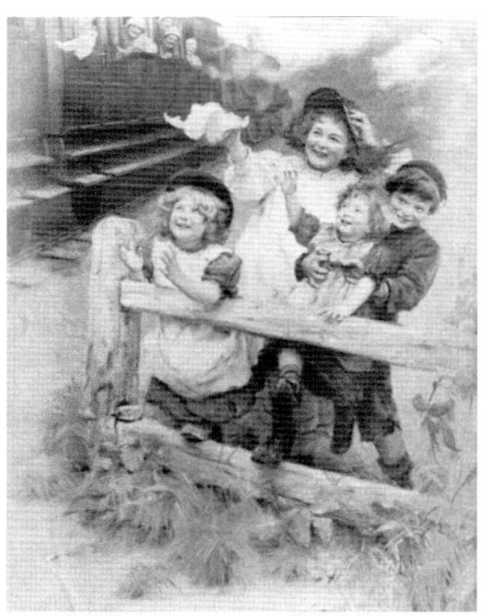

Home Again

No Admittance *signed and dated 1900*

Details of original painting unknown.

A return to the schoolroom theme of *Hard Pressed*, 1898. Not to be confused with *No Thoroughfare*, c.1902, the next year's Fine Art Society follow-up publication.

Sepia photogravure, 22½ins x 17½ins (57.5cm x 45cm), engraved by The Art Photogravure Company and published by The Fine Art Society, 100 Artist's proofs @ 4 guineas, India prints @ 1 guinea.

This Way! *signed and dated 1900*

Oil on canvas, 36ins x 28ins (91.5cm x 71.5cm). Owned in 1991 by Haynes Fine Art who titled it *Homeward Bound*.

In his address book Elsley noted "Hilda Francis, 23 Maitland Park Villas, Haverstock Hill, N.W. – do for *This Way* generally".

Black and white photograph in *Black and White Handbook to the Royal Academy*, 1901, p.28, and *The Sketch*, 8th May 1901, p.111.

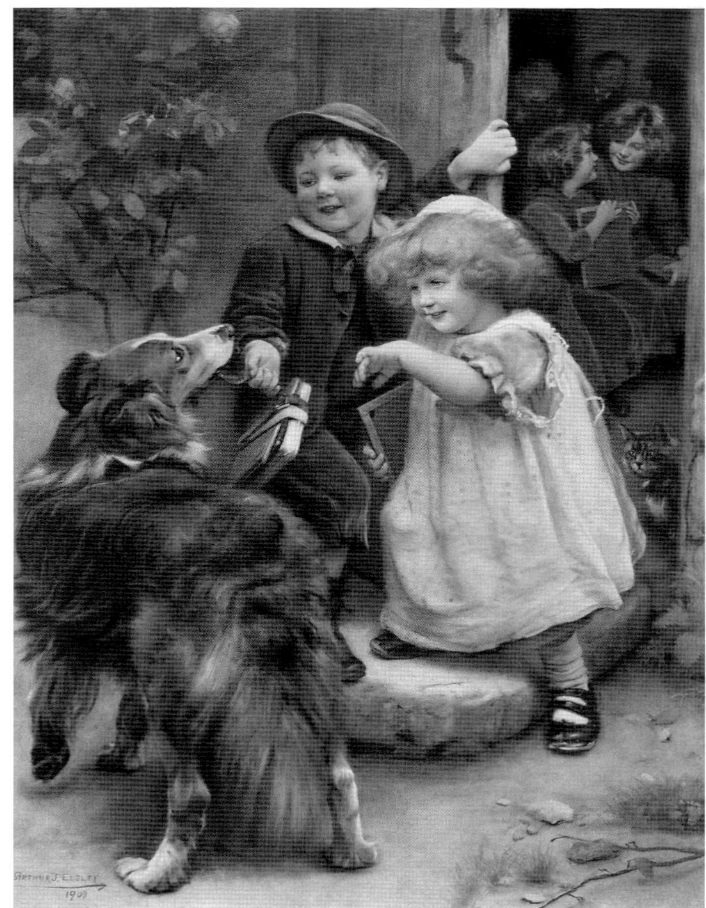

No Admittance

Photogravure, 23ins x 17¾ins (59cm x 46cm), engraved by B. Pratt, copyright James Connell & Sons, 116 St. Vincent St., Glasgow, 200 Artist's proofs @ 4 guineas, India prints @ 1 guinea. **See page 64**.

You Mustn't Pull *signed and dated 1901*

Details of original painting unknown.

This is similar in composition to *Make Haste!*, Royal Academy, 1895 and *Out Of Reach*, 1908.

Sepia photogravure, 26¼ins x 18¼ins (67cm x 47cm), copyright C.W. Faulkner, 1902. The first work known to have been reproduced by Charles William Faulkner, though the copyright of *Their First Swim* c.1897-1900 was owned by Faulkner in 1904. This was the beginning of a long association and friendship, leading to the inclusion of Faulkner's children in Elsley's later works. Black and white postcard published by Faulkner, c.1909.

Colour chromolithograph, 24ins x 18ins (61.5cm x 46.5cm), Frisby's Boot Co., 1908 calendar with the title printed bottom right on image not signed or dated. There was possibly another poor-quality colour chromolithograph produced of this, probably a tea calendar also not signed or dated.

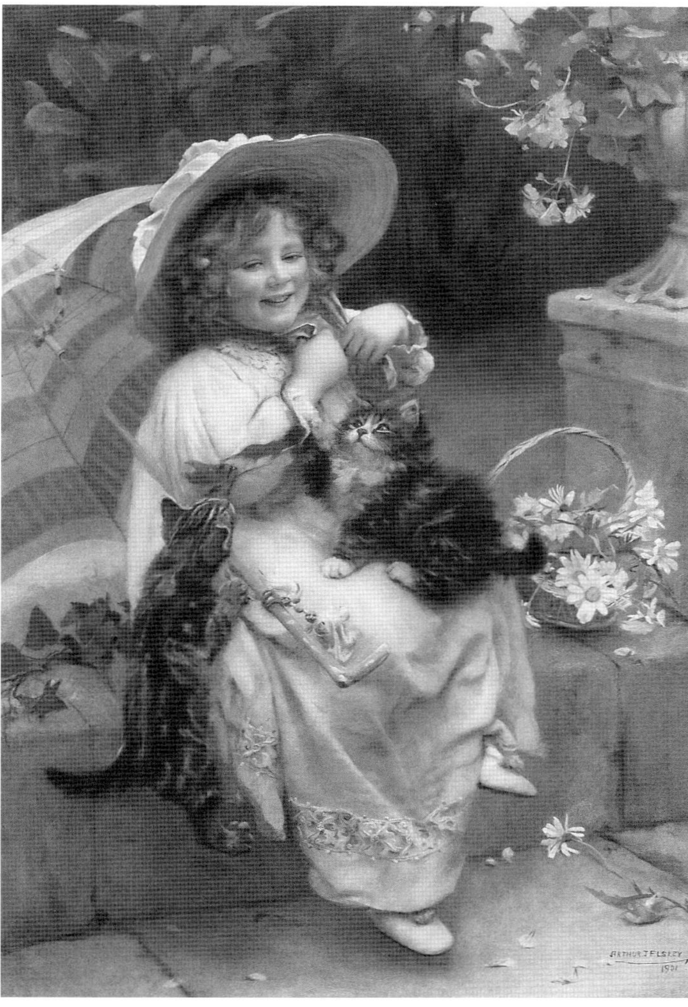

You Mustn't Pull

Kiss And Be Friends *signed and dated 1901*

Oil on canvas. Auctioned at Sotheby's, London, 29th January 1947, titled *Kiss And Be Friends* (Version I or II?).

This painting and *Which May I Keep?*, 1901, were a return to the use of St. Bernards as models. They were a very popular breed at this time, and Paderewski, the famous pianist, kept one as his favourite dog, ("Paderewski At Home by W. Adlington", *Pearson's Magazine*, December 1898, p.707).

Version I

Background shows room interior.

Photogravure, 26ins x 18ins (66.5cm x 46.5cm), copyright C.W. Faulkner & Co. 1902, signed and dated 1901. **See page 68**.

Version II

A version was reproduced as a black and white page in *Home Words* magazine, date unknown, called *Live Nobly Love Nobly*.

Colour photolithograph print, 10ins x 7$^{1}/_{4}$ins (25.5cm x 18.5cm), called *Kiss and Be Friends*, copyright Faulkner. In this version the signature is higher, there is no date, and the background is now a curtain. **See next page**.

Which May I Keep? *signed and dated 1901*

Details of original painting unknown.

Black and white photograph in *The Royal Magazine*, Vol. IX No.53, March 1903, entitled *Which May I Keep?*, copyright Berlin Photographic. American colour calendar manufactured by Osbourne Company, New Jersey, 1906. Elsley notes in his address book the company's London and New York addresses. **See page 68**.

[Pick-a-Back] *signed and dated 1901*

Details of original painting unknown.

In 1901 Elsley made oil sketches of the River Lea at Broxbourne. The background for this work was probably sketched in this area of Hertfordshire which was only a short train journey from North London.

Hand-tinted photogravures, 22$^{3}/_{4}$ins x 17ins (58.5cm x 43cm), plate size, 28ins x 21ins (71.5cm x 54cm), the original plates are still produced by Thomas Ross & Co.

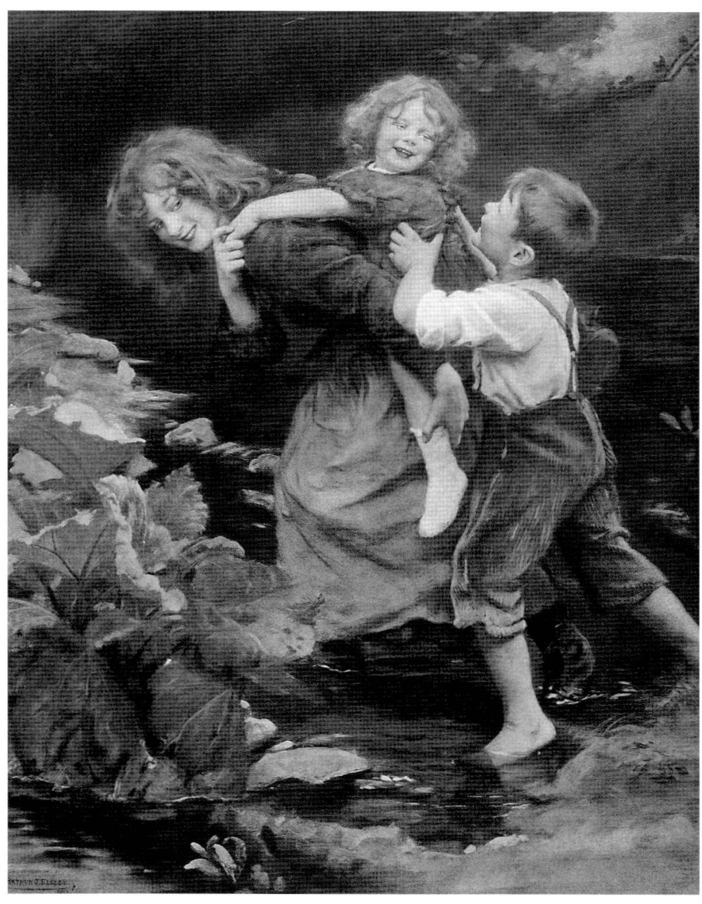

[Pick-a-Back]

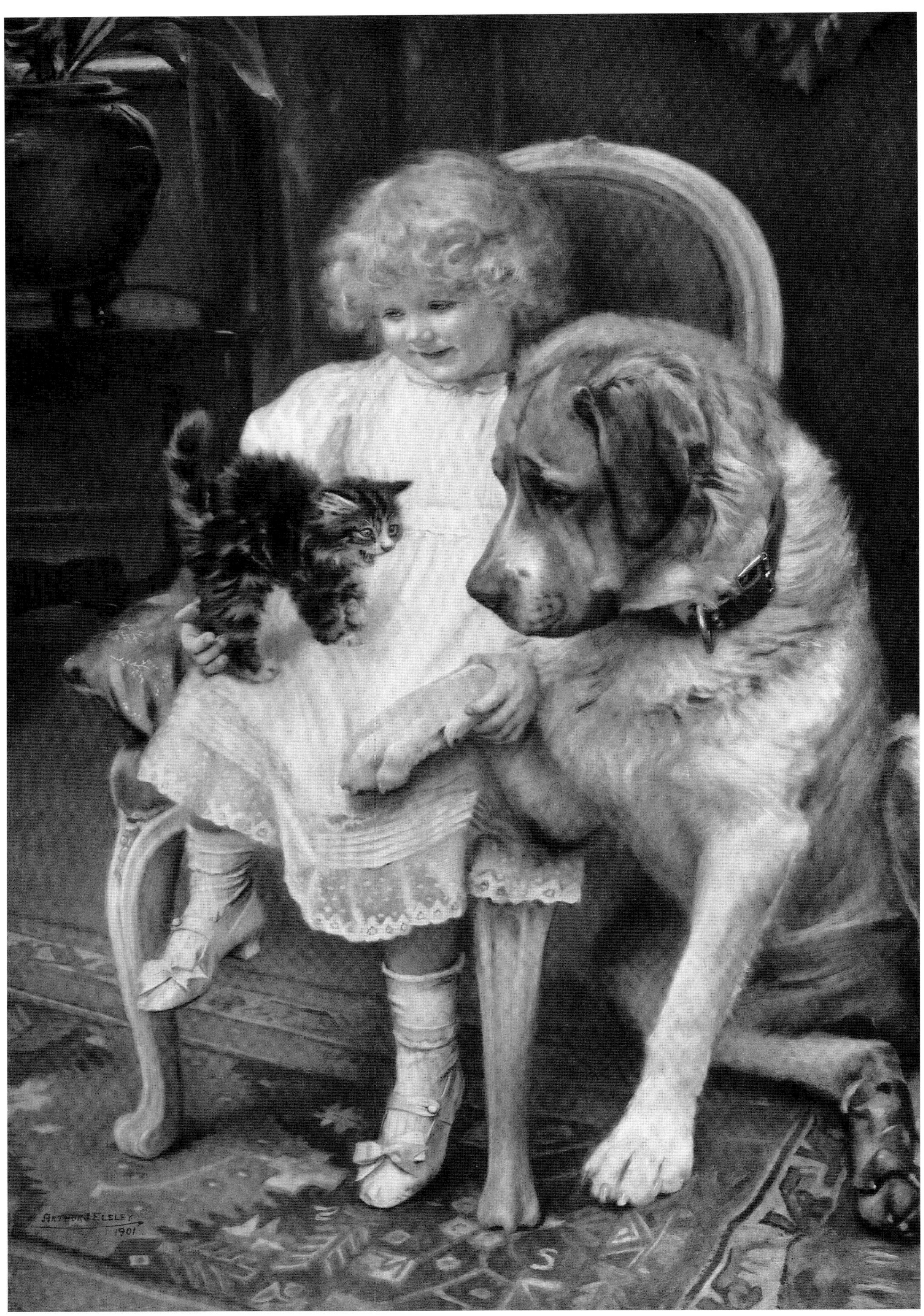

Kiss And Be Friends. Version I. **See page 47**.

COLOUR PLATES

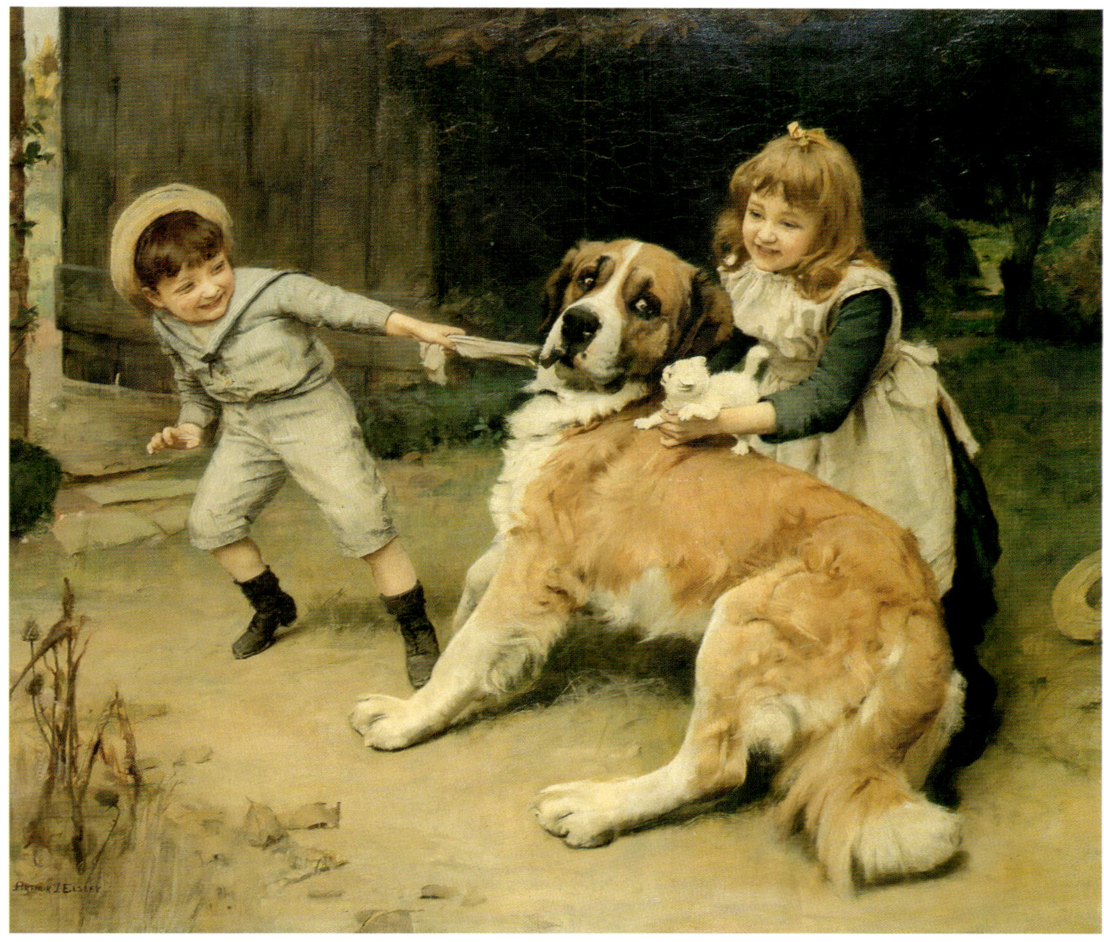

Victims, c.1891. **See page 16**.

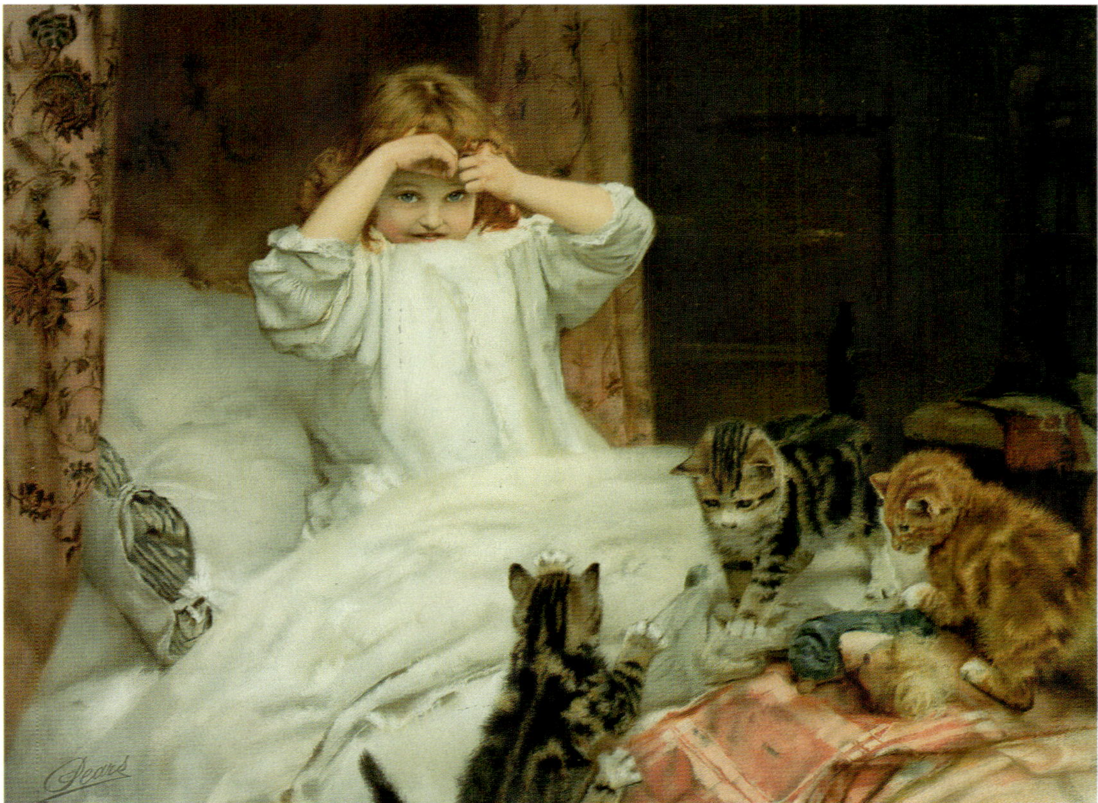

Surprised / The Invaders, c.1893. **See page 21**.

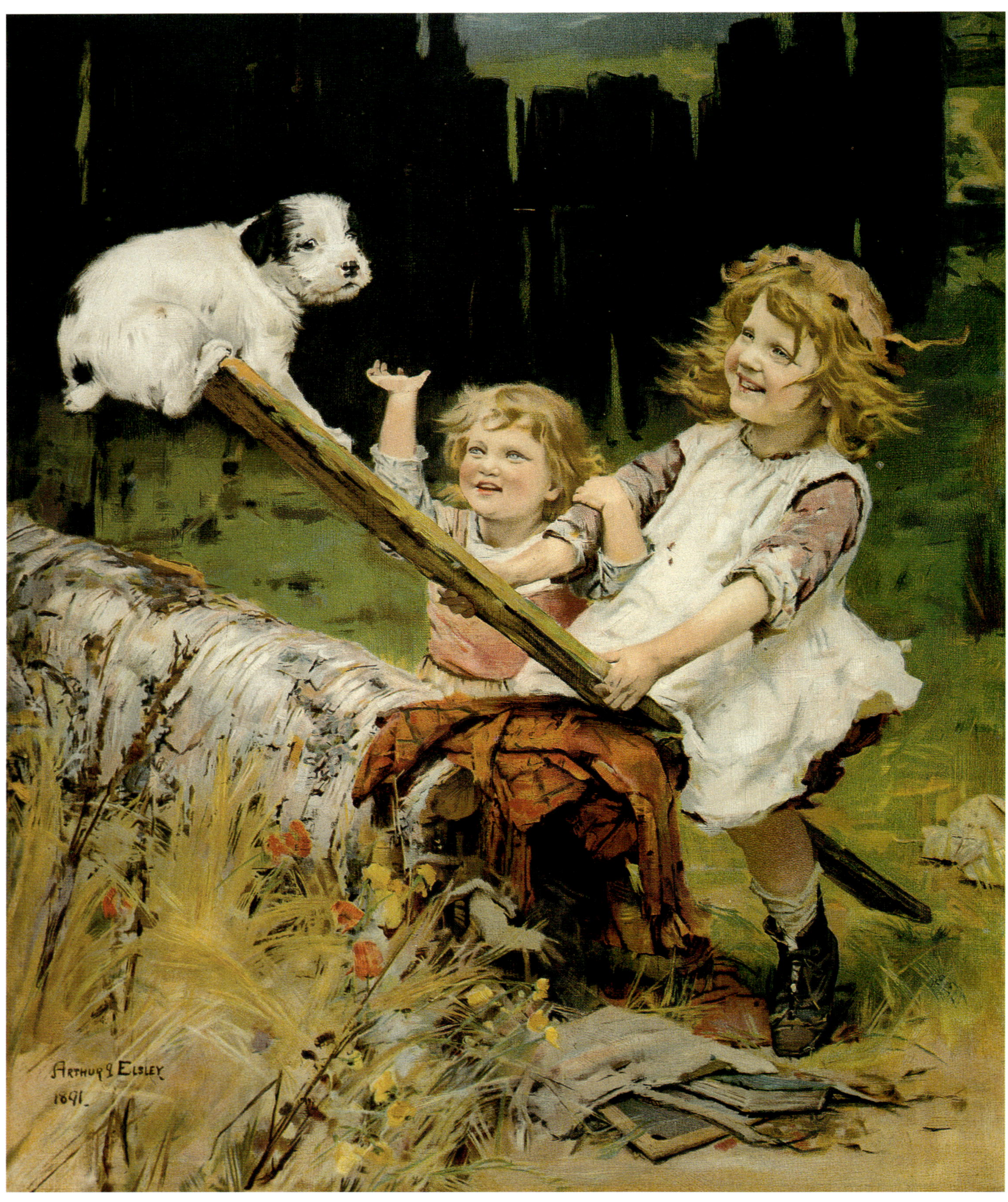

Happy Days / The See-Saw, 1891. **See page 16**.

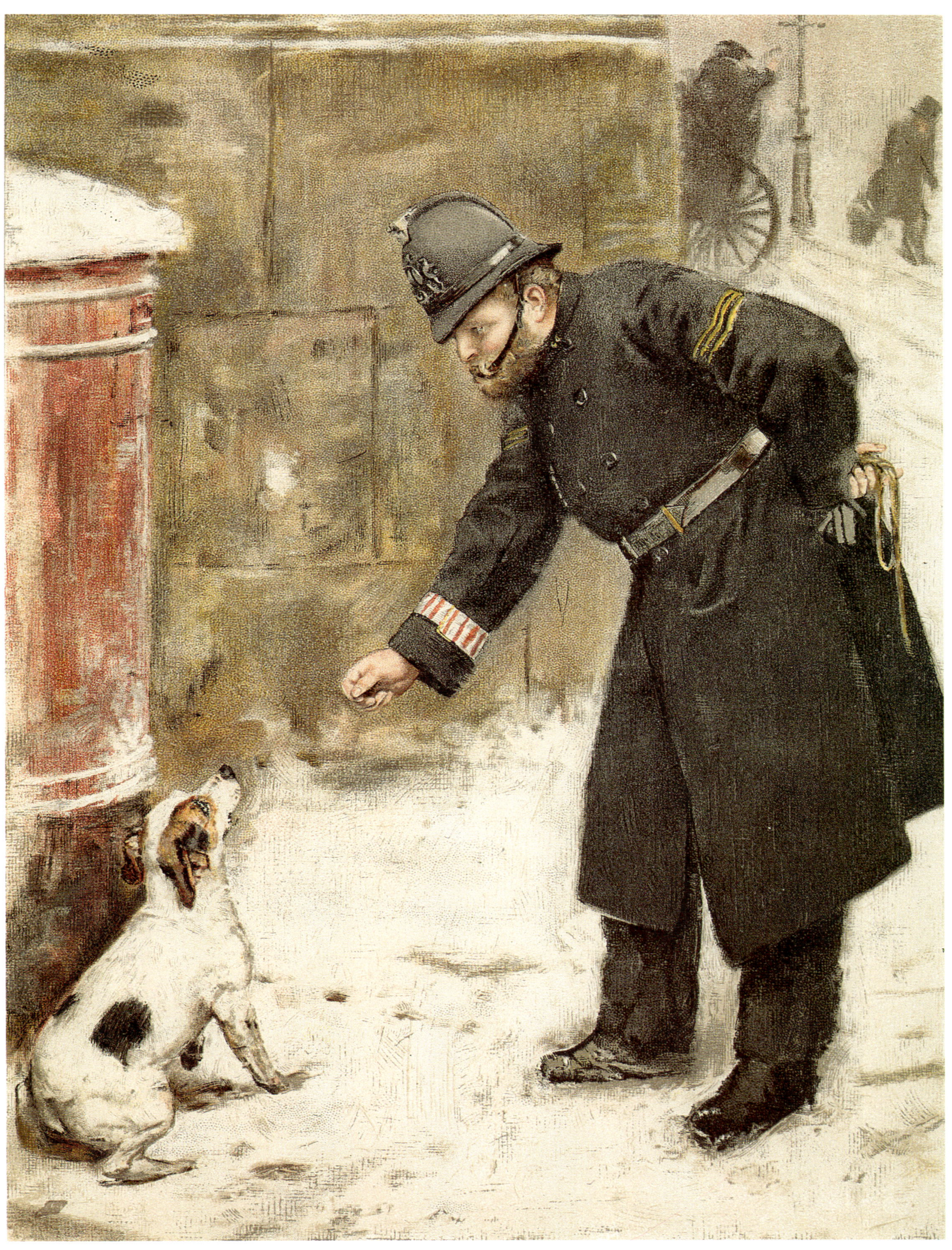

Doubtful Kindness, c.1891. See page 18.

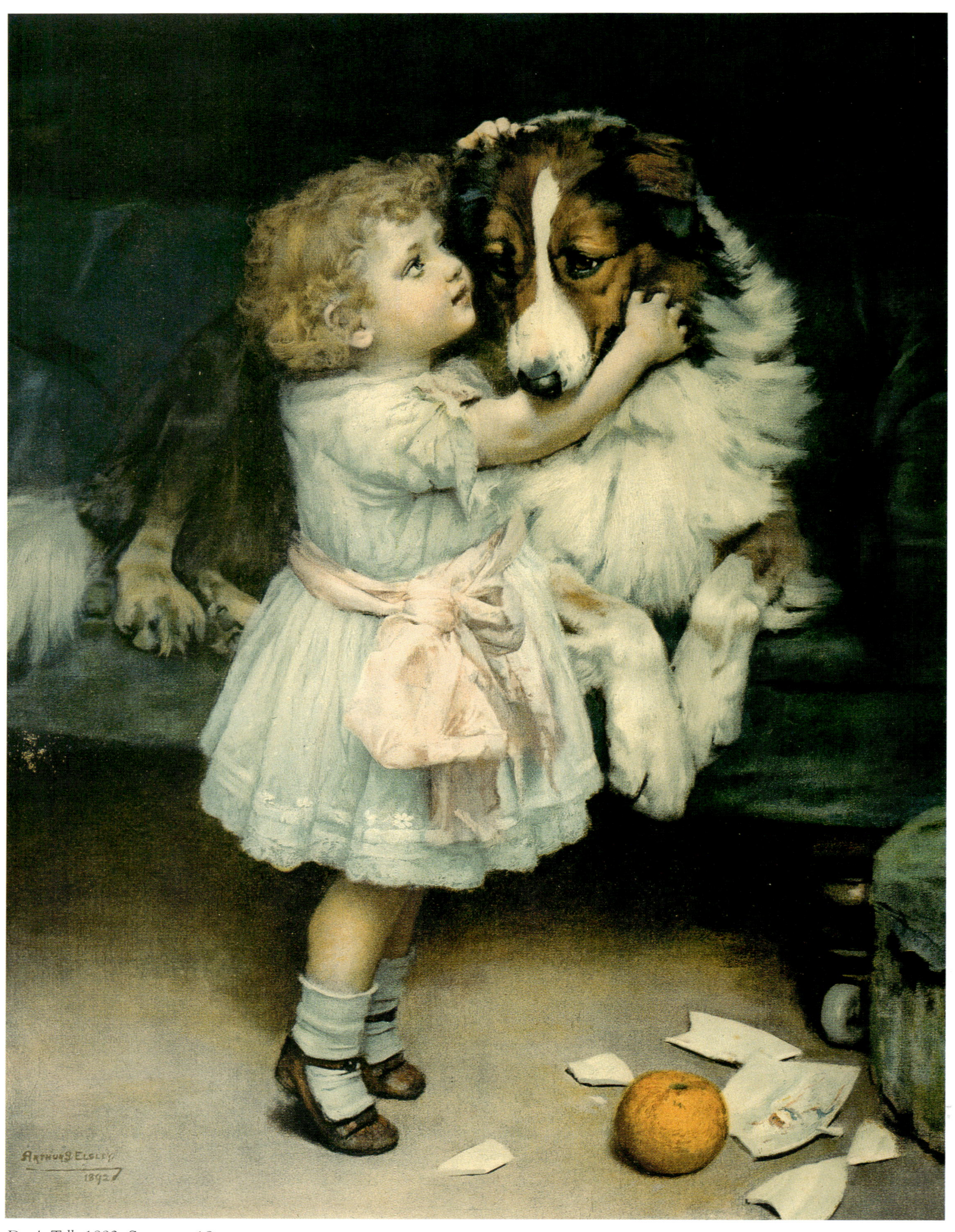

Don't Tell, 1892. **See page 18.**

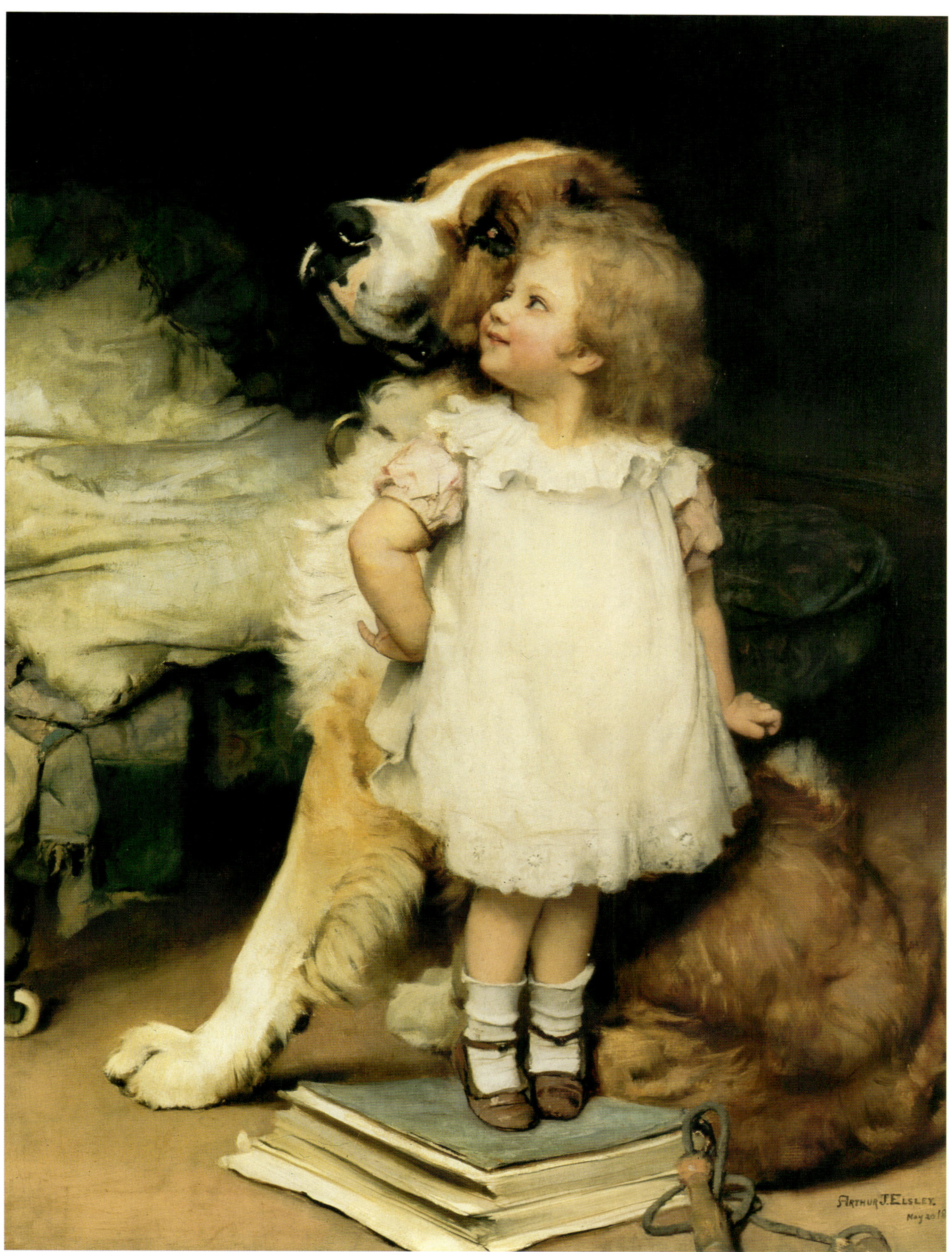

I'se Biggest, Version II, 1892. **See page 18**.

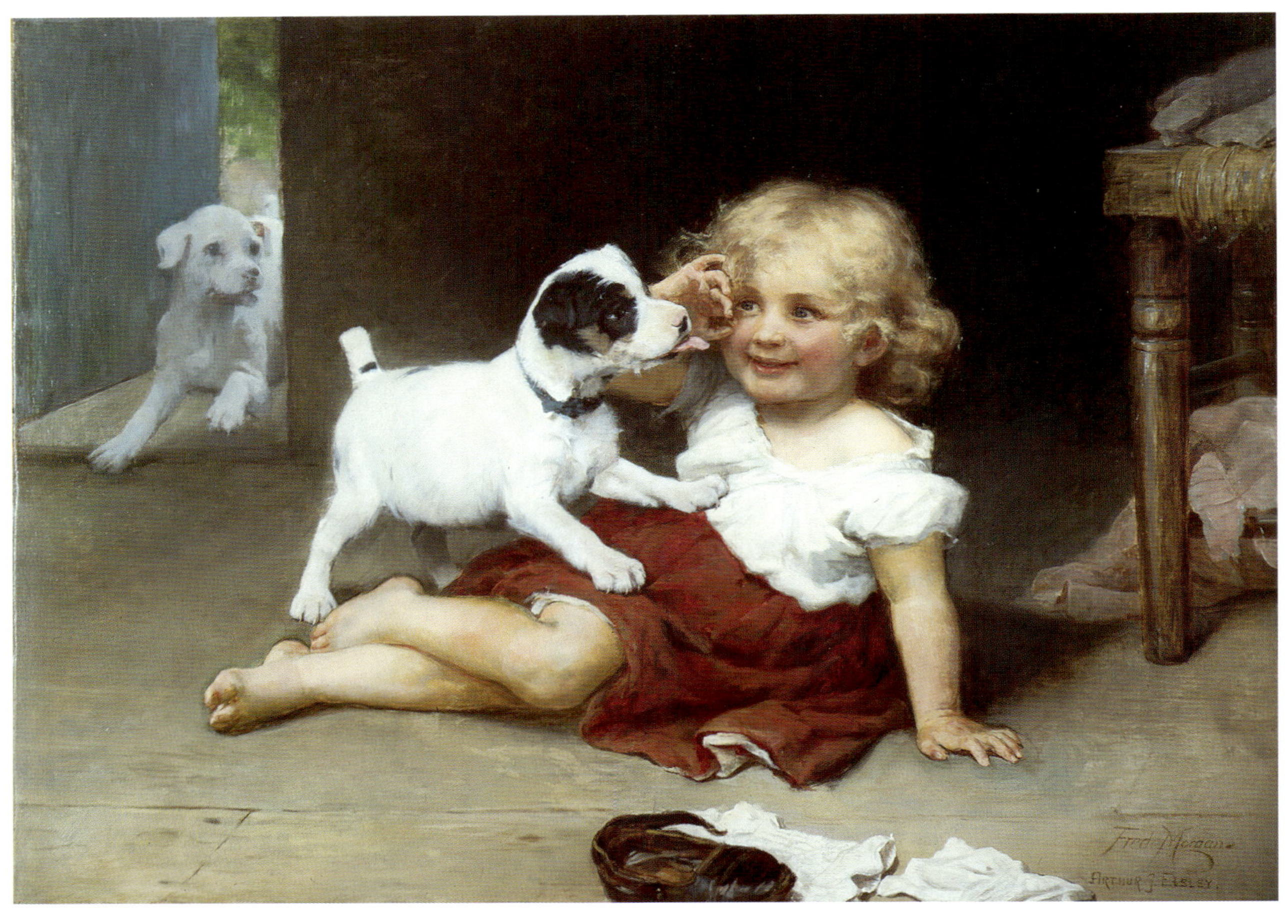

Ruff Play by Fred Morgan and Arthur J. Elsley, c.1889. **See page 13**.

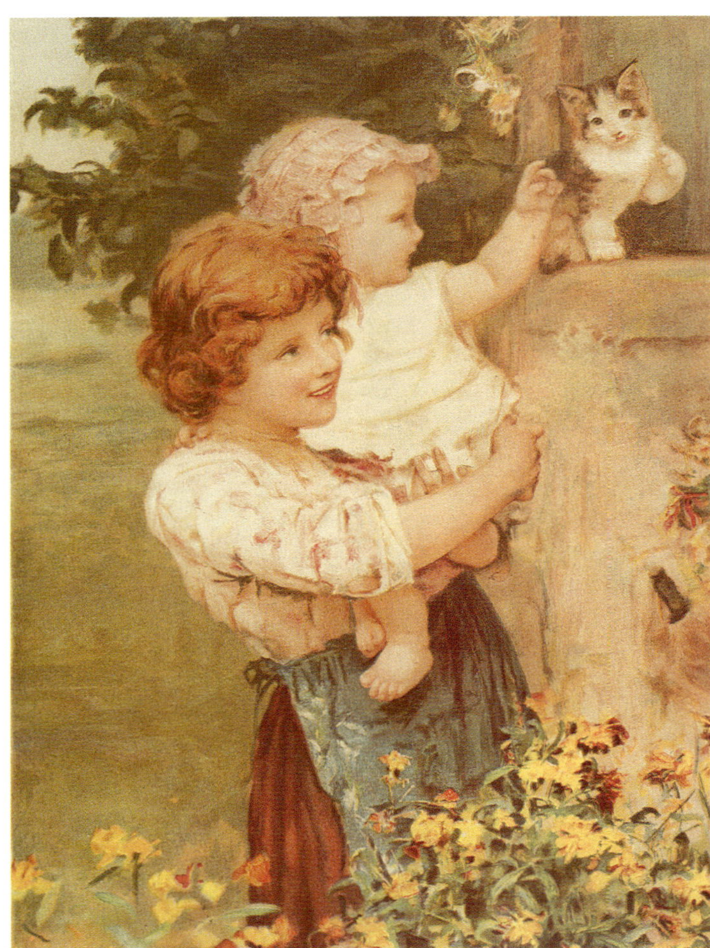

Shake Hands / In Children's Happy Hour, c.1890. **See page 18**.

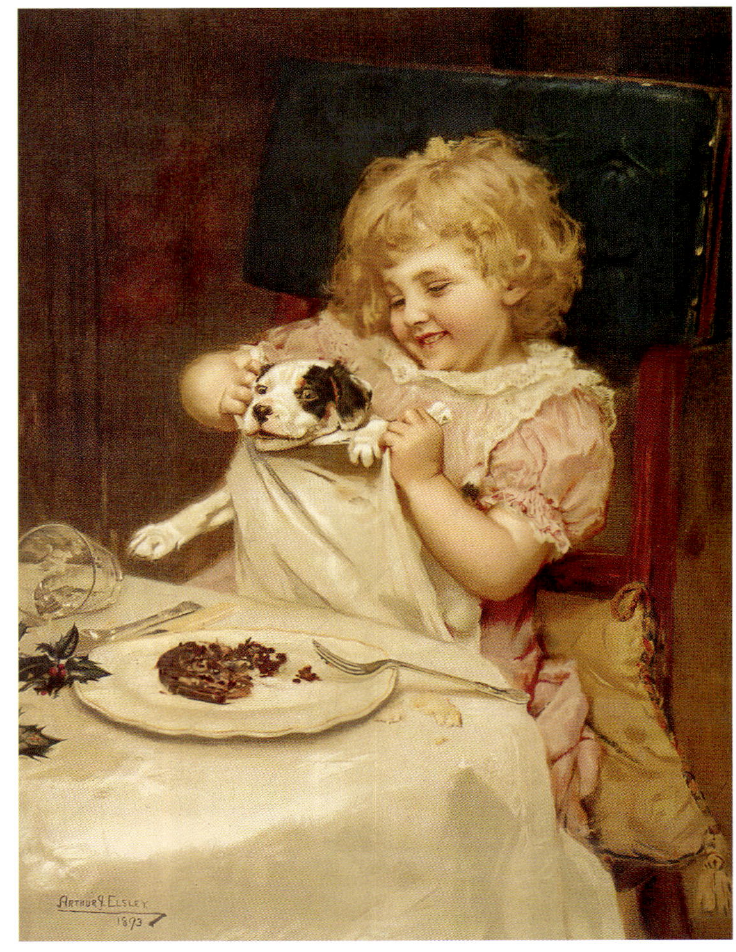

Wait A Minute / Plum Pudding, 1893. **See page 24**.

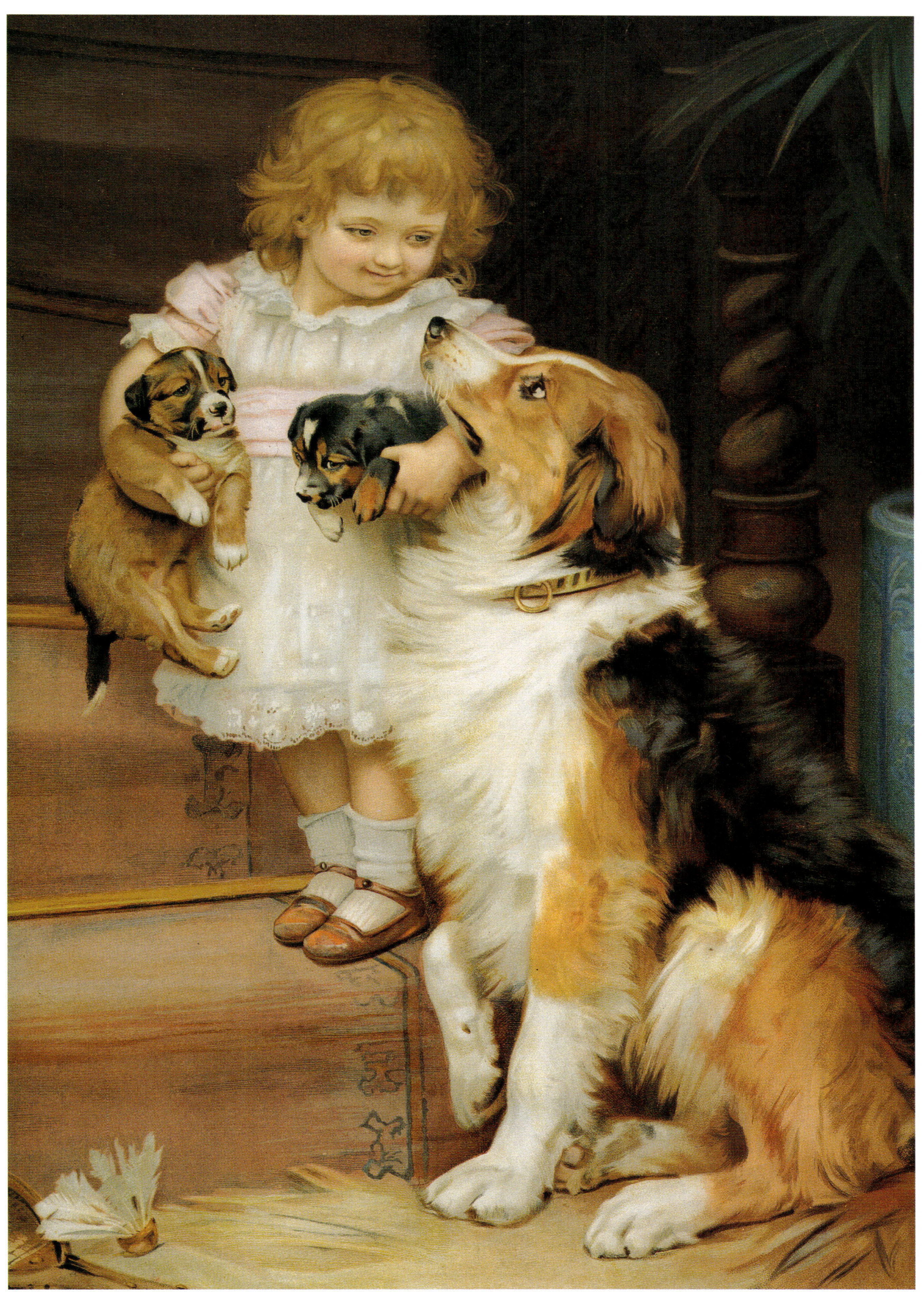

Which Hand Will You Have? / You Can Trust Me, c.1893. **See page 25**.

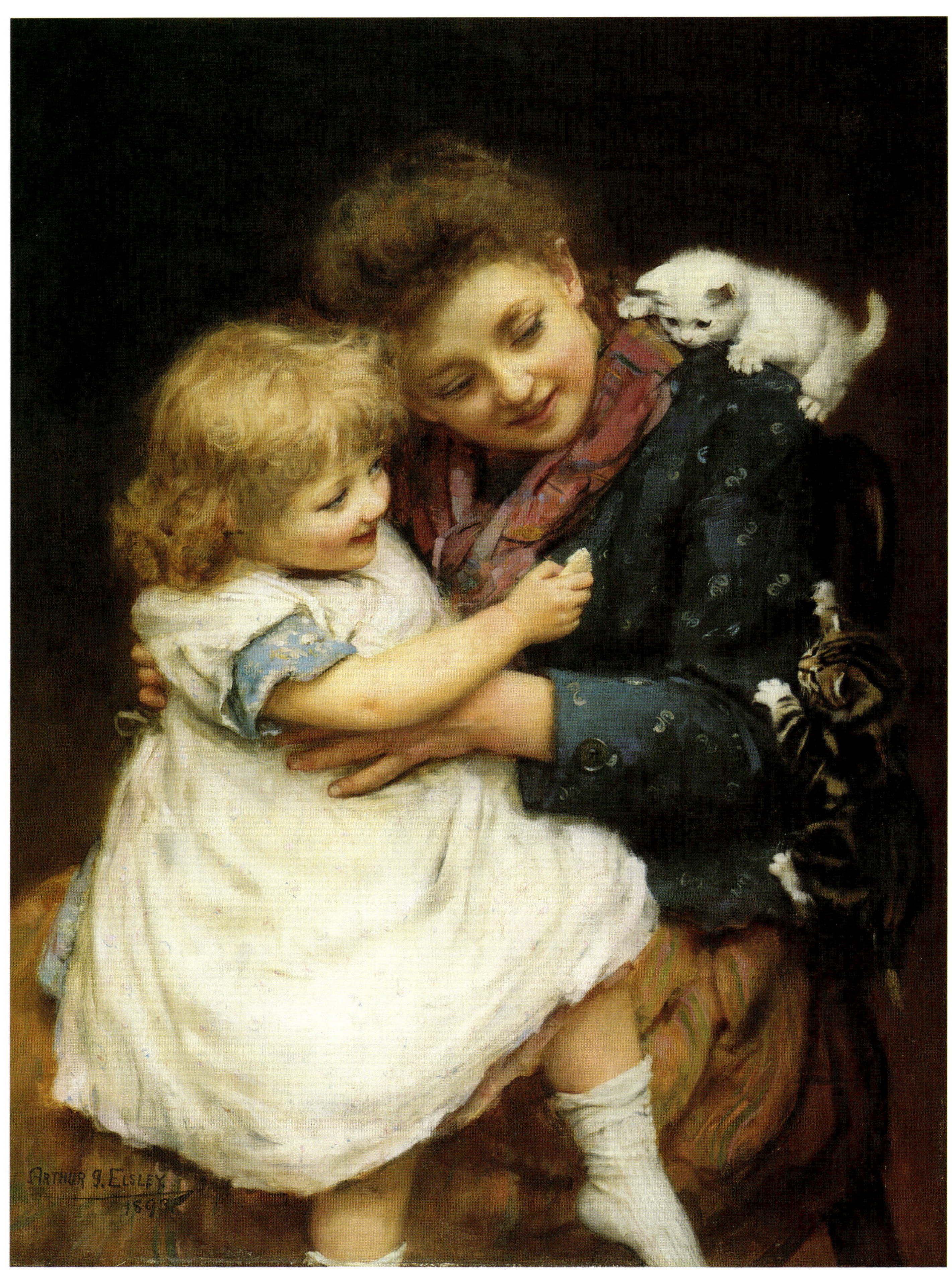

[Play Time], 1893. **See page 22.**

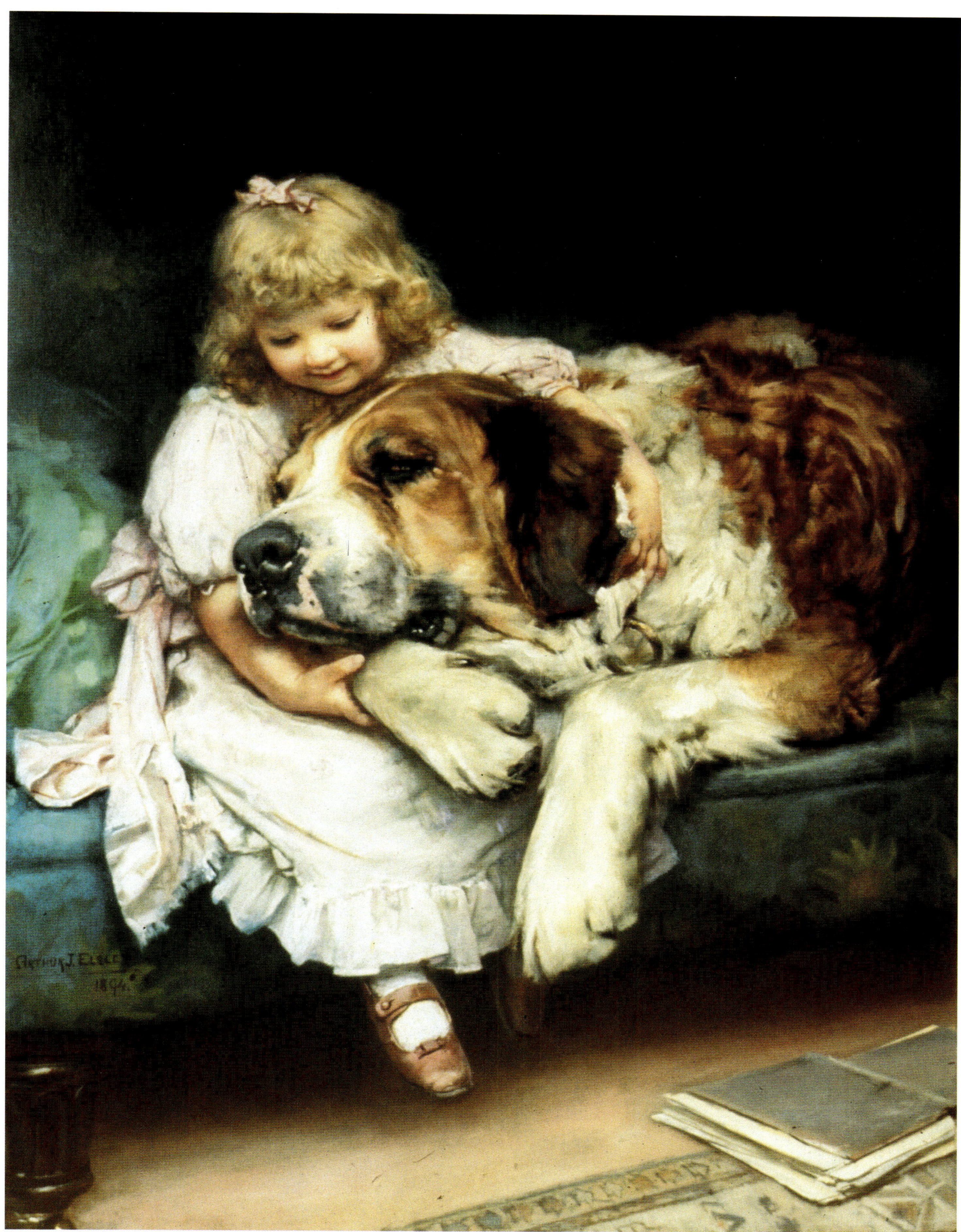

So Tired!, 1894. **See page 25**.

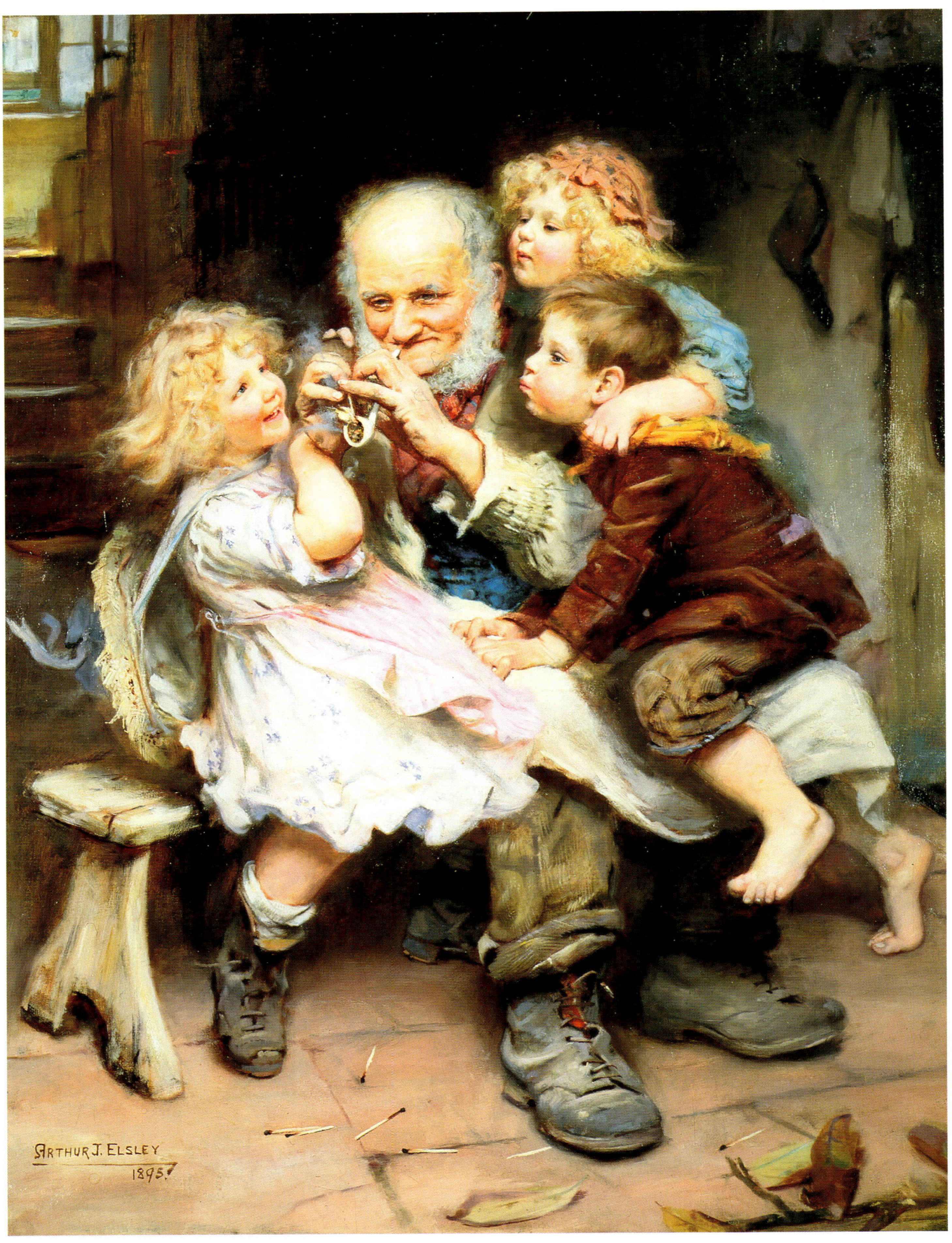

Adverse Winds, 1895. **See page 36**.

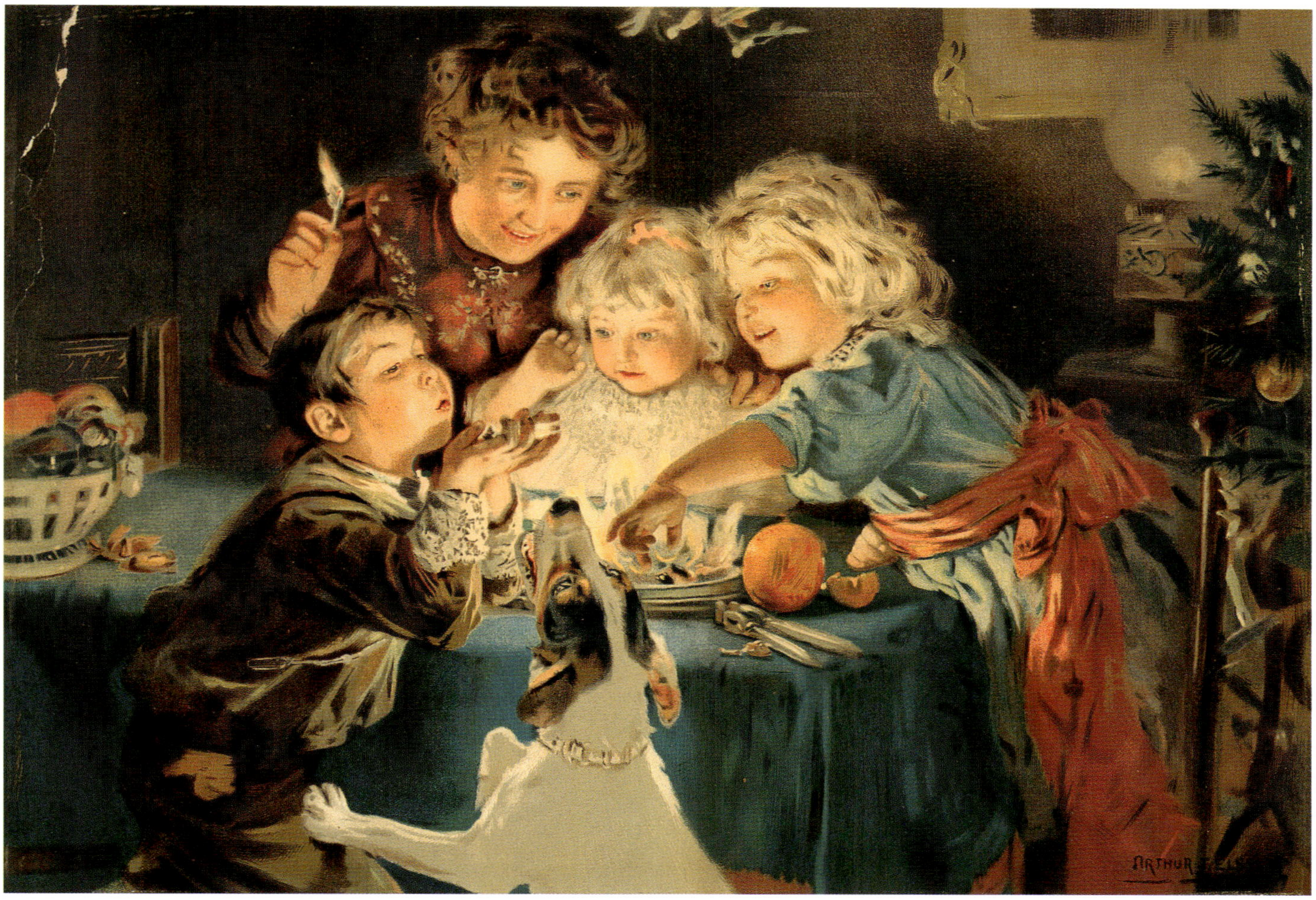

Snapdragon, c.1894. **See page 30**.

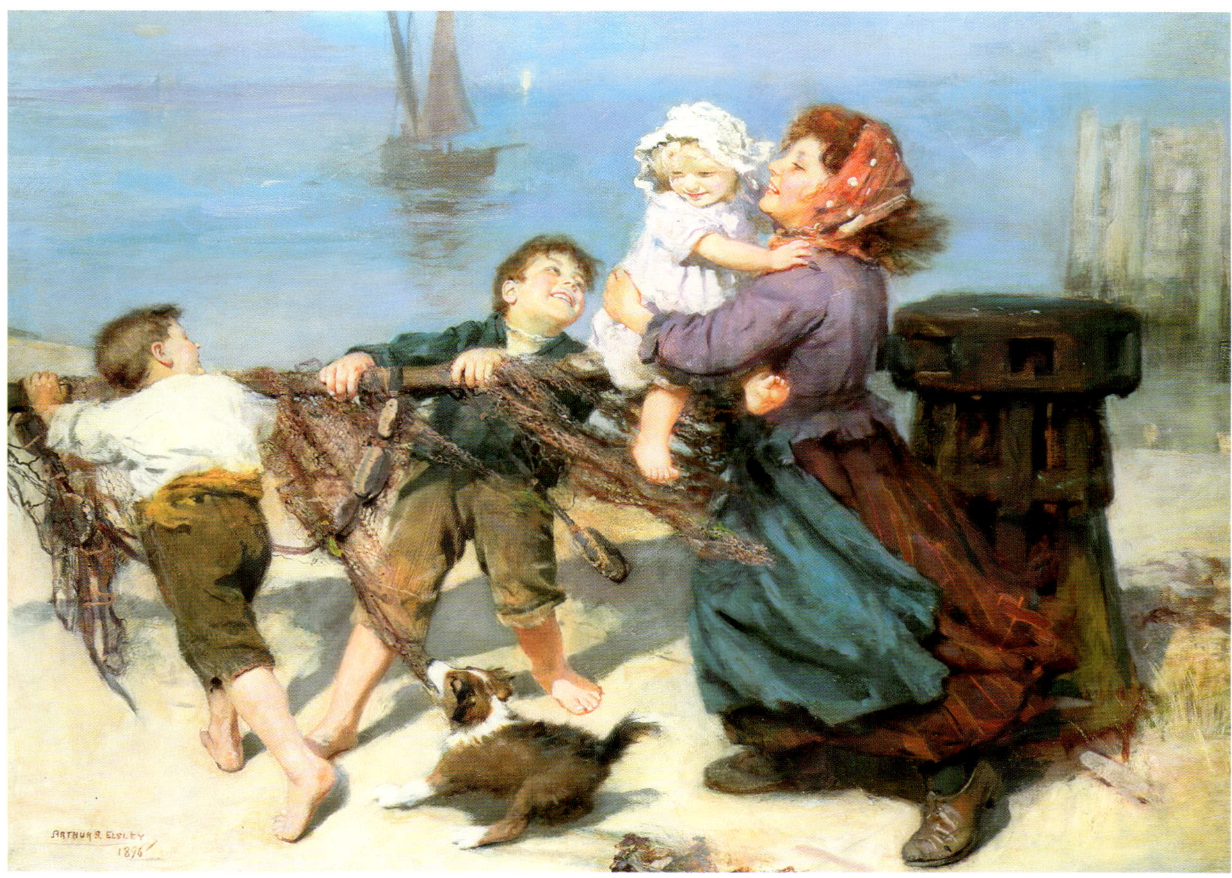

[Heave-Ho], 1896.
See page 38.

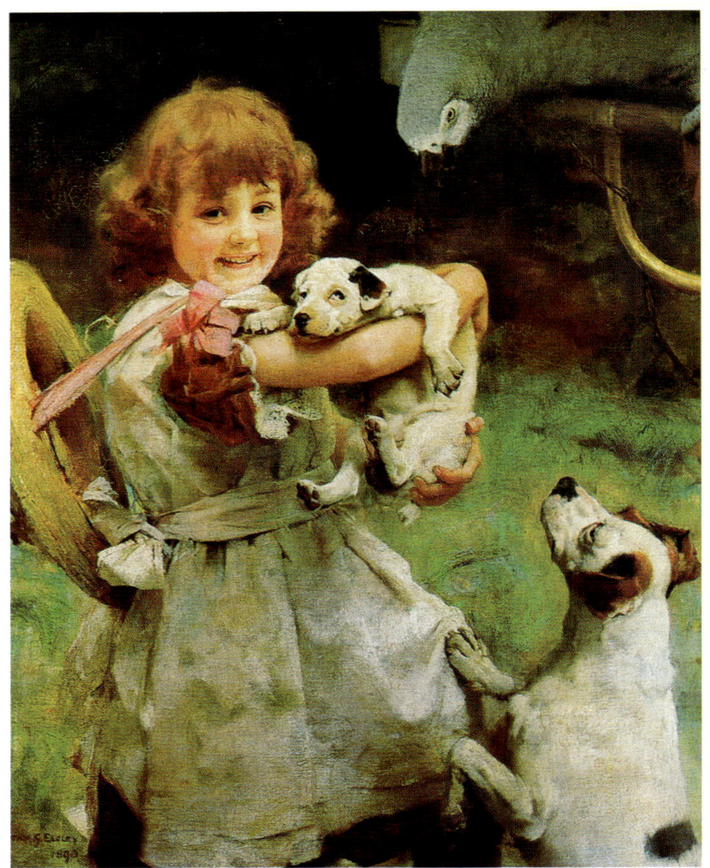

More Frightened Than Hurt, 1890. **See page 15**.

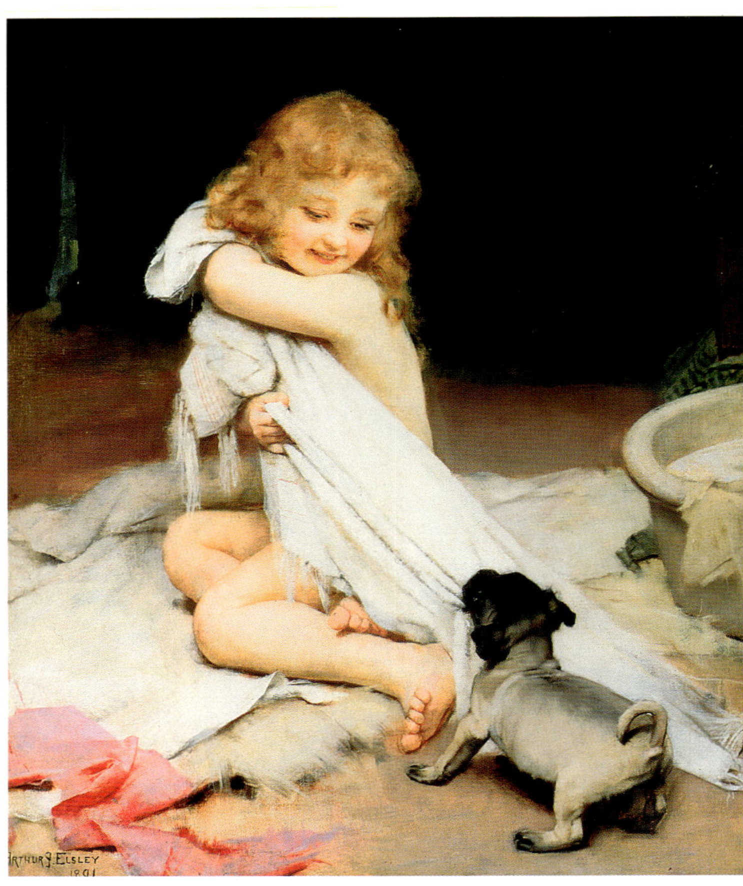

Go Away Sir!, 1891. **See page 16**.

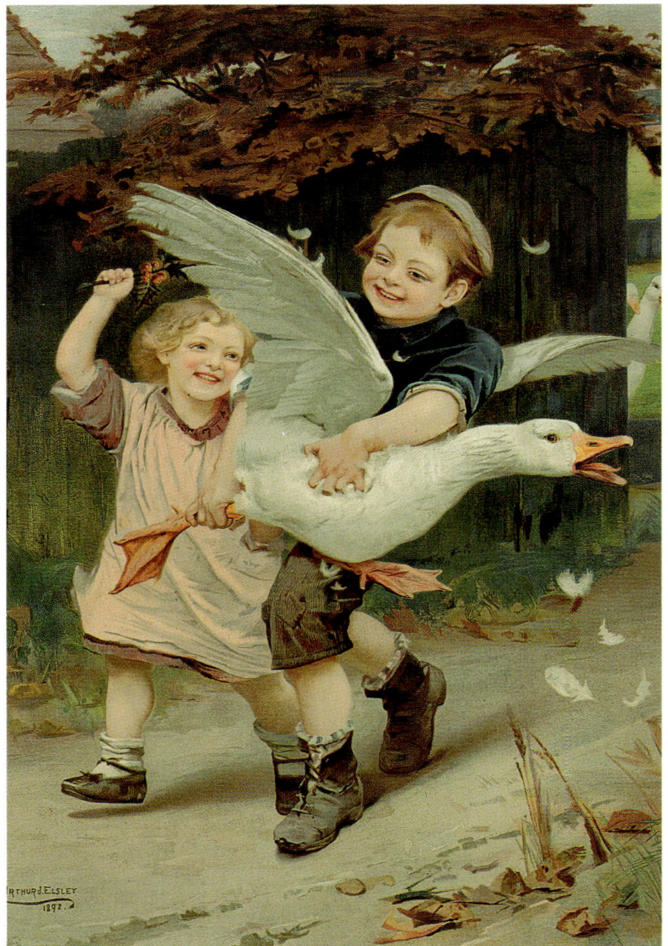

Our Christmas Goose, 1892. **See page 21**.

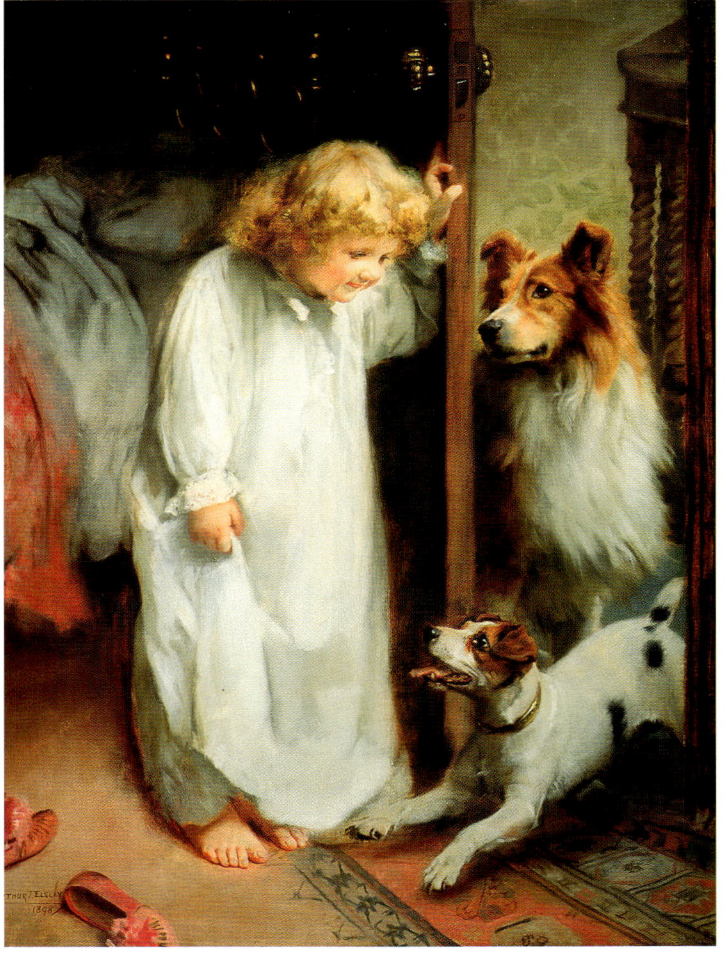

Hard Pressed / Time To Get Up, 1898. **See page 41**.

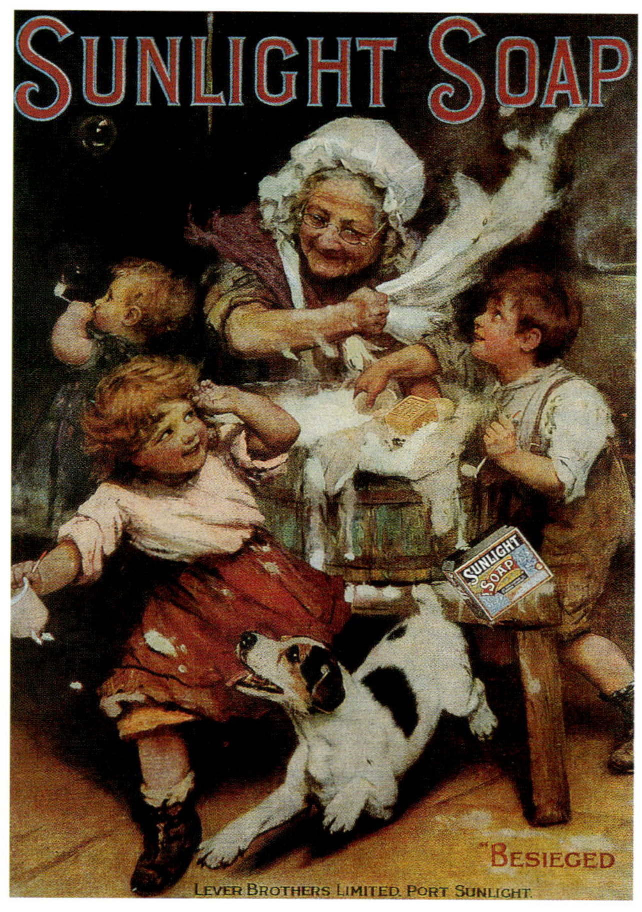

Besieged, 1893. **See page 24**.

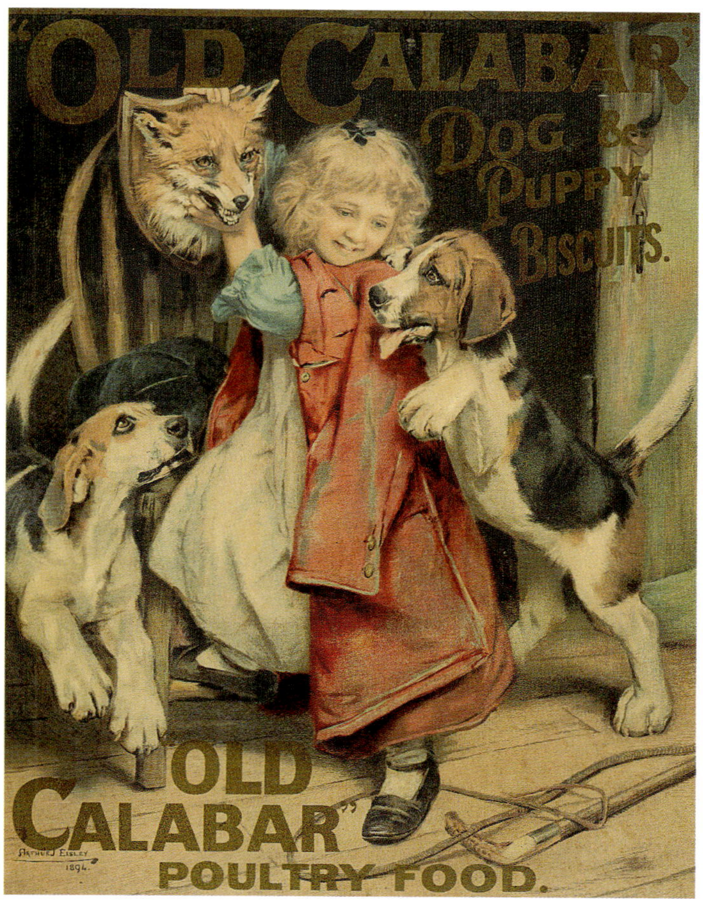

Tally Ho!, 1894. **See page 27**.

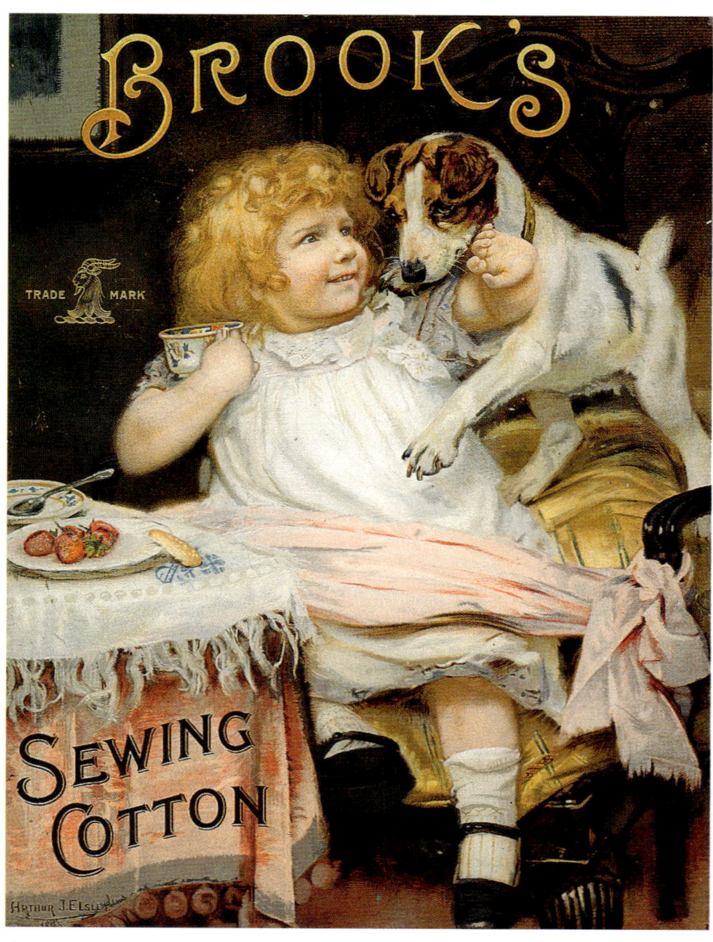

[An Uninvited Guest], 1895. **See page 35**.

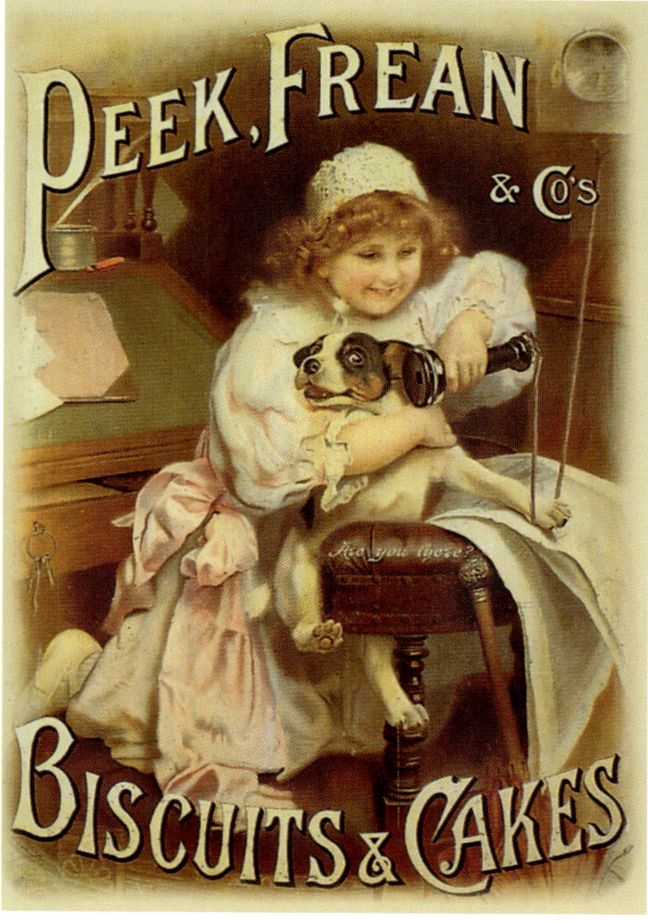

Are You There?, c.1896. **See page 39**.

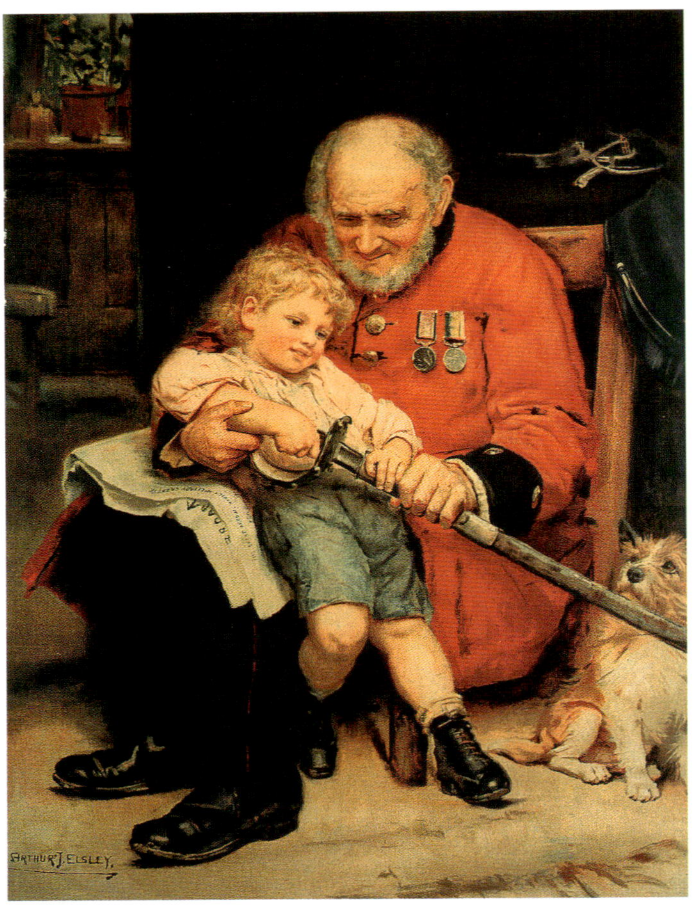

A Young Briton, 1895. **See page 34**.

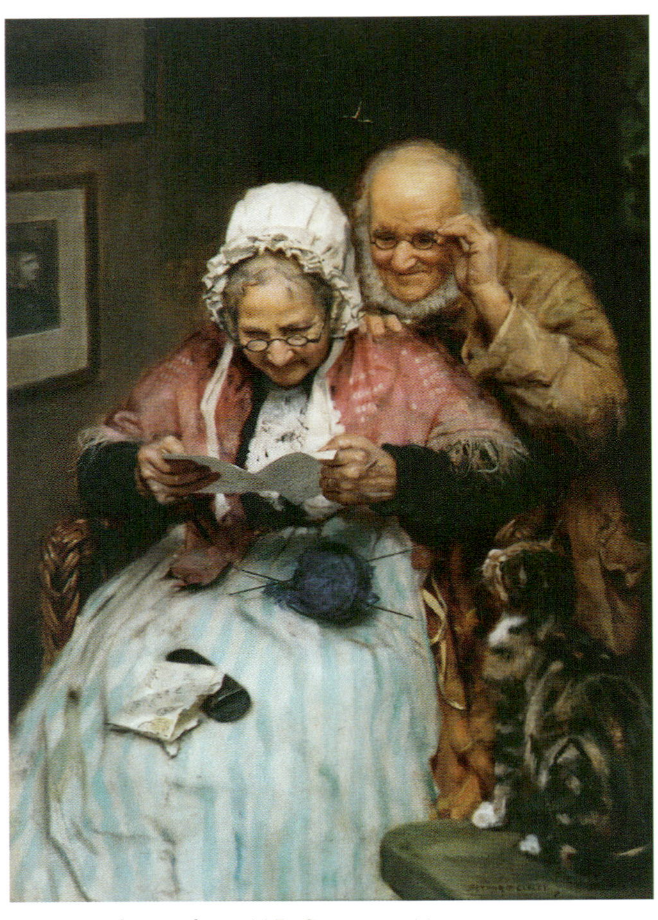

Homeward Bound, c.1897. **See page 40**.

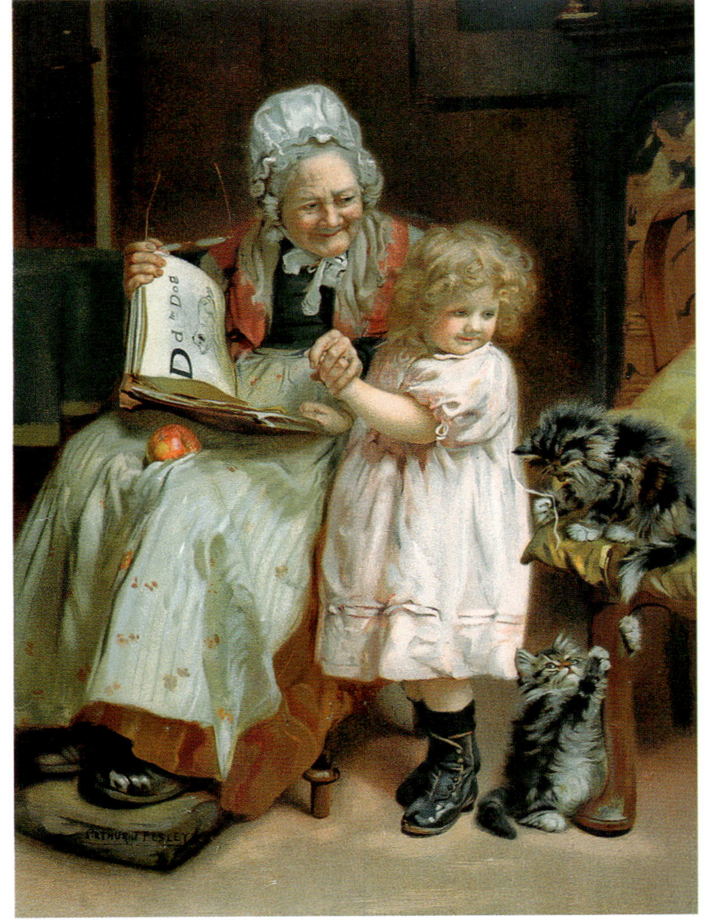

Divided Attention, c.1898. **See page 42**.

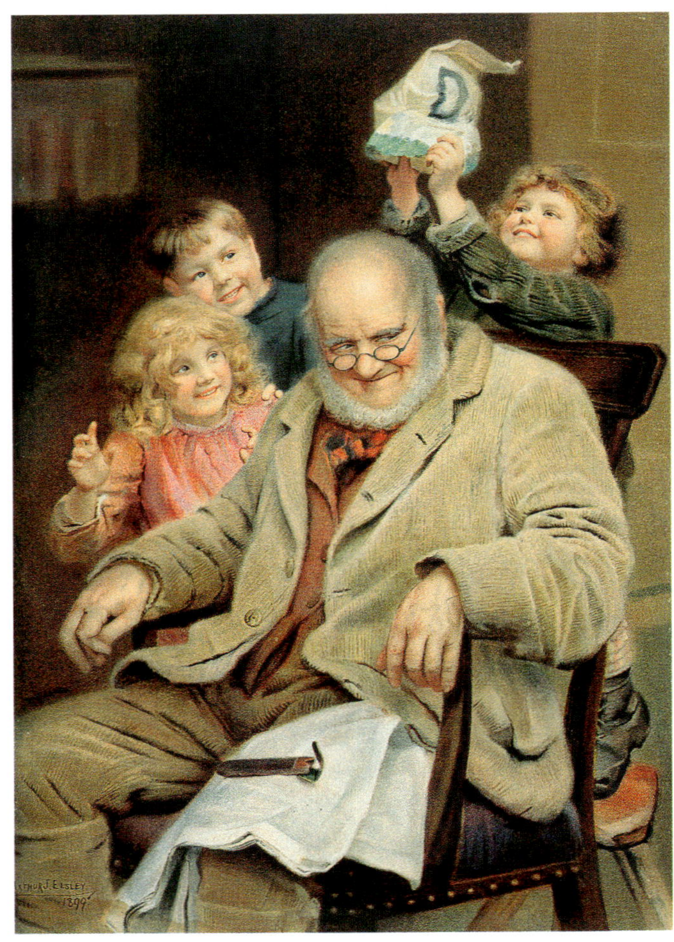

Caught Napping, 1899. **See page 42**.

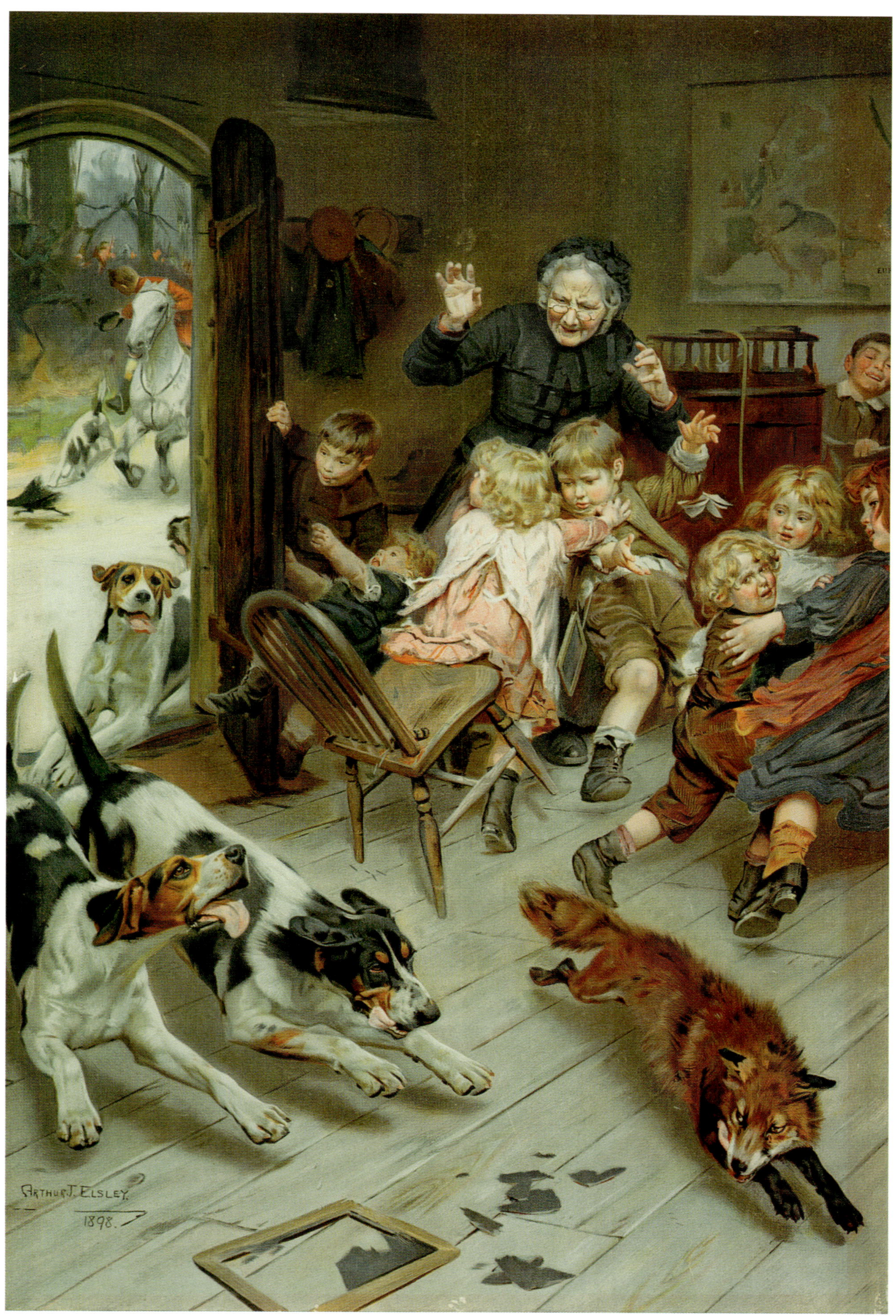

Any Port In A Storm / Late For School, 1898. **See page 41**.

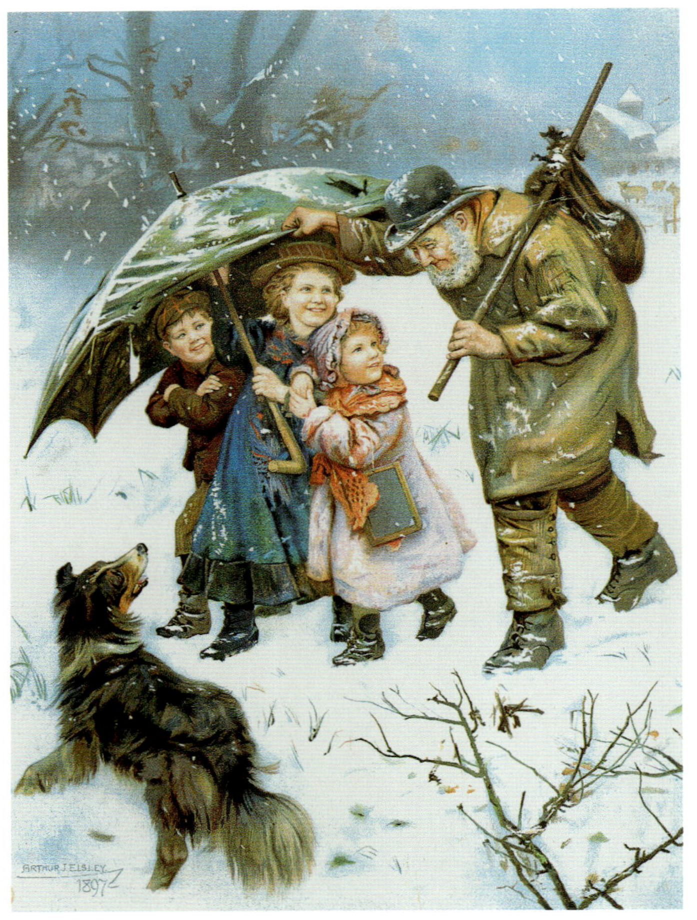

Any Room For Me?, 1897. **See page 40**.

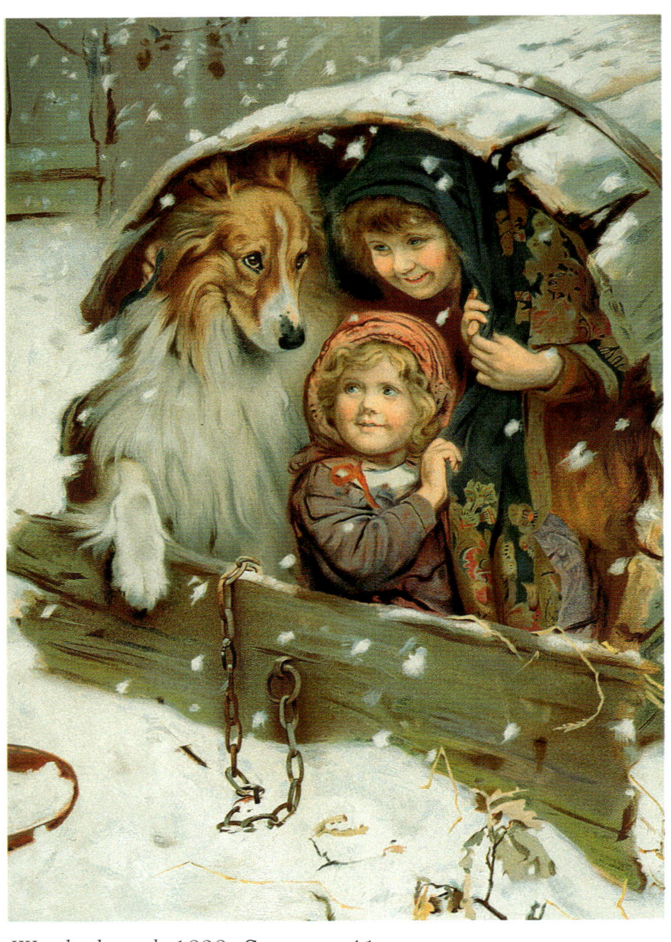

Weatherbound, 1898. **See page 41**.

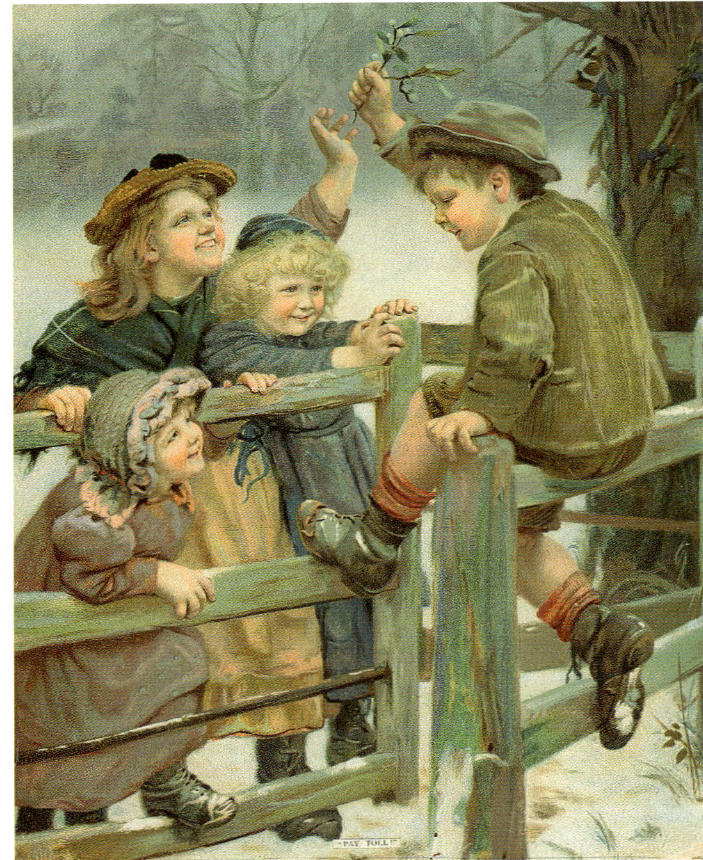

At Bay / Pay Toll, 1898. **See page 42**.

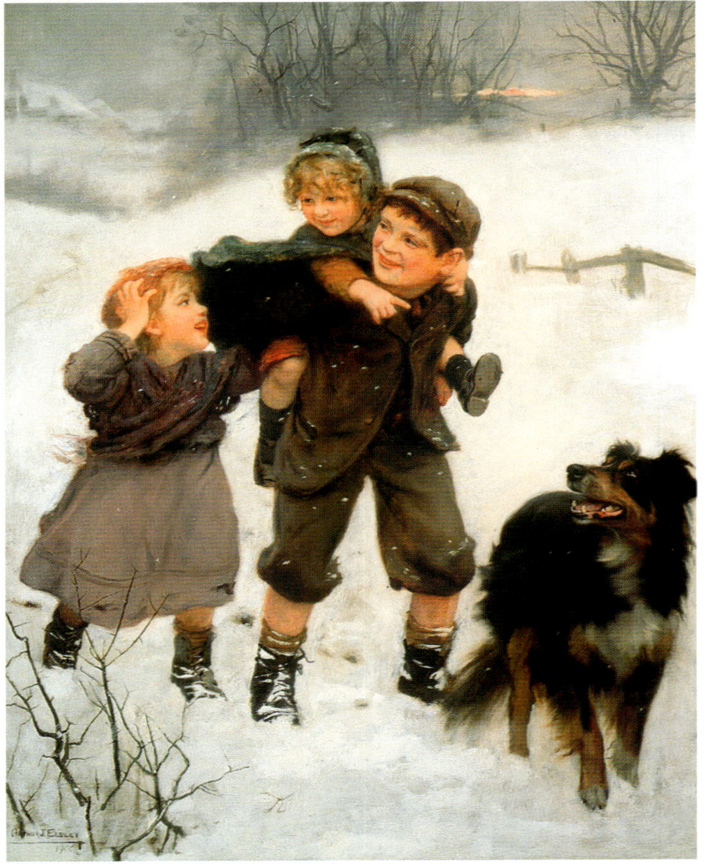

This Way, 1900. **See page 46**.

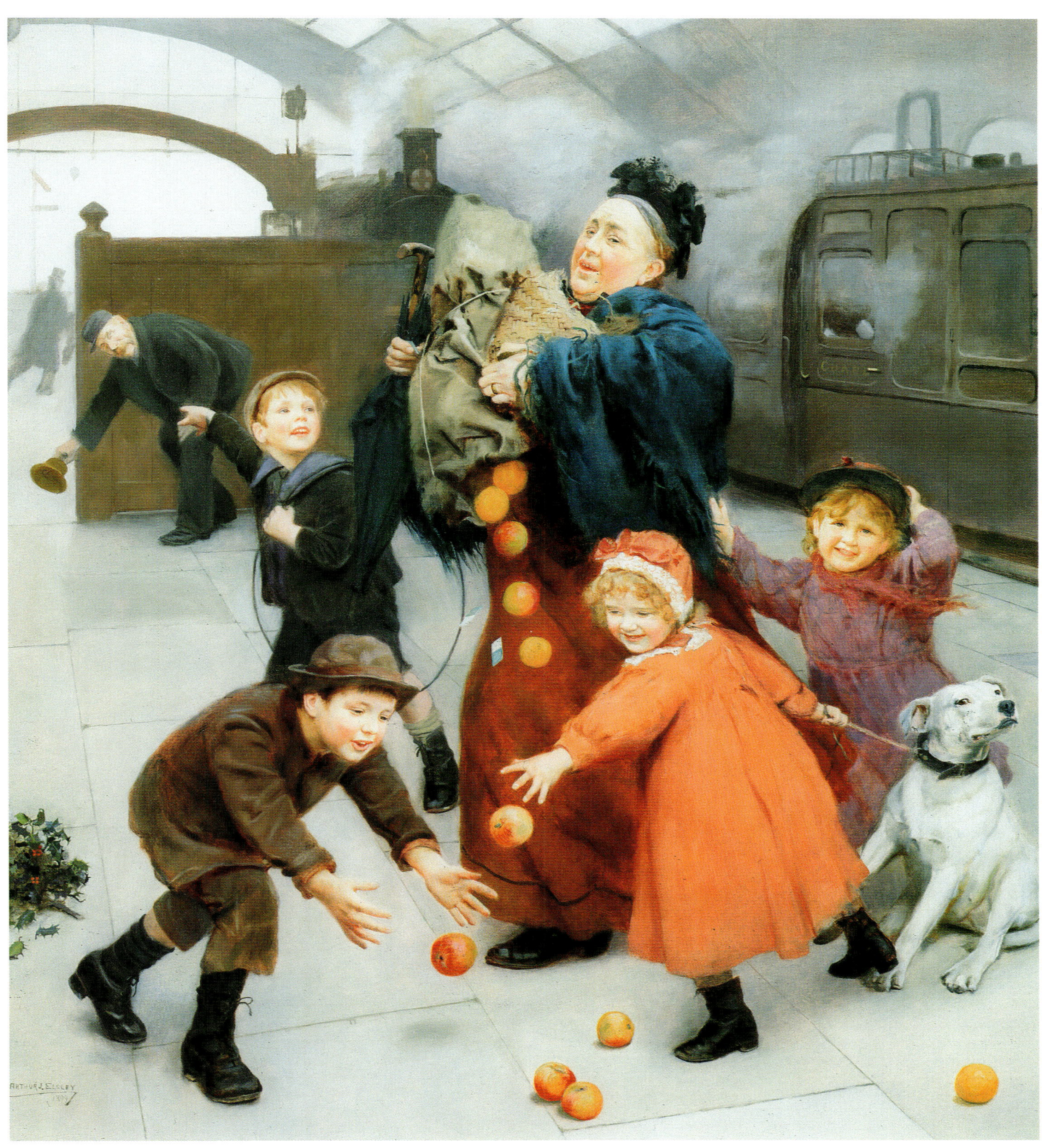

More Haste – Less Speed, 1899. **See page 44**.

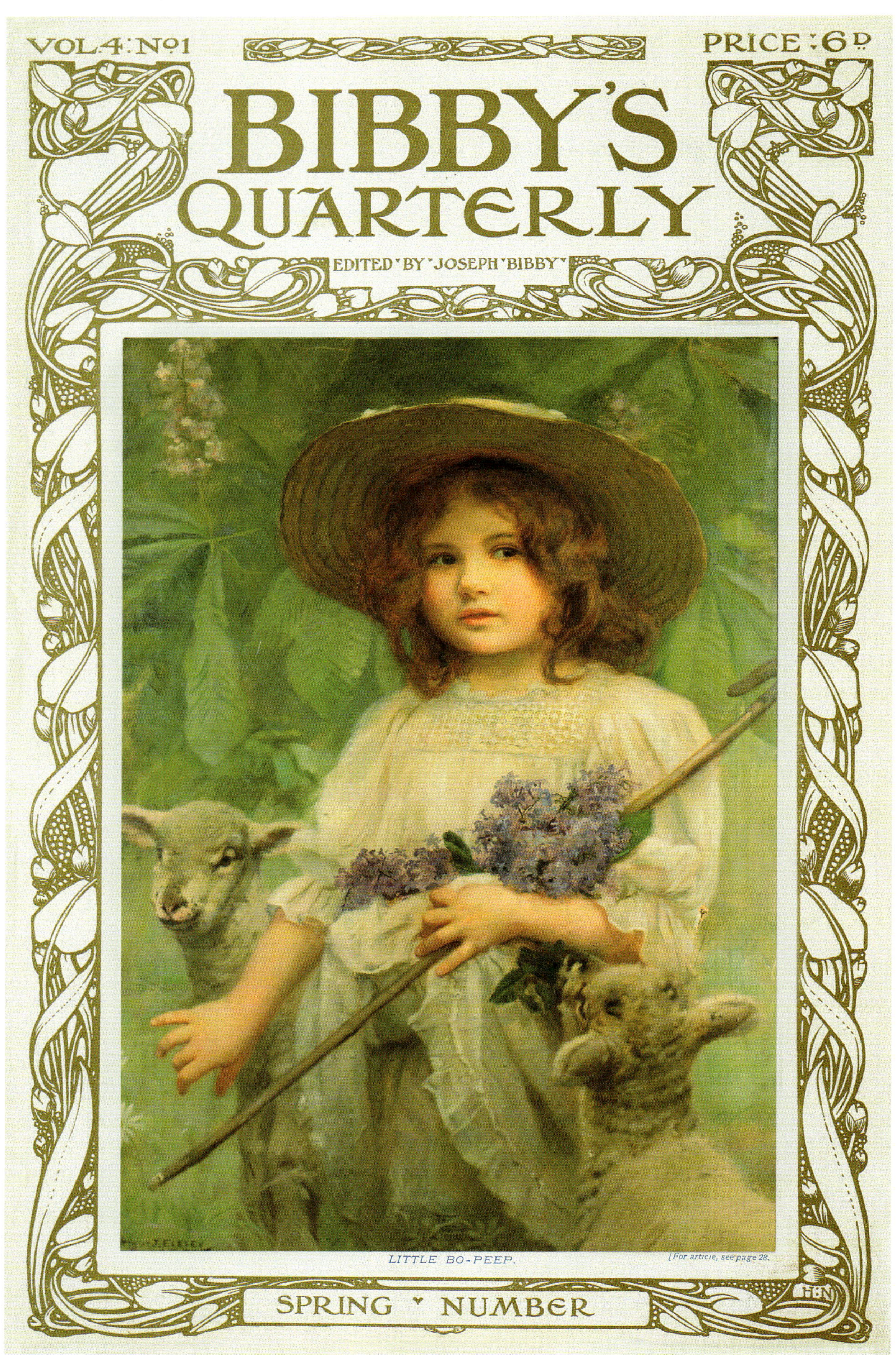

Little Bo-Peep, 1900. **See page 45**.

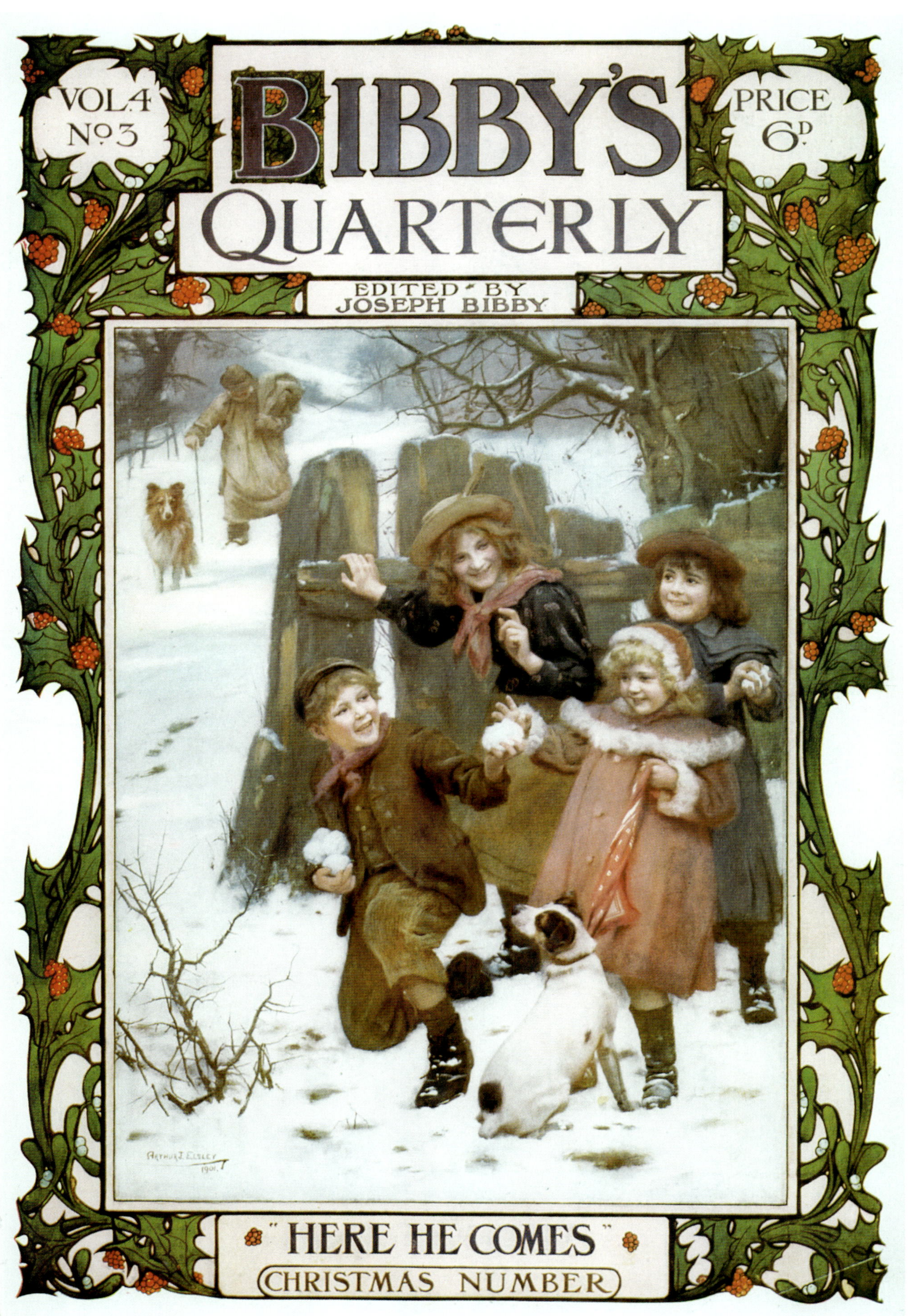

Hold Up / Here He Comes, 1901. **See page 89**.

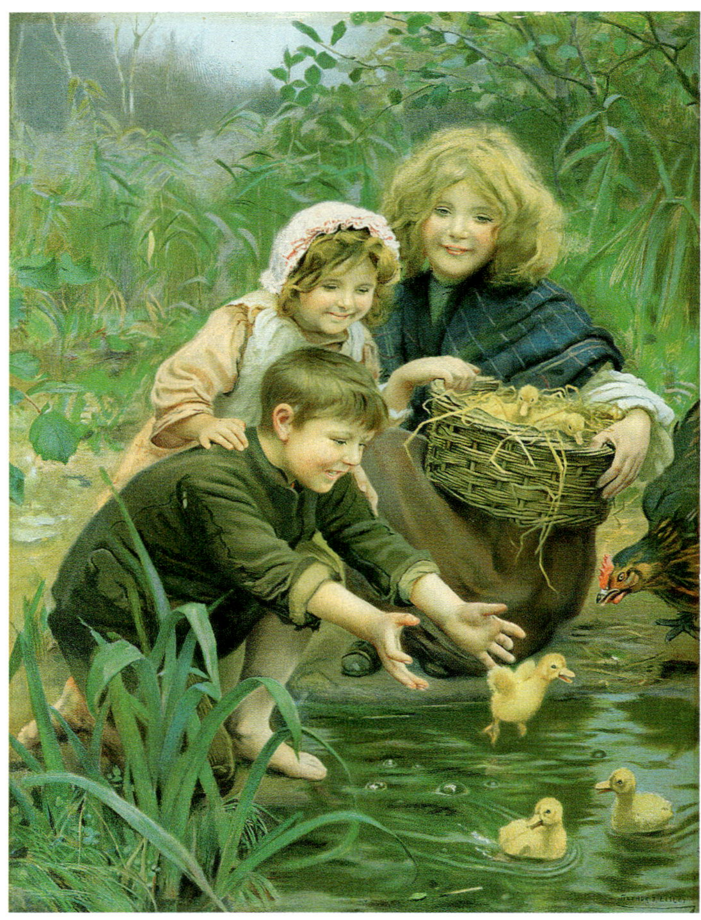

Their First Swim, c.1897. **See page 40**.

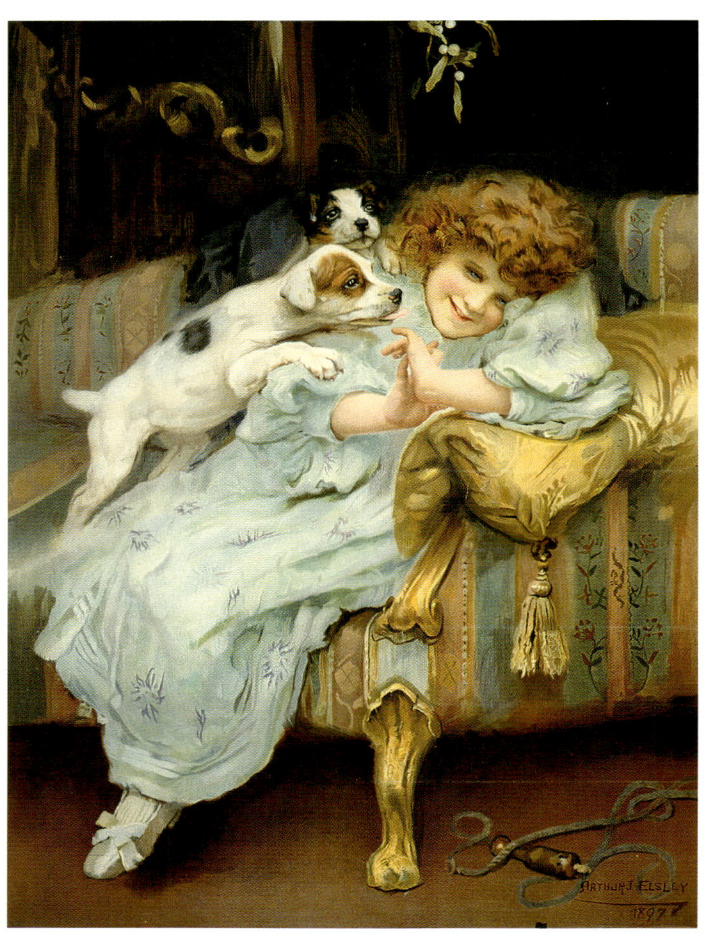

Under The Mistletoe, 1897. **See page 40**.

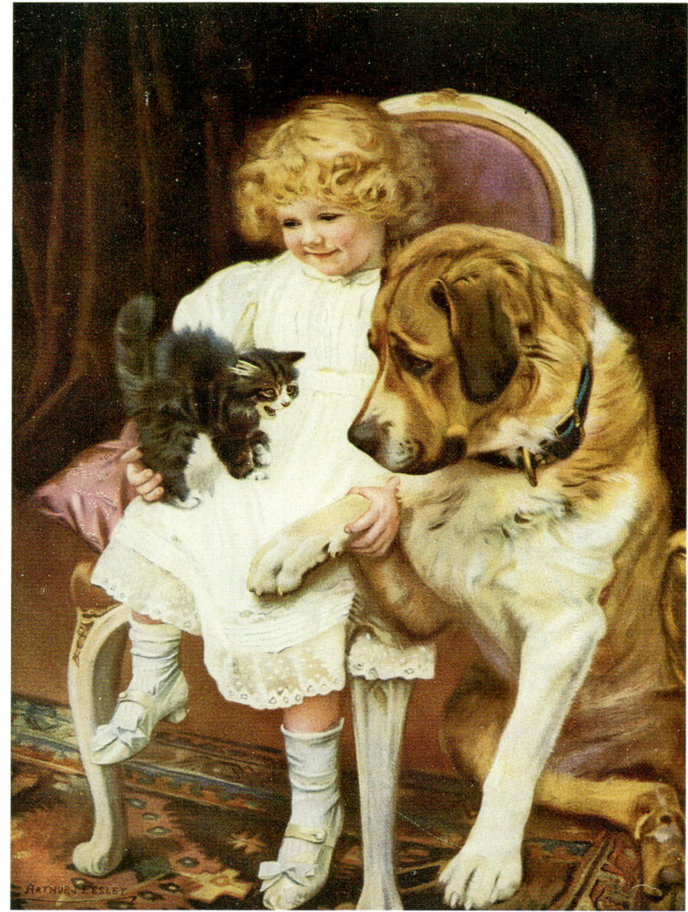

Kiss And Be Friends, Version II, 1901. **See page 47**.

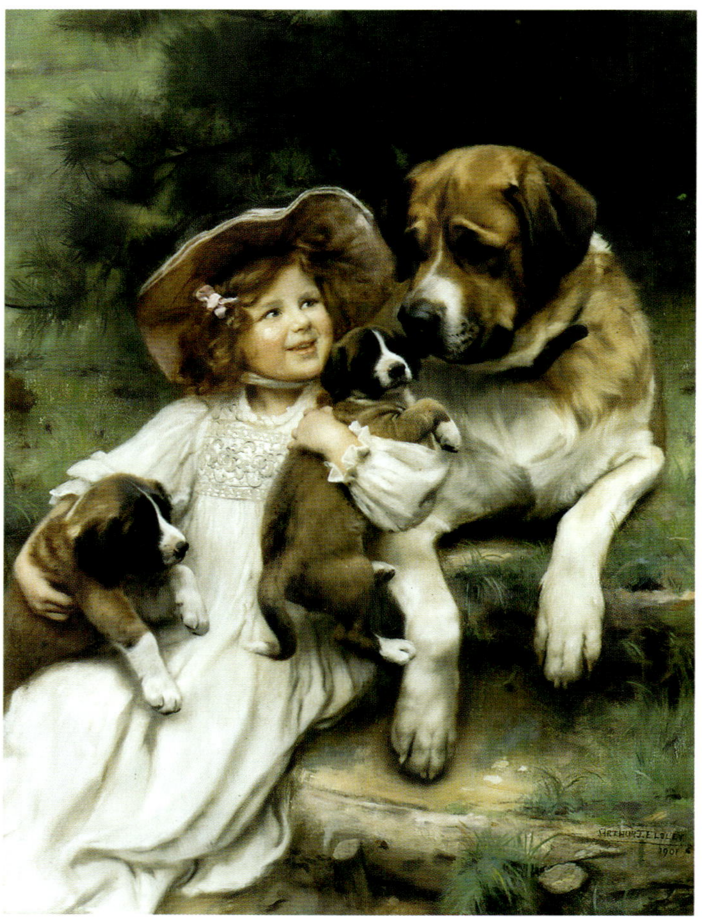

Which May I Keep?, 1901. **See page 47**.

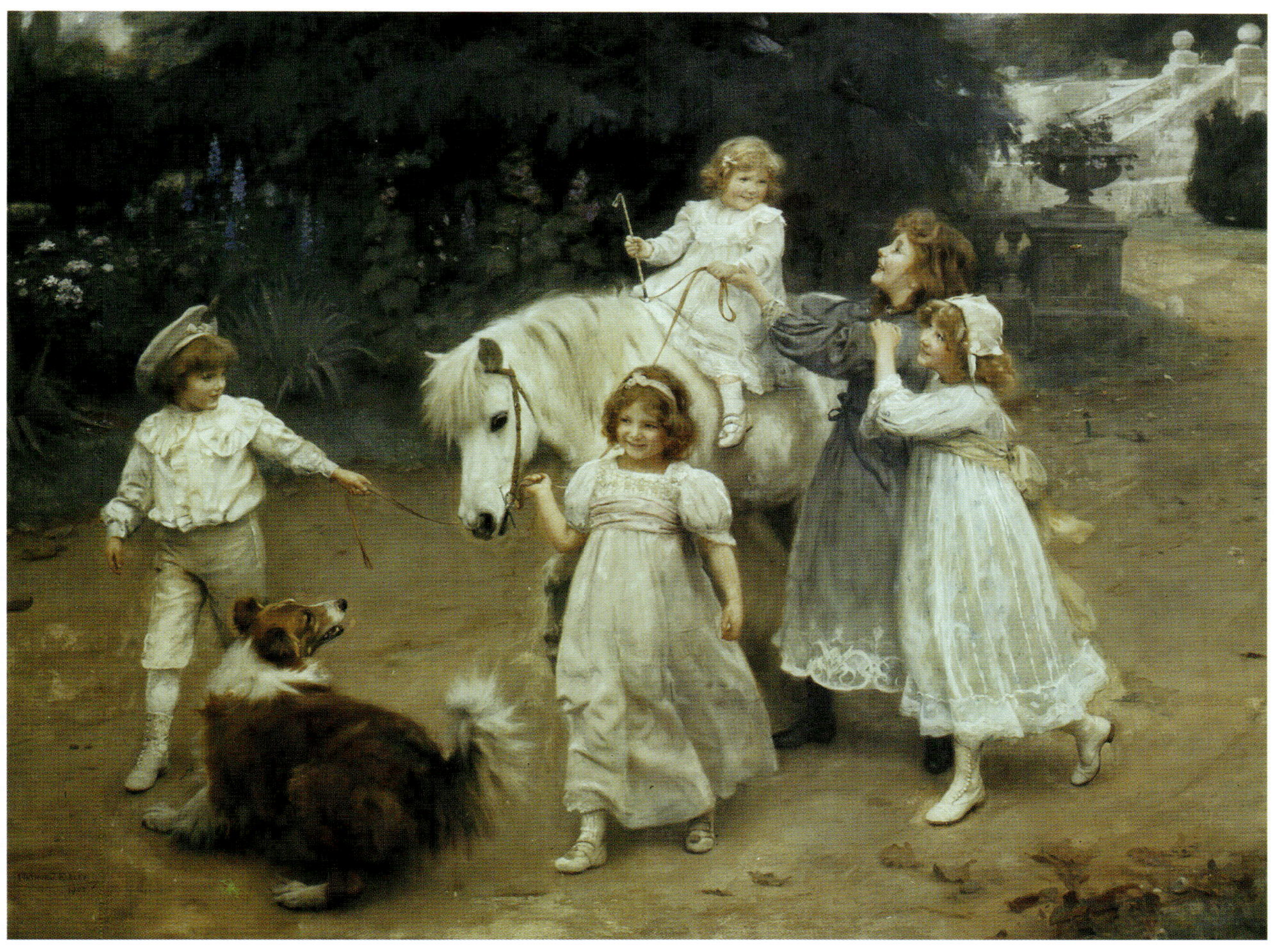

Golden Hours, 1903. **See page 93**.

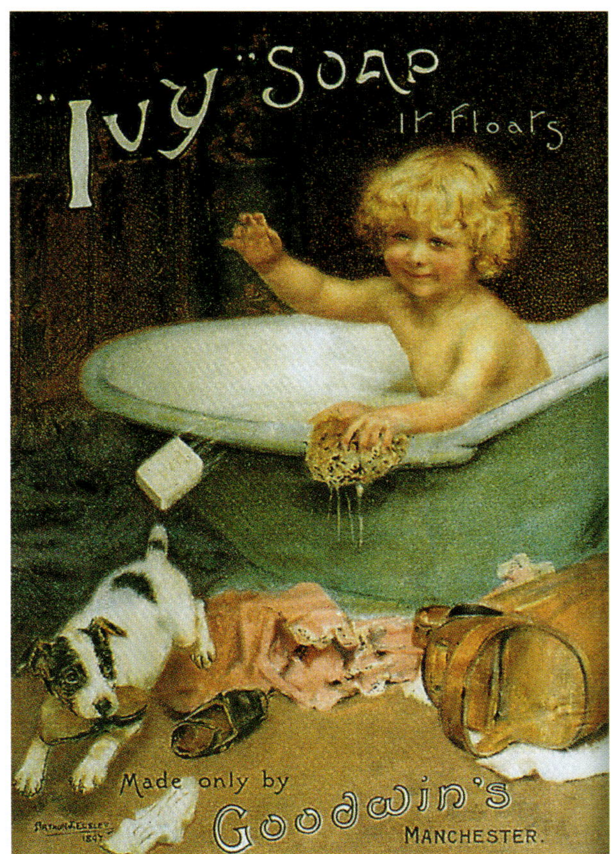

[A Clean Getaway] / Ivy Soap Advertisement, 1897. **See page 40**.

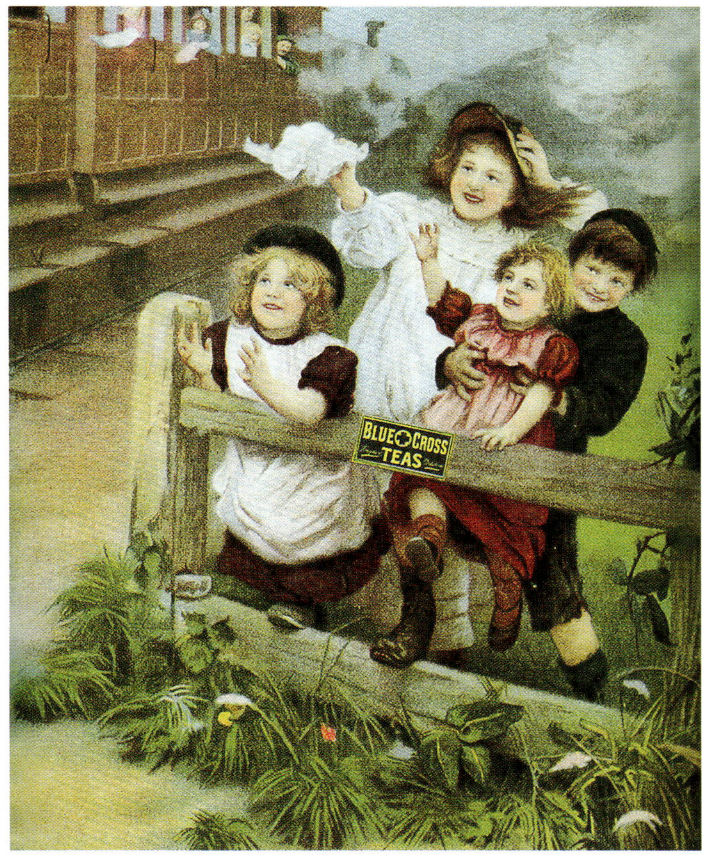

Home Again, c.1900. **See page 46**.

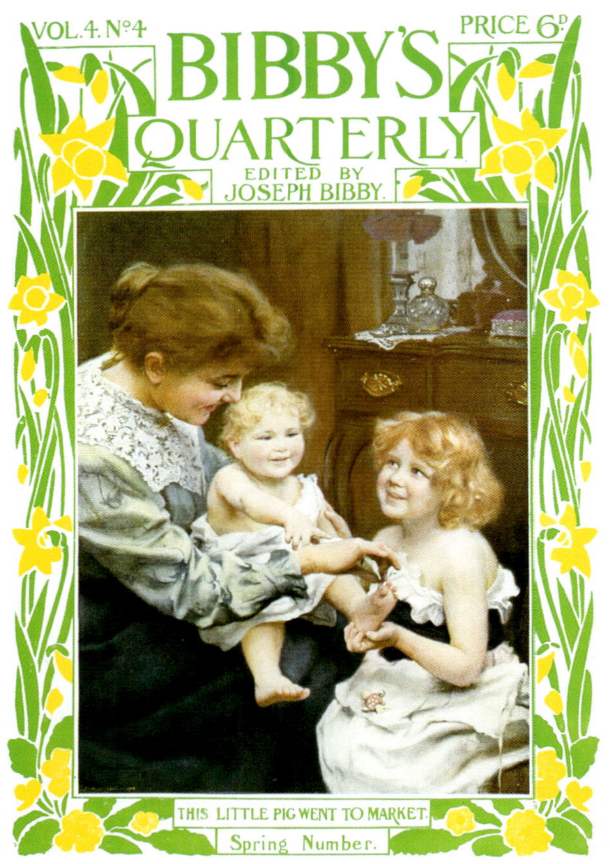

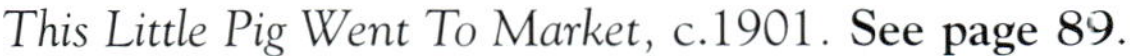

This Little Pig Went To Market, c.1901. **See page 89**.

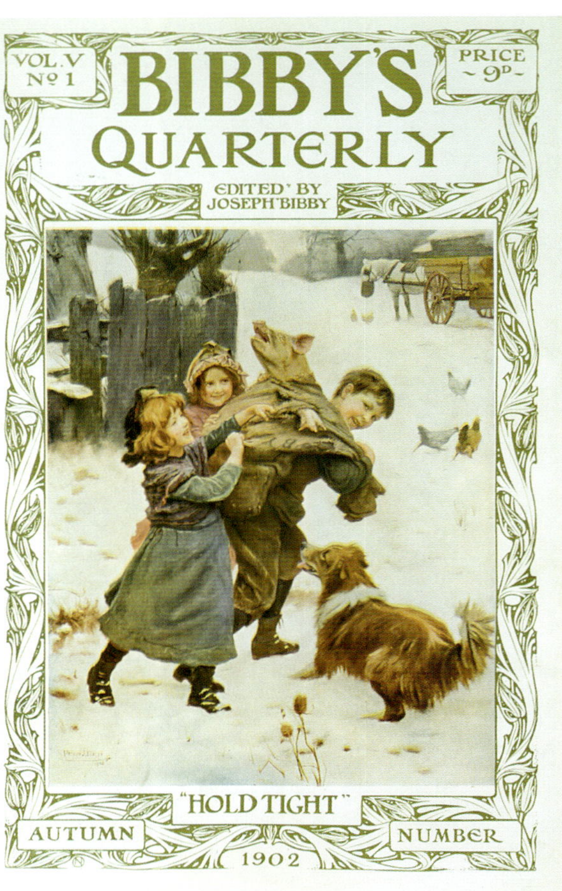

Hold Tight, 1902. **See page 92**.

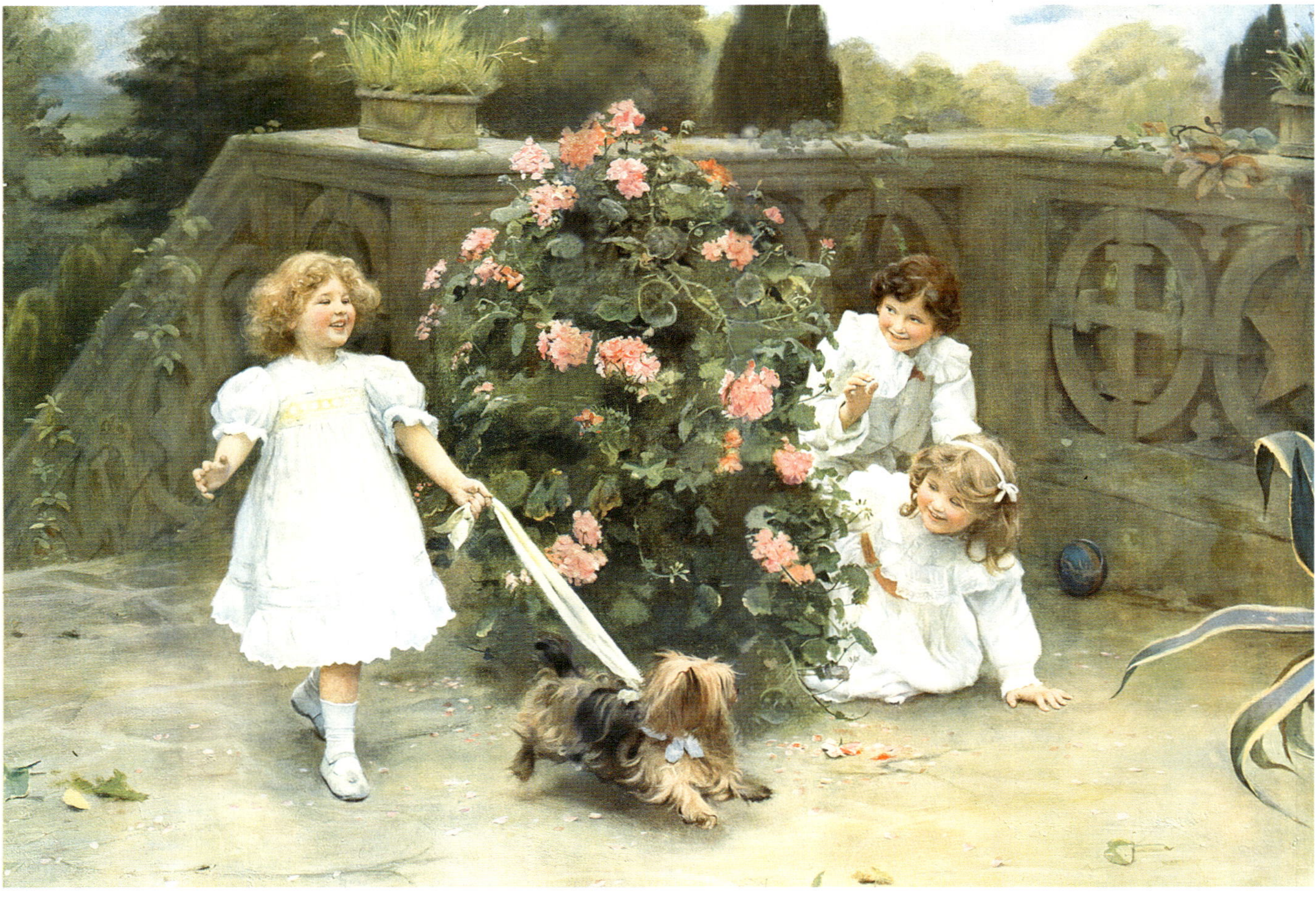

Here They Are!, 1907. **See page 107**.

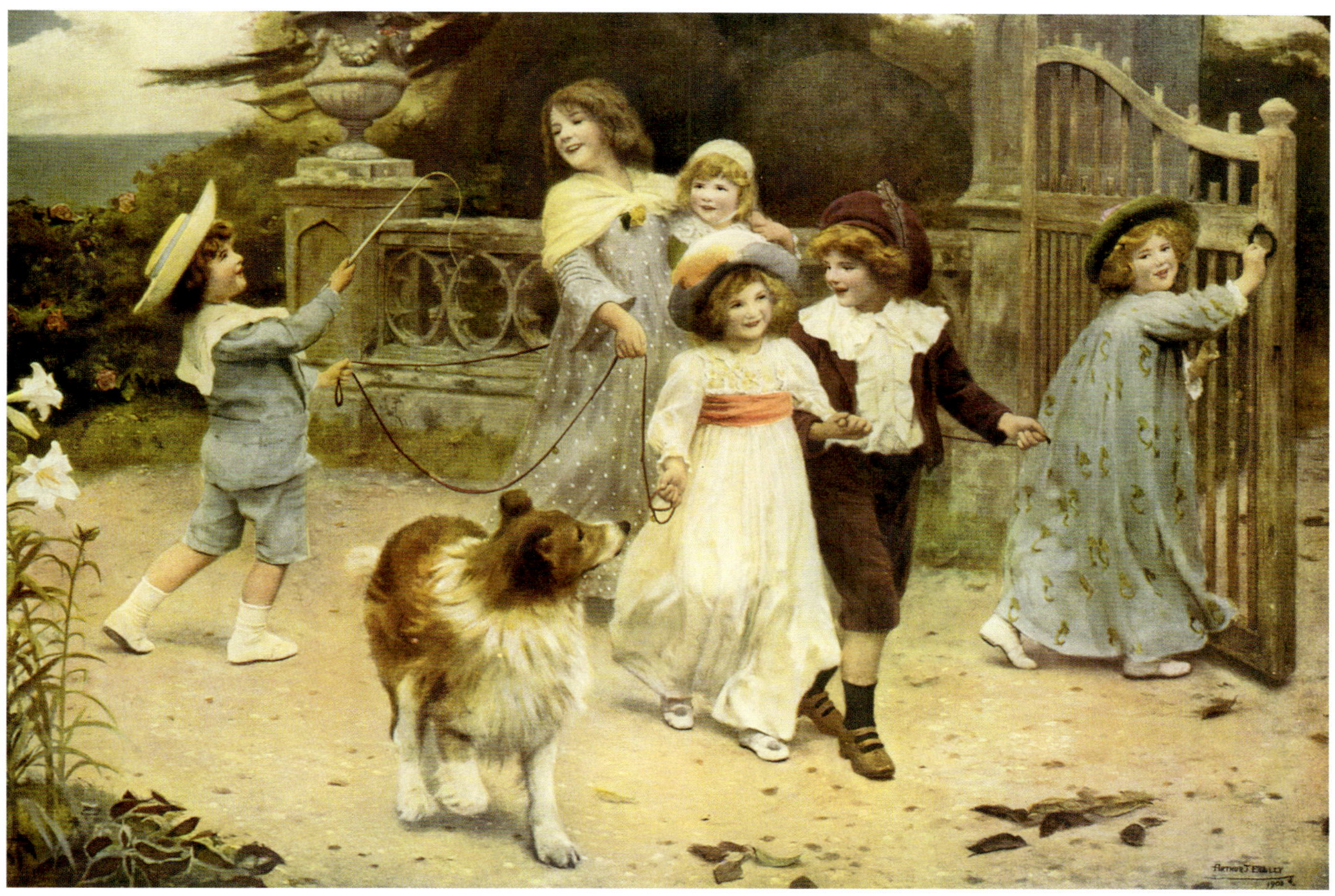

The Home Team, 1903. **See page 94**.

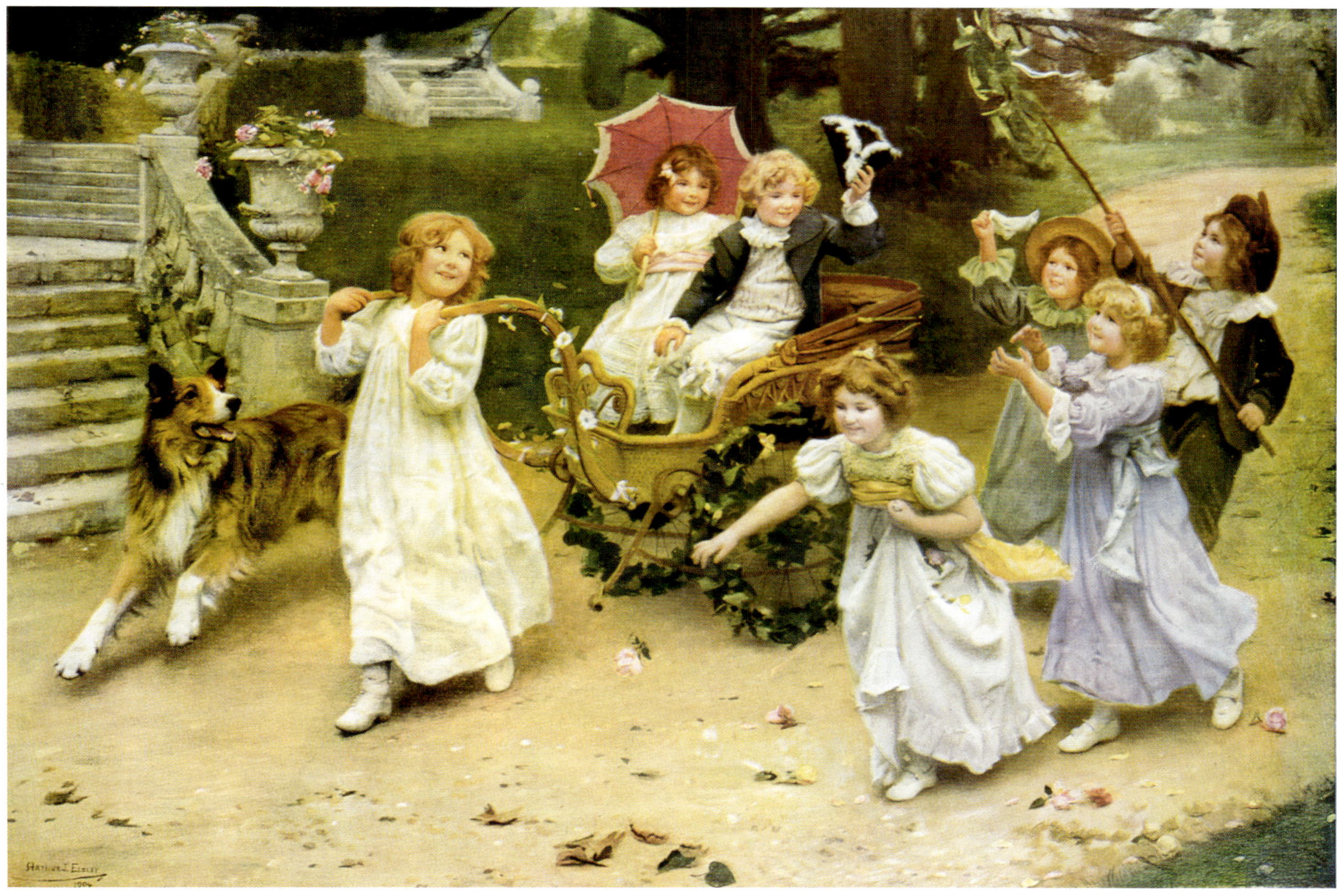

The Happy Pair / A Royal Procession, 1904. **See page 97**.

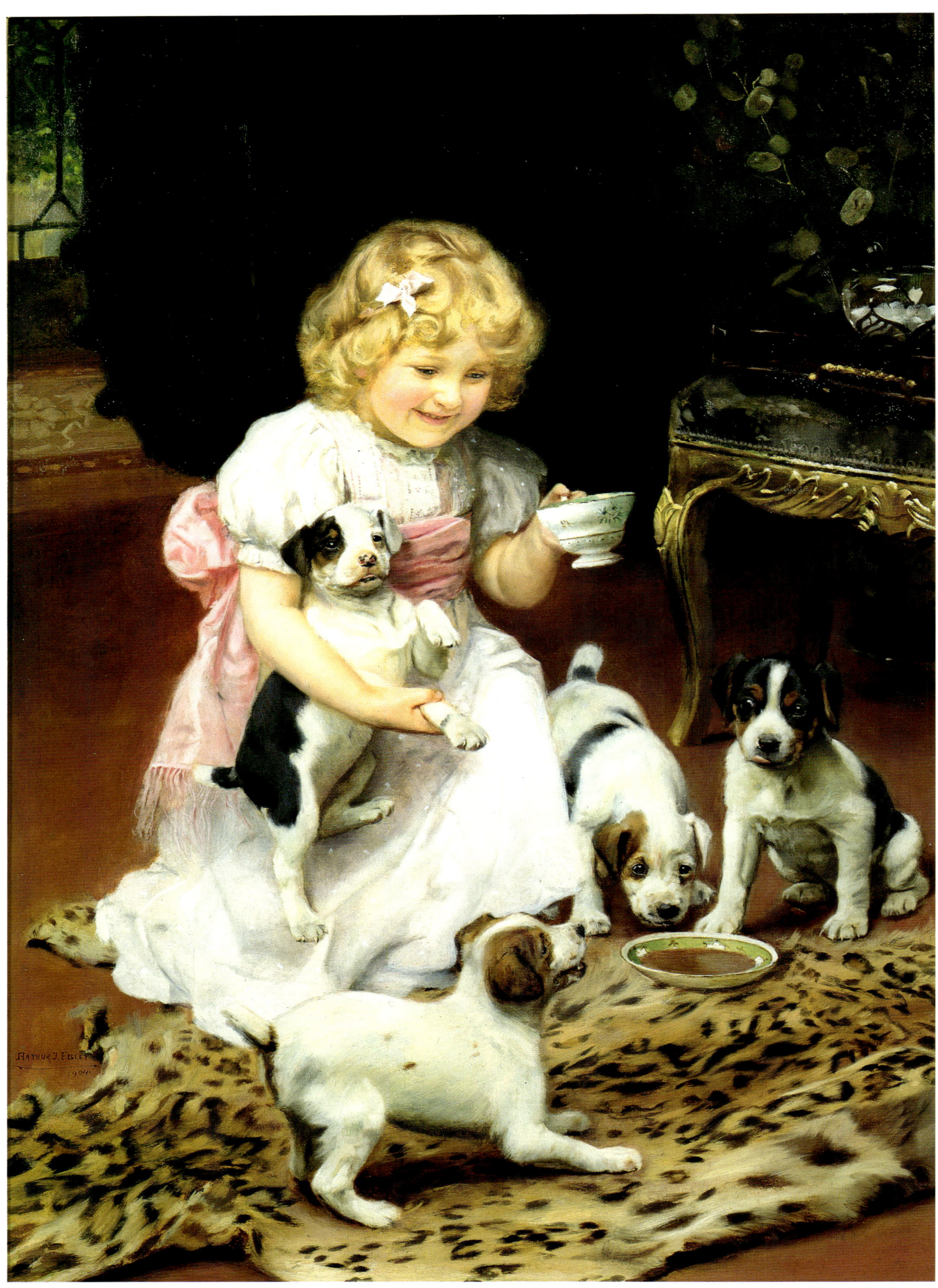

Too Hot, 1904. **See page 97**.

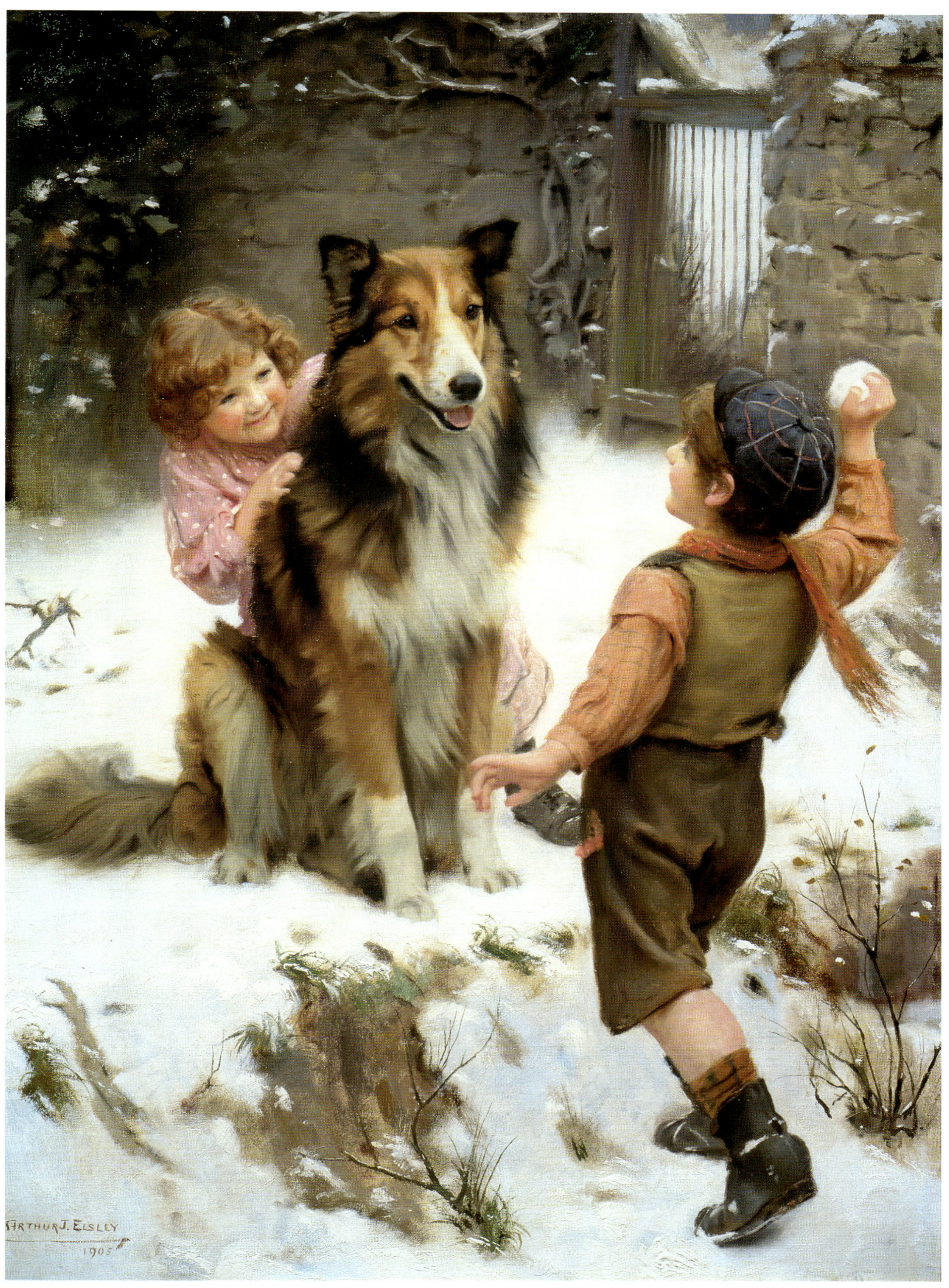

You Dursn't, 1905. **See page 97**.

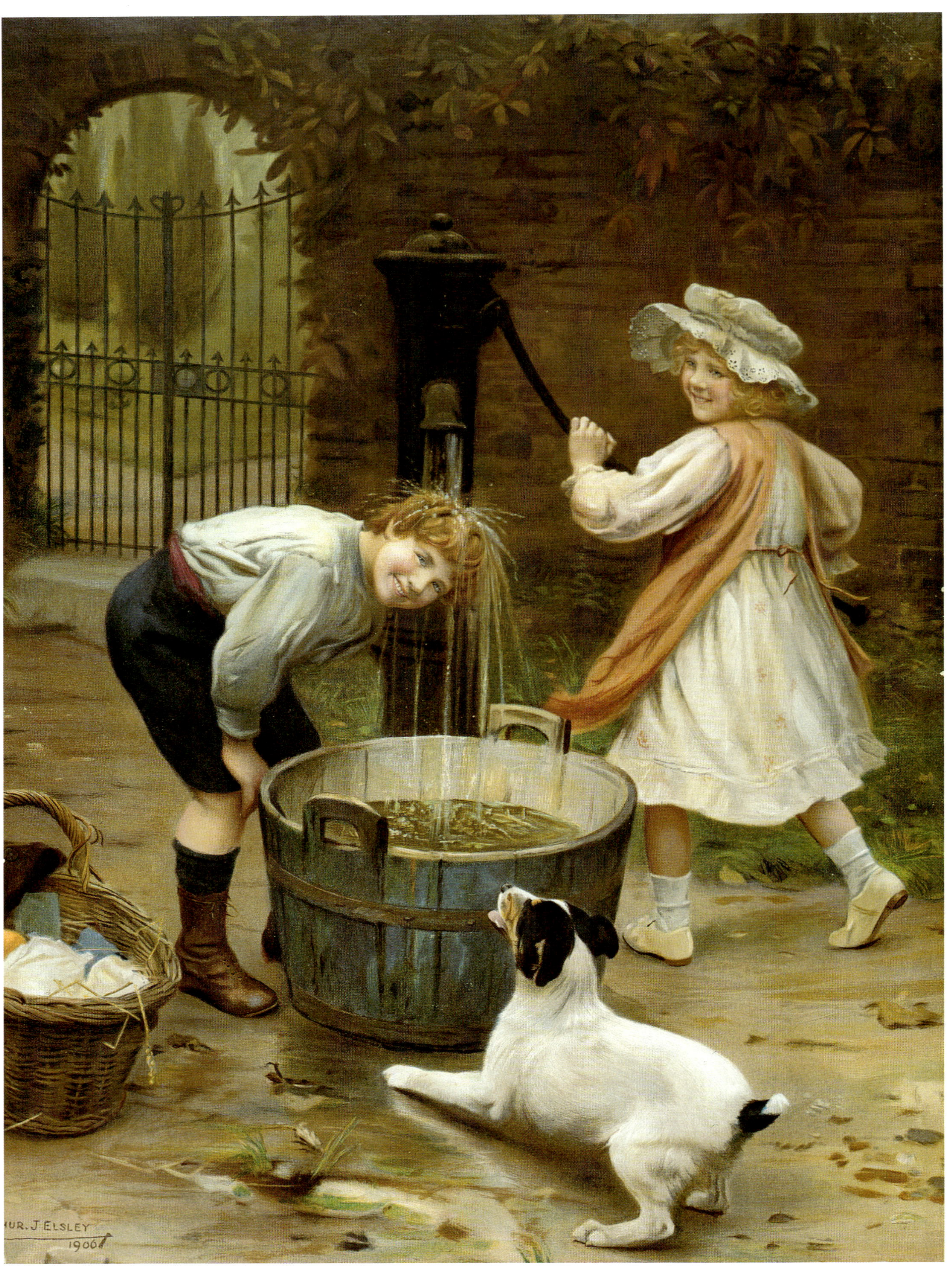

Cooling His Yed / My Turn Next, 1906. **See page 104**.

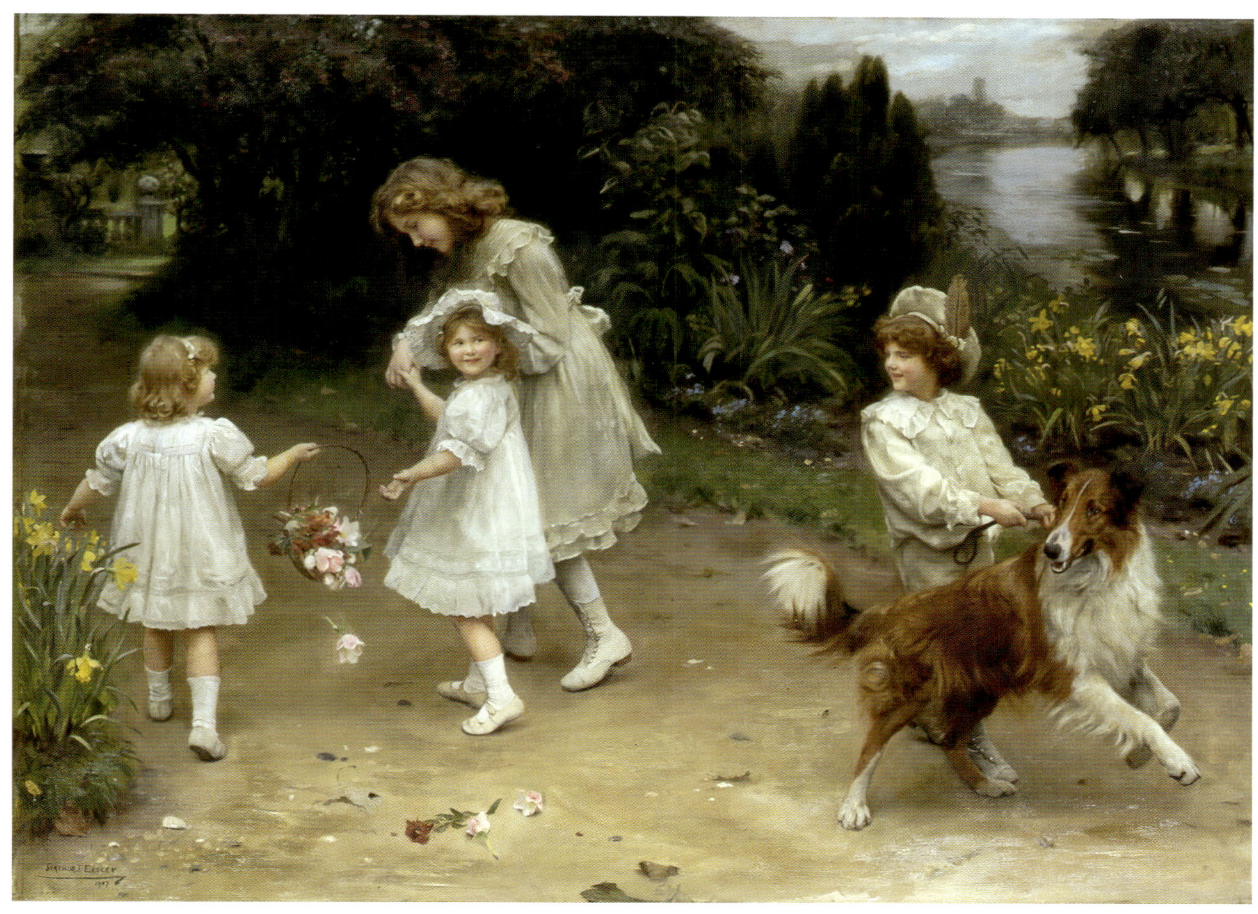

Love At First Sight, 1907. **See page 107**.

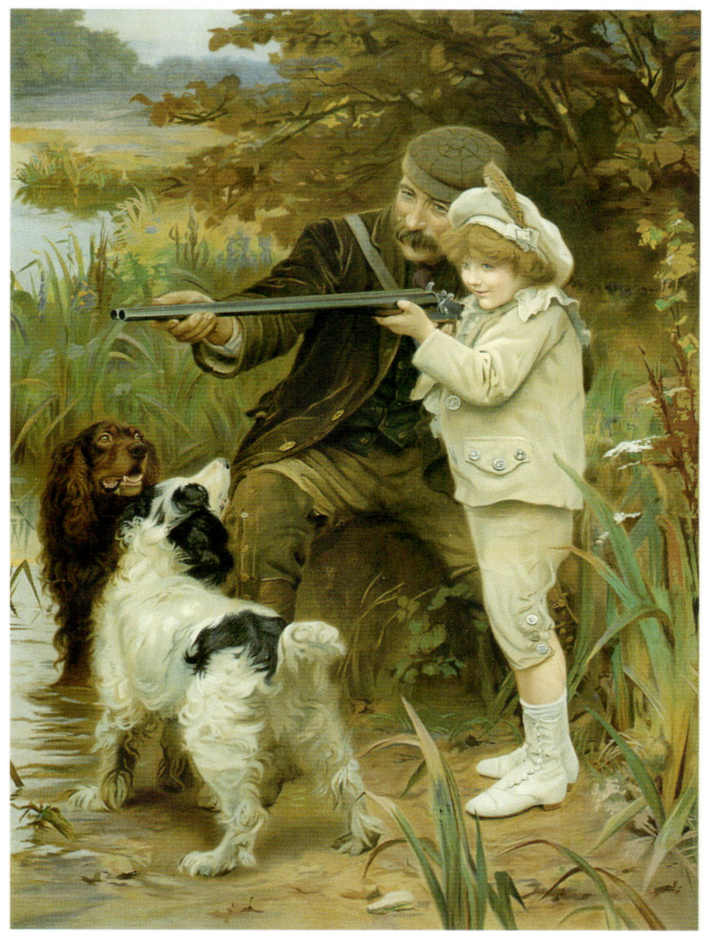

His First Shot, 1903. **See page 96**.

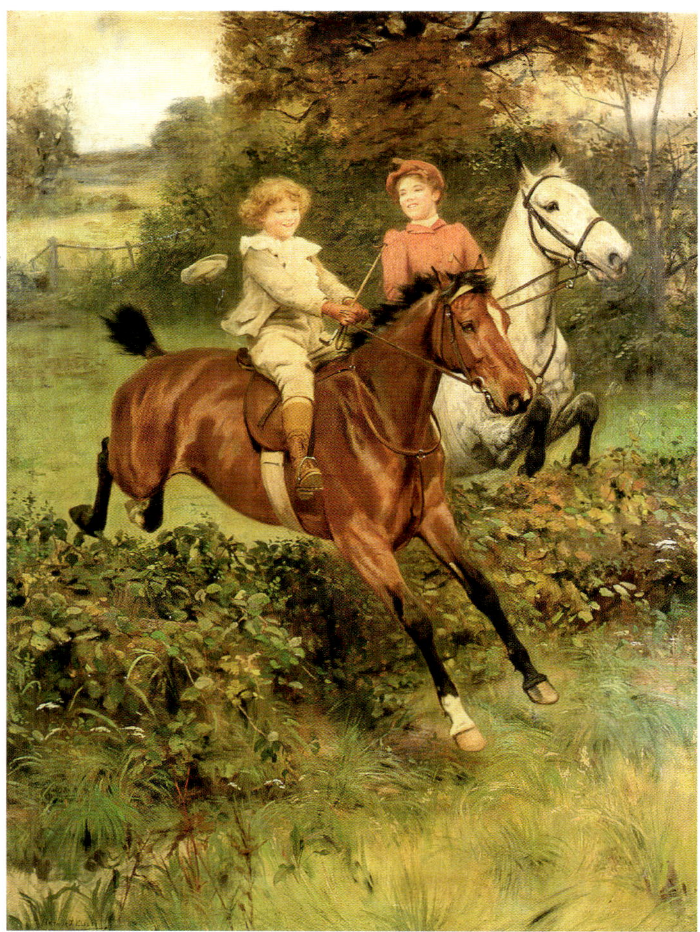

His First Fence, 1904. **See Page 97**.

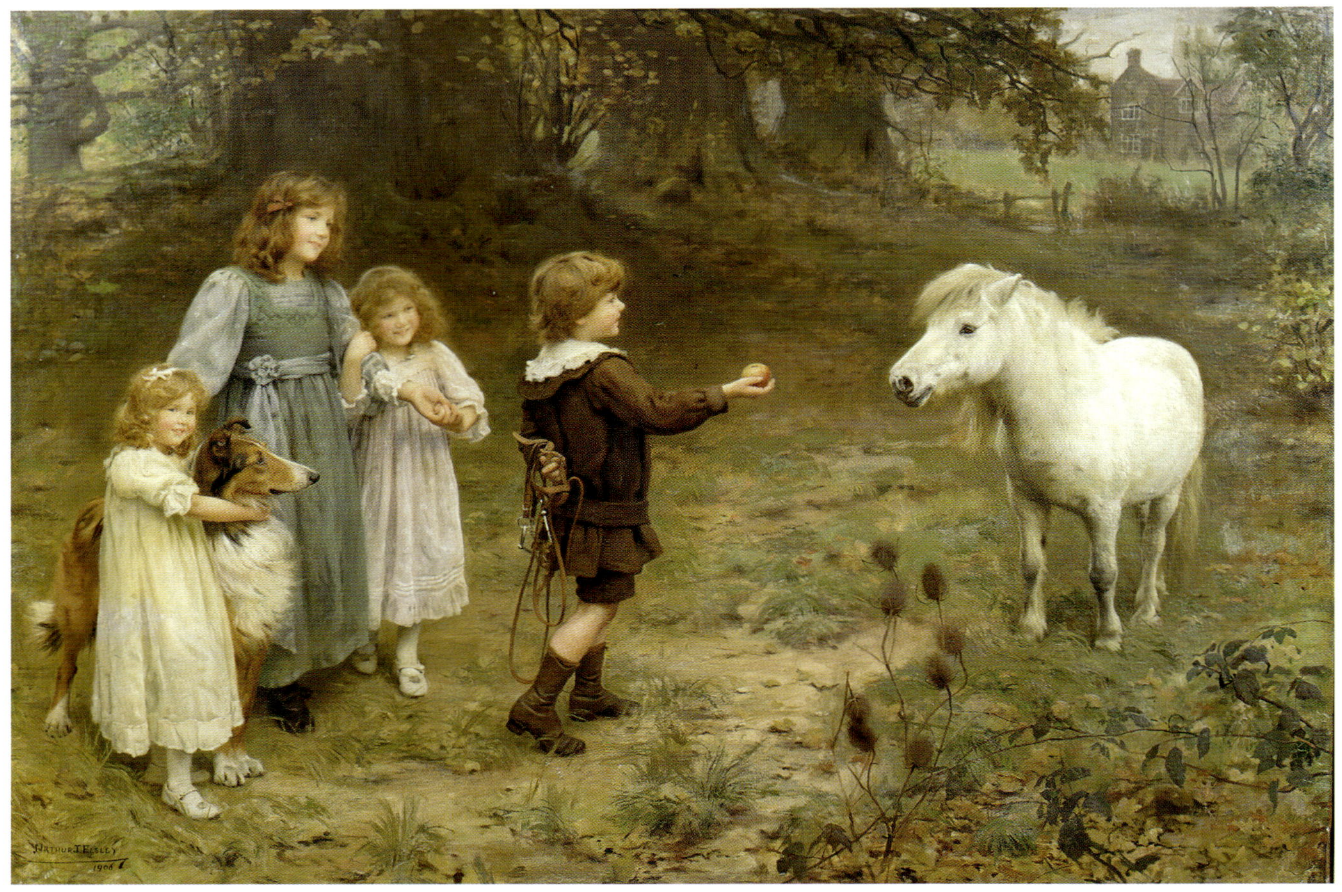

A Tempting Bait, 1906. **See page 102**.

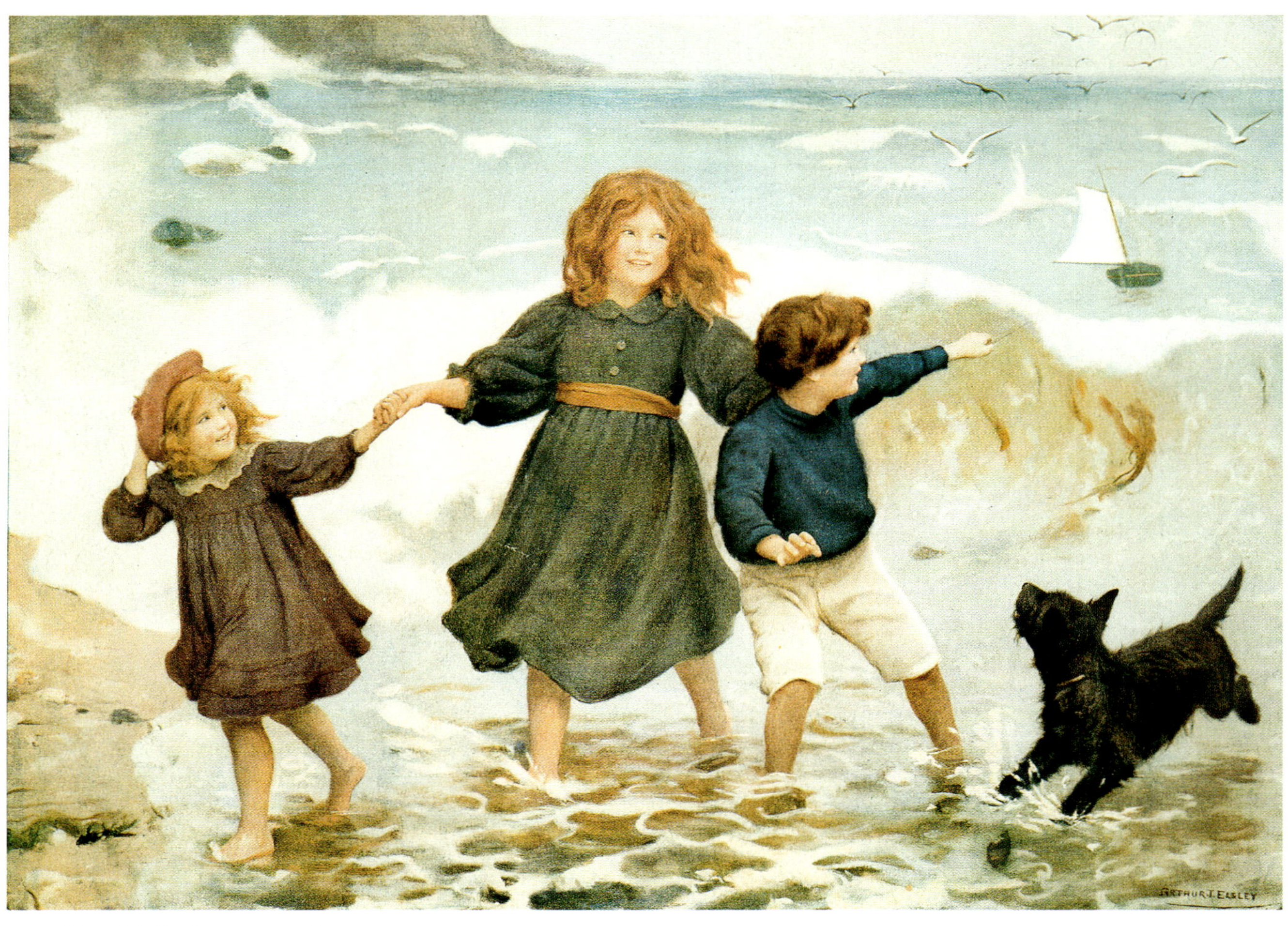

Look Out, 1908. **See page 113**.

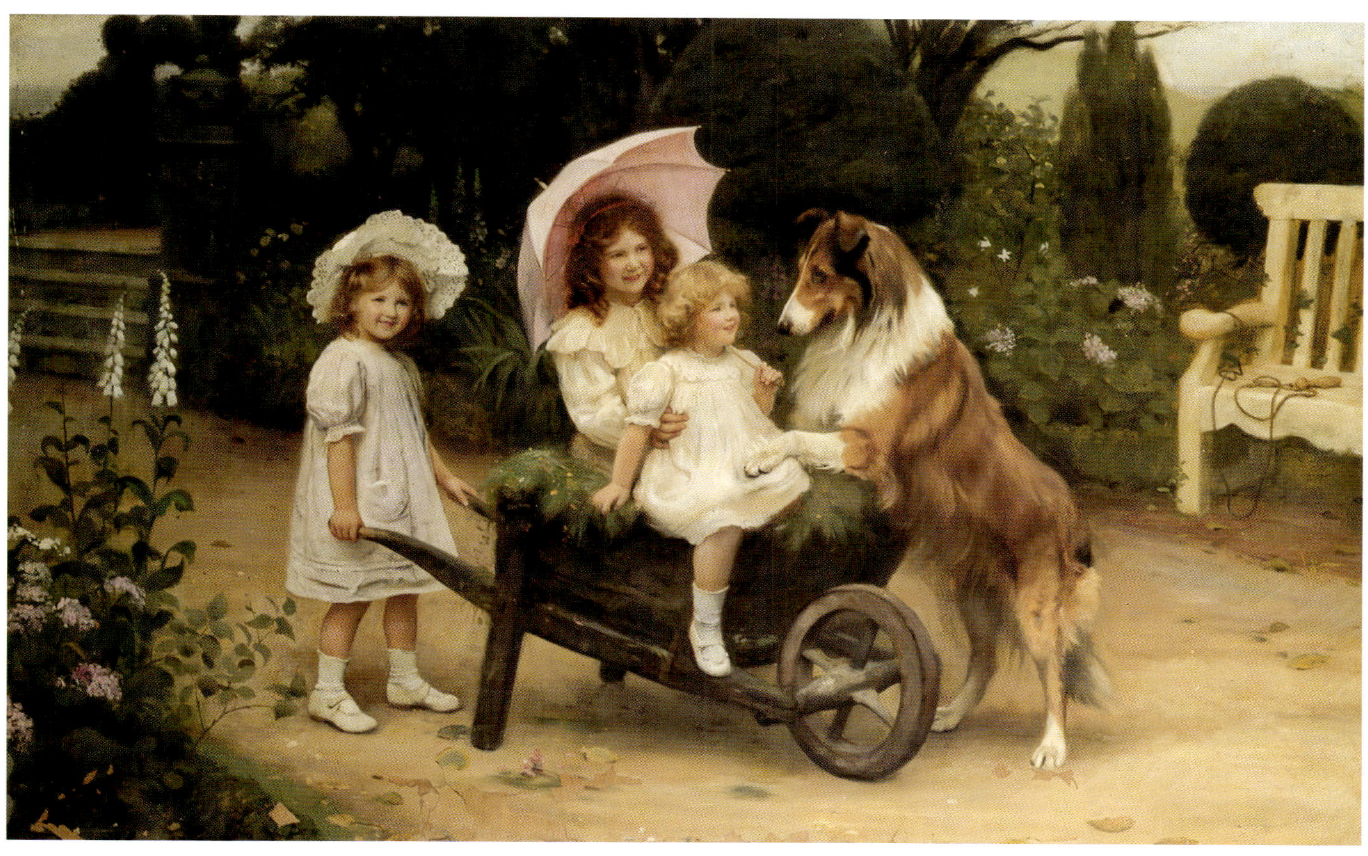

Jump Up / Bon Amis / Take Me Too / Jump In, 1908. **See page 107**.

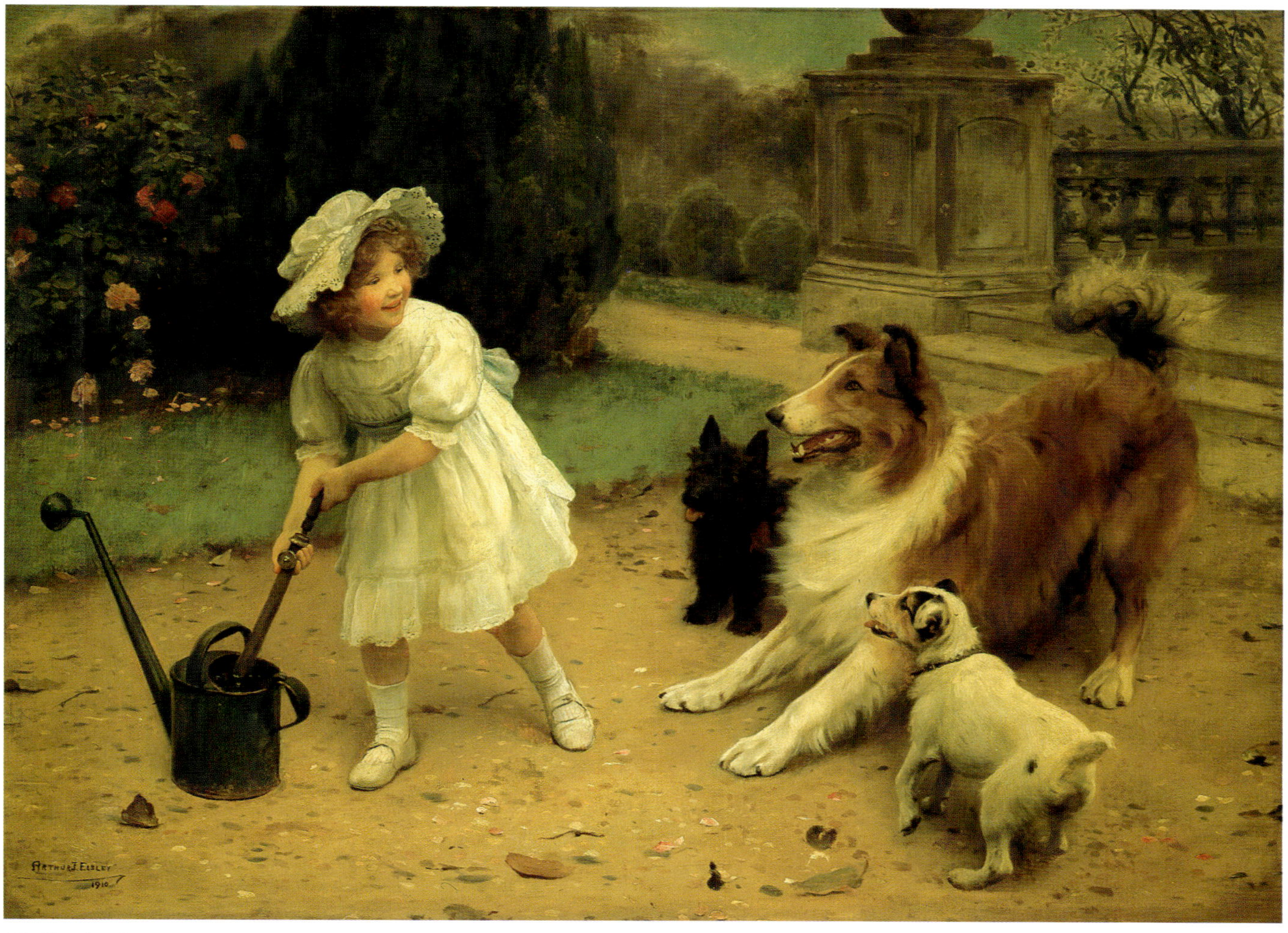

Shall I? / Whose Turn First?, 1910. **See page 117**.

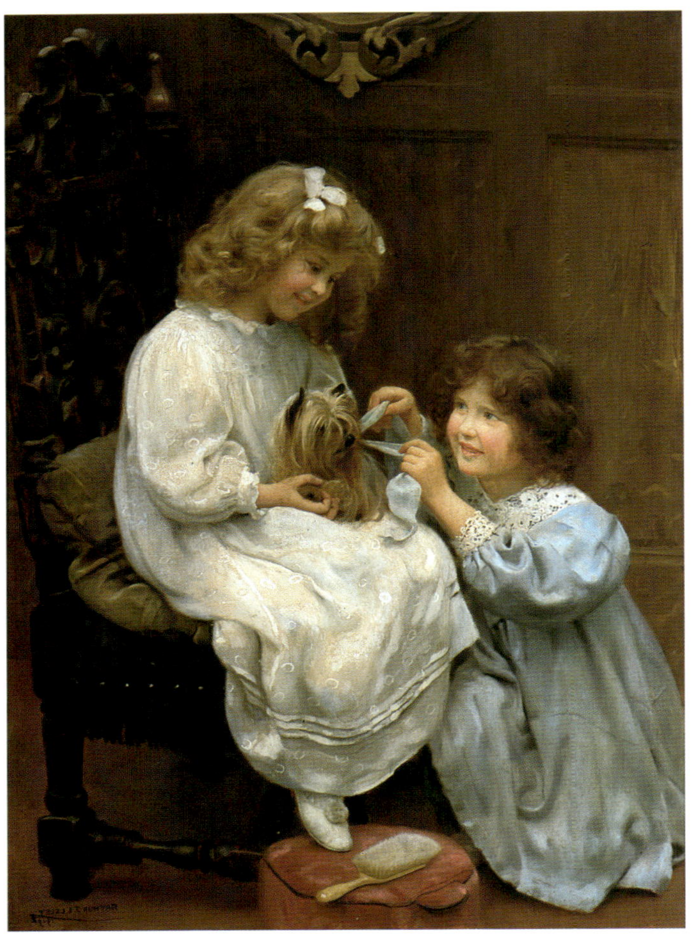

Finishing Touches, 1909. **See page 113**.

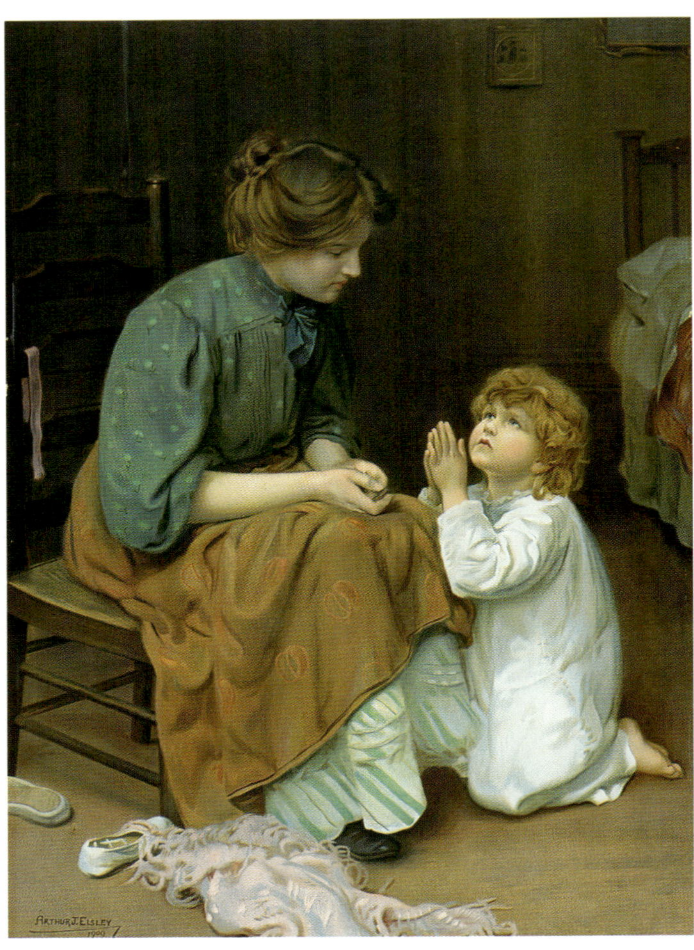

God Bless Daddy, 1909. **See page 113**.

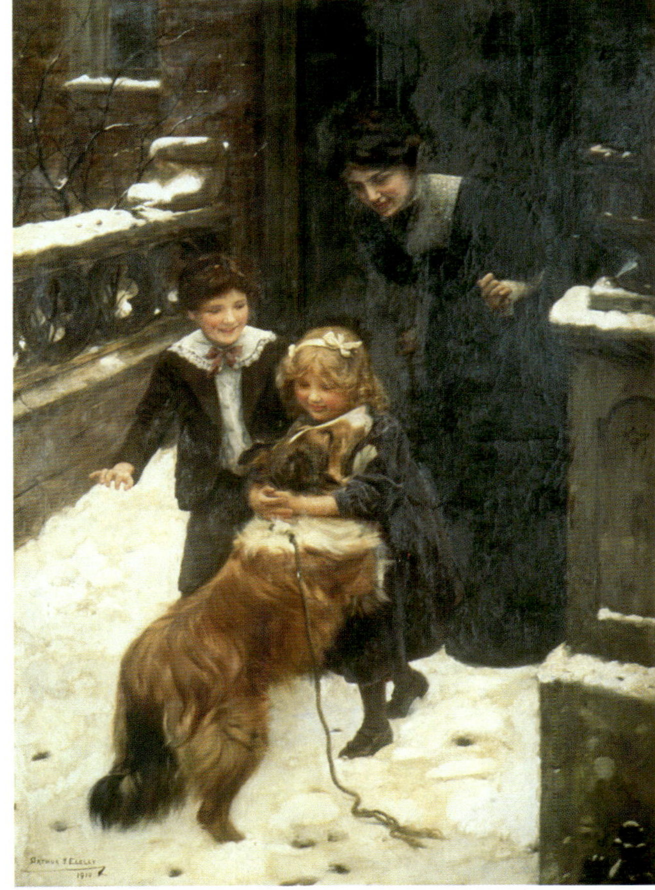

Home Again, 1910. **See page 117**.

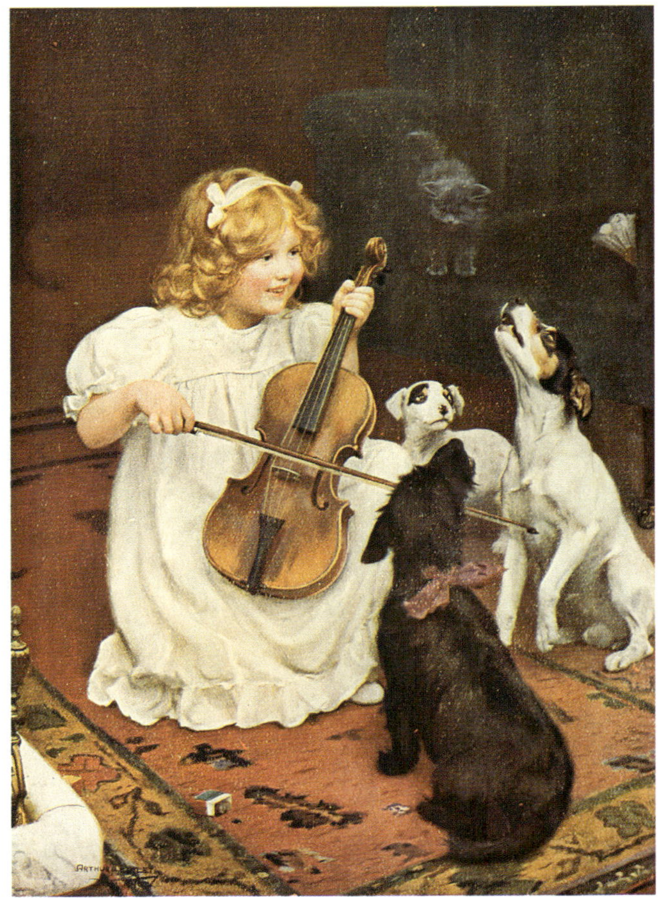

A Broken Melody, 1909. **See page 114**.

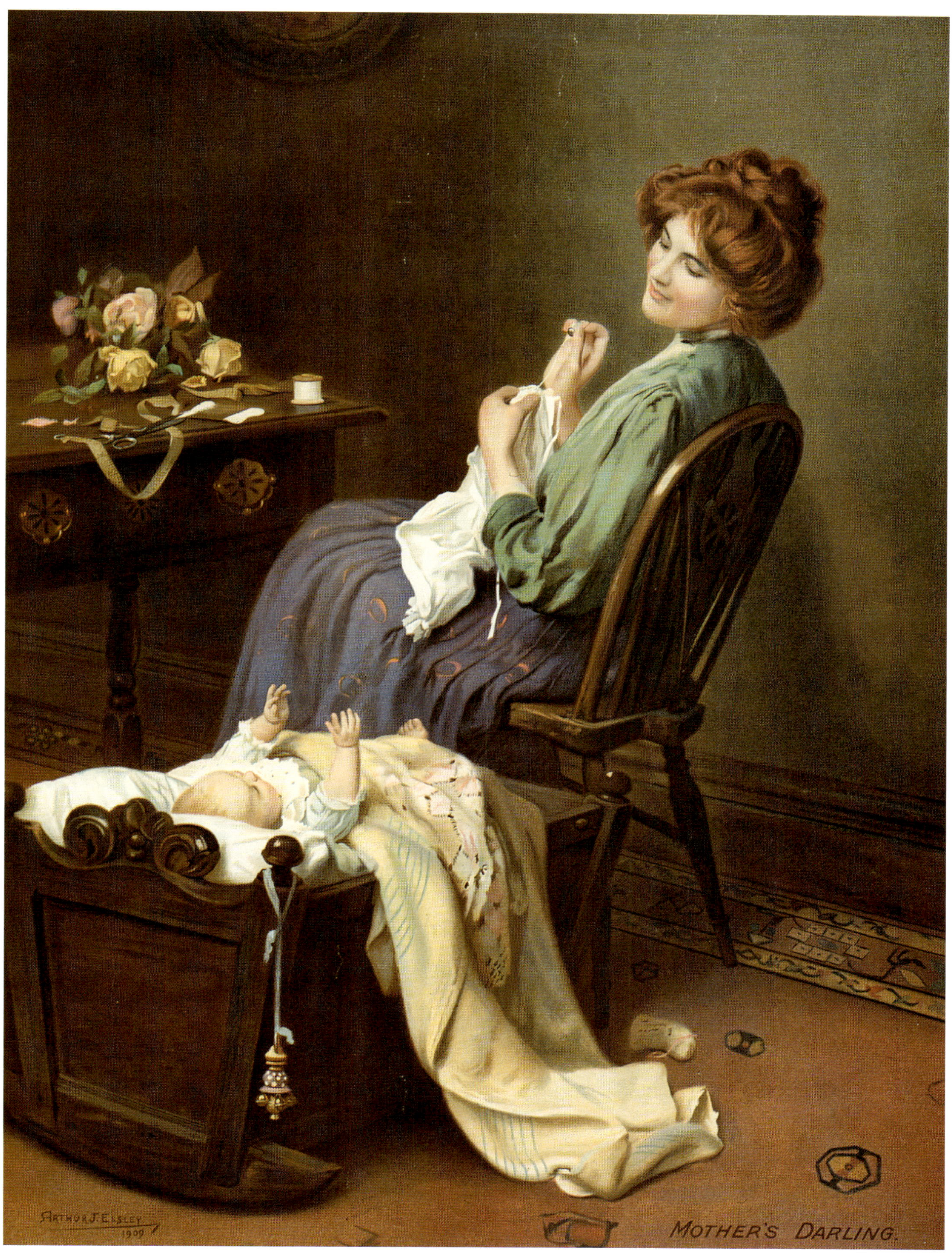

Mother's Darling, 1909. **See page 113**.

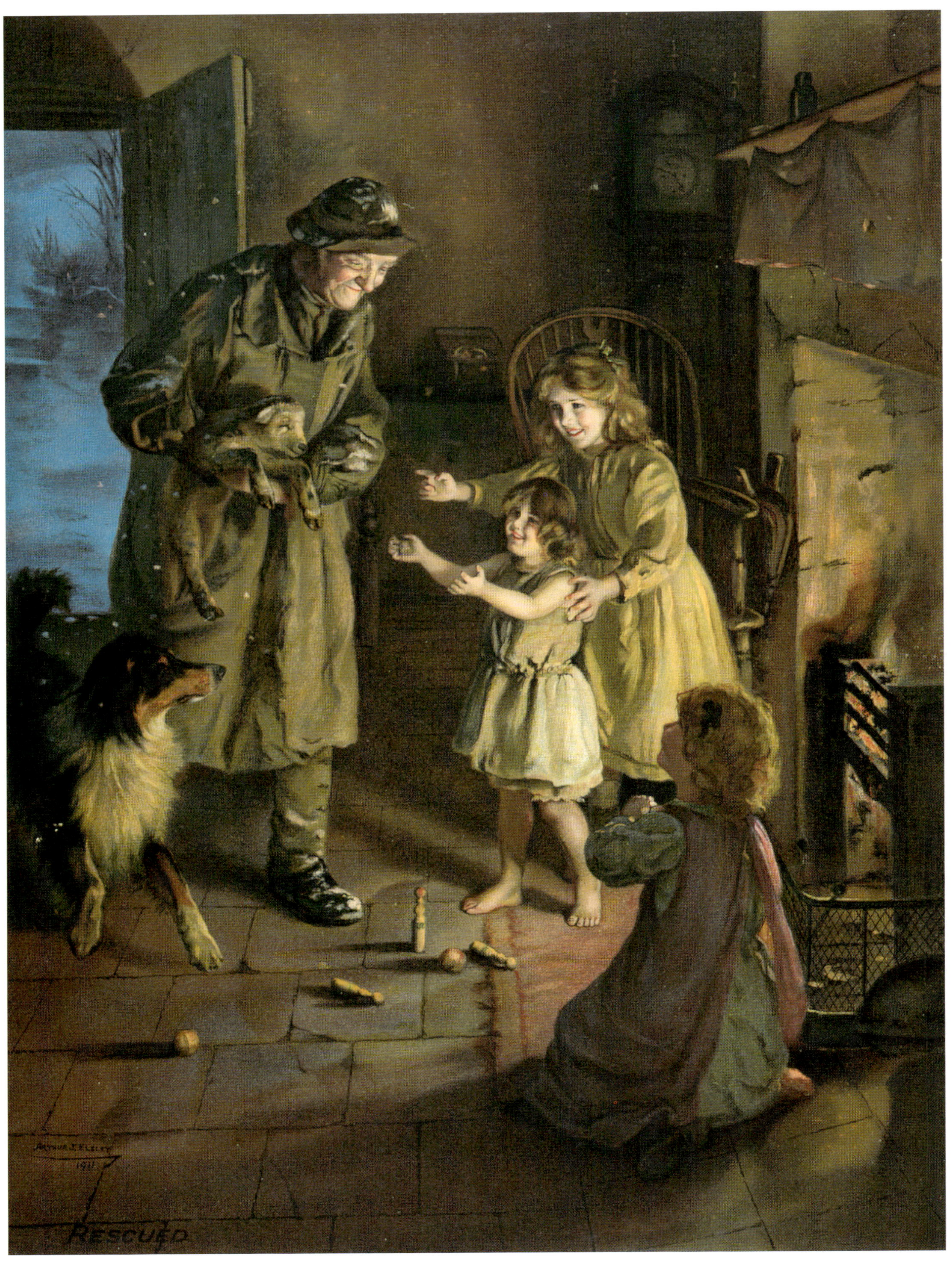

Rescued, 1911. **See page 119**.

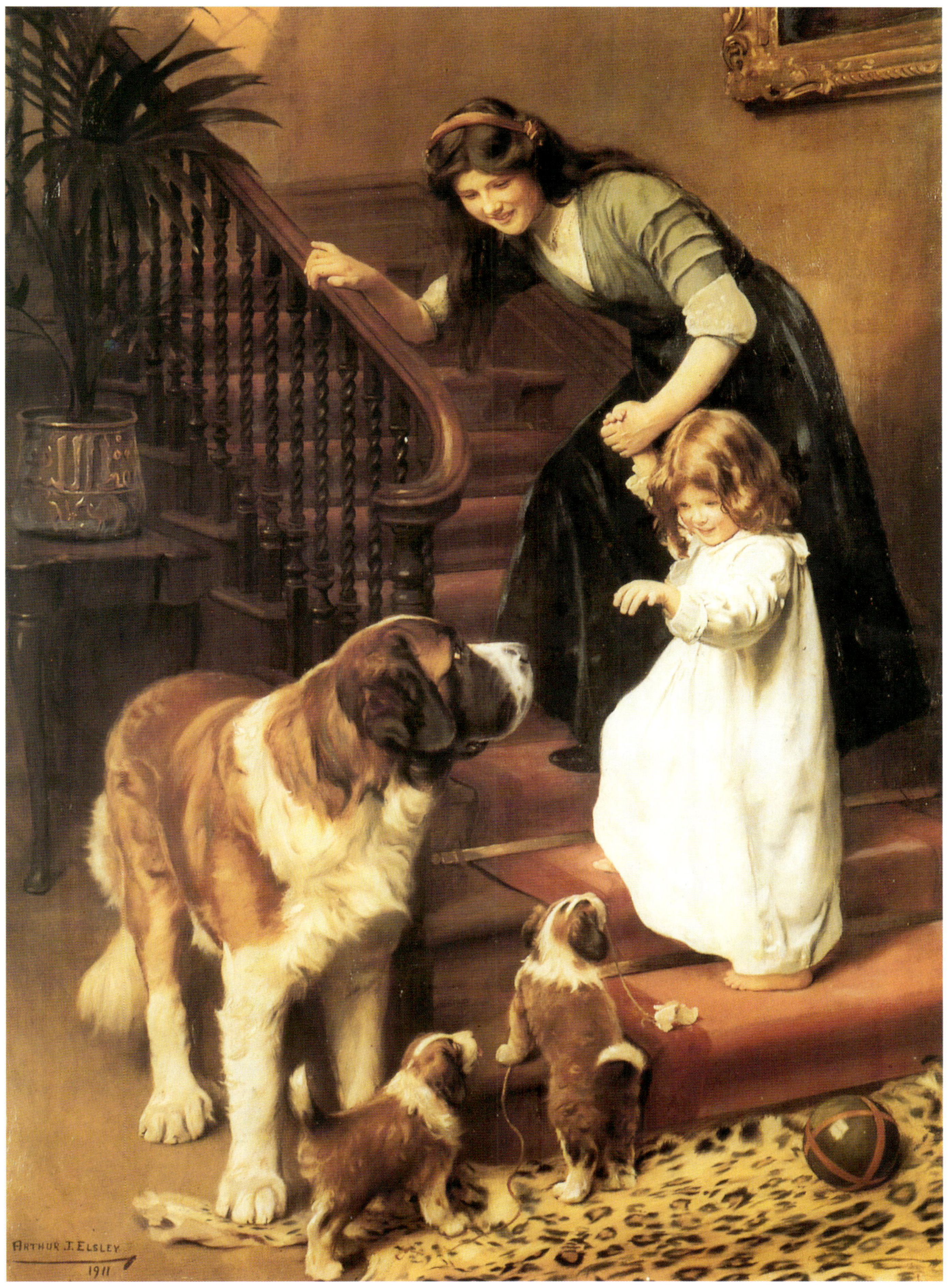

Goodnight, 1911. **See page 118**.

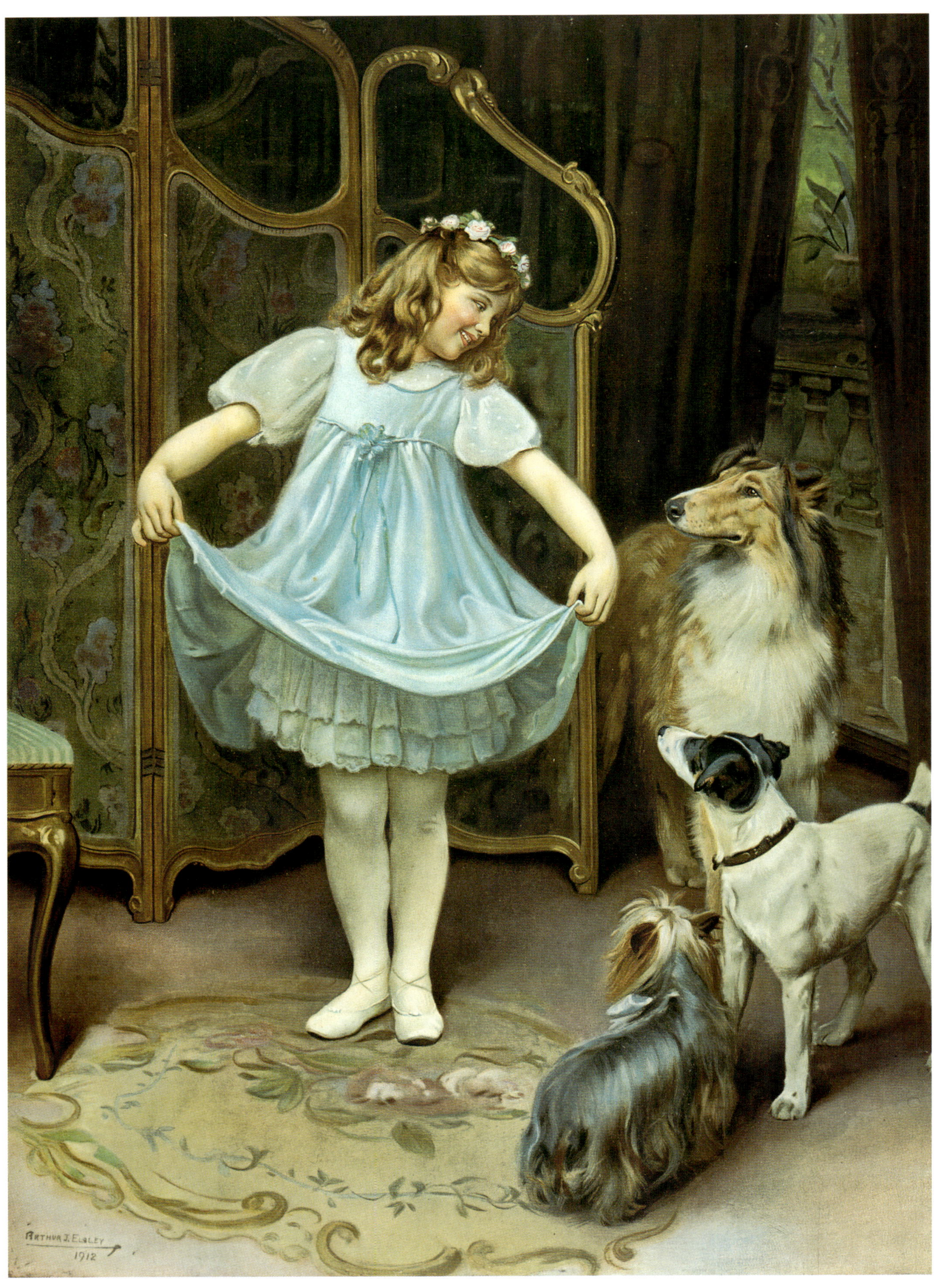

[The New Dress], 1912. **See page 120**.

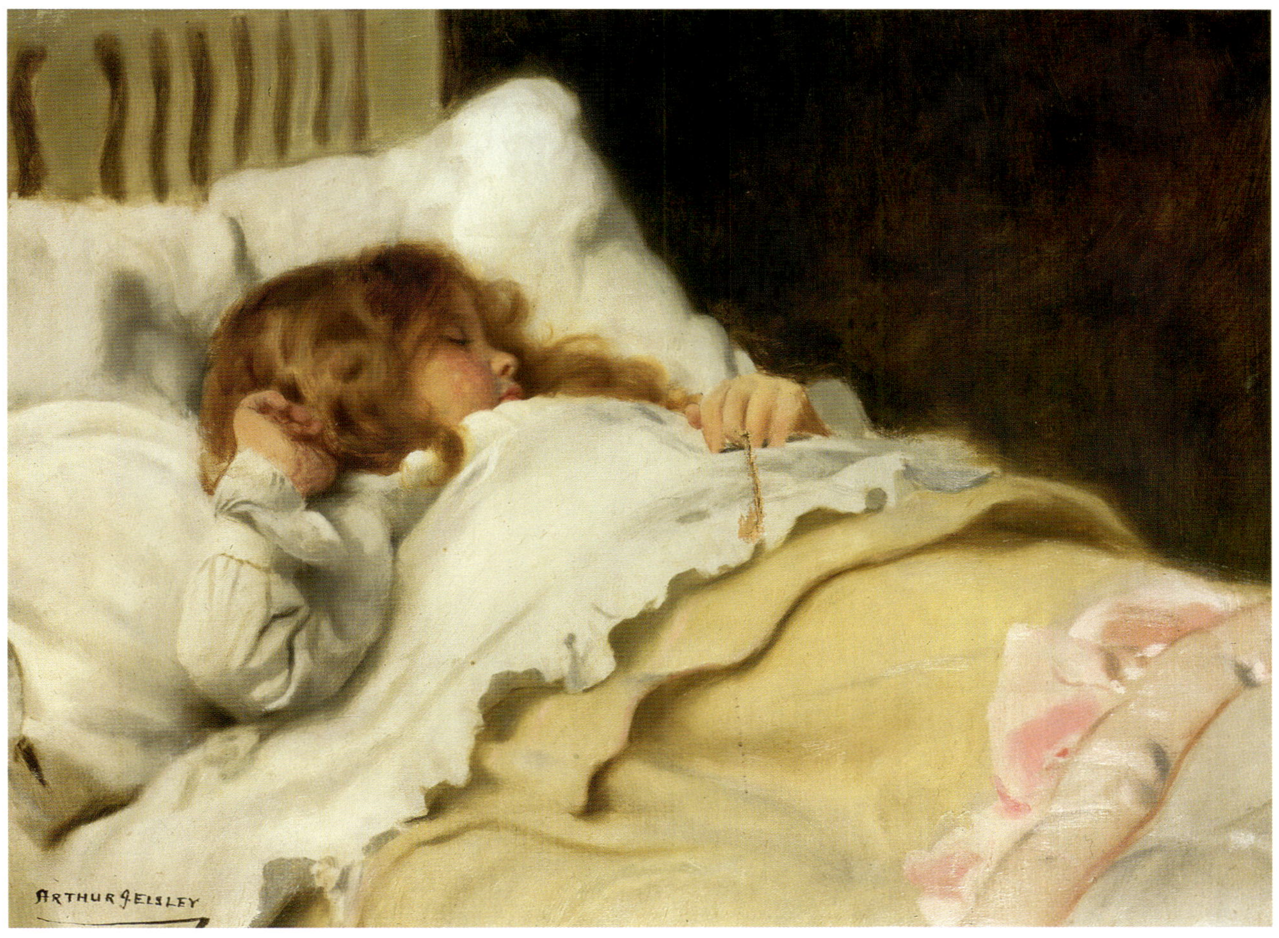

Fitful Slumber, 1909. **See page 115**.

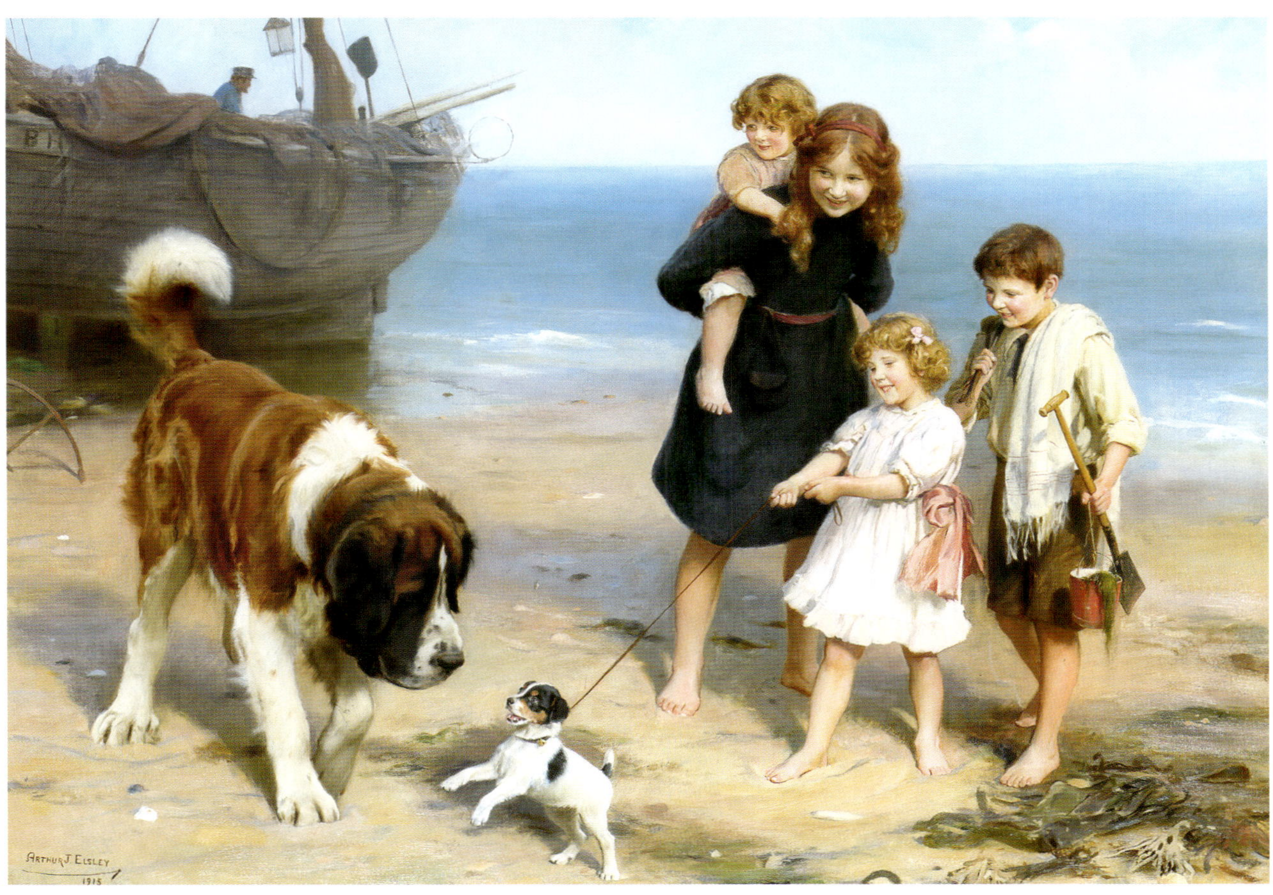

Who's Afraid?, 1915. **See page 126**.

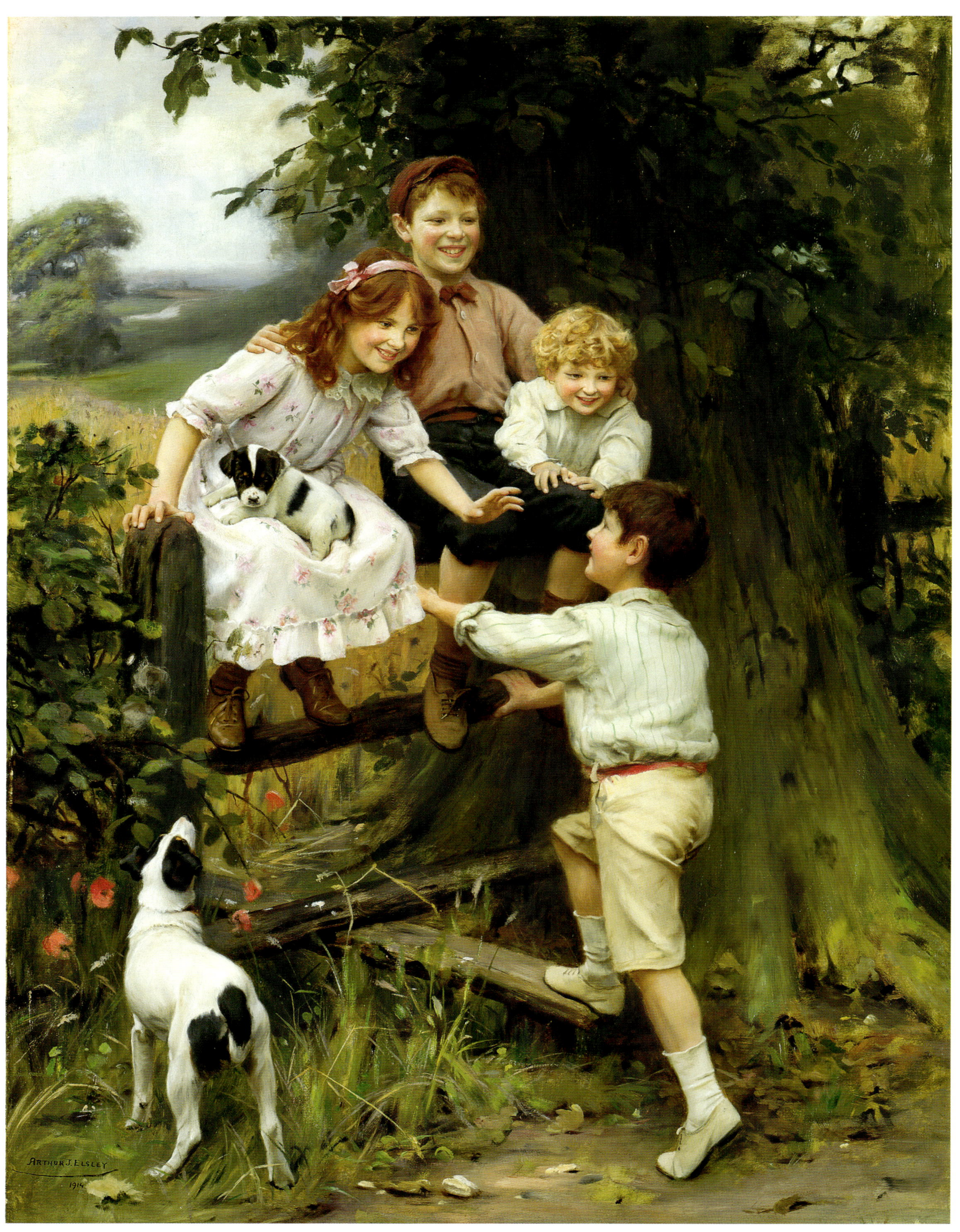

[Guarding The Stile], 1914. **See page 125**.

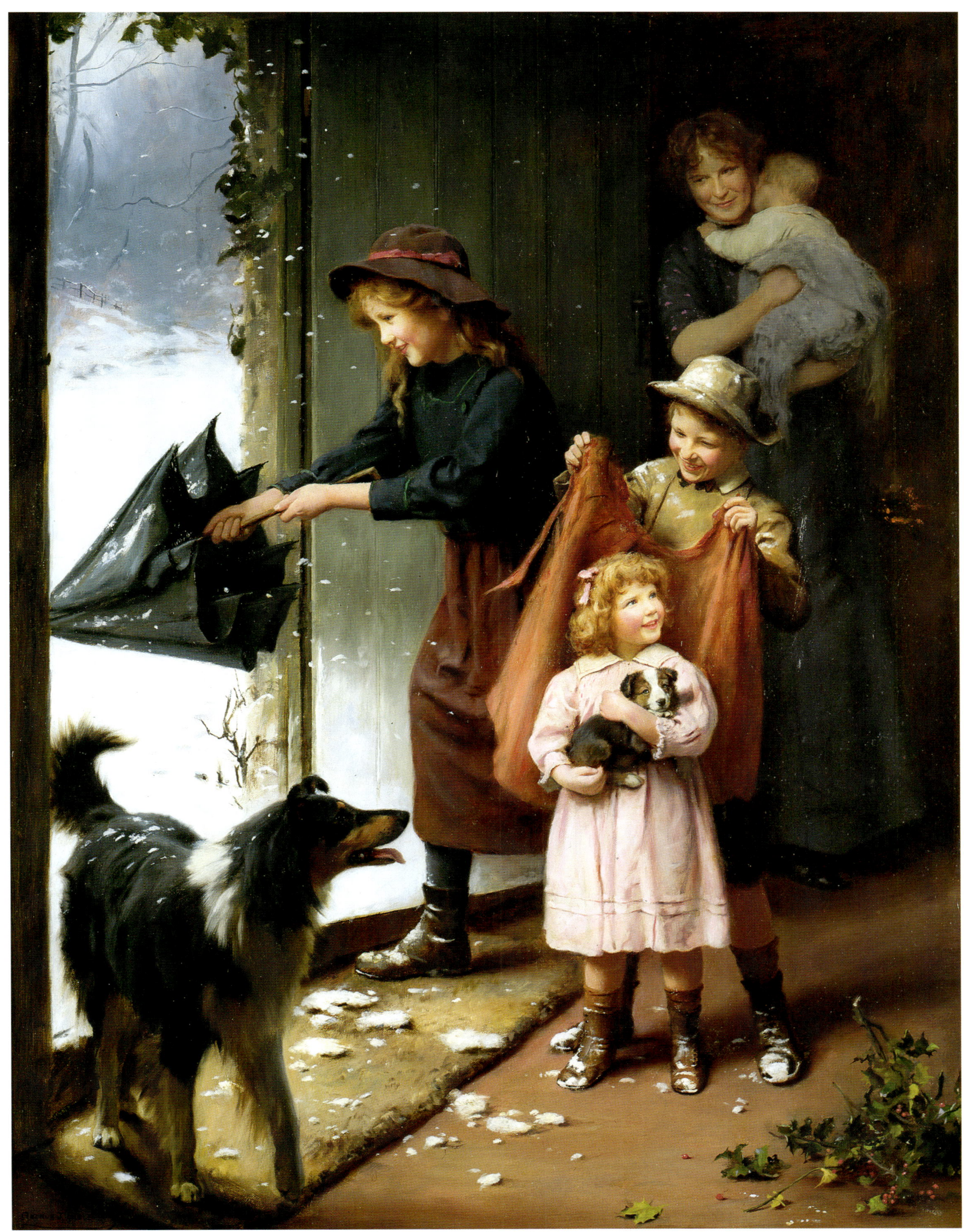

[Home At Last], c.1918. **See page 129**.

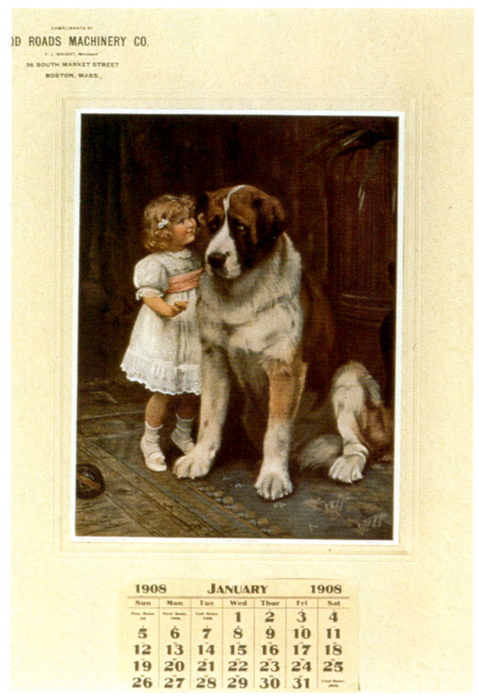

Private And Confidential, 1906.
See page 104.

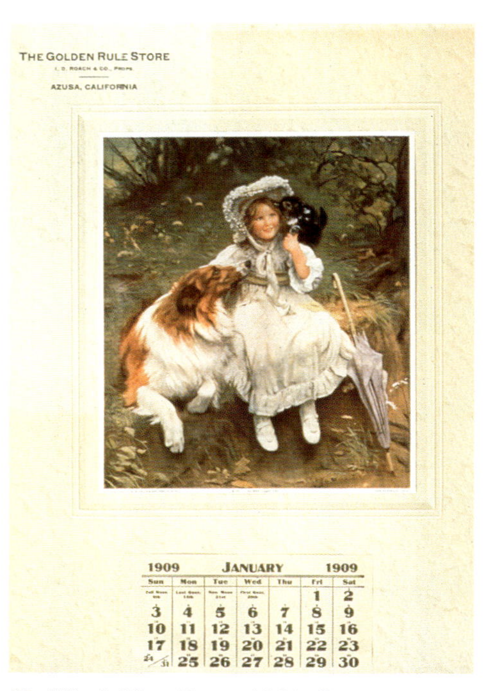

He Won't Hurt You, c.1908. **See page 111**.

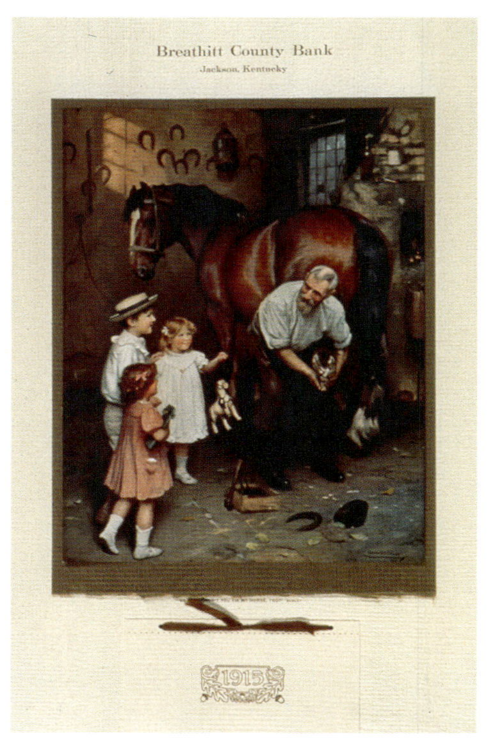

Won't You Fix My Horse Too?, 1912.
See page 121.

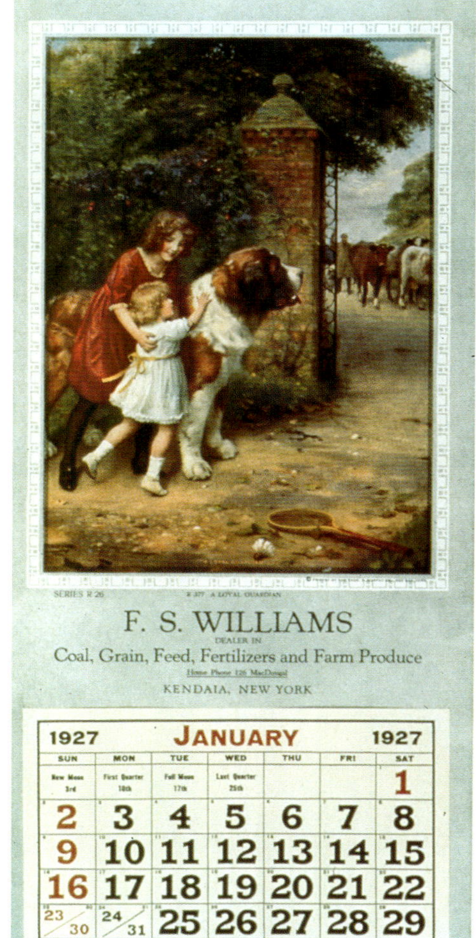

A Loyal Guardian, 1922. **See page 131**.

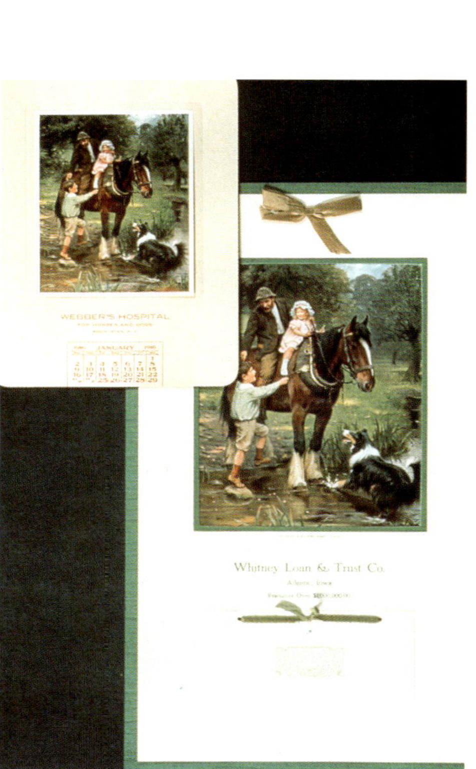

A Helping Hand, 1913. **See page 124**.

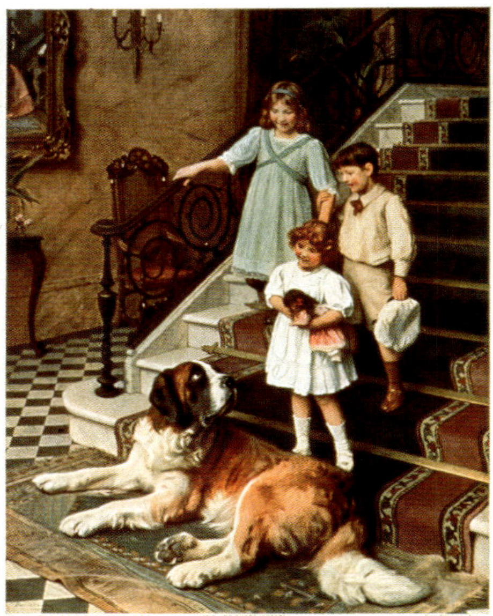

No Thoroughfare, 1917. **See page 129**.

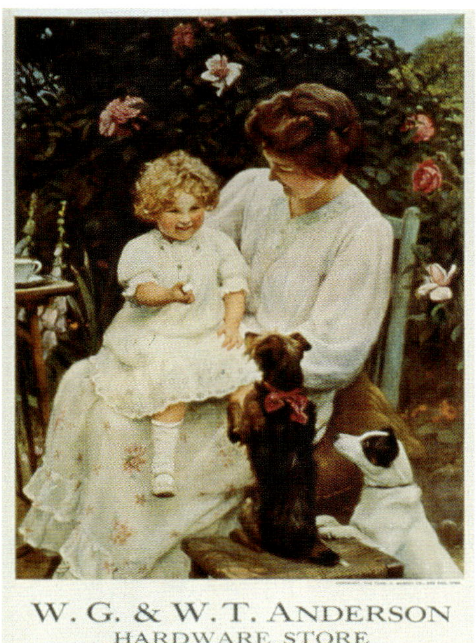

W. G. & W. T. ANDERSON
HARDWARE STORE
BAXTER, TENN.
WILLINGNESS AND EQUIPMENT TO SERVE WELL

1922			JANUARY			1922
SUN	MON	TUE	WED	THU	FRI	SAT
1	2	3	4	5	6	7
8	9	10	11	12	13	14
15	16	17	18	19	20	21
22	23	24	25	26	27	28
29	30	31	First Quar. 6th	Full Moon 13th	Last Quar. 20th	New Moon 27th

Who Speaks First, 1919. **See page 130.**

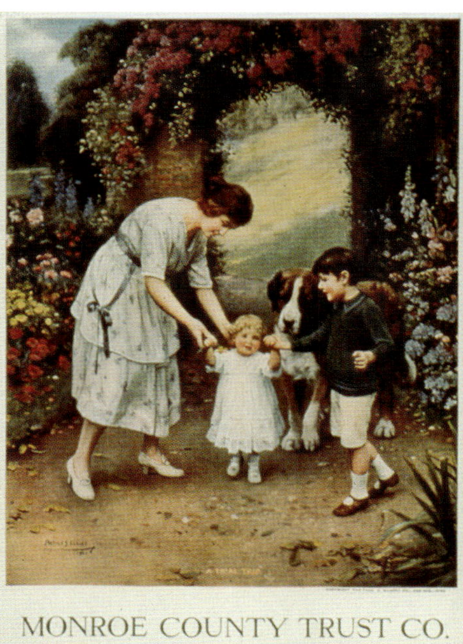

MONROE COUNTY TRUST CO.
COURTEOUS ACCOMMODATIONS
PARIS, MISSOURI

1924			JANUARY			1924
SUN	MON	TUE	WED	THU	FRI	SAT
New Moon 6th	First Quarter 13th	1	2	3	4	5
6	7	8	9	10	11	12
13	14	15	16	17	18	19
20	21	22	23	24	25	26
27	28	29	30	31	Full Moon 21st	Last Quarter 29th

A Trial Trip, 1921. **See page 131.**

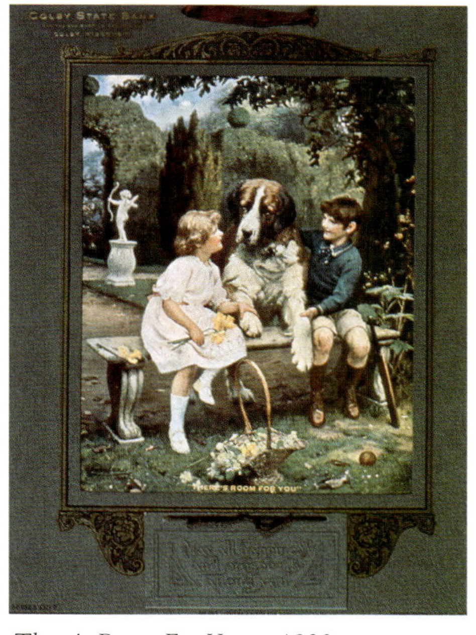

There's Room For You, c.1920. **See page 131.**

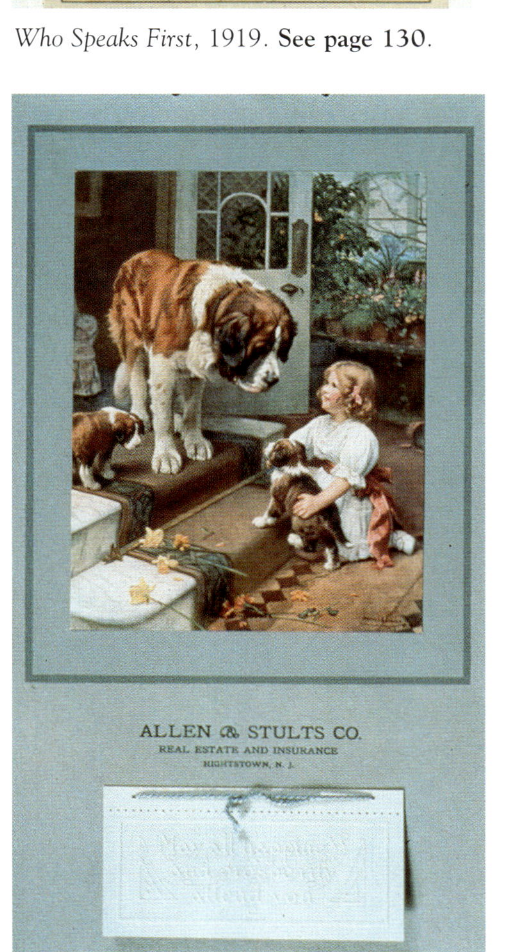

Here He Comes, 1917. **See page 128.**

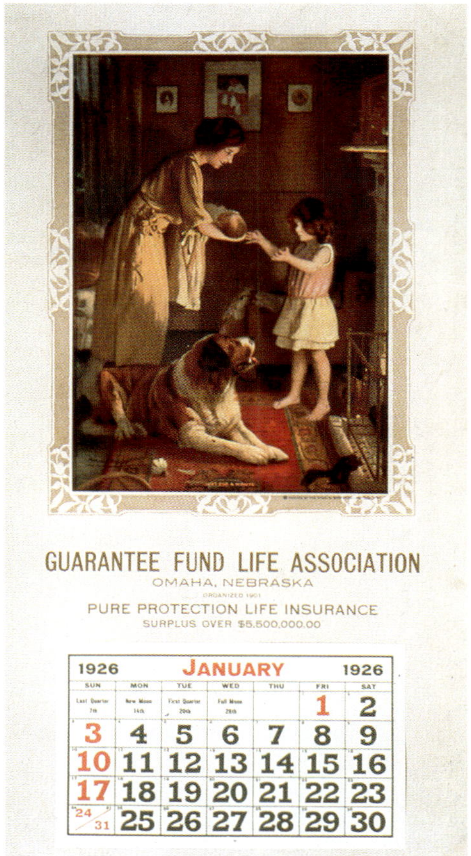

1926			JANUARY			1926
SUN	MON	TUE	WED	THU	FRI	SAT
					1	2
3	4	5	6	7	8	9
10	11	12	13	14	15	16
17	18	19	20	21	22	23
24/31	25	26	27	28	29	30

Just For A Minute, c.1920. **See page 131.**

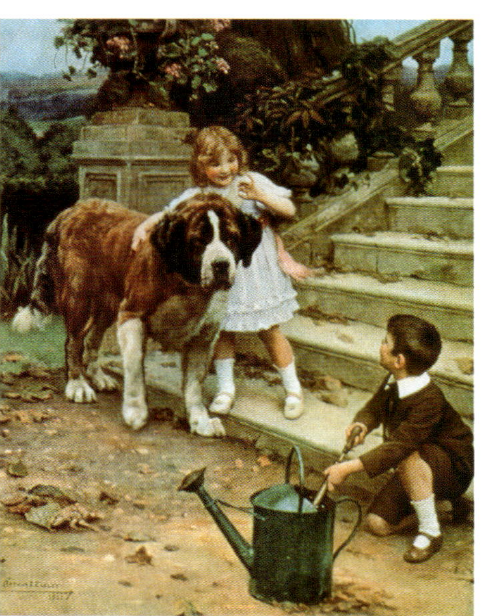

L. J. CHERRIER
PLUMBING AND HEATING
FRANKLIN, N. H.

1923			JANUARY			1923
SUN	MON	TUE	WED	THU	FRI	SAT
	1	2	3	4	5	6
7	8	9	10	11	12	13
14	15	16	17	18	19	20
21	22	23	24	25	26	27
28	29	30	31			

You Dare, 1921. **See page 131.**

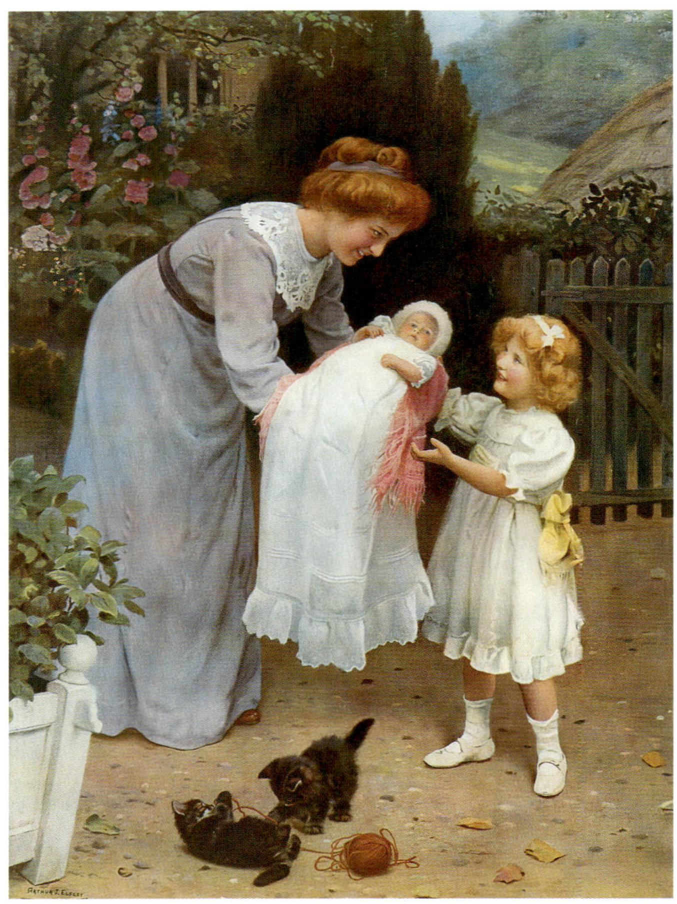

Do Be Careful, 1912. **See page 120**.

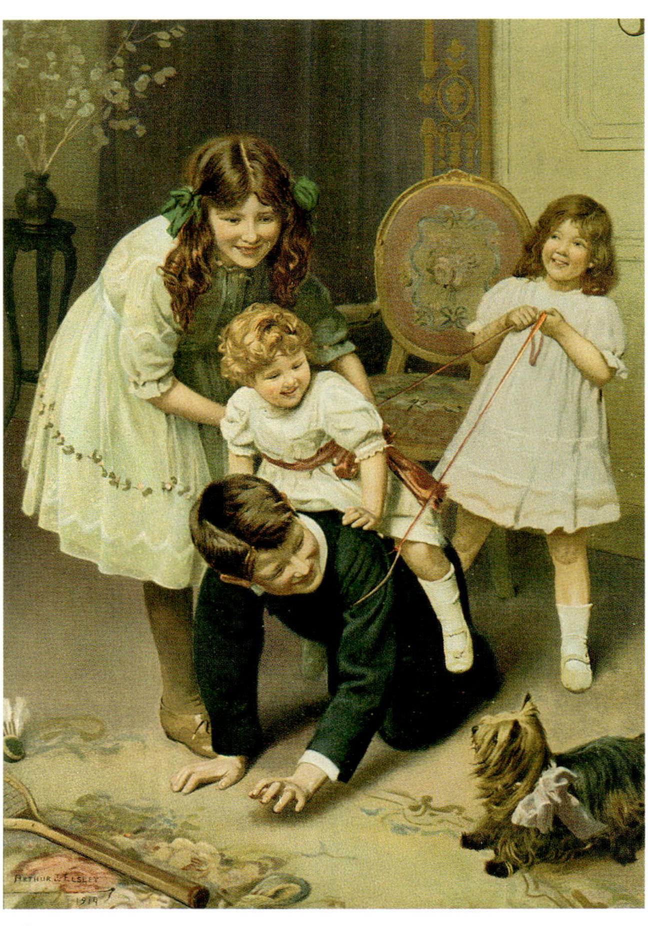

The War Horse, 1914. **See page 125**.

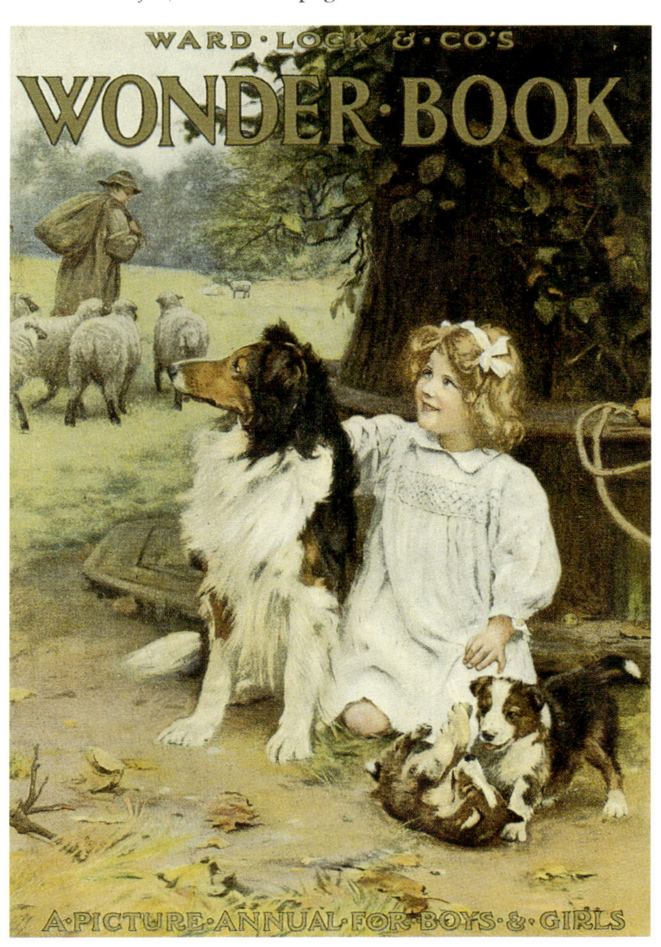

'Twixt Love And Duty, 1919. **See page 130**.

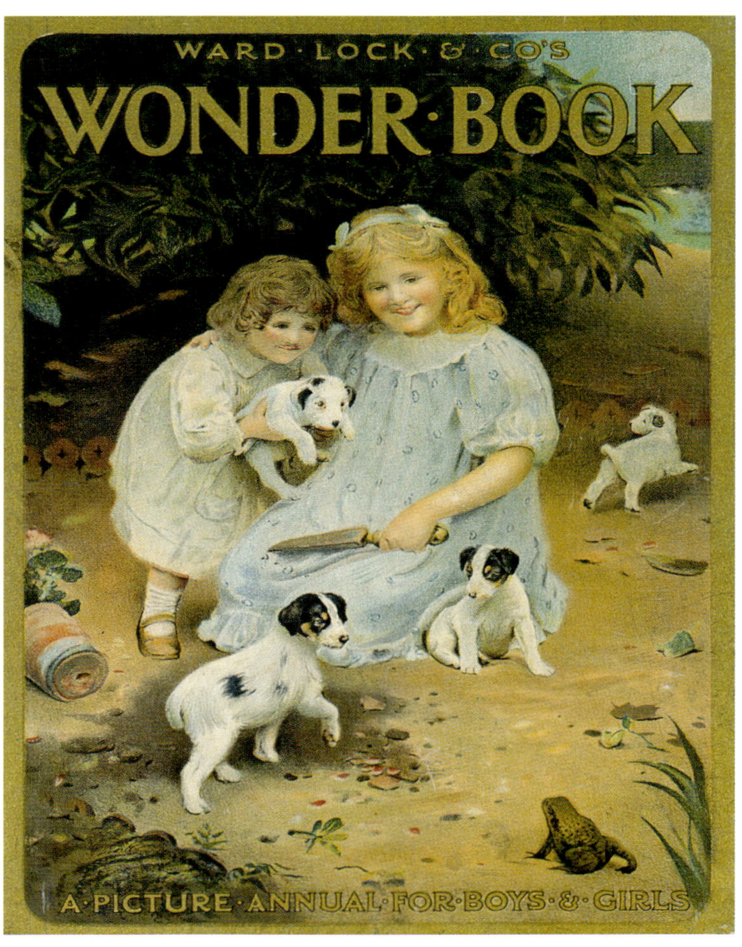

An Uninvited Guest, c.1919. **See page 129**.

One At A Time *signed and dated 1901*

Details of original painting unknown.

The black collie is listed in Elsley's address book as belonging to a Miss Cottrell of 15a High Street, but he does not give any further information. This is a very similar composition to *Her New Love*, 1902. The same collie appears in *This Way*, 1900, and the same hat is in *Little Bo Peep*, 1900.

Burgundy photograph, 7¾ins x 5¾ins (19.5cm x 14.5cm), in an unknown magazine in 1903.

Large sepia photogravure engraved by Blechinger & Leykauf and published by C. Klackner, 150 Artist's proofs @ 3 guineas, India prints @ 1 guinea.

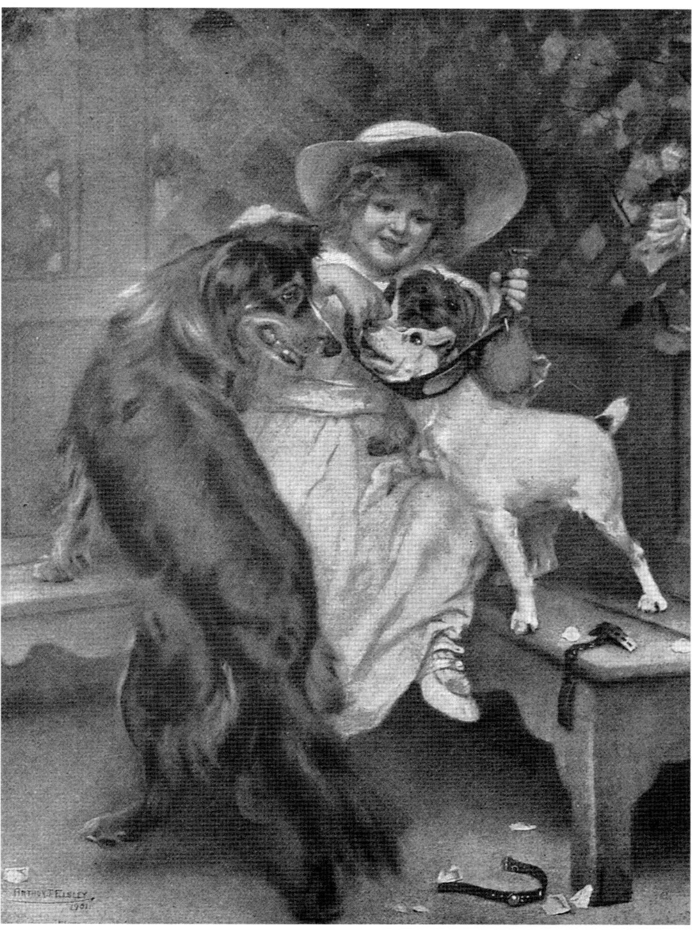

One At A Time

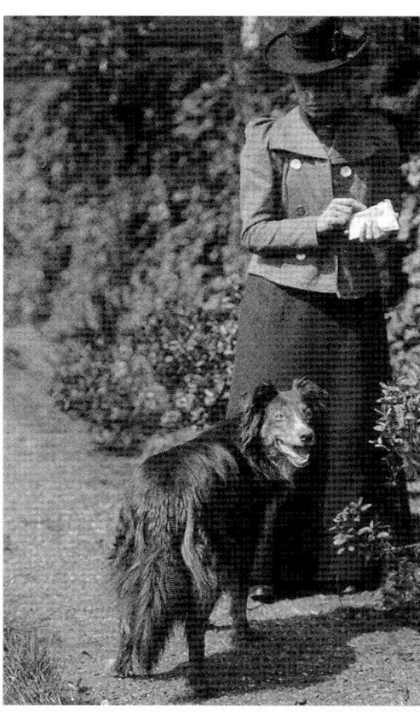

Source photograph of Emm and a dog for *One At A Time*.

Hold Up / Here He Comes *signed and dated 1901*

Oil on canvas, 35ins x 27ins (89cm x 69cm). Exhibited at the Royal Academy, 1901 (No.890), where it was sold for £175 on 13th June 1901. Originally owned by Bibby's, and later donated to The Royal Liverpool Children's Hospital where it still hangs. An oil sketch, 9¾ins x 8ins (24.5cm x 20.5cm), of the older girl was sold at the Studio Sale (Lot 24). Not to be confused with a work of the same title reproduced as an American colour calendar manufactured by Thos. D. Murphy Co., 1921 and 1934.

Snowballing has long been a popular theme for artists, including John Morgan, Royal Academy 1865; also Fred Morgan's painting of children in the snow with a basket over their heads and an old man carrying faggots on his back in the distance.

Sepia photogravure, 21ins x 15¾ins (54cm x 40cm), and a smaller version, 8½ins x 6½ins (21.5cm x 16.5cm), both copyright *Bibby's Quarterly*. Colour cover, 13½ins x 9ins (34.5cm x 23cm), image 9¼ins x 7ins (23.5cm x 18cm), *Bibby's Quarterly - Literary Supplement*, Vol.4 No.3, Christmas 1901, called *Hold Up*. Reproduced in colour in *This England*, Winter 1981, p.14. **See page 67.**

This Little Pig Went To Market *circa 1901*

Possibly oil on canvas, 37½ins x 27ins (95.5cm x 69cm), sold at Christie's, London, on 1st August 1930. It is uncertain if it was this version or the work of the same title painted c.1911-2 and reproduced in *Mother and Home*, Christmas 1915.

This was a popular subject for artists of the period, and Arthur Drummond's work with this same title was reproduced as a Bovril print in 1909.

Colour cover, 13¼ins x 9ins (33.5cm x 23cm), image 9¼ins x 7ins (23.5cm x 18cm), signed not dated, *Bibby's Quarterly - Literary Supplement*, Vol.4 No.4, Spring 1902. **See page 70.**

Spring Songs / Baby's Birthday
signed and dated 1902

Details of original painting unknown, *Spring Songs* was exhibited at the Royal Academy in 1902 (No.533), and was unsold. Also exhibited at Birmingham, Spring 1903 (No.148), priced 80 guineas. The oil painting entitled *Baby's Birthday*, measuring 39ins x 52ins (99.5cm x 133cm), was auctioned at Christie's, London, on 30th January 1904 (Lot 120), bought by Lister for £105.

This, together with *I Sent A Letter To My Love*, his other Royal Academy exhibit that year, was the first of his more adventurous, large scale, multi-figured works. Other artists painting similar works called the subject *The Battle Of The Flowers*. Elsley incorporated a head and shoulders oil sketch on board, 9ins x 7½ins (23cm x 19cm), which was sold at his Studio Sale (Lot 19). The terrier belonged to the wife of Elsley's younger brother Edwin. It was called Khaki, the colour of the British army's cotton field uniform introduced in 1899 and popularised during the

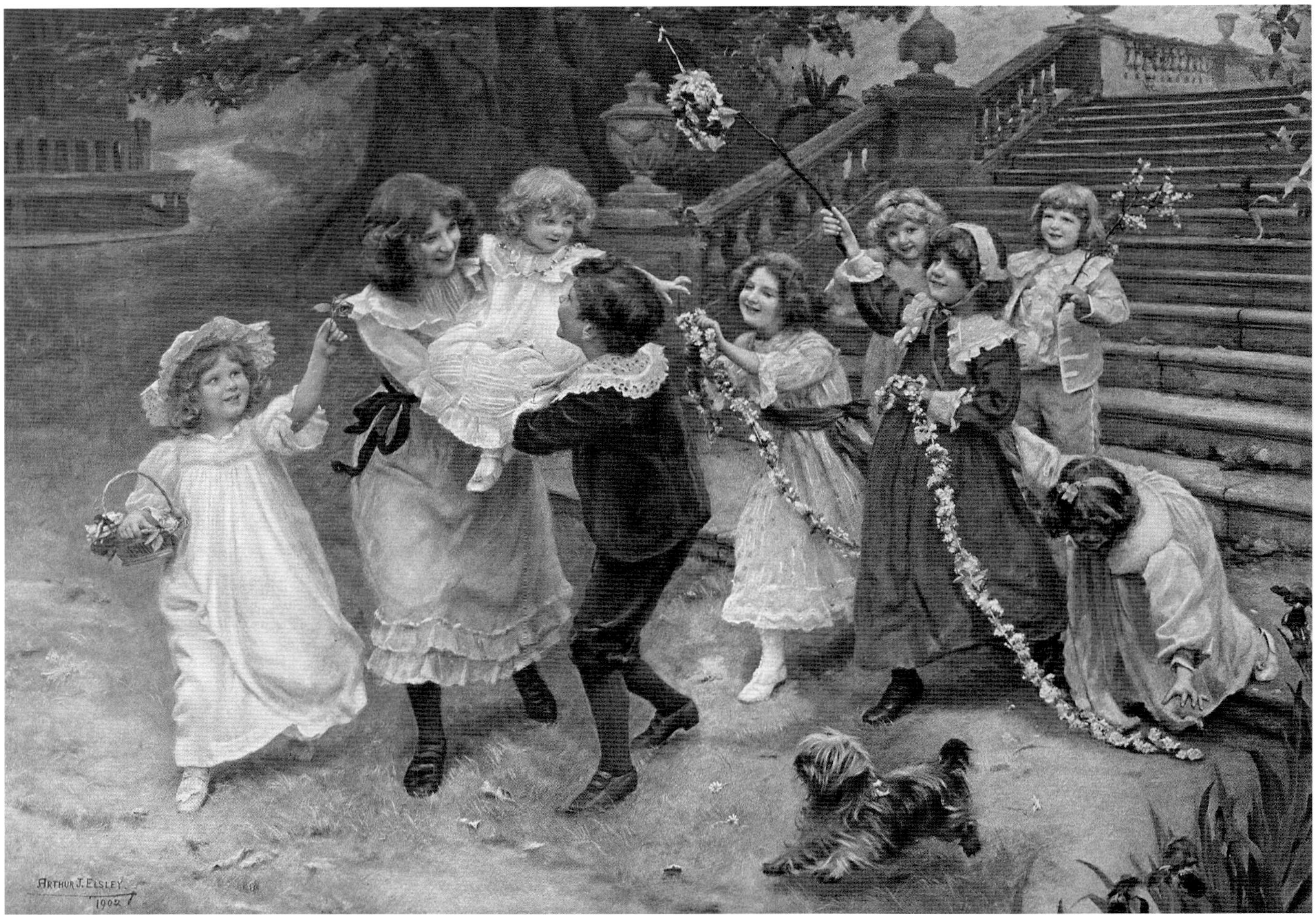

Spring Songs / Baby's Birthday

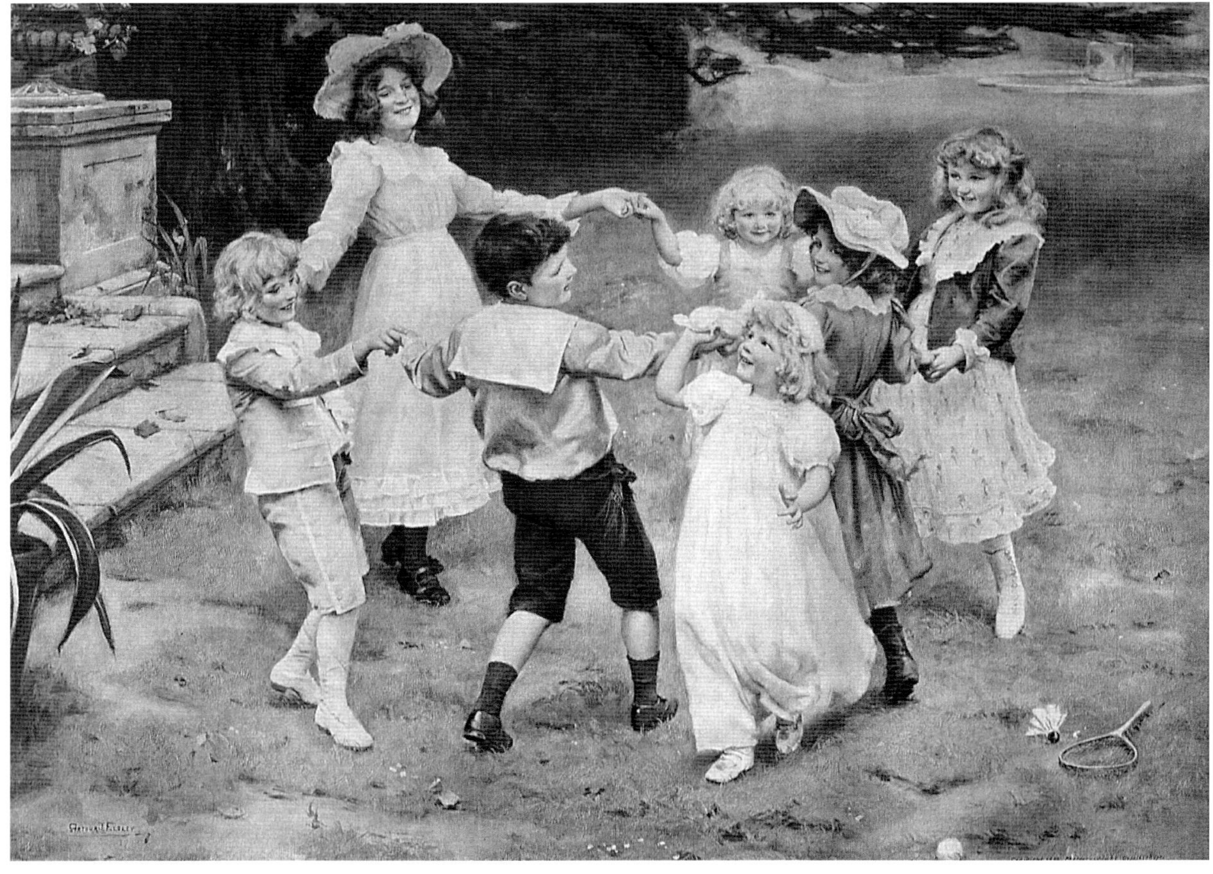

I Sent A Letter To My Love

Boer War. Extract from *The London Magazine*, December 1904, pp.630-632:

> "A similar incident, the sight of two children carrying a baby, suggested the beautiful picture called *Baby's Birthday*. The natural difficulties of the subject were enhanced by the necessity of having two or three children at the same time; and to discover two or three different models exactly suited to one's purpose is by no means easy.
>
> The reason the little ones in Mr Elsley's pictures sometimes seem at first sight alike is that he selects the same type of child, and in this way people confuse the generic child with the particular one. Childhood, to the artist, is invariably fair in colour, its face bright and smiling – for it knows nothing of the cares and troubles of life – and its cheeks are plump and rosy. True, there are numbers of dark children; but they never appear either so young or so merry as the fair ones, and for this reason do not suit his purpose so well."

Large sepia photogravure engraved by F. Hanfstaengl, copyright Frost & Reed, 200 Artist's proofs @ 4 guineas, India prints @ 1 guinea. (Artist's proofs still available in Frost & Reed's May 1908 and January 1913 catalogues.) Sepia photogravure, 13ins x 18ins (33cm x 46.5cm), presented with *Weldon's Ladies' Journal*, Christmas 1911, copyright Frost & Reed.

I Sent A Letter To My Love

signed and dated 1902

Details of original painting unknown. Exhibited at Royal Academy, 1902 (No.712), and sold for £250 on 27th July 1902.

This painting depicts a popular children's dance. Compositions of circular dancing were a popular artistic device used by both John and Fred Morgan, e.g. John's *Playing at Soldiers*, c.1882, and Fred's *Ring-a-Ring-a-Roses-Oh!*, Royal Academy, 1885. The song is, apparently, American. Its earliest appearance in print was in 1879, and it is often known by the words *Atisket, Atasket* or *Itisket, Itasket*. Ella Fitzgerald revived the song in 1938.

Black and white photograph, *The London Magazine*, December 1904, p.625.

Sepia photogravure, 15½ins x 20¼ins (39.5cm x 51.5cm), presented with the *Lady's Pictorial*, Christmas 1906, copyright Berlin Photographic 1902. Also seen as a crystoleum.

Primroses *signed and dated 1902*

Oil on canvas, 26½ins x 19¼ins (67.5cm x 49.5cm). This work was given to the Brighton Museum and Art Gallery by Marjorie Wheatley in 1971. Until then it had remained in the family and had not been exhibited or reproduced.

A Touch Of Nature *signed and dated 1902*

Details of original painting unknown. This was one of the series of hunt paintings which began with *Late for School*, 1898, and the follow up to *Forbidden Ground*, 1899, which also featured Franciscan monks. It was probably painted

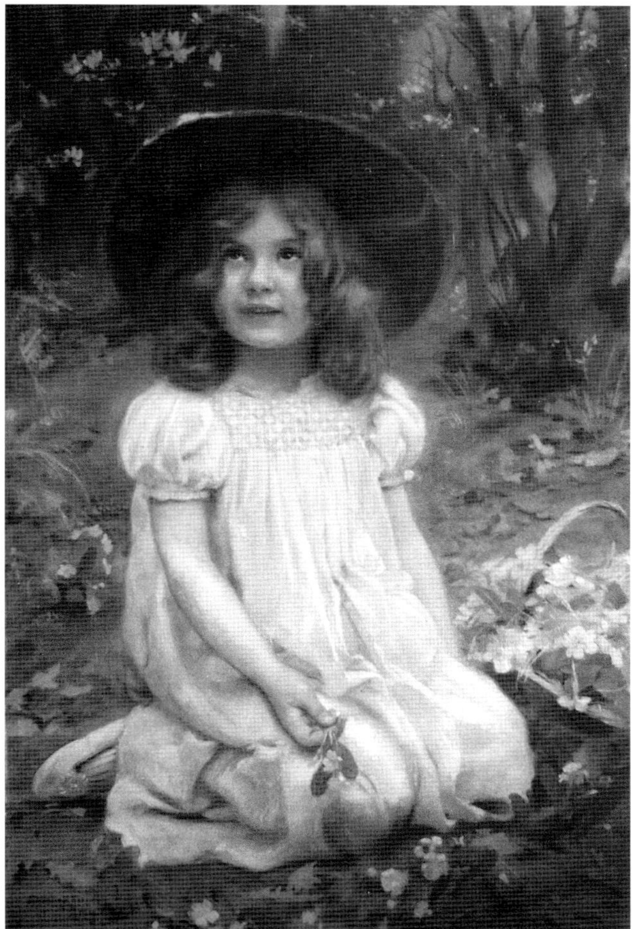

Primroses

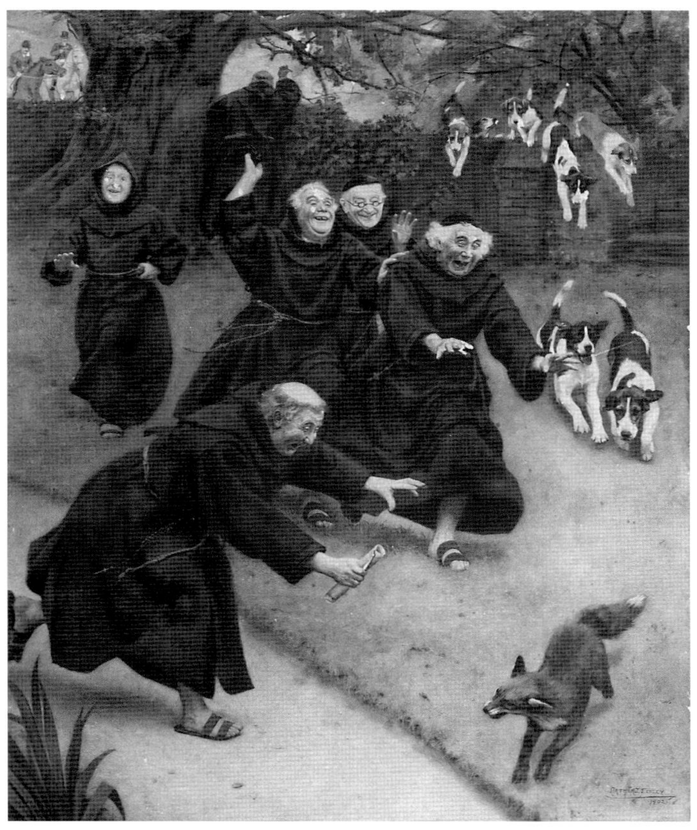

A Touch Of Nature

around the same time as the others, but not completed until 1902. Today, this work could, perhaps, be interpreted as the monks trying to rescue the fox, but Elsley's audience would have only seen the thrill of the chase.

Sepia photogravure, 20ins x 16ins (51cm x 40.5cm), and small version, 8¼ins x 6½ins (21cm x 16.5cm), printed by McCorquendale & Co., copyright *Bibby's Quarterly*, possibly *No Thoroughfare*. Not to be confused with the American colour calendar with the same title manufactured by Thos. D. Murphy Co., 1919. Nor to be confused with *No Admittance*, c.1901, this is the follow up to the Fine Art Society publication of 1901.

Large sepia photogravure engraved by R. Paulsusaen and published by The Fine Art Society, 100 Artist's proofs @ 4 guineas, India prints @ 1 guinea.

[Children On Beach] *signed and dated 1902*

Oil on canvas, 32½ins x 40¼ins (81.5cm x 102cm). Auctioned in Sweden in 1976. Unrecorded as a print.

[A Harbour Scene] *date unknown*

Oil on canvas, 22¾ins x 37¾ins (58.5cm x 96cm). Auctioned in Denmark, (Lot 380) date unknown. Unrecorded as a print.

Hold Tight *signed and dated 1902*

Oil on canvas, approximately 35ins x 27½ins (89cm x 70cm). The painting was almost certainly owned by Bibby's and then donated to The Royal Liverpool Children's Hospital, Heswall. It now hangs in The Royal Liverpool Children's Hospital, Alderhey, Eaton Road, Liverpool, L12.

Not to be confused with the painting of the same title, Royal Society of British Artists, 1897.

Colour cover, 14¼ins x 9¼ins (37cm x 23.5cm), image 9ins x 7ins (23cm x 18cm), *Bibby's Quarterly - Literary Supplement*, Vol.V No.1, Autumn 1902. **See page 70.**

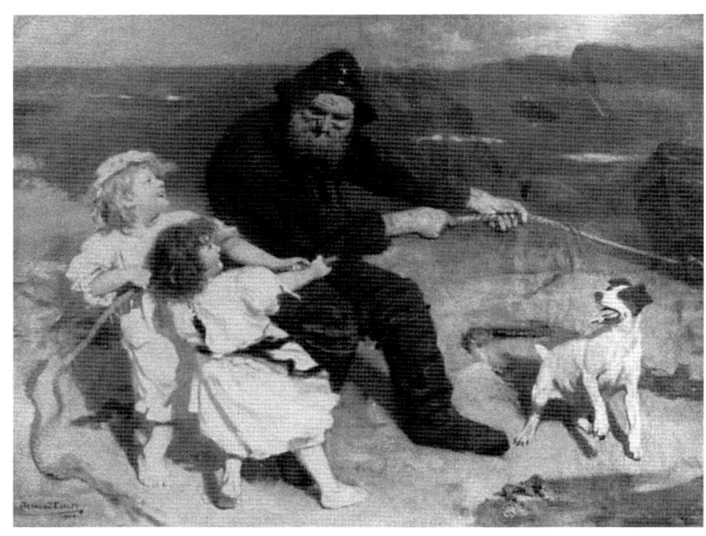

A Harbour Scene

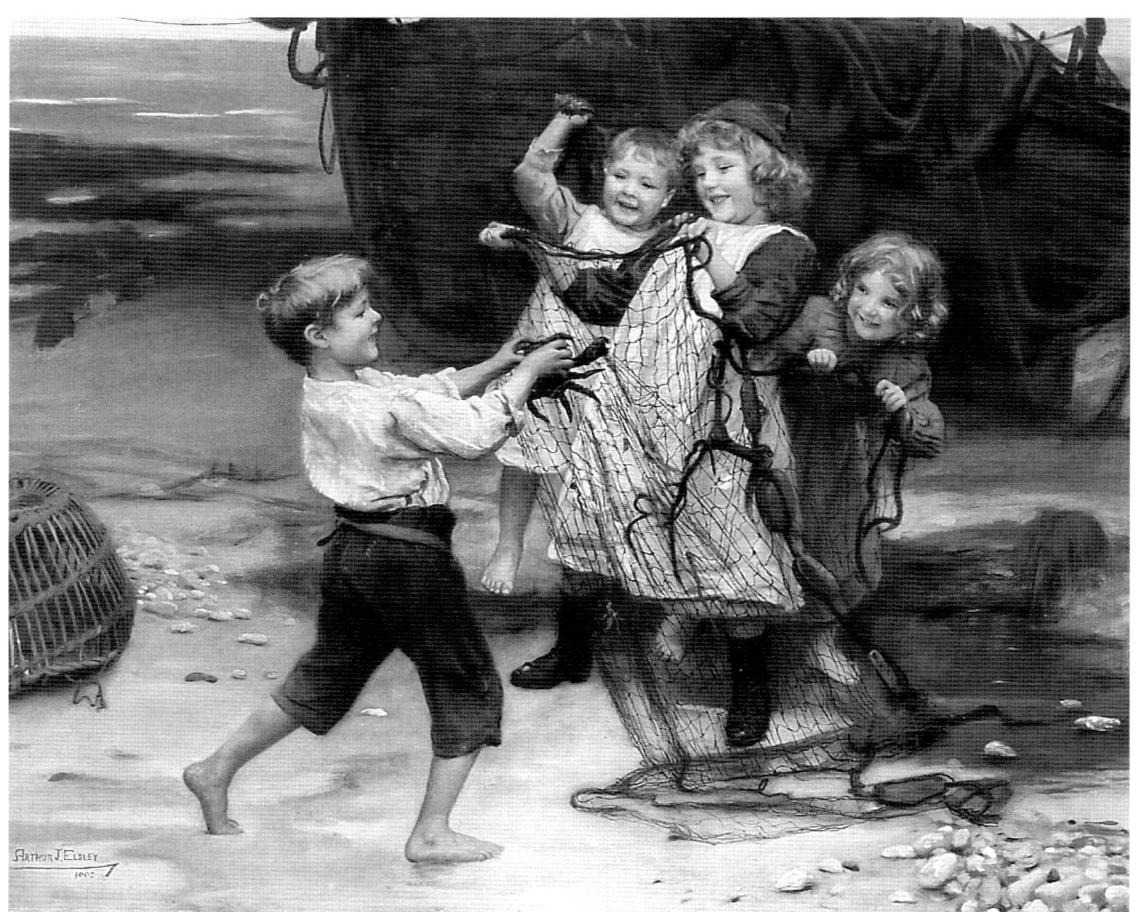

[Children On Beach]

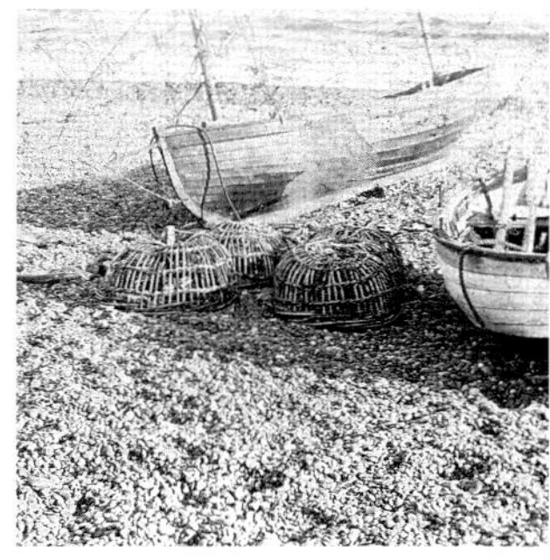

Source photograph for *[Children On Beach]*.

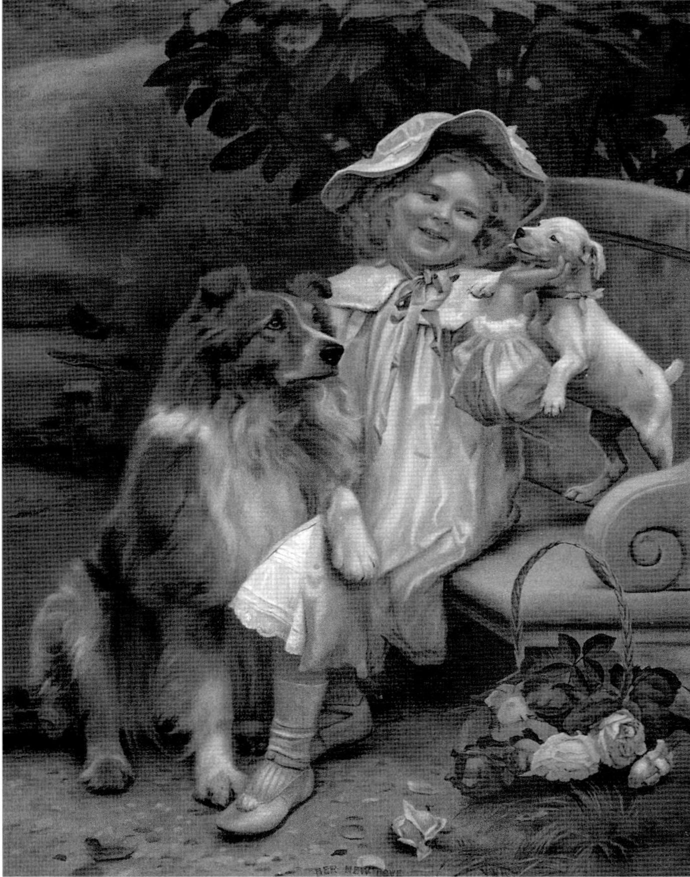

Her New Love

Her New Love *signed and dated 1902*

Details of original painting unknown. Possibly exhibited in Birmingham, Autumn 1903 (No.100), priced £100, copyright reserved.

This work appears to have been painted earlier, but bears the date 1902 and is a very similar composition to *One at a Time*, 1901.

Sepia postcard Faulkner & Co. Ltd., c.1904. Reproduced as a magazine page entitled *Have You Quite Forgotten Me?*

Sepia photogravure, 12¾ins x 8¾ins (32.5cm x 22cm), presented with *Weldon's Illustrated Dressmaker*, Christmas 1904, copyright Landeker & Brown, London. This version is signed and dated 1902. At the same time their sister publication *Weldon's Bazaar of Children's Fashions* featured *Divided Attention*, c.1898, in the same format. Colour chromolithograph, 24¼ins x 18ins (62cm x 45.5cm), probably a calendar, signature and date removed, title printed on bottom of image.

Ladies First *signed and dated 1902*

Oil on canvas, 29½ins x 22½ins (75cm x 57.5cm). Exhibited at the Royal Academy, 1903 (No.286), and was unsold. Owned by Haynes Fine Art in 1992.

This work features Old Bruce, the same collie as in *Bath Time*, 1900.

Modern colour print entitled *High Expectations* published by Felix Rosenstiel's Widow & Son.

Small colour photolithograph, 8ins x 6ins (20.5cm x 15cm), presented with *Horner's Penny Stories*, date unknown. Also produced as a colour chromolithograph calendar, no copyright given.

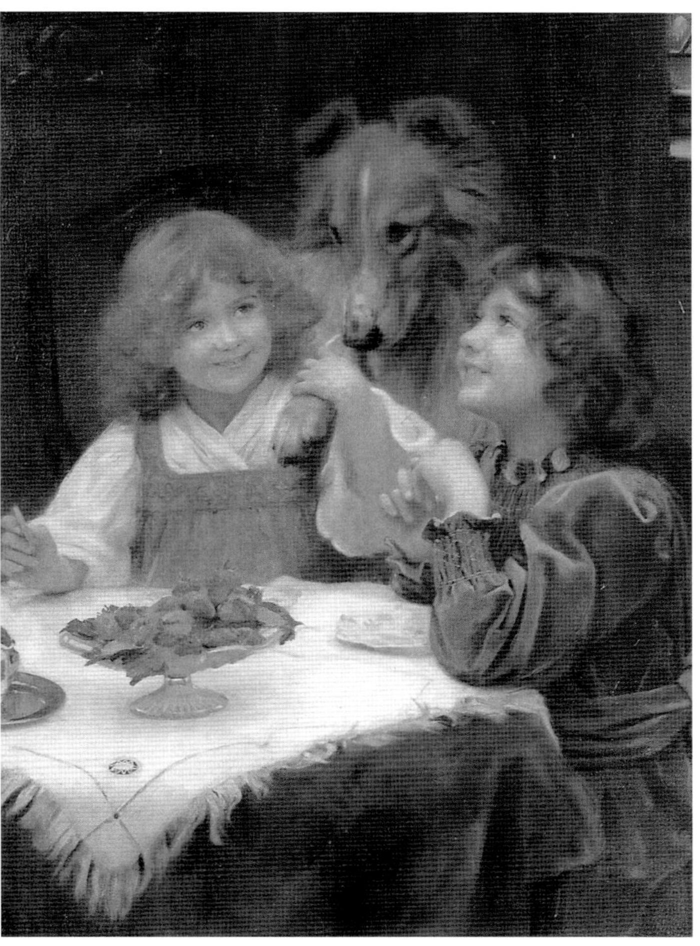

Ladies First

Golden Hours *signed and dated 1903*

Oil on canvas, 44ins x 61ins (112cm x 155.5cm). Exhibited at the Royal Academy, 1903 (No.391), and was unsold. The Royal Academy Hanging Committee must have considered this an important work as it was "hung on the line" in Gallery VII. In each room there was a line at eye level where all the best works were hung. Also exhibited in Liverpool, Autumn 1903 (No.863), price £250, copyright reserved. Paintings unsold at Royal Academy Summer Exhibitions were frequently sent on to the Walker Art Gallery, Liverpool, Autumn Exhibition. This had been the case with Elsley's works in 1885, 1888 and 1889. So popular was this practice that the Walker Art Gallery had a special cellar to store the works. Extract from *The London Magazine*, December 1904, p.632:

> "One of those little misadventures to which child life is liable, happened in connection with *The First Ride*. The pony was painted at Hoddesdon, Herts., and Mr. Elsley arranged with the people to whom it belonged to get a

child to sit on it, so that he might paint the pony and child together. The day appointed for the sitting was very wet, and, thinking that the parents would not allow the child to go out, he did not go into the country. Next day, however, he went. The pony was brought out. 'Where is the child?' he asked.

'Oh, the child was here yesterday,' they said. 'But as we did not know you were coming to-day they did not send her up.' A messenger went for the little one, and returned with the answer, 'She can't come, for she's gone to the 'orspital with the scarlet fever.'

Eventually a child was found to deputise for the original model. Mr. Elsley painted the pony, which he measured carefully; and on his return to London he reproduced the measurements by padding an apple-barrel, on which another child rode with supreme satisfaction to itself as a 'pretence gee'."

The First Ride was Elsley's early working title and the farm mentioned in this extract was Manor Farm, Wormley, Hoddesdon. *Bibby's Quarterly*, Summer 1908:

> "Mr. Elsley is master of these bright scenes of childhood. He knows all the ingredients that compose the children's paradise; a pony and a dog, a lovely garden and romping spirits untouched by any shade of care. The original is owned by our good friends and neighbours Mr. Charles W. Ashcroft, Oxton, Birkenhead."

Almost certainly an American colour calendar manufactured by Thos. D. Murphy Co., 1906. Modern print printed by The Medici Society Ltd. Black and white photograph in *Royal Academy Notes* 1903, p.96, and *Bibby's Quarterly Summer*, 1908, copyright Berlin Photographic.

Sepia photogravure, 11½ins x 15¼ins (29cm x 39cm), *Weldon's Ladies' Journal* Christmas 1906, copyright 1903, Berlin Photographic. **See page 69**.

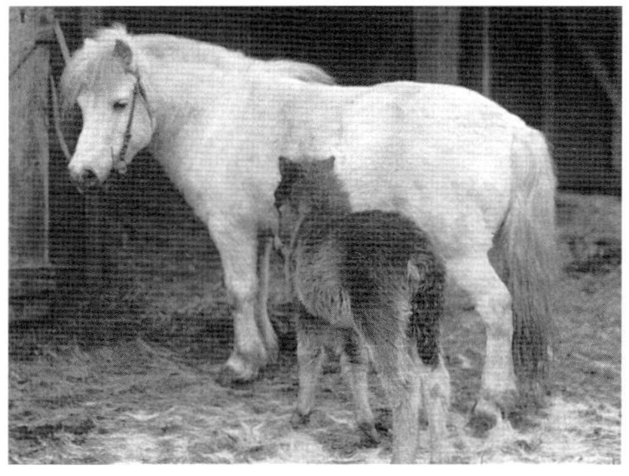

Source photograph of the pony in *Golden Hours*.

The Home Team *signed and dated 1903*

Details of original painting unknown. This appears to be an adaptation of Fred Morgan's *Sea Horses*, Pears print, 1894.

Modern print by Rosentiel's entitled *The Home Team*.

Sepia photogravure approximately the same size as *A Royal Procession*, 20½ins x 27½ins (52cm x 70.5cm), copyright Louis Wolff. Colour photolithograph, 9½ins x 14ins (24cm x 35.5cm), supplement to the *Review of Reviews Annual*, date unknown. A pair with *A Royal Procession*, signed and dated 1904. **See page 71**.

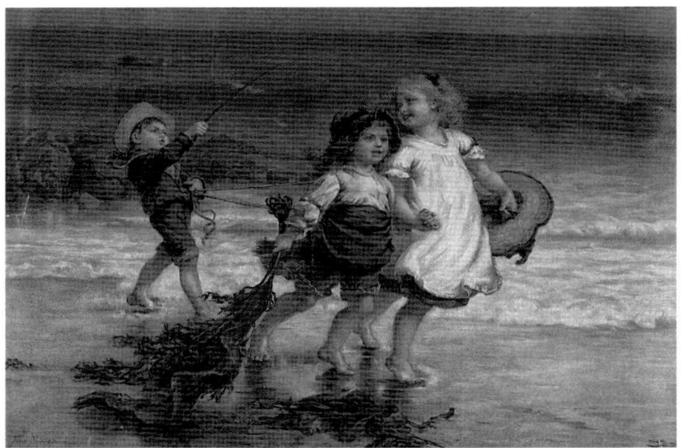

Sea Horses by Fred Morgan, Pears print, 1894.

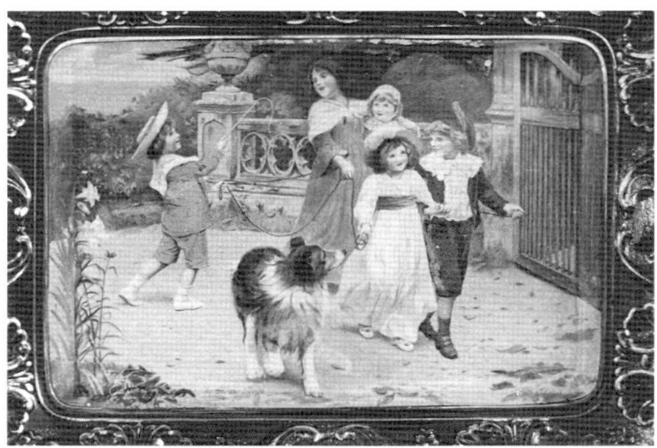

Pottery plaque of *The Home Team* (without the character on the right), 12ins x 9ins (30.5cm x 23cm) produced by Empire Works, Stoke-on-Trent. Backstamp used until 1912.

Pick-a-Back *signed and dated 1903*

Oil on canvas, 35ins x 26ins (89cm x 66.5cm). The same collie and screen appear in *The New Dress*, 1912.

The Antiques Trade Gazette, 25 December 1993, described it as:

> "...the sort of Edwardian chocolate box painting that makes Modernists reach for their flame-throwers and greeting card manufacturers reach for their chequebooks. In fact, such was the saccharine appeal of this painting...showing a young girl giving a collie puppy a piggy-back in an Edwardian interior – accompanied by the puppy's watchful mother – that (the auctioneers) were contacted by two greetings cards manufacturers with an eye to possible reproduction. (The) vendor who had been left it by an aunt, who in turn had bought it 'for a few pennies' some years ago."

Sepia photogravure, 26ins x 18¾ins (66.5cm x 48cm), copyright C.W. Faulkner & Co. 1904.

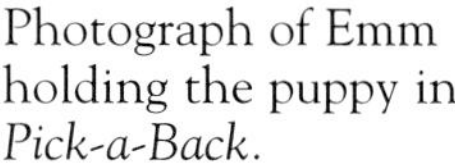

Photograph of Emm holding the puppy in *Pick-a-Back*.

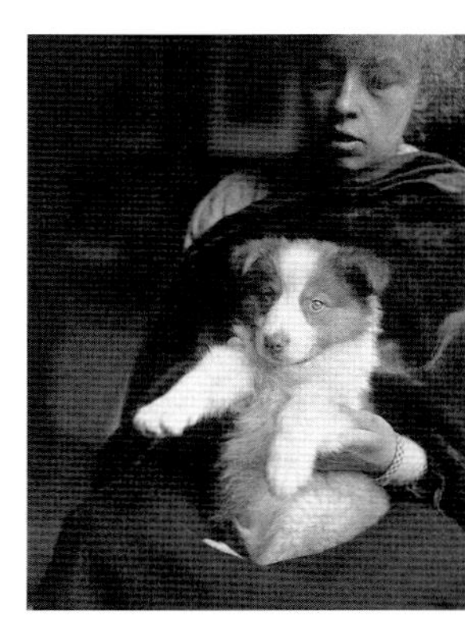

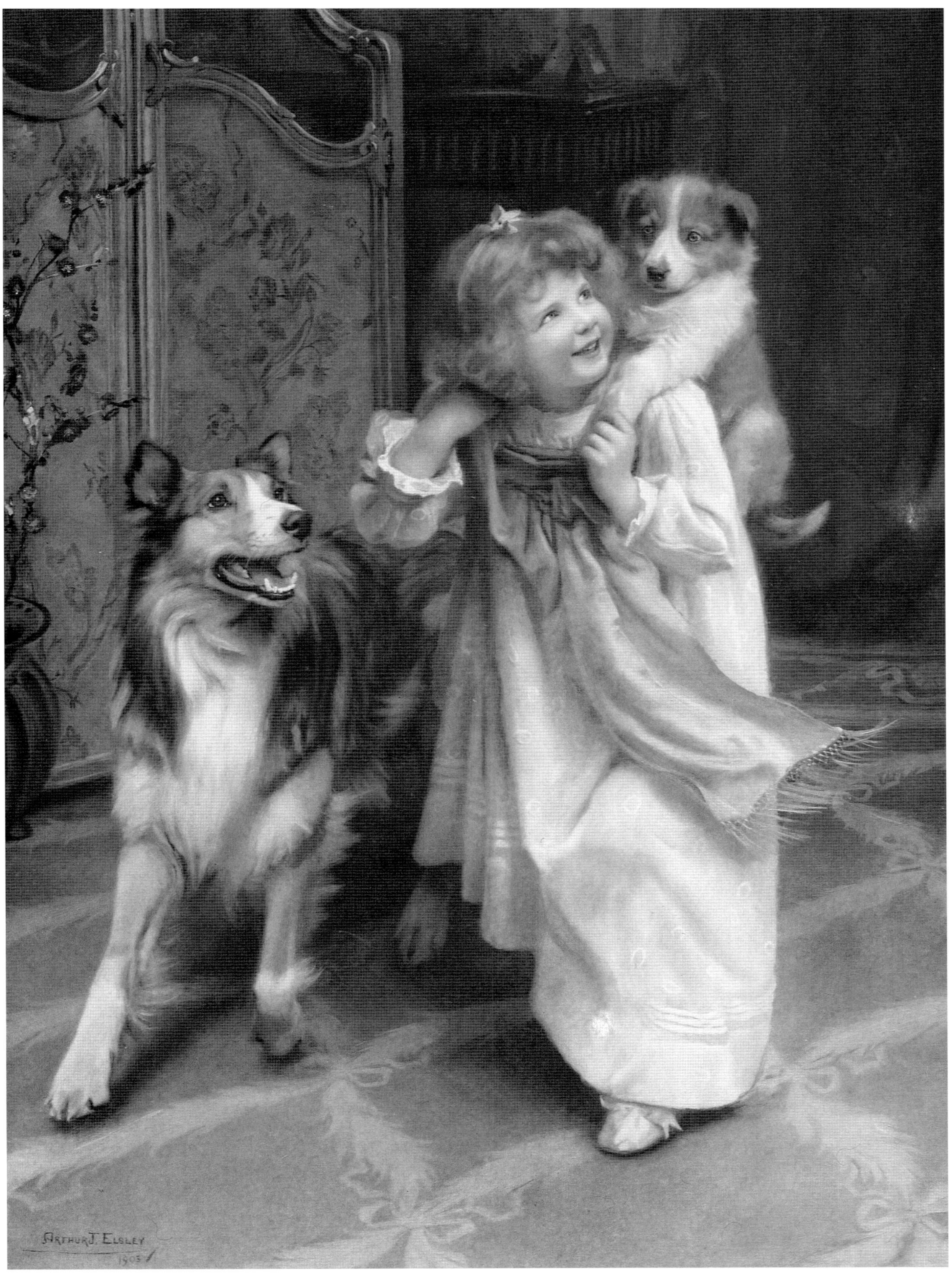

Pick-a-Back

You Must Stay There! *signed and dated 1903*

Almost certainly *Just Keep Them There*, an oil painting, 33ins x $21^{1}/_{2}$ins (83.5cm x 55cm), signed and dated 1903. It was bought by De Casseres at Christie's, London, in 1931.

The tub in this picture was at the end of Elsley's garden next to his studio, and also in *Divided Affection*, Royal Academy, 1899. Black and white photograph, *The Windsor Magazine*, Vol.39 No.229, January 1914.

Sepia photogravure, 26ins x 17ins (66.5cm x 43cm), published by C.W. Faulkner & Co.

His First Shot *signed and dated 1903*

Oil on canvas, 43ins x 33ins (109.5cm x 84cm).

The painting is unusual in not featuring a girl. Charles Burton Barber's paintings often featured a peacock feather in the cap.

Colour chromolithograph, 23ins x $16^{1}/_{2}$ins (59cm x 42cm), possibly a calendar. **See page 75**.

Safe And Sound *circa 1904*

Details of original painting unknown.

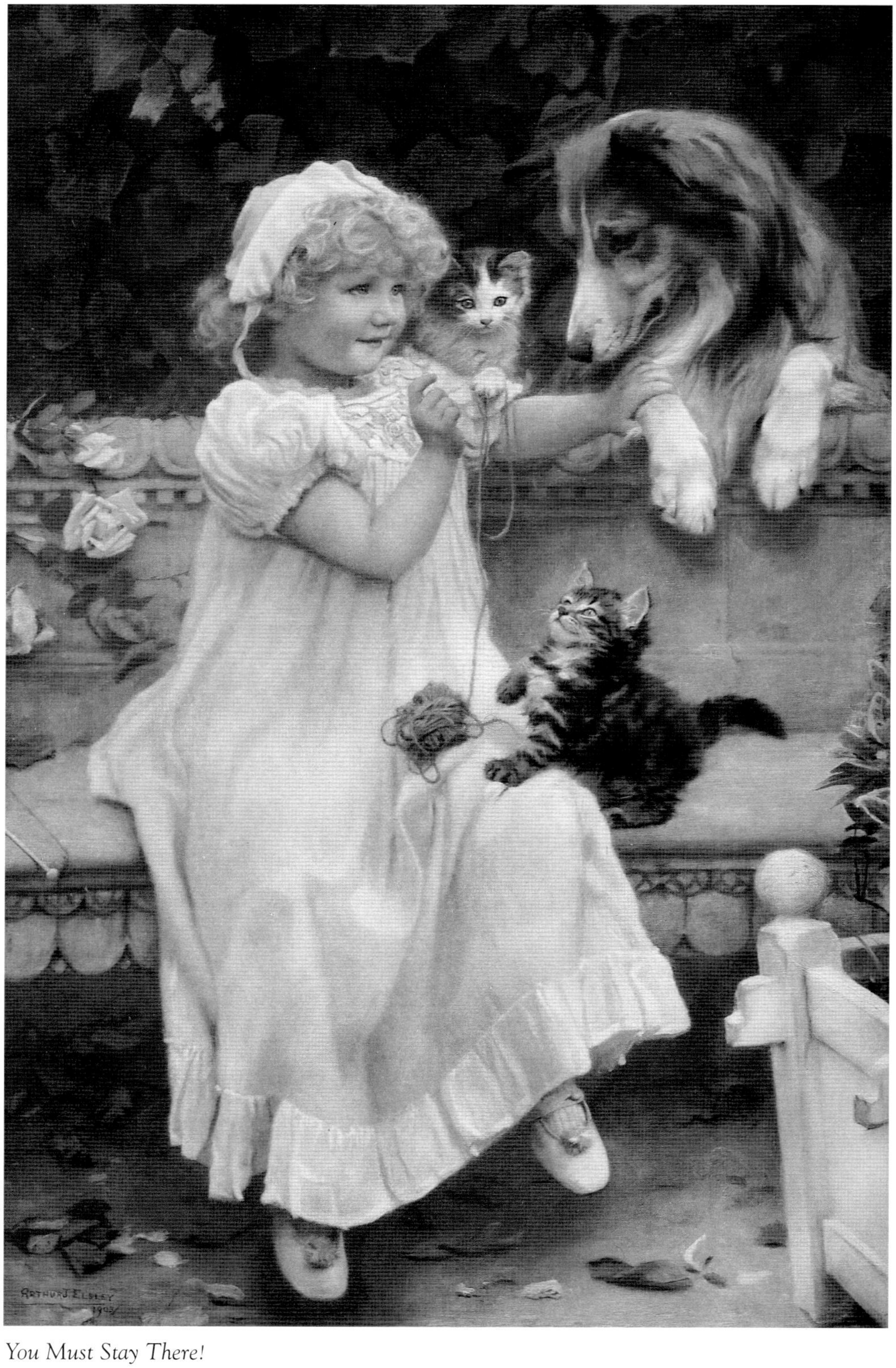

You Must Stay There!

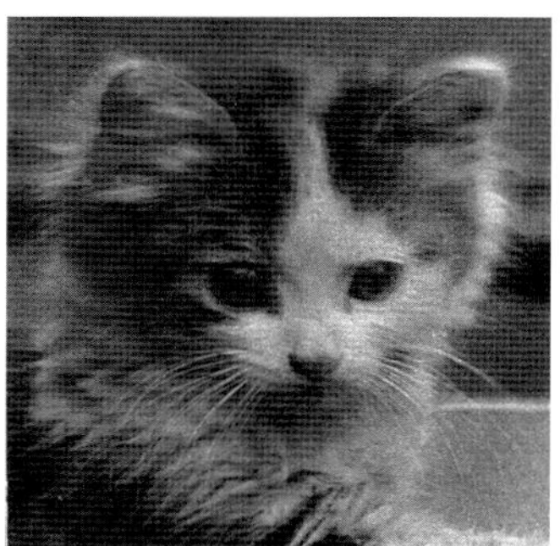

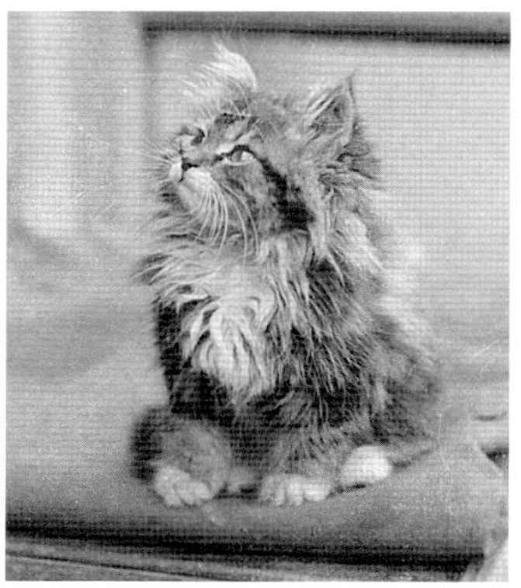

Top and above, source photographs for *You Must Stay There!*

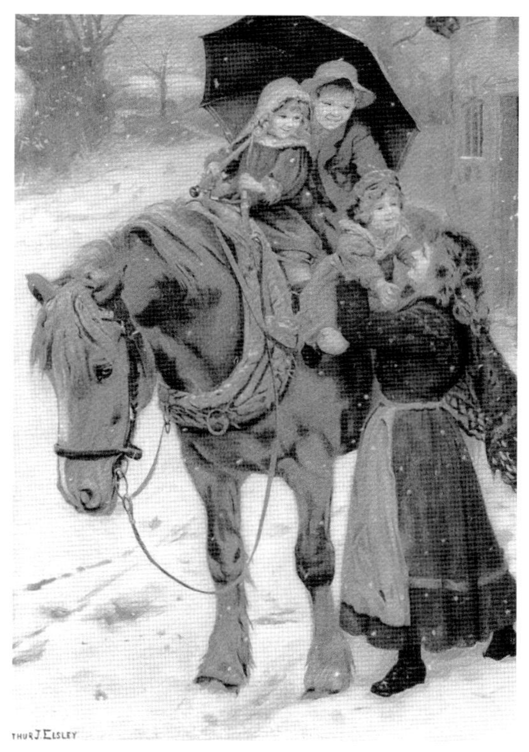

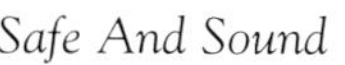

Safe And Sound

His First Fence *signed and dated 1904*

Oil on canvas, 40ins x 30ins (102cm x 76.5cm). Owned in 1994 by Haynes Fine Art who called it *Race You Home*.

This is the last in the series of hunt paintings and features the same horse (reversed) as is depicted in *Forbidden Ground*, signed and dated 1899. This picture is similar to the work of Thomas Blinks who collaborated with Morgan on *HM Queen Alexandra, Her Grandchildren and Dogs*, Royal Academy, 1902.

Colour chromolithograph, 23¼ins x 16½ins (59.5cm x 42cm), almost certainly a calendar. The image had been cropped at the sides and bottom thus removing the signature. A detail from this work cropped left, right and bottom including the loss of his signature called *His First Fence*, 17ins x 13¼ins (43cm x 33.5cm), was used for a calendar in 1910, printed by Thomas Forman & Sons, Nottingham. **See page 75.**

Too Hot *signed and dated 1904*

Oil on canvas, 33ins x 23¾ins (84cm x 61cm). Owned by Fine Art of Oakham in 1992, now called *Tea Time*.

Modern colour print entitled *Tea-Time* published by Felix Rosenstiel's Widow & Son.

Sepia photogravure, 18ins x 13ins (46.5cm x 33cm), copyright C.W. Faulkner & Co. Later reproduced as a black and white photolithograph calendar, 23ins x 17ins (59cm x 43cm). **See page 72.**

The Happy Pair / A Royal Procession

signed and dated 1904

A signed oil sketch of the head of the girl who was pulling the pram was sold at the Studio Sale (part of Lot 22).

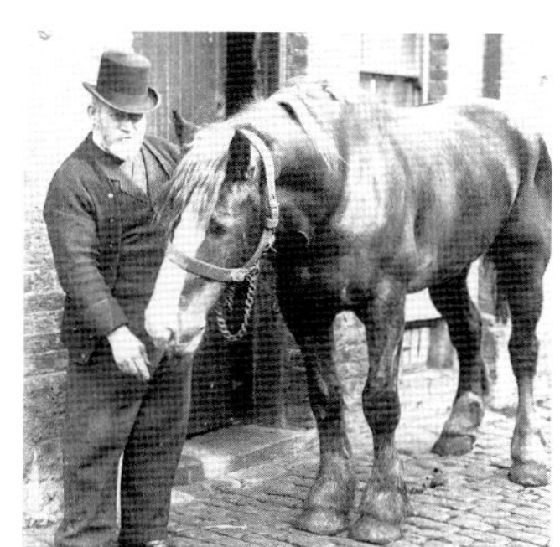

Source photograph for *Safe And Sound*.

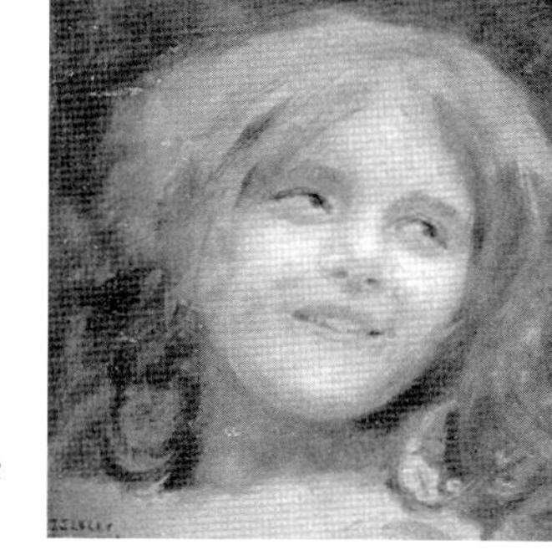

Oil sketch of head, *The Happy Pair*.

Modern print The Medici Society Ltd., London. Used for the colour lid of a McVitie & Price biscuit tin as part of their Yuletide Favourites range for Christmas 1938.

Sepia photogravure, 20½ins x 27½ins (52cm x 70.5cm), copyright Louis Wolff, 1904. Also reproduced as a large colour chromolithograph (details unknown), and later as a colour photolithograph supplement, 9½ins x 14ins (24cm x 35.5.cm), to the *Review of Reviews Annual*, date unknown, reproduced as a pair with *The Home Team*, signed and dated 1903. **See page 71.**

You Dursn't *signed and dated 1905*

Oil on canvas, 35½ins x 25¼ins (90.5cm x 64.5cm). Owned in 1994 by Haynes Fine Art entitled *You Daresn't*.

Black and white photogravure, 13½ins x 9½ins (34.5cm x 24cm), copyright unknown. Not to be confused with the American colour calendar manufactured by Thos. D. Murphy Co., 1923, entitled *You Dare!* and painted in 1921. Reproduced as a colour chromolithograph advertising calendar for J.B. Bowler Mineral Water Company of Bath. **See page 73.**

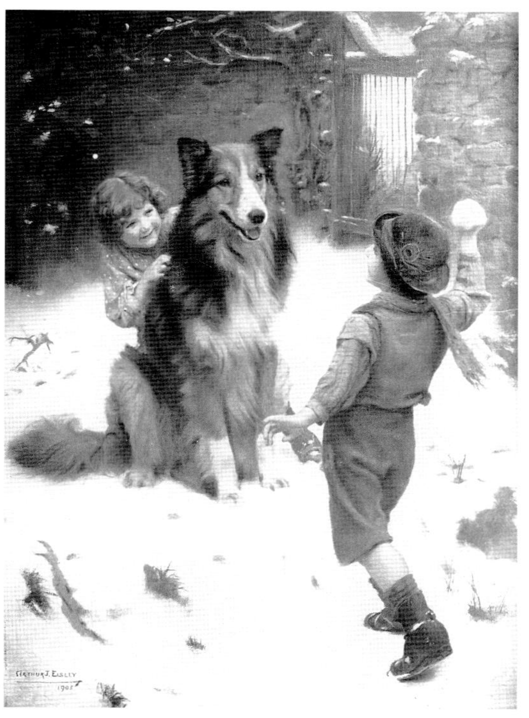

You Dursn't. Unfinished version, the boy is wearing a hat not a cap.

Good Night! / Puppy Love *signed and dated 1905*
Details of original painting unknown. Exhibited at the Royal Academy, 1905 (No.289), and was sold for 175 guineas on 4th August 1905.

cf. *Bedtime*, Royal Academy, 1914-1915, copyright Louis Wolff & Co., 1905. Black and white photograph in *Wife and Home*, October 1929, p.9. Accompanied by a poem by Muriel Arnott:

To My Little Girl
My darling, when, in childish fun,
You coax our pups to play,
The dear old mother dog looks on
With eyes which seem to say,
'Please hold them safely in your arms,
And never let them stray!'

And I, a mother, breathe a prayer
That you may ever be
Kept safe and happy; that my love
May guard you tenderly.
I say to life, 'Be kind to her,
She means so much to me!' "

Modern Italian reproduction entitled *Puppy Love*.

Sepia print, 17ins x $12^{1}/_{2}$ins (43cm x 32cm), in *Madame*, 18th November 1905. Medium size sepia print, *The Queen Newspaper*, Christmas 1913.

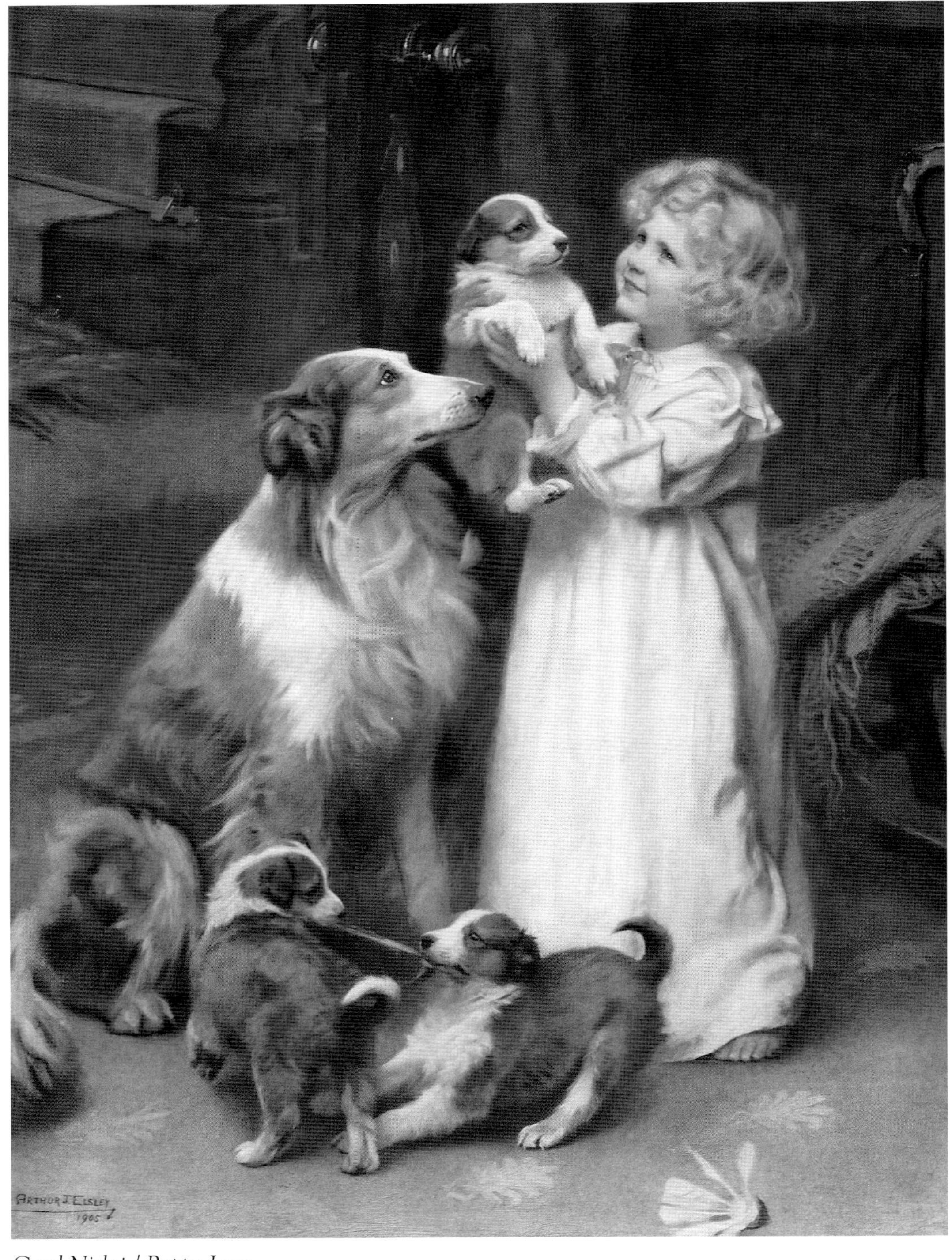

Good Night! / Puppy Love

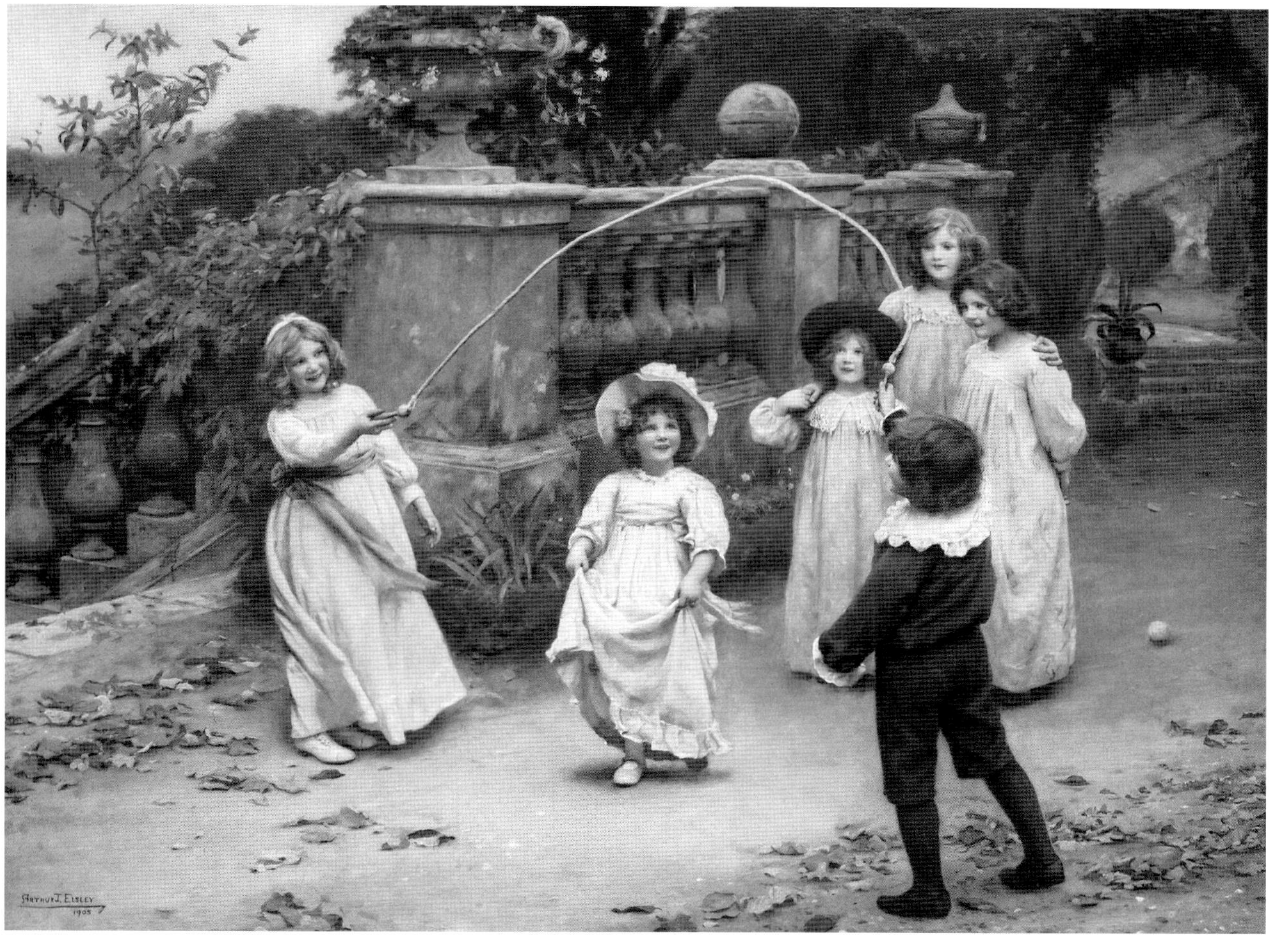
Baby's Turn / A Skipping Match

Baby's Turn / A Skipping Match

signed and dated 1905

Oil on canvas, 42ins x 50ins (107cm x 128cm). Exhibited at the Royal Academy, 1905 (No.416), and was unsold, and "hung on the line" in Gallery VII.

The girl skipping in this picture was Barbara Cook, daughter of the artist Walter F. Cook. The Elsley and Cook families were great friends and often went on holiday together.

Black and white photograph in *Royal Academy Notes*, 1905, p.98.

Sepia photogravure, 20½ins x 26¾ins (52cm x 68.5cm), copyright C.W. Faulkner & Co., 1906. Sepia photogravure, 15½ins x 20ins (39.5cm x 51cm), presented with *The Queen, The Lady's Newspaper,* Christmas 1906. Elsley provided the artwork for *The Queen* presentation print every Christmas from 1906-1915, except in 1907.

Won't You Try / A Passive Resister / Come Along *signed and dated 1905*

Details of original painting unknown. Exhibited at the Royal Academy, 1905 (No.524), entitled *Won't You Try* and was unsold. Photograph in the Elsley Collection shows more of the upper part of the painting, including a sailing boat in the sea, and the boots (bottom left) are in a slightly different position. The shape of the towel is different, more detail is visible on the print showing the pattern and fringe. cf. *Tug Of War*, 1889.

Black and white postcard entitled *Come Along*, published by The Rotary Photo Co., as part of their Opalette series, c.1909. The image is framed in an oval. Possibly an American colour calendar manufactured by Thos. D. Murphy Co., 1928 and 1930, entitled *Come Along Then.*

Small sepia photogravure entitled *A Passive Resister* was presented with *Weldon's Bazaar of Children's Fashions,* Christmas 1906.

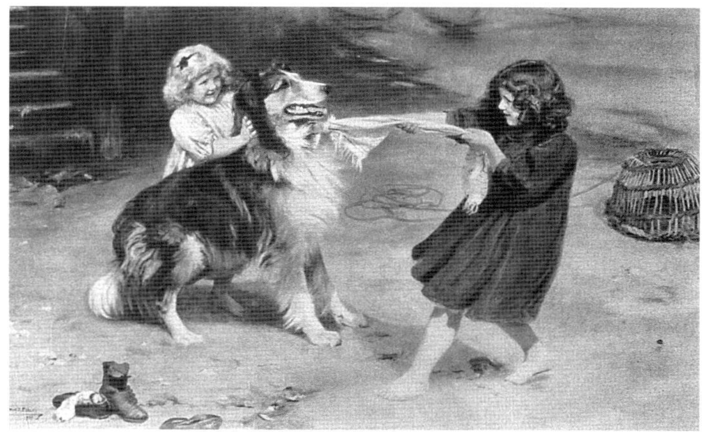
Won't You Try / A Passive Resister / Come Along

Favourite Of The Litter *signed and dated 1905*

Oil on canvas, 40ins x $19^{1}/_{2}$ins (102cm x 50cm).

Not to be confused with *Pick Of The Litter*, 1908. cf. Fred Morgan's *The Yacht Race / The Coming Nelson*, 1899, Charles Burton Barber's work, and Elsley's *Pick-a-Back*, signed and dated 1901.

Sepia photogravure, 30ins x $14^{3}/_{4}$ins (76.5cm x 37.5cm), published C.W. Faulkner & Co., signed and dated 1905.

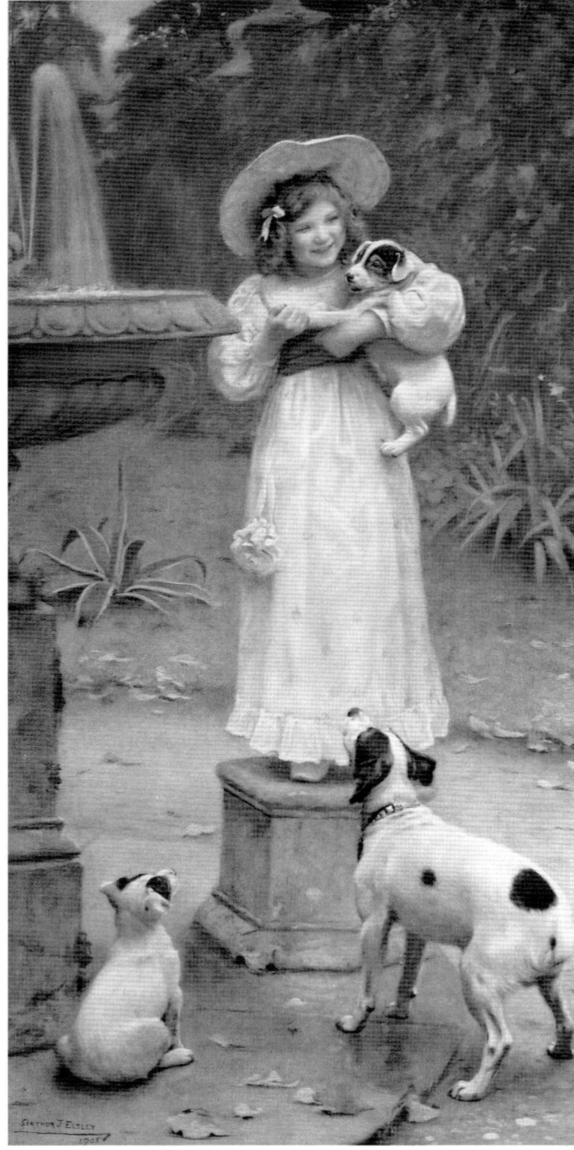

Favourite Of The Litter

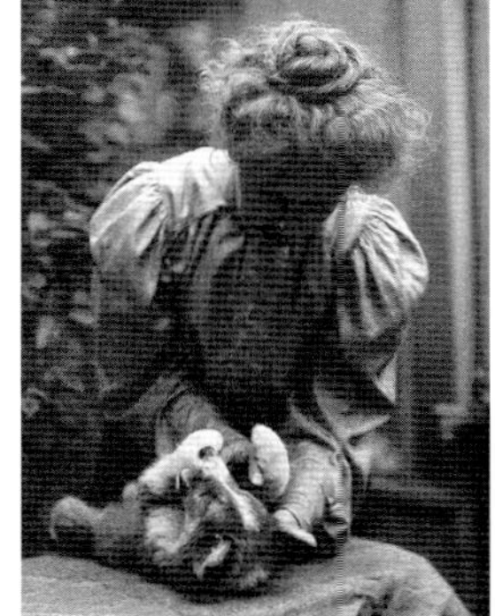

Photograph of Emm and puppy in *Try Again* and *'Twixt Love and Duty*. **See page 88**.

Open Your Mouth And Shut Your Eyes *signed and dated 1905*

Details of original painting unknown.

The girl in this picture is Elsley's daughter, Marjorie. This is the first of many occasions in which she features in his work. Fred Morgan exhibited a painting with the same title in 1883, but the subject was two girls and a cat.

Black and white double-page engraving in German magazine, and black and white single page in smaller magazine, c.1910.

Sepia photogravure, 26ins x 19ins (66.5cm x 49cm). Copyright Louis Wolff & Co, London, 1906. Produced as a crystoleum.

Try Again *signed and dated 1906*

Details of original painting unknown.

Elsley's daughter, Marjorie, is the youngest girl in the picture. The garden tub features again. cf. *A Dead Heat*, signed and dated 1893.

Sepia photogravure, $27^{1}/_{2}$ins x 20ins (70.5cm x 51cm), copyright Louis Wolff, 1907. Medium size sepia photogravure entitled *Try Again*. Large colour chromolithograph, $24^{3}/_{4}$ins x $19^{1}/_{4}$ins (63.5cm x 49.5cm), entitled *Try Again*. Medium size colour chromolithograph, Frisby's Boot Co., calendar c.1912 printed on image.

Produced as a crystoleum.

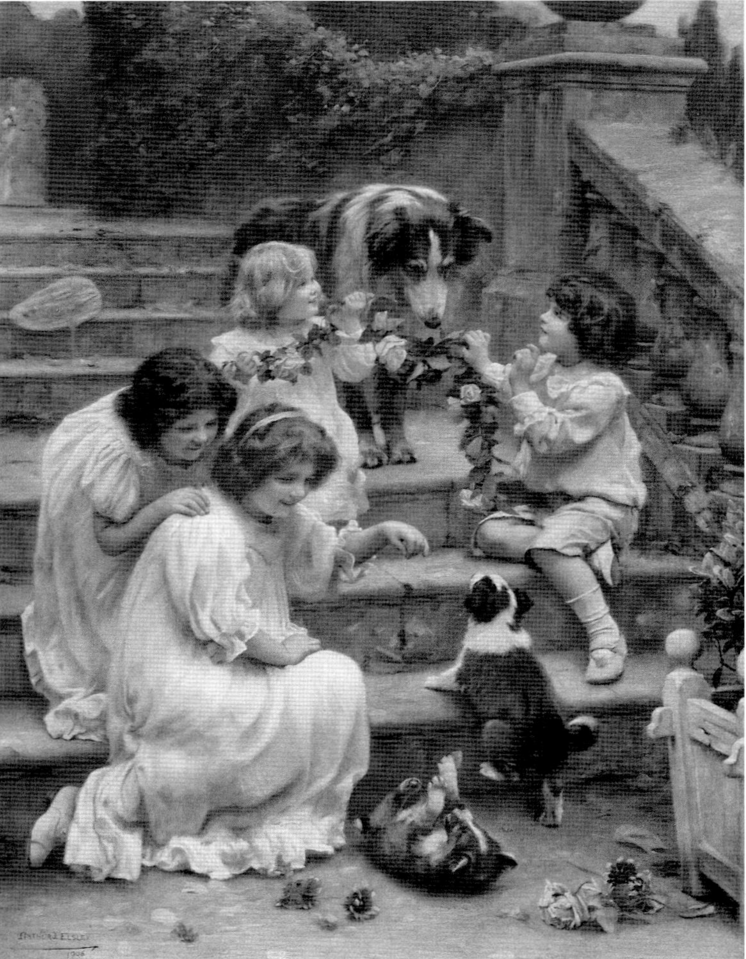

Try Again

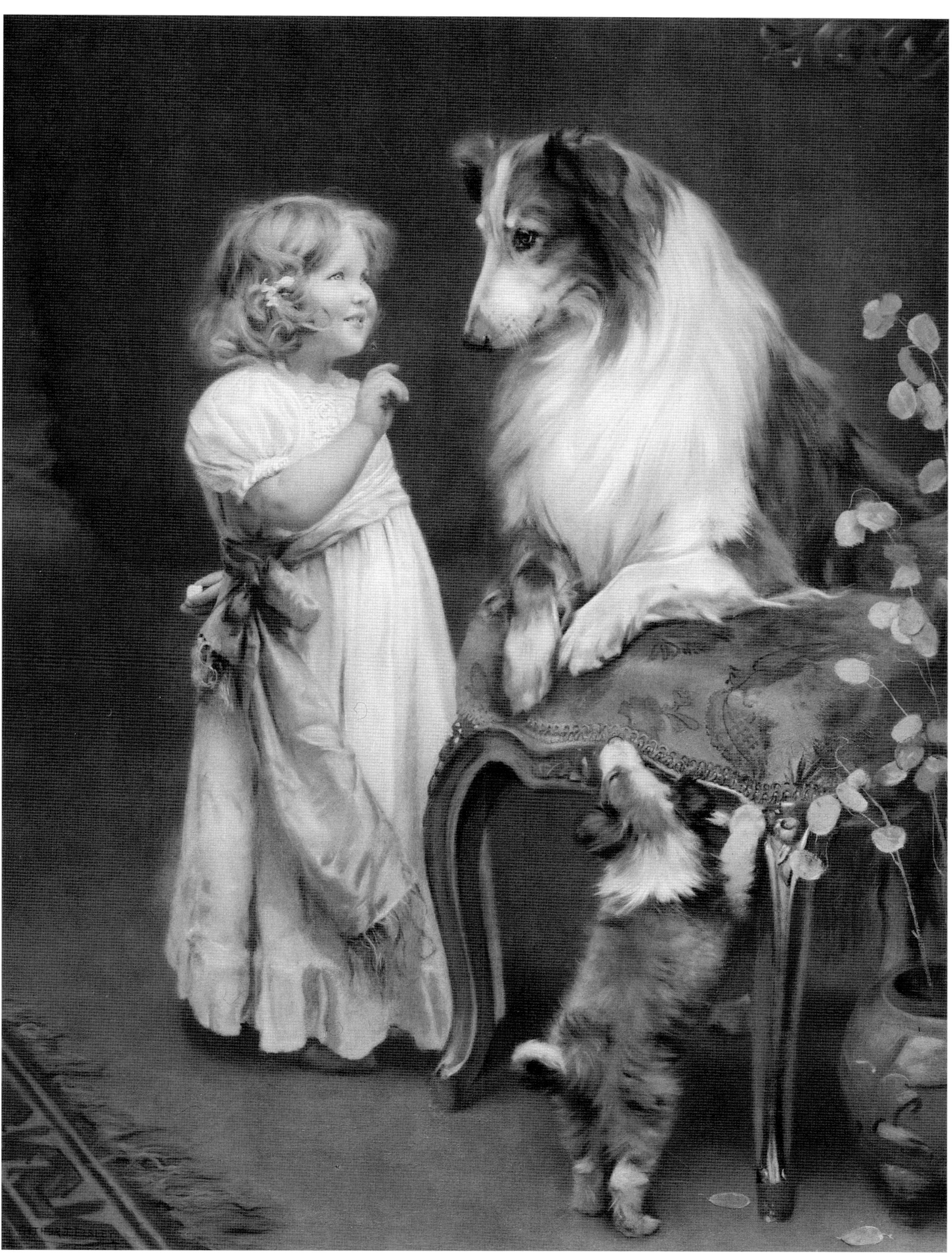

Open Your Mouth And Shut Your Eyes

A Tempting Bait *signed and dated 1906*

Oil on canvas, 40ins x 58ins (102cm x 148.5cm). Exhibited at the Royal Academy, 1906 (No.43), but was unsold. Also exhibited Liverpool, Autumn 1906 (No.831), no price given. The painting is now in the Russell-Cotes Art Gallery and Museum, Bournemouth.

Possibly painted in the New Forest. Marjorie is the little girl holding the collie and Dolly Brennan is the taller girl. Extract from *Bulletin of the Russell-Cotes Art Gallery and Museum*, December 1936, p.48:

> "The anecdote told by *A Tempting Bait* needs for its amplification no text. The academic laws of composition are fulfilled in the careful arrangement of the group of children balanced by the large mass of high light (the pony). There is a faint complementary colour balance between the dresses of the two younger girls – made unobtrusive by the interposition of a grey-blue dress. The artist has carried on the tradition of a highly finished, botanically accurate foreground similar to the one in Lucy Kemp Welch's *Gipsy Horse Drovers* painted twelve years before."

Sepia photogravure, 19½ins x 28¼ins (50cm x 72cm), issued by Bovril in May 1906. This was the first of twelve works to be reproduced by Bovril which were obtained by collecting coupons on Bovril jars. Signed proof prints were also available of the later ones in exchange for a larger number of coupons. **See page 76**.

One, Two, Three! Go! *signed and dated 1906*

Oil on canvas, 39¾ins x 29½ins (101cm x 76cm). Auctioned as *One, Two, Three, Off!* at Sotheby's, Los Angeles, in 1980.

Marjorie was only three and was painted with longer legs to make her taller. The model for the old man is the same as used by Fred Morgan in many of his works between 1898 and 1903, including *The Sunshine of His Heart*, 1898.

Black and white small magazine page, publication unknown.

Sepia photogravure, 24ins x 17¾ins (61.5cm x 46cm), published by Hildesheimer & Co Ltd., London, copyright 1907, entitled *One, Two, Three, Go!* Black and white photogravure, 10¼ins x 7½ins (25cm x 19cm), presented with *The Sunday Circle*, no date given, signed and dated 1906, entitled *One, Two, Three! Go!*

The Little Doctor *signed and dated 1906*

Details of original painting unknown.

This work was inspired by Charles Burton-Barber's earlier work of the same title, signed and dated 1889.

Sepia photogravure, 25¾ins x 18¾ins (66cm x 48cm), copyright C.W. Faulkner & Co., 1907. Sepia photogravure, 20½ins x 14ins (52cm x 35.5cm) presented with *The Queen, The Lady's Newspaper*, Christmas 1909, date below signature now removed. Colour chromolithograph calendar 1911 for *Frisby's Boot Store*, 24¾ins x 19¼ins (63.5cm x 49.5cm). Also produced as a calendar for Matthews Brothers.

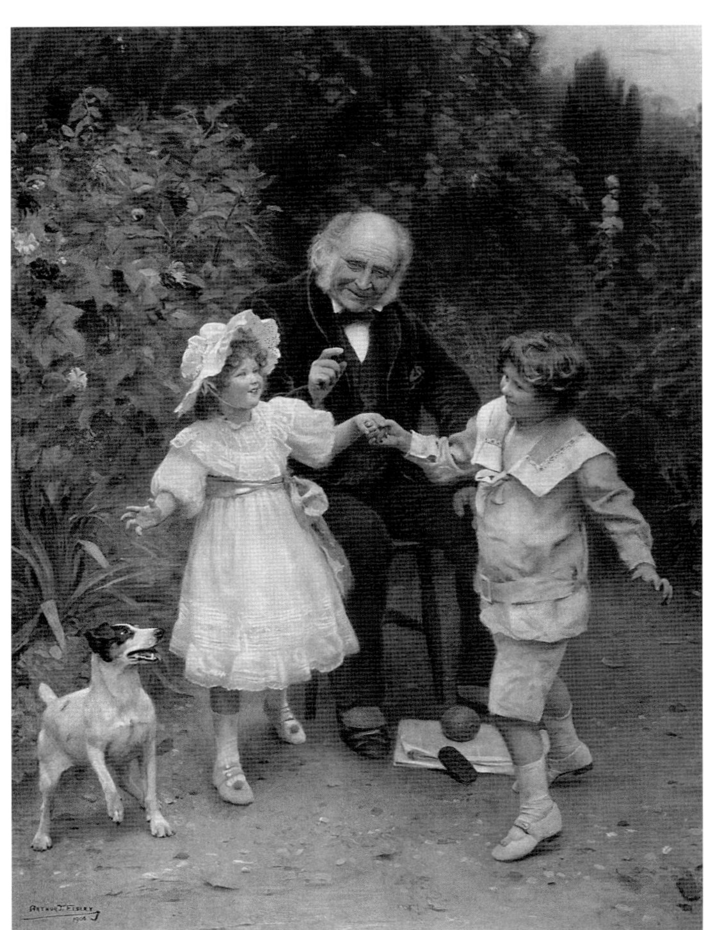

One, Two, Three! Go!

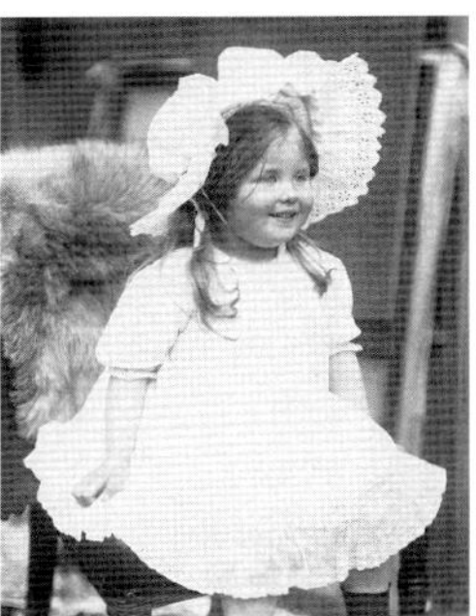

Source photograph of Marjorie used for *One, Two, Three! Go!*

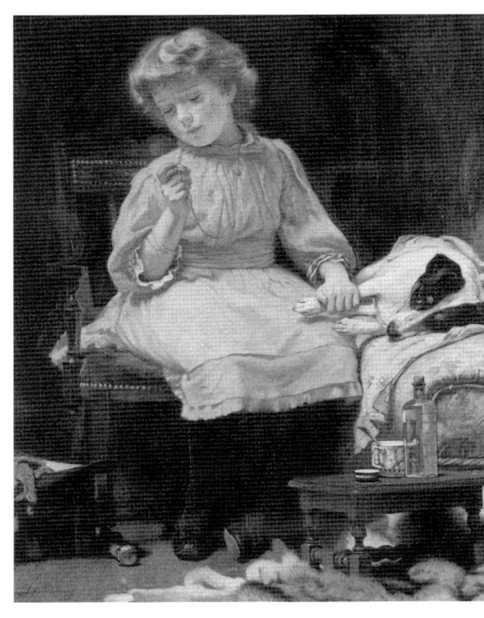

The Little Doctor by Charles Burton Barber.

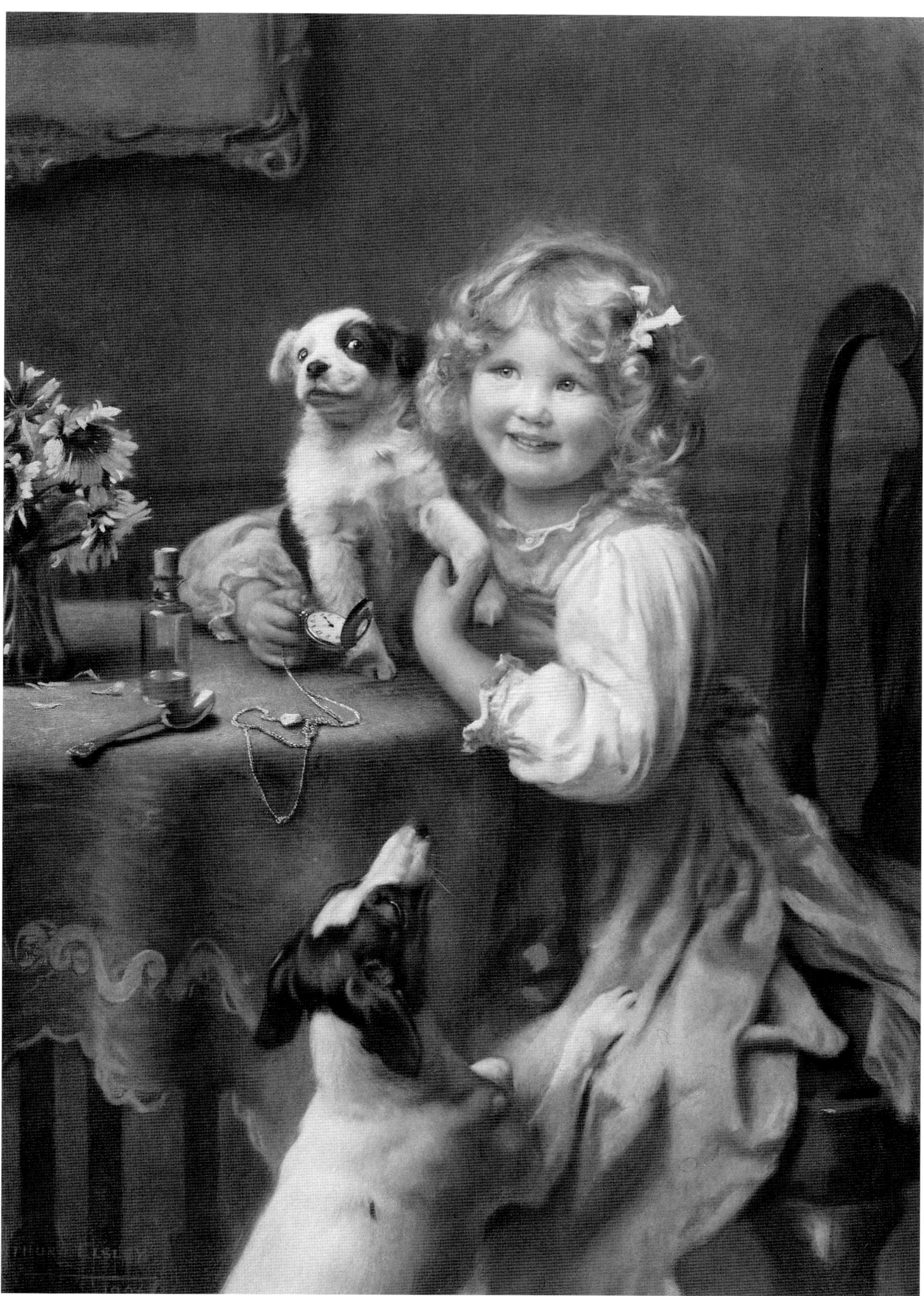

The Little Doctor

Cooling His Yed / My Turn Next
signed and dated 1906
Details of original painting unknown.

Poor-quality colour chromolithograph print, 23¾ins x 17½ins (61cm x 45cm), called *Cooling His Yed*, details unknown. Also a colour chromolithograph calendar for Blue Cross Tea, 22ins x 16½ins (56.5cm x 42cm). In this version a packet of Blue Cross tea replaces the white package in the shopping basket (bottom left). This was the second Elsley to be used by Blue Cross – the first was *The Home Coming*, 1900. Colour photolithograph 9¼ins x 6¾ins (23.5cm x 17cm), presented with *Horner's Penny Stories*, 11th April 1914. **See page 74**.

Keeping Watch *signed and dated 1906*
Details of original painting unknown.

The demand for his paintings was so great that Elsley had to work at speed, often on two at a time because of changes in light in the studio. He painted this work with the aid of photographs of Marjorie sleeping, and one of the St. Bernard.

Published as a print in U.S.A., copyright 1907.

Private And Confidential *signed and dated 1906*
Details of original painting unknown.

Marjorie is the model, standing in the same position as in *Bedtime / Goodnight*, 1914.

American colour calendar manufactured by Thos. D. Murphy Co., 1908. **See page 86**.

Not Caught Yet *signed and dated 1906*
Details of original painting unknown.

Marjorie doesn't appear in this work. The same boy appears in *His First Shot*, 1903. A head and shoulders oil sketch, 9ins x 8ins (23cm x 20.5cm), of the older girl was auctioned at the Studio Sale (part of Lot 18). The sundial was copied from a photograph in *Country Life* magazine.

Sepia photogravure, 9½ins x 12½ins (24cm x 32cm), presented with *Weldon's Bazaar of Children's Fashions*, December 1909, copyright Hildensheimer & Co., London. It was reproduced as a pair with Morgan's *A Tug of War*, which was presented with *Weldon's Illustrated Dressmaker* of the same date.

Source photograph for *Keeping Watch*.

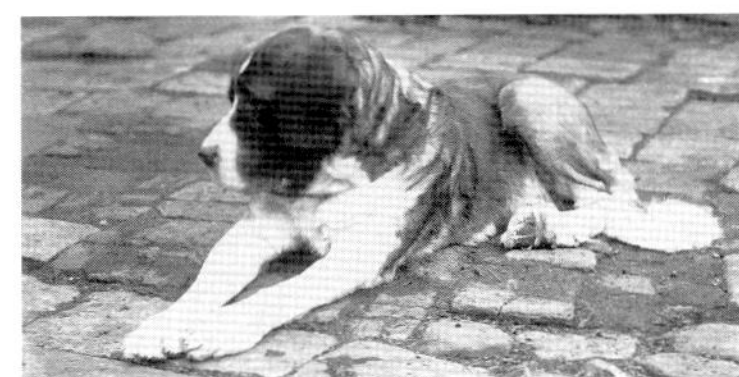

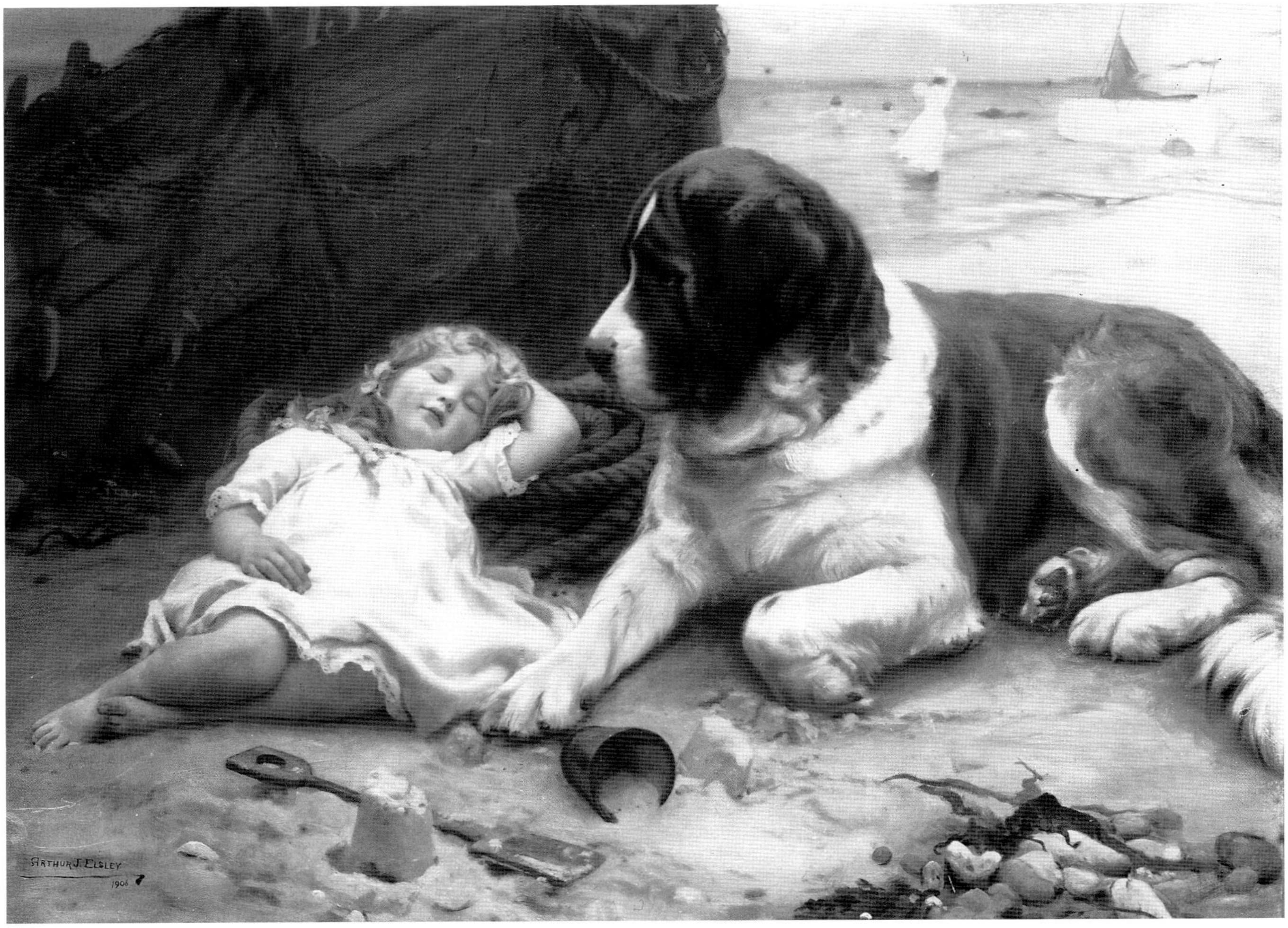

Keeping Watch

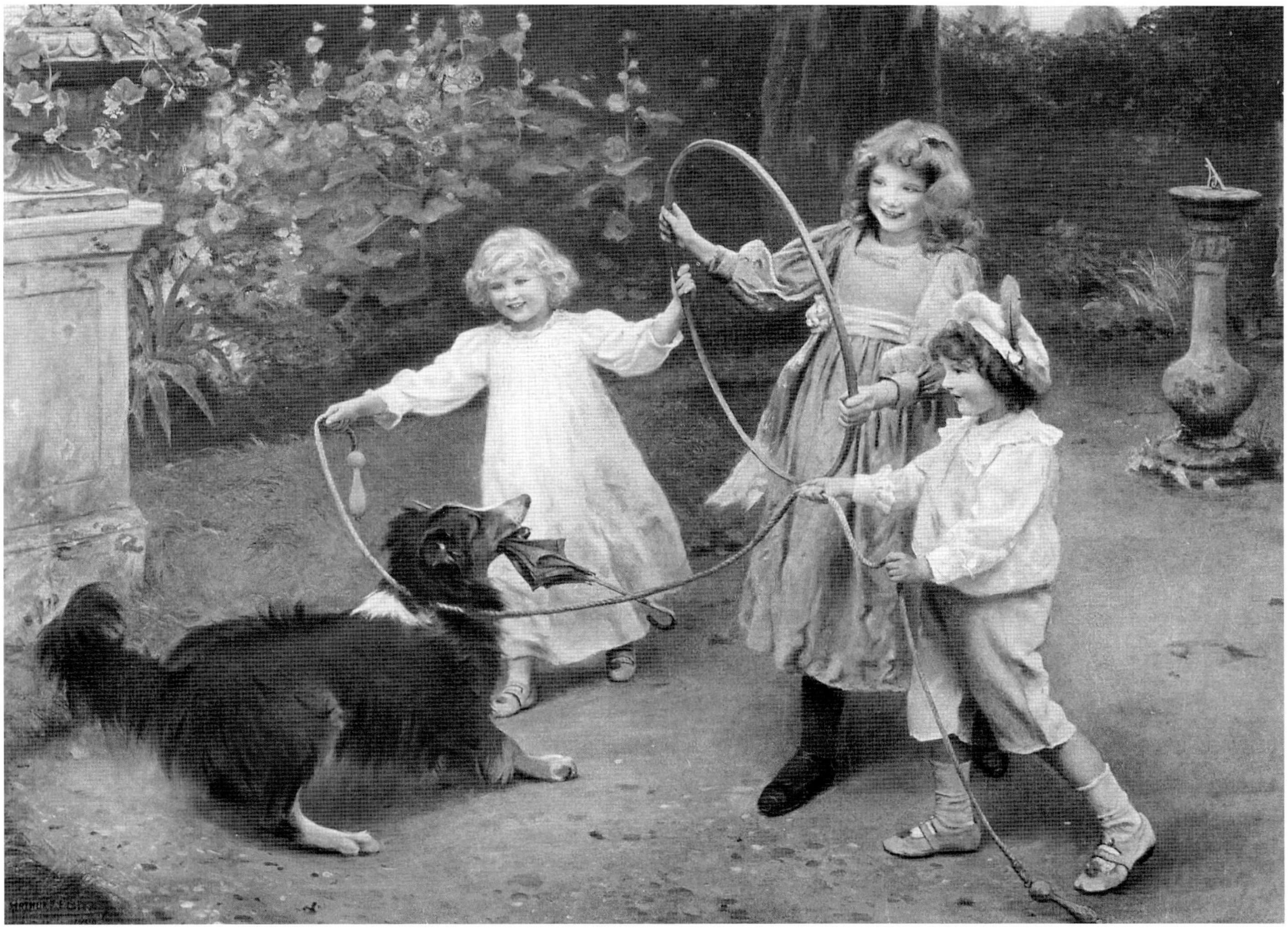

Not Caught Yet

Never Mind *signed and dated 1907*
Oil on canvas, 46ins x 34¼ins (117cm x 87.5cm). Exhibited at the Royal Academy, 1907 (No.832), in Gallery XI and was unsold.

The studio had a separate door from the garden and, even though Marjorie appeared with many different children in her father's works, she didn't actually meet many of them. Elsley used children from the street as

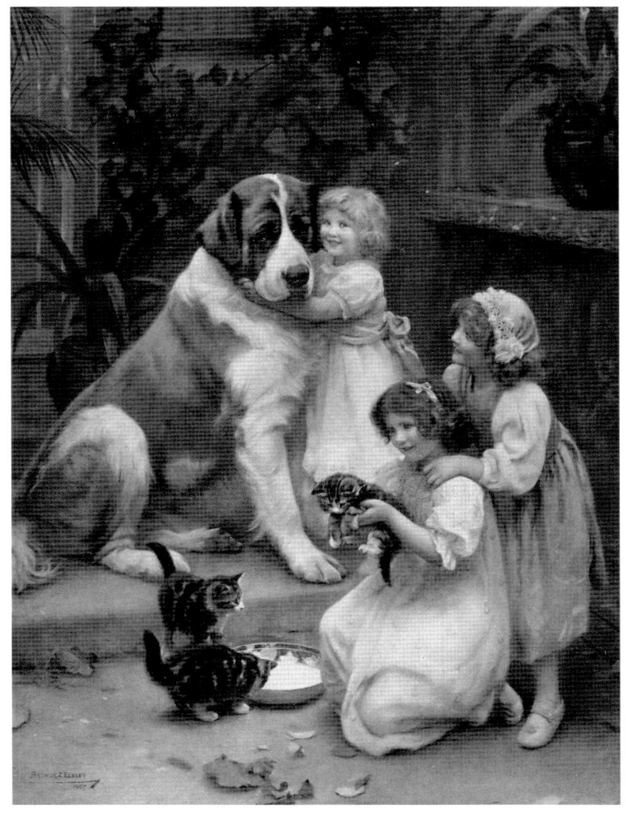

Never Mind

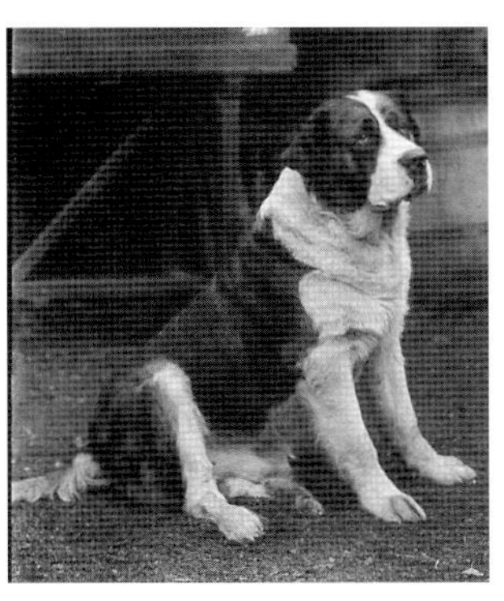

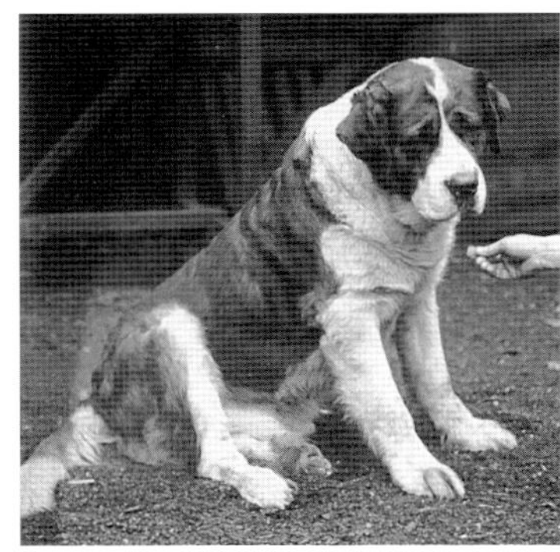

Source photographs of the head and the body of the St. Bernard in *Never Mind*.

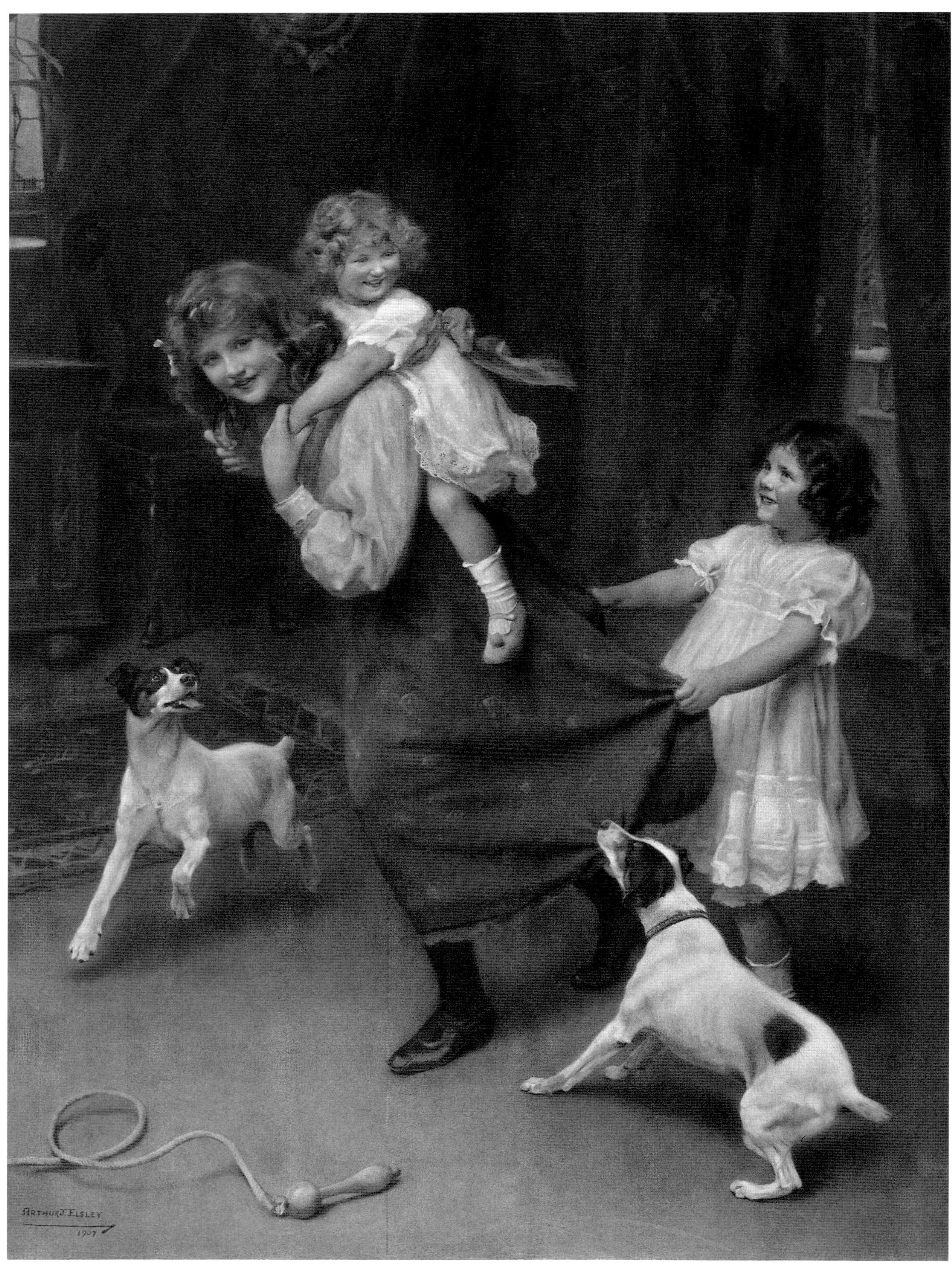

Pickaback / Gee-Up

models, many of whom had diseases and lice! Marjorie, a delicate child, was kept in the main house and went into the studio only when the other children weren't there.

Marjorie remembers that the St. Bernard featured in this work was owned by Miss Mumford, a nurse who lived at South Woodford. One hot summer afternoon when she came to collect the dog, some workmen were mending the road nearby and had a large butt of water into which the dog leaped and refused to leave. In desperation the owner walked off, ignoring him. When he finally scrambled free there was water everywhere.

Fred Morgan also used this title for his Royal Academy exhibit of 1884, but it was a different subject.

Black and white photograph in *Royal Academy Notes*, 1907, p.139. Sepia photogravure, 27½ins x 20¼ins (70.5cm x 51.5cm), published by Louis Wolff & Co., in 1907. Copyright Louis Wolff & Co. Produced as a small colour photolithograph calendar print in 1925 for Joseph Frisby Ltd., (Frisby Footwear), copyright now Bemrose Cooke.

Modern colour print entitled *Family Favourites* published by Felix Rosenstiel's Widow & Son.

Pickaback / Gee-Up *signed and dated 1907*

Oil on canvas almost certainly sold as *Whoa Back*, measuring 39ins x 28½ins (99.5cm x 72.5cm) at Christie's, London, 20th April 1925. It was bought for 17 guineas by W.W. Sampson, a top London art dealer.

The little girl holding the skirt was named Ivy and she had two sisters and a brother who were also named after flowers: Rose, Ivy, Lily, and (Sweet) William! The dog next to her belonged to Emm's cousin, Lily Coccioletti, and was called Spot.

Colour postcard produced by Hildershiemer, c.1914.

Sepia photogravure, 24ins x 17¾ins (61.5cm x 46cm), copyright Hildershiemer. Medium size sepia photogravure presented with *The Illustrated London News*, Christmas 1908, called *Pickaback*. Re-issued in *Weldon's Illustrated Dressmaker*, Christmas 1911, as a small sepia photogravure, 13ins x 9ins (33cm x 23cm), now called *Gee Up*, still signed and dated 1907. This version shows slightly less of the right-hand side of the painting. Medium size colour chromolithograph calendar produced for Nectar Tea.

Here They Are! *signed and dated 1907*

Details of original painting unknown.

cf. *The Home Team*, 1903, and *Shall I? / Whose Turn First*, 1910, in which the roses are similar.

Colour photolithograph, 14½ins x 21ins (37cm x 54cm), probably a calendar. Image trimmed at the bottom removing signature and date to disguise later use. **See page 70**.

Love at First Sight *signed and dated 1907*

Oil on canvas, 42ins x 56ins (107cm x 143cm).

The same boy in the white outfit and feathered hat features in *His First Shot*, 1903, and *Not Caught Yet*, 1906. Elsley loved the countryside and painted landscapes for pleasure. The background is taken from one he painted at Broxbourne, Hertfordshire, signed and dated 1901. It was sold at the Studio Sale (Lot 17).

Modern colour print entitled *Love at First Sight* published by Felix Rosenstiel's Widow & Son.

Sepia photogravure, copyright Louis Wolff, 1904. Also reproduced as a crystoleum. **See page 75**.

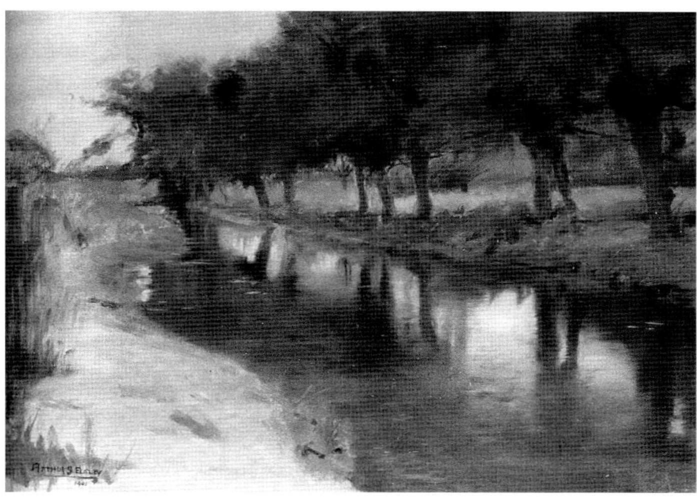

Broxbourne, Hertfordshire, 1901.

Jump Up / Bon Amis / Take Me Too / Jump In *signed and dated 1908*

Oil on canvas, 28¼ins x 44ins (72cm x 112cm).

When this painting was auctioned it was inscribed *Jump Up* on its original frame. This is an excellent study of a collie. Marjorie is pushing the wheelbarrow, and the seat was at the bottom of the garden outside Elsley's studio.

Sepia card (smaller than a postcard) entitled *Happy Days and Happy Hours*, c.1910.

Sepia photogravure, 14¼ins x 21ins (36cm x 54cm), published by Landeker & Brown, entitled *Jump In*. Medium size sepia photogravure published by Landeker & Brown, entitled *Bon Amis*. Small sepia photogravure, 8¾ins x 13¾ins (22cm x 35cm) presented with *Weldon's Bazaar of Children's Fashion*, Christmas 1908, wrongly called *Take Me Too*. There must have been confusion at Faulkners and somehow the titles of this and a Fred Morgan painting were transposed when licensed to Weldon's. This version shows slightly more of the image on both sides and slightly less of the leaves at the bottom right of the picture. Poor-quality colour chromolithograph, 17¾ins x 27¾ins (46cm x 71cm), probably a calendar, entitled *Jump In* and a poor-quality chromolithograph calendar for 1914, 15¾ins x 20¾ins (40cm x 53cm). The image has been closely trimmed and the signature and date removed. **See page 77**.

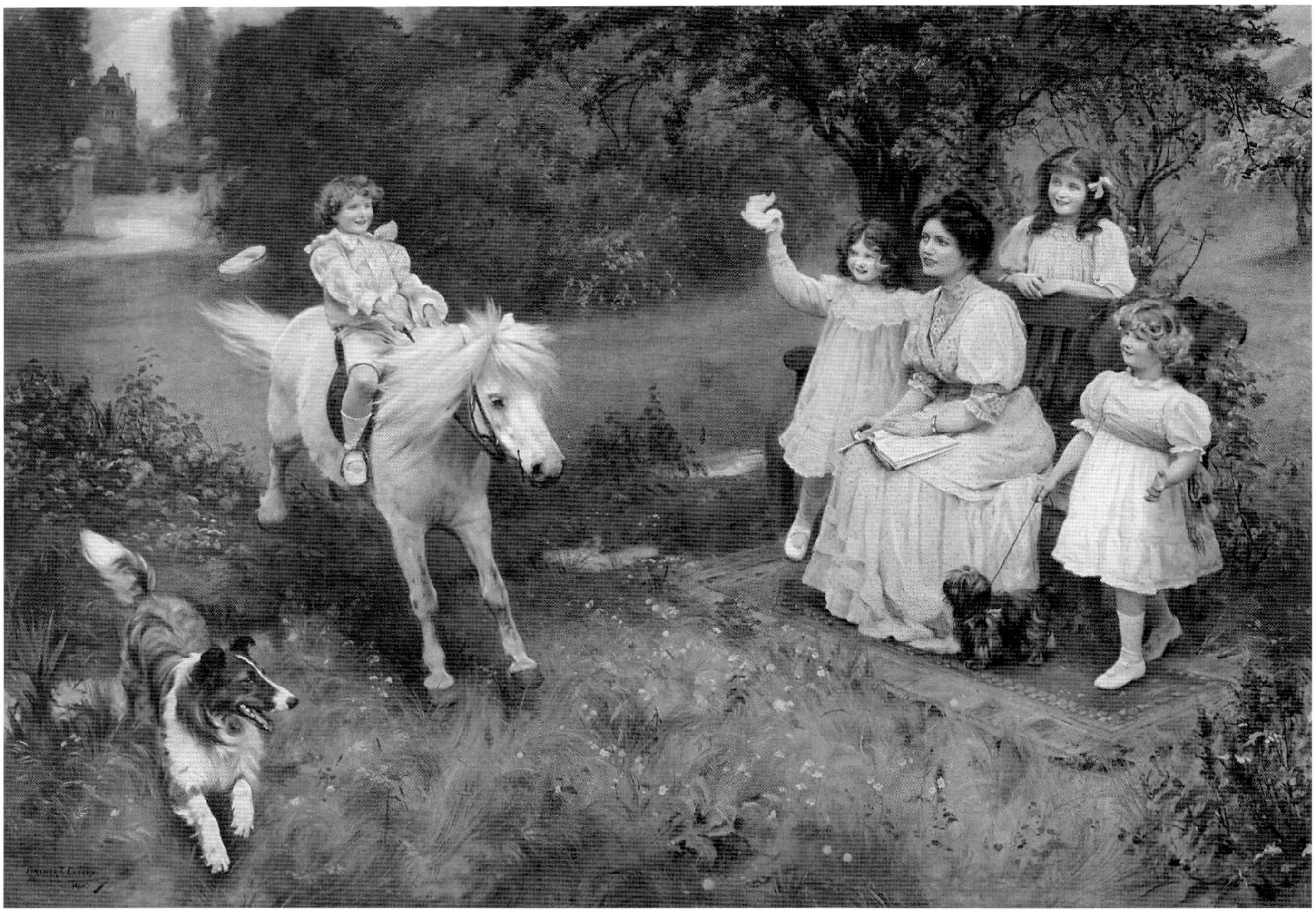

Well Done

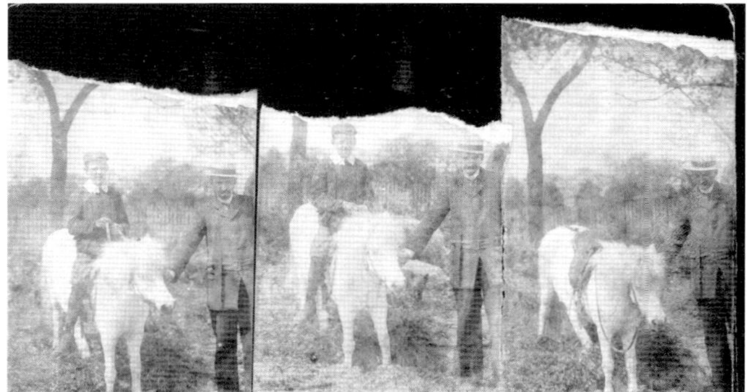

Source photograph for *Well Done*.

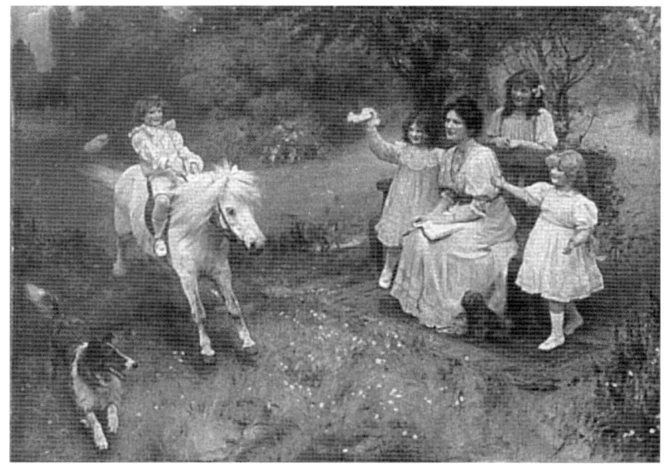

Photograph of unfinished *Well Done*.

Well Done *signed and dated 1907*

Oil on canvas, 42ins x 59ins (107cm x 151.5cm). Auctioned at Christie's on 19th December 1924, and was bought by Mitchell for 50 guineas.

Elsley was a keen photographer and took a series of three photographs of the pony. He showed sepia photographs of his works to potential publishers – Charles Faulkner, who purchased the copyright, (and also reproduced many of Fred Morgan's works) was well-known for suggesting changes to the paintings he published. A photograph of this work prior to completion differs in a few details. The waving handkerchief of the girl on the left has been changed; Scamp, the dog, is sitting down but in the completed version is standing; and the girl on the right is holding her hand outstretched but, in the completed version, she is holding the dog's leash.

Sepia photogravure, $19\frac{1}{4}$ins x $27\frac{1}{2}$ins (49.5cm x 70.5cm), issued by Bovril in 1907, copyright C.W. Faulkner.

A Faithful Guardian *signed and dated 1908*

Details of original painting unknown.

Elsley used his photographs of the St. Bernard and of the geese for this composition. Not to be confused with an American calendar *A Loyal Guardian*.

No print is recorded.

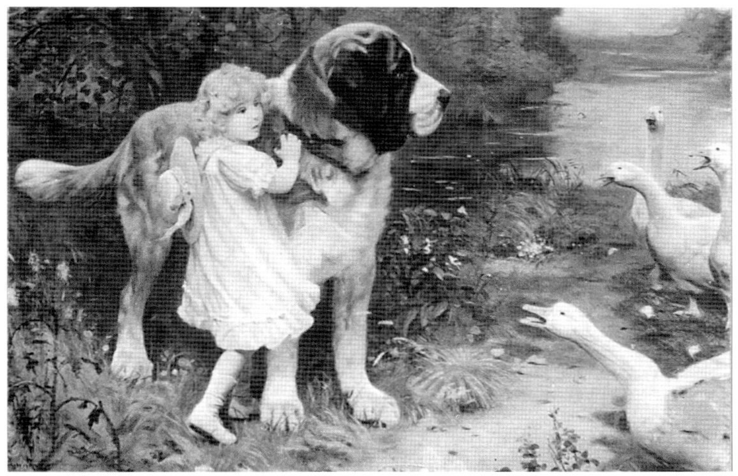

A *Faithful Guardian* with source photograph below.

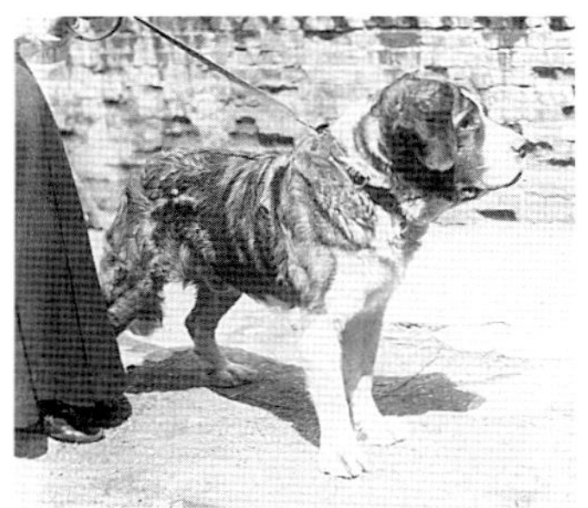

The First Love Letter *signed and dated 1908*

Details of original painting unknown. Exhibited at the Royal Academy, 1908 (No.548), and was unsold.

The children in the background are playing Diabolo, which was the latest craze introduced in 1907. The game literally means "the devil-on-two-sticks".

Sepia photogravure, $20\frac{1}{2}$ins x $27\frac{1}{2}$ins (52cm x 70.5cm), copyright Louis Wolff 1908.

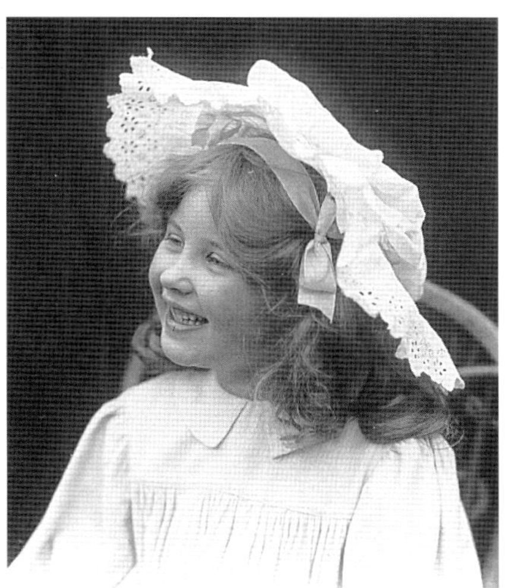

Source photograph of Marjorie, *The First Love Letter.*

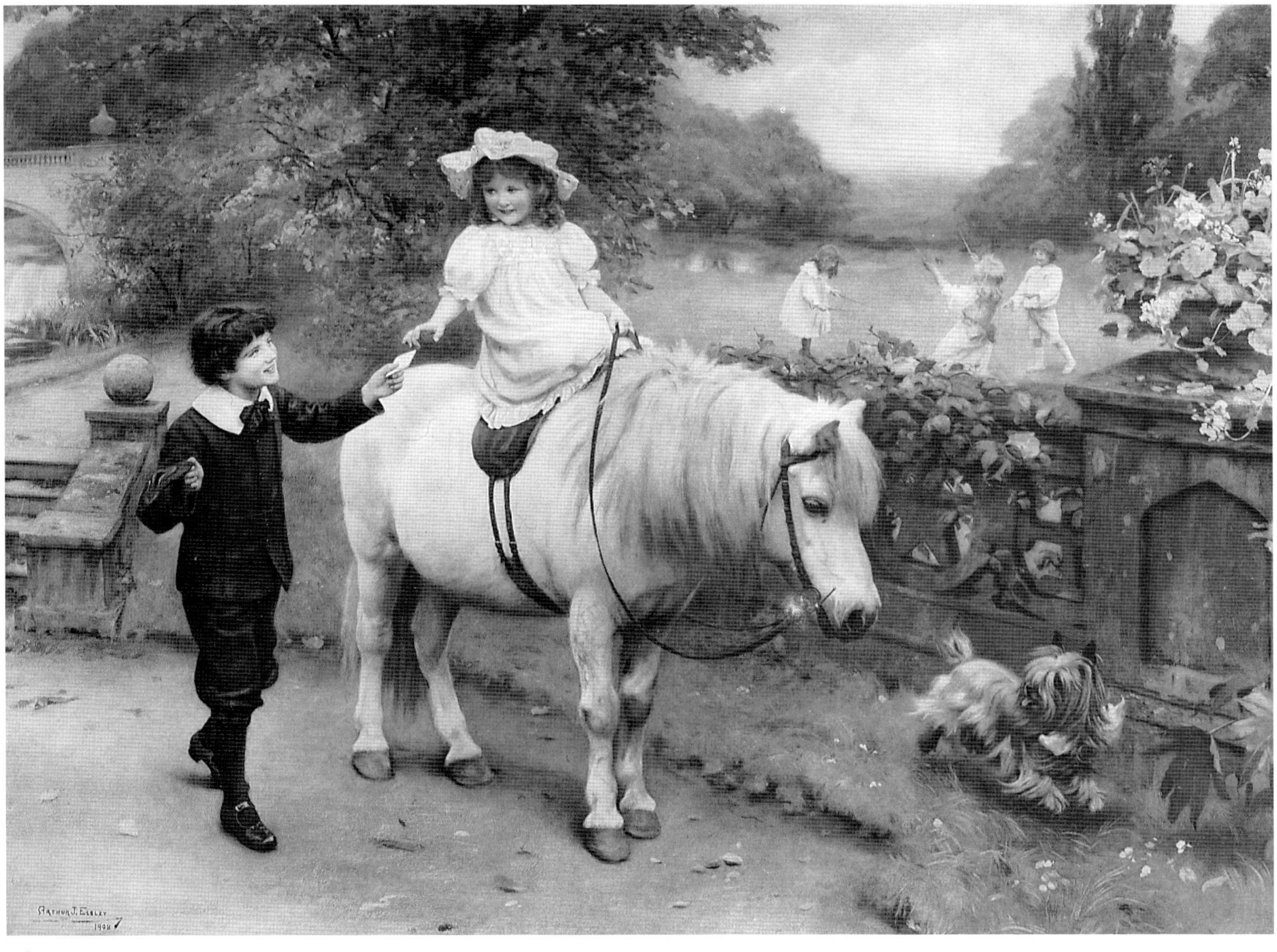

The First Love Letter

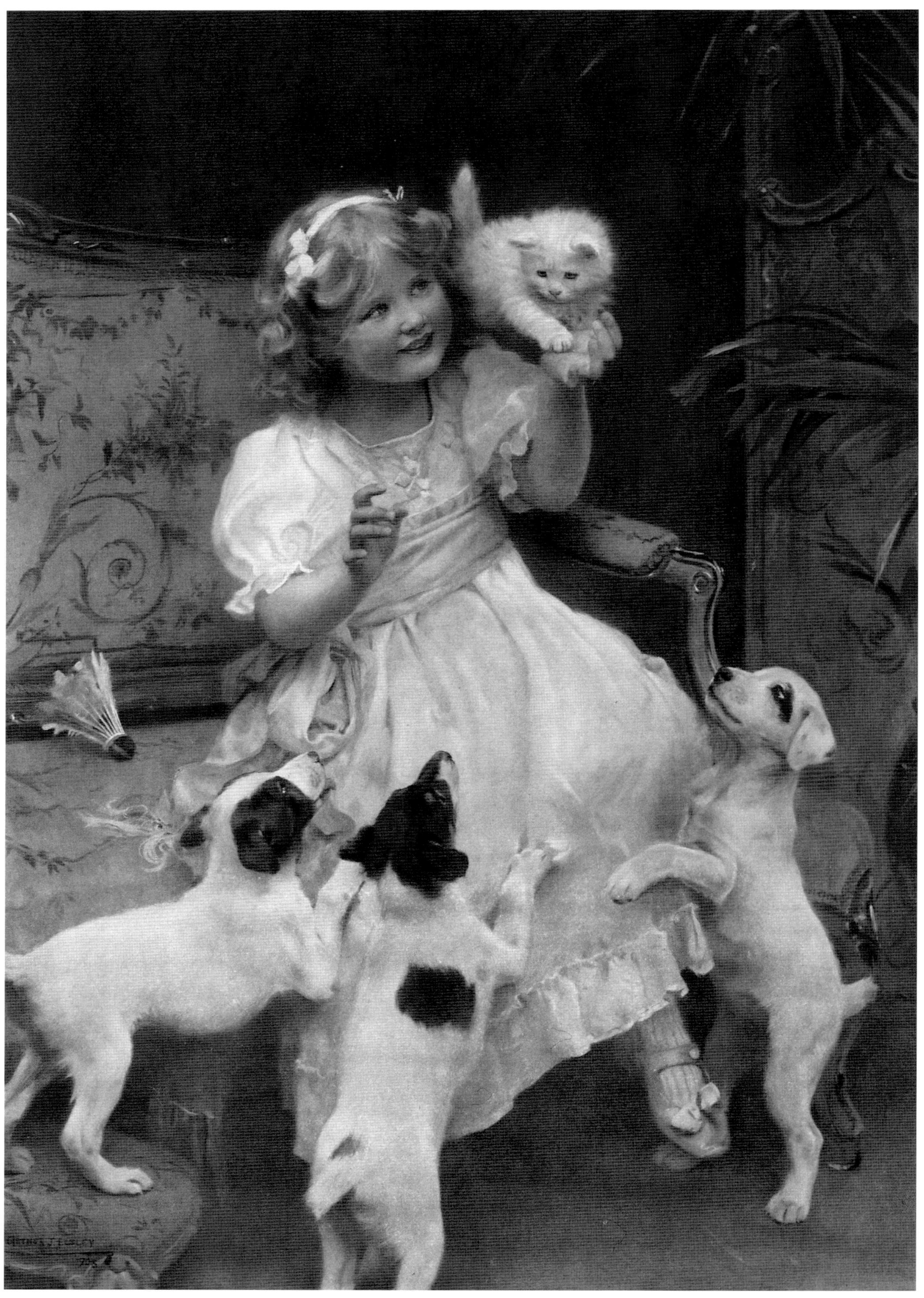

Out Of Reach

Out Of Reach *signed and dated 1908*

Oil on canvas, 36ins x 25¼ins (91.5cm x 64.5cm).

Marjorie again features in this work.

Sepia photogravure, 20¾ins x 14¼ins (53cm x 36cm), presented with *The Queen, The Lady's Newspaper*, Christmas 1908. Small colour photolithograph presented with the first issue of *Cassells Family Circle*.

Pick Of The Litter / The Huntsman's Pet *signed and dated 1908*

Details of original painting unknown. Exhibited at Liverpool, Autumn 1908 (No.1043), entitled *Pick Of The Litter*, price £150, copyright already reserved. Not to be confused with a print entitled *Favourite Of The Litter*, 1905.

Elsley took a photograph of four people wearing fancy dress in his studio, including one in a huntsman's outfit. In his address book he noted "The Artists Costume Supply" at 13 Upper Phillmore Place, Kensington. He also noted a model, G.F. Riches of 161 Purves Road, Willesden, as having a huntsman's costume.

Sepia photogravure, 20ins x 15ins (51cm x 38cm), called *The Huntsman's Pet*, issued by Bovril in July 1908, copyright C.W. Faulkner. Also reproduced as a sepia photogravure, 18¼ins x 15ins (47cm x 38cm), copyright unknown with the title *The Huntsman's Pet* printed on the bottom right of this version.

He Won't Hurt You *circa 1908*

Details of original painting unknown.

Features Marjorie in a similar pose to *Out Of Reach*, 1908, with a collie and black kitten.

American colour calendar manufactured by Thos. D. Murphy Co., 1909. **See page 86.**

Hide And Seek *signed and dated 1908*

Oil on canvas, 36ins x 28ins (91.5cm x 71.5cm).

Ships carrying produce from the U.S.A. had spare capacity for the return journey and the economic recession in Britain created difficulties for artists when selling their paintings at home. The cheap freight charges encouraged many artists and dealers to seek patrons across the Atlantic. Elsley found a ready market with the United States calendar manufacturer Thos. D. Murphy Co., who bought this work and numerous others. Ironically, Murphy employed representatives to sell their reproductions in Britain prior to the Great War.

American colour calendar entitled *Hide and Seek* manufactured by Thos. D. Murphy Co., 1910 and 1926.

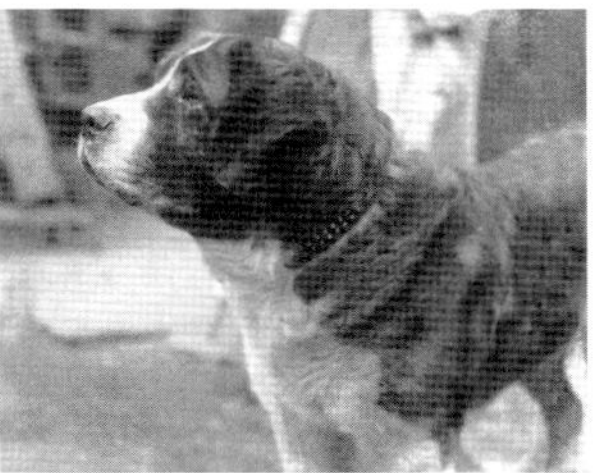

Source photograph for *Hide And Seek*.

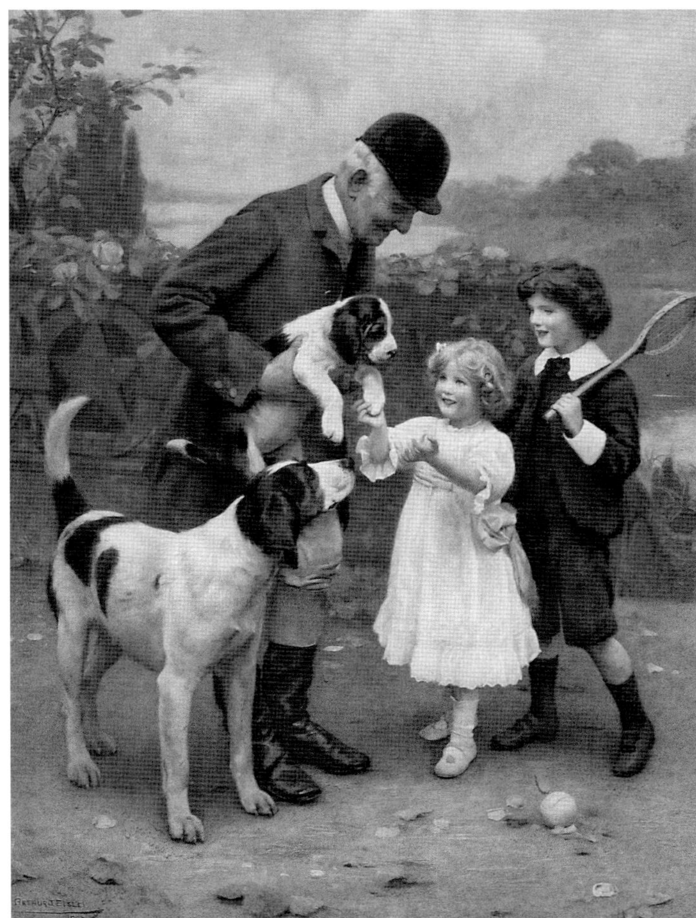

Pick Of The Litter / The Huntsman's Pet

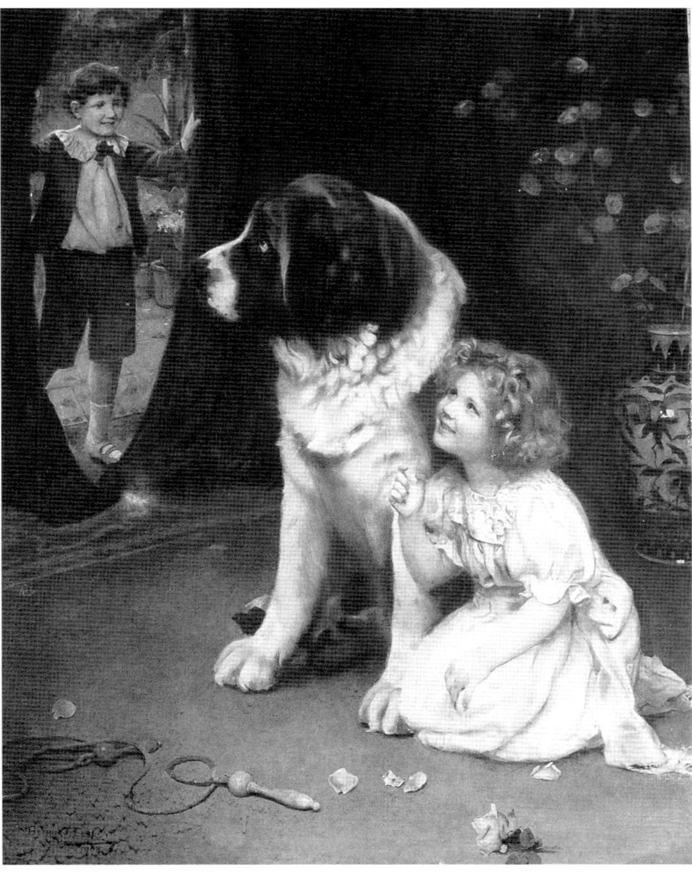

Hide And Seek

[Title Unknown] *circa 1908*

Details of original painting unknown.

This painting is on an easel in Elsley's studio during one of his photography sessions with Miss Mumford's St. Bernard (**see page 119**), and it pre-dates her move to Sandgate, Kent in 1909. The girl sitting in an armchair was nicknamed 'Queenie' (after Queen Alexandra). She is reading a book whilst watching over a baby in a cradle. On the other side is a St. Bernard also keeping watch.

No print recorded.

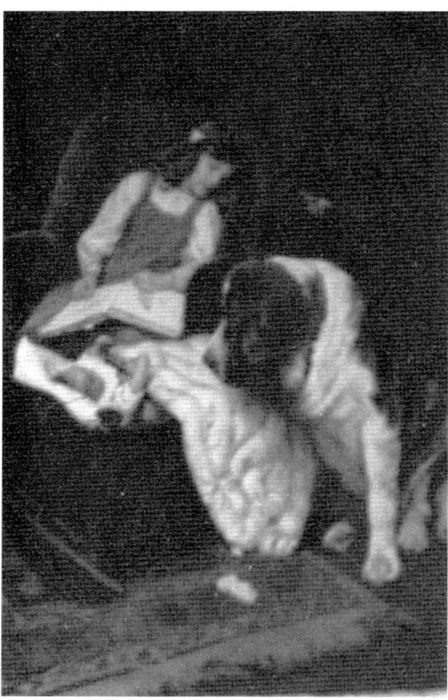

[Title Unknown]

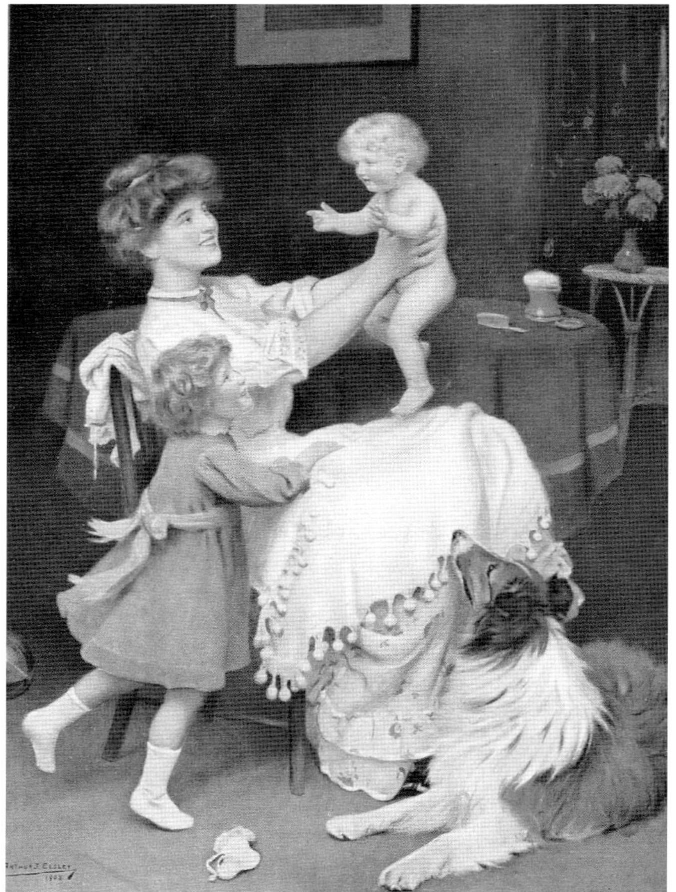

Mother's Treasure

Mother's Treasure *signed and dated 1908*

Details of original painting unknown.

"Specially painted from life for the proprietors of Neave's Food" printed on blotter, 10½ins x 8ins (26.5cm x 20.5cm), with calendar for 1910. Neave's Food was for infants, invalids, growing children and the elderly. Sold in tins and packets it was manufactured by Josiah R. Neave & Co., Fordingbridge, England. Not to be confused with *Mother's Treasures*, 1911.

Baby's Bath Time *circa 1908*

Oil on canvas, 40ins x 28ins (102cm x 71.5cm), signed not dated. Almost certainly Christie's, London (Art Sales Index 1931/2).

Mother and naked baby are the same models as in *Mother's Treasure*, 1908. Marjorie (left of bath), is the mirror image to *Hide and Seek*, 1908. The startled terrier is a mirror image, similar to the one in the *Ivy Soap Advertisement* painted in 1897.

Not to be confused with *The Ivy Soap Advertisement*, 1897, or *Before the Bath*, 1900.

No print recorded.

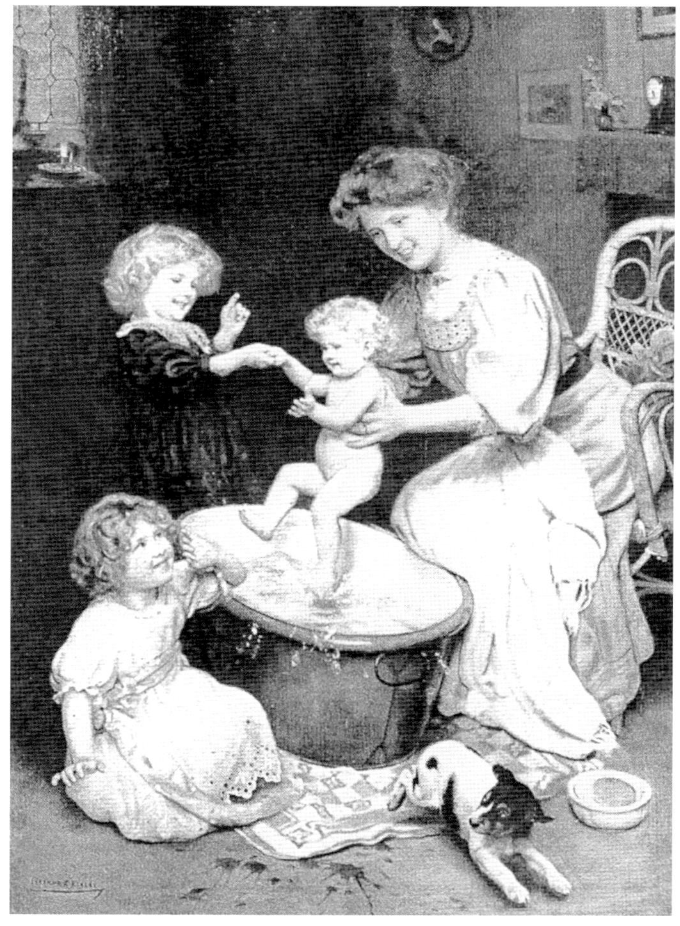

Baby's Bath Time

Look Out *signed and dated 1908*

Details of original painting unknown.

This work pre-dates *The Rescue Party,* 1909, and was possibly painted at Folkestone. The Scottie is a different dog to the usual breeds, and appears again in *As Good As Ever,* 1912. It was at about this time that Emily, Elsley's mother, died when Marjorie was five years old.

Colour photolithograph on slightly textured paper, 9ins x 12ins (23cm x 30.5cm), presented with *The Sunday Companion*, Summer No. 1913. **See page 76.**

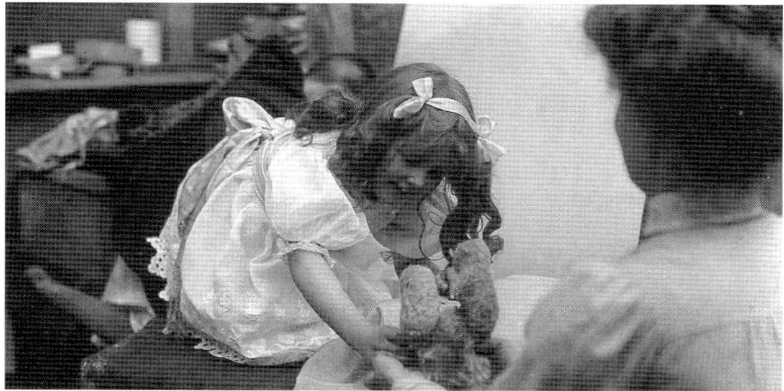

Marjorie and Emm in the studio, source photograph for *There's Room For You.*

There's Room For You / Room For One More *signed and dated 1909*

Details of original painting unknown. Exhibited at the Royal Academy, 1909 (No.271), entitled *There's Room For You* and was unsold.

Marjorie was photographed reaching forward to grab a cuddly toy from her mother. In the painting she is now reaching for a puppy.

Not to be confused with *Any Room For Me*, 1897, *Room For One More*, 1910, or *There's Room For You*, 1920 (22).

Sepia photogravure, 24ins x 15½ins (61.5cm x 39.5cm), presented with *The Illustrated London News,* Christmas 1910, entitled *Room For One More.* Sepia photogravure, 12¾ins x 9ins (32.5cm x 23cm), presented with *Home Fashion*, Christmas 1915, now called *There's Room For One More.* The title was possibly changed to avoid confusion with a 1910 painting reproduced as an American calendar in 1913.

Finishing Touches *signed and dated 1909*

Oil on canvas, 35ins x 25½ins (89cm x 65.5cm). Almost certainly auctioned at Christie's, London, on 21st June 1935 entitled *The Pet Dog,* and bought by Waters for 4 guineas.

The show dog arrived at the studio with its hair, which Elsley was very careful to avoid getting into knots, neatly plaited in ribbons.

Colour front cover Ward Lock & Co.'s *Wonder Book, A Picture Annual for Boys and Girls* (published 1917), called *Finishing Touches.*

Medium size sepia photogravure (size and publication unknown). Colour chromolithograph, 20½ins x 15ins (52cm x 38cm), calendar print 1911. **See page 78.**

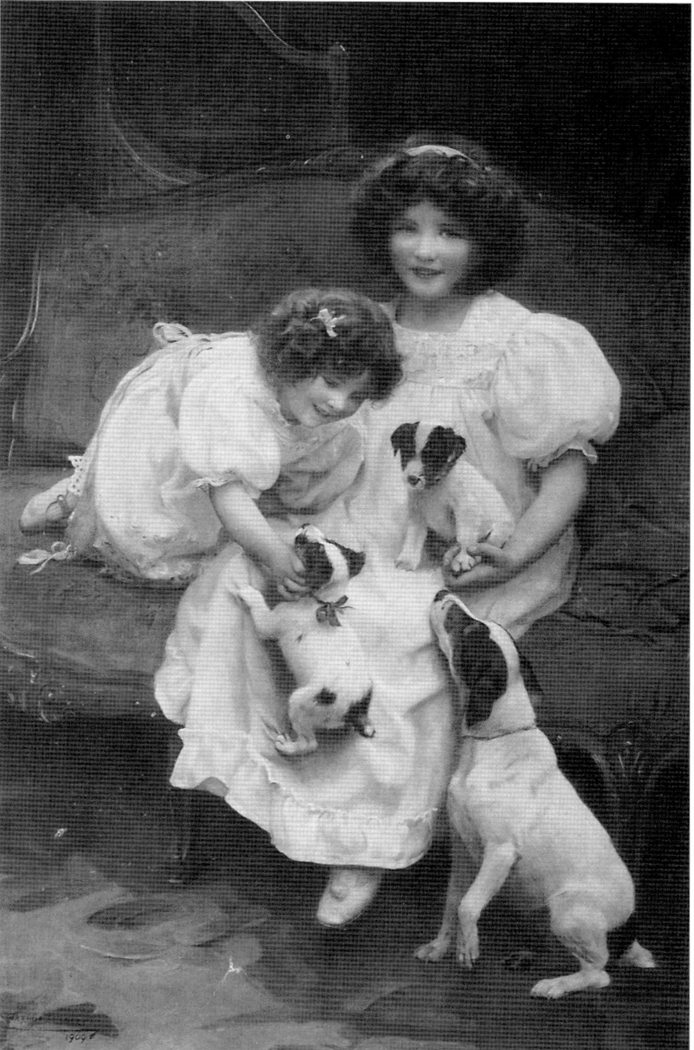

There's Room For You / Room For One More

God Bless Daddy *signed and dated 1909*

Details of original painting unknown.

This picture and *Mother's Darling* are unusual as neither feature animals.

Colour chromolithograph calendar, 23¾ins x 18ins (61cm x 46.5cm), for The Queen Tea Co., (produced as a pair with *Mother's Darling*, 1909).

This is a very rare print. **See page 78.**

Mother's Darling *signed and dated 1909*

Details of original painting unknown.

Printed on blotter, 10½ins x 8ins (26.5cm x 20.5cm), with 1913 calendar for Neave's Food who had earlier published *Mother's Treasure*, 1908, for their 1910 blotter.

Colour chromolithograph, 24ins x 17¾ins (61.5cm x 46cm), 1914 calendar for Frisby's Boot Co. The title *Mother's Darling* is printed bottom right on the image. Also reproduced as a calendar for The Queen Tea Co., where the title appears below the picture. **See page 78.**

A Broken Melody *signed and dated 1909*

Oil on canvas, 37ins x 27ins (94.5cm x 69cm).

The painting was auctioned at Christie's, London, 27th November 1931. It was the property of the late Sir Edward Sharp, Bart and was bought by the London dealer W.W. Sampson for 14 guineas.

Elsley's painting was based on Charles Burton Barber's 1887 work entitled *The Lost Chord* which was reproduced as a chromolithograph print by *The Illustrated London News* in 1896 and re-named *Symphony*.

From an early age Marjorie excelled at her music lessons and went on to graduate from The Royal College of Music, whilst also attending the St John's Wood Art School. This led to a career in teaching both these subjects and she played the piano into her late eighties and enjoyed painting until her death.

Sepia photogravure, 12½ins x 9½ins (32cm x 24cm), presented with *Weldon's Bazaar of Children's Fashion*, December 1910, called *A Broken Melody*. It was reproduced as a companion to *Full Inside*, 1899, presented with *Weldon's Illustrated Dressmaker* of the same date. Colour photolithograph page illustrating "The Child and His Dumb Friends" by Laurence North in *The Windsor Magazine*, December 1911, p.177, now called *Chorus Gentlemen!* **See page 78.**

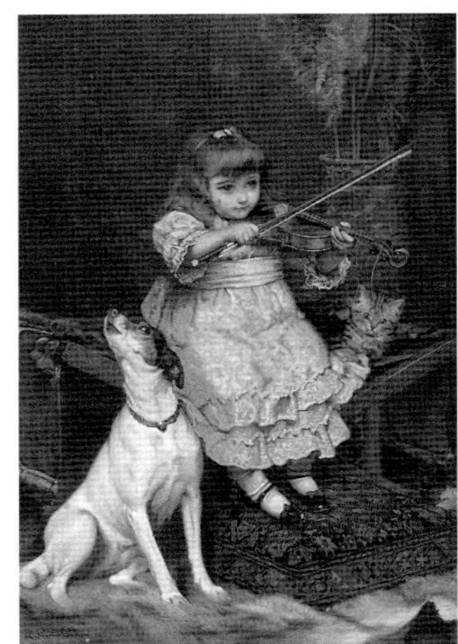

The Lost Chord, 1887, by Charles Burton Barber.

The Rescue Party *signed and dated 1909*

Details of original painting unknown.

When Marjorie was six years old, she suffered from glandular fever. Miss Mumford, the owner of the St. Bernard featured in *Never Mind!*, 1907, had moved from Woodford to run The Bevan Nursing Home at 6 Devonshire Terrace, Sandgate, Near Folkestone, Kent. In October the Elsley family went to Sandgate while Marjorie was convalescing, and during this time he painted the work. Incidentally, Miss Mumford was the first female constable in the First World War.

The girls are 'Queenie' and Marjorie but the boy hasn't been identified. The St. Bernard substitutes for the donkey traditionally used for children's rides on the beach. This composition returns to Elsley's much earlier style of windswept hair (e.g. *Here's Father*, 1894) and follows on from *Look Out!*, 1908. Modern postcard printed by The Medici Society. Unrecorded as a print.

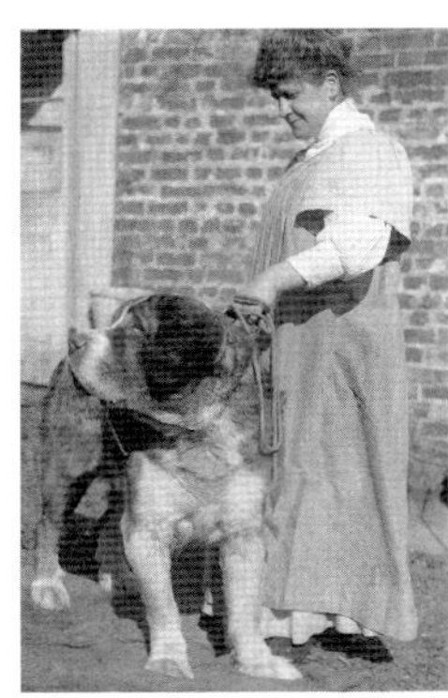

Source photograph of Miss Mumford with her St. Bernard, *The Rescue Party*.

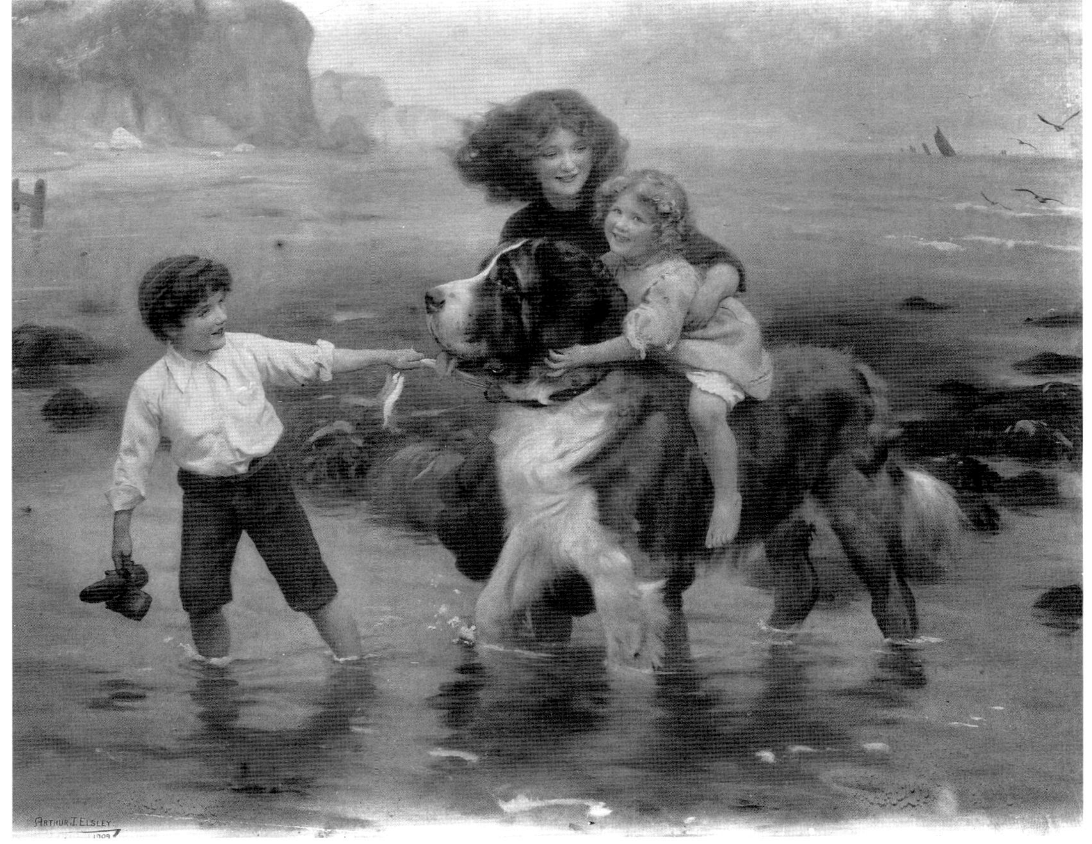

The Rescue Party

Wake Up It's Christmas Morning

signed and dated 1909

Oil on canvas, 34ins x $25\frac{1}{2}$ins (86.5cm x 65.5cm).

This work is painted with great affection and has lovely touches, particularly the peacock feather in the hat. The older girl is Queenie of whom a head and shoulders oil sketch, $9\frac{1}{2}$ins x $7\frac{1}{4}$ins (24cm x 18.5cm), hung in the Elsley home until the Studio Sale (Lot 21). She married an American at the end of the First World War, and went to live in the United States. Marjorie's bed was taken into the studio so that her father could paint it. An oil on canvas study, 19ins x 25ins (49cm x 64cm), signed and dated 1909, showed Marjorie asleep in bed. The painting was kept by Marjorie until some confidence tricksters tried to steal it from her in the early 1980s. She then decided to auction it at Sotheby's, London, on 1st October 1986 (Lot 378). It was given the title *Fitful Slumber.* **See page 83.** 'Queenie' and Marjorie also appear together in an unfinished painting with Marjorie holding a doll.

Charles Burton Barber featured a similar theme in his work *The Morning Call (Le Reveil Matin)*, c.1883. Elsley's contemporary, Maude Goodman, painted a similar work entitled *Santa Claus* in 1901. 'Queenie' is positioned over the sleeping child like Santa Claus in the popular poster for Tom Smith Christmas Crackers first used in 1906.

Colour photolithograph in contemporary magazine called *Our Darling's Birthday Morning.* Colour photolithograph page called *Wake Up!*, used to illustrate Jessie Pope's article "The Children's Season" in *The Windsor Magazine*, December 1910. Modern print published by Stephen Selby Collection.

Sepia photogravure, $20\frac{1}{2}$ins x 16ins (52cm x 40.5cm), presented with *The Illustrated London News*, Christmas 1911, by permission of Berlin Photographic.

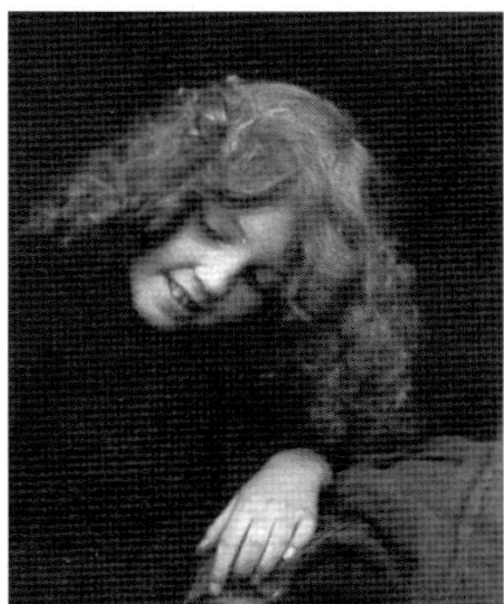

Photograph of 'Queenie'.

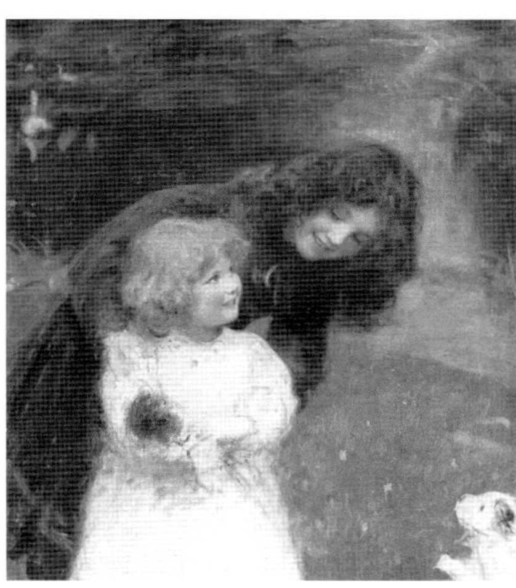

Unfinished painting of 'Queenie' and Marjorie.

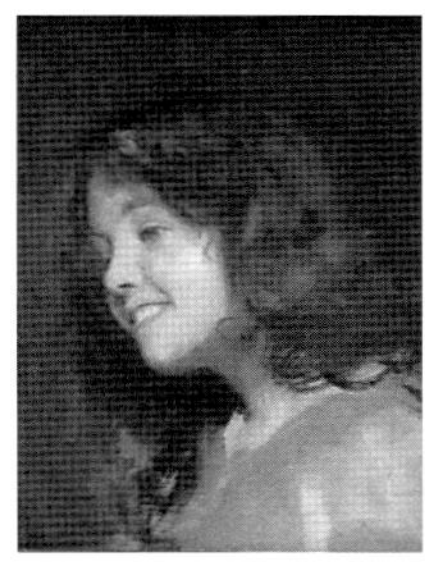

Painting of 'Queenie'.

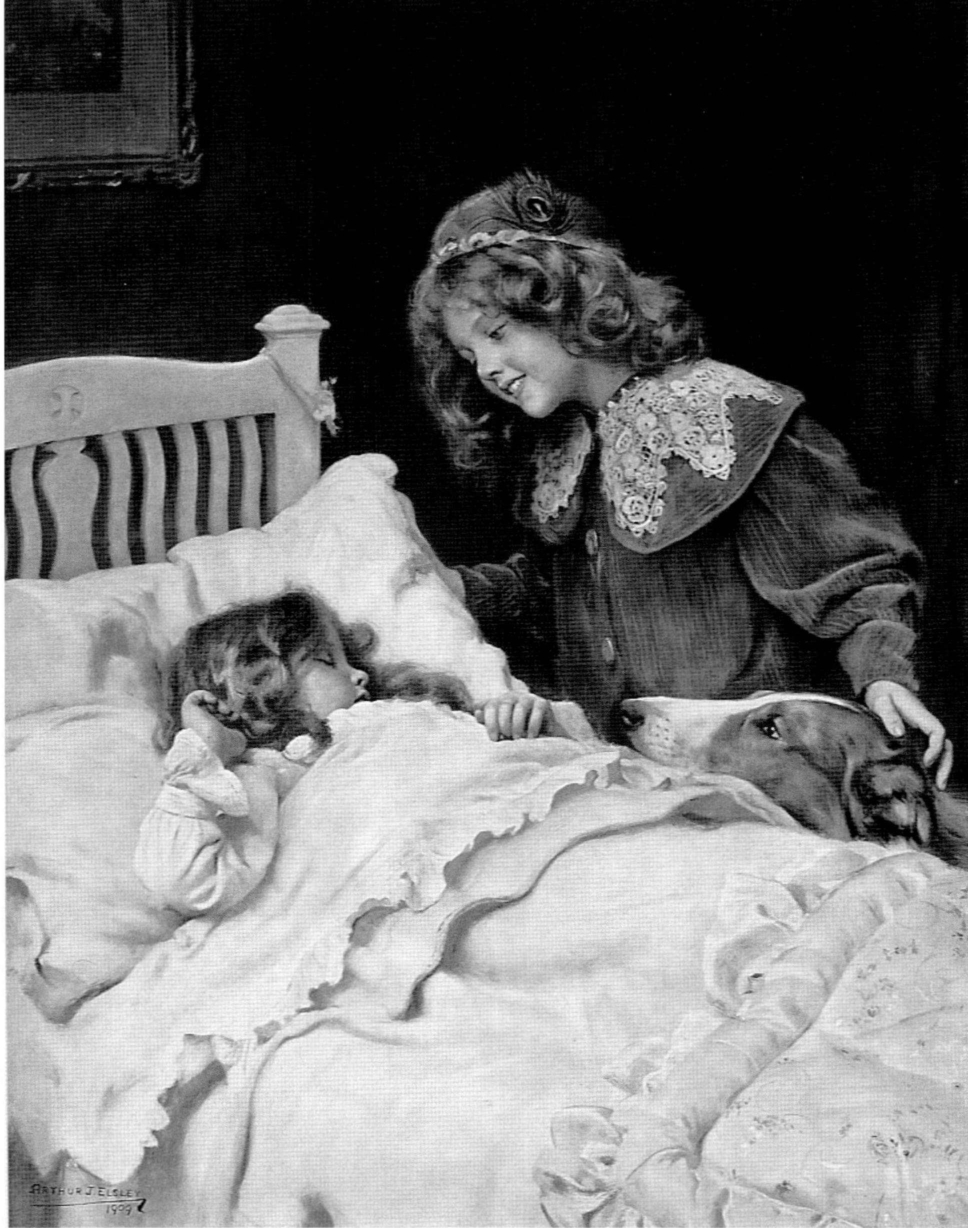

Wake Up It's Christmas Morning

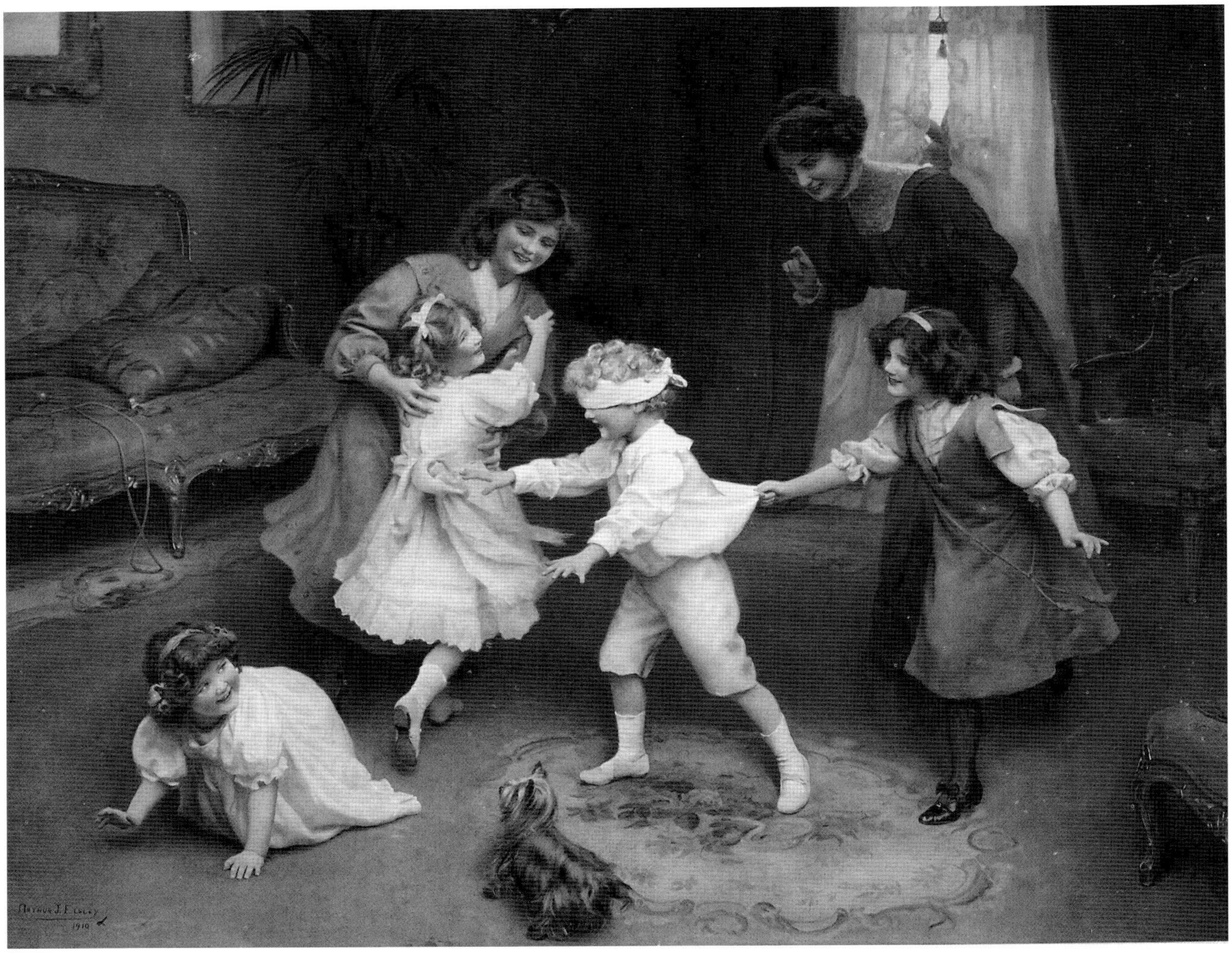

Blind Man's Buff

Blind Man's Buff *signed and dated 1910*

Details of original painting unknown. Exhibited at the Royal Academy, 1910 (No.746), and was unsold.

One of Elsley's many parties for Marjorie inspired this work. This popular children's game was painted by many artists in the early nineteenth century, including Sir David Wilkie, R.A. Fred Morgan's Royal Academy exhibit in 1898 entitled *Sunshine of His Heart* was of a grandfather playing the game with a group of children.

As a little girl Marjorie had to turn the corners of the prints so her father could sign the Artist's proofs, sometimes up to 250 copies. In an interview "Mr Dendy Sadler At Play", *Cassell's Magazine*, November 1897, p.583, the popular artist said it was the custom for the painter to sign proof prints on selling the copyright to a publisher:

> "He, in return, presents the artist with six artist's proofs...very often he is only too glad to buy them back when there is a very successful issue. ...sometimes this has to be done at very awkward times; but there, it is all a part of the business."

Black and white photograph, *Royal Academy Pictures*, 1910, p.160.

Sepia photogravure, 20¼ins x 25ins (51.5cm x 64cm), produced by Bovril in 1910, copyright C.W. Faulkner.

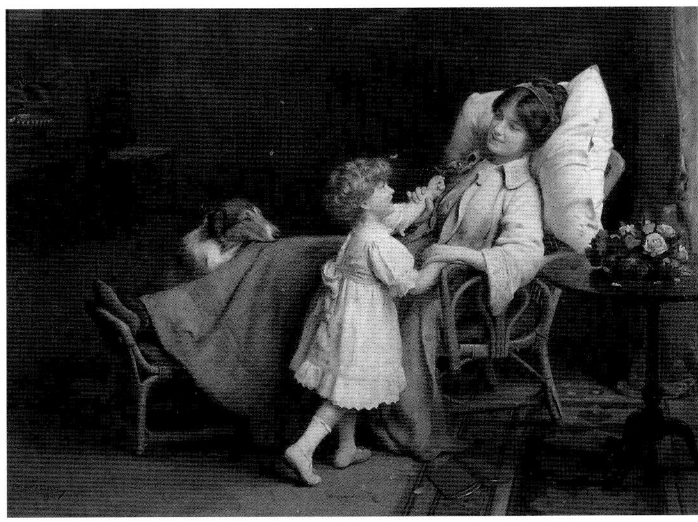

Well On The Mend

Well On The Mend *signed and dated 1910*

Oil on canvas, 36ins x 24ins (91.5cm x 61.5cm).

Reproduced as a colour advertising show-card for Wincarnis, the Great Health Restorer.

Home Again *signed and dated 1910*
Oil on canvas, 42½ins x 29½ins (108.5cm x 75.5cm). Owned by Haynes Fine Art in 1992.

Prior to the birth of Marjorie, Elsley kept a collie. The model for this painting was owned by a Miss Watson. It had been lost and its return, with a rope tied around its neck, inspired this work.

Not to be confused with *Home Again / The Home Coming*, 1900. Colour photolithograph page in *The Windsor Magazine*.

Sepia photogravure, 20½ins x 14¼ins (52cm x 36cm), presented with *The Queen Newspaper*, December 1910, copyright C.W. Faulkner. **See page 79**.

Shall I? / Whose Turn First? *signed and dated 1910*
Details of original oil unknown. Now owned by Haussner's Restaurant, Baltimore, U.S.A.

The collie's head was painted from the same photograph used for *You Mustn't Touch*, c.1897.

Sepia photogravure, 17½ins x 24ins (45cm x 61cm), copyright Hildershiemer 1910, entitled *Shall I?* (this print is not signed and dated). Sepia photogravure presented with *The Illustrated London News*, Christmas 1912, now called *Whose Turn First?* **See page 77**.

Room For One More *signed and dated 1910*
Details of original painting unknown.

A St. Bernard on the riverbank, a boy sheltering under umbrella and Marjorie with outstretched hand. Not to be confused with a painting of the same title, 1909.

American colour calendar manufactured by Thos. D. Murphy Co., 1913.

Little Sister / [possibly Safe Across]
signed and dated 1910
Details of original painting unknown.

'Queenie' helps Marjorie walk across a stream on a gangplank with a St. Bernard walking alongside them in the stream.

St. Bernard's were a particularly popular breed in America at this period and this may have been produced for the American market only. Possibly *Safe Across* an American colour calendar manufactured by Thos. D. Murphy Co. 1929, and 1931.

Unrecorded as a print.

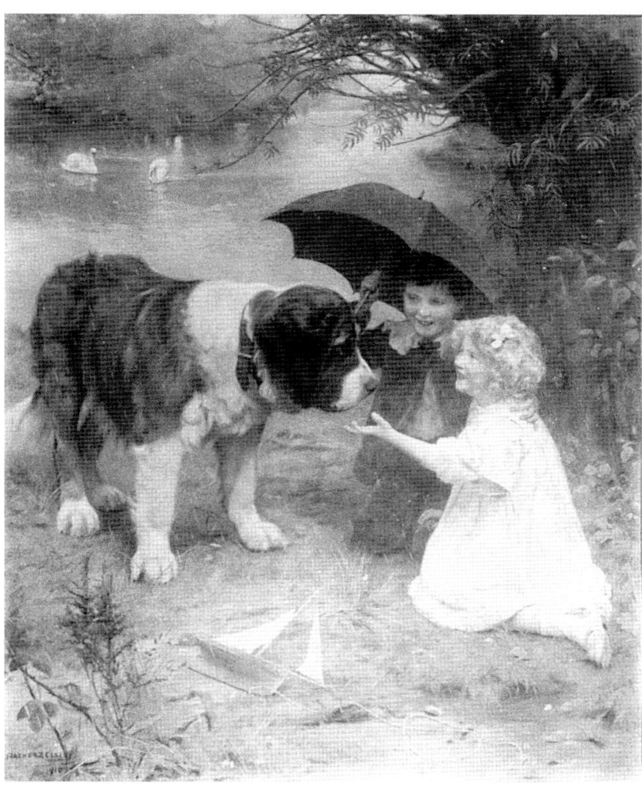

Room For One More

Source photograph for *Room For One More.*

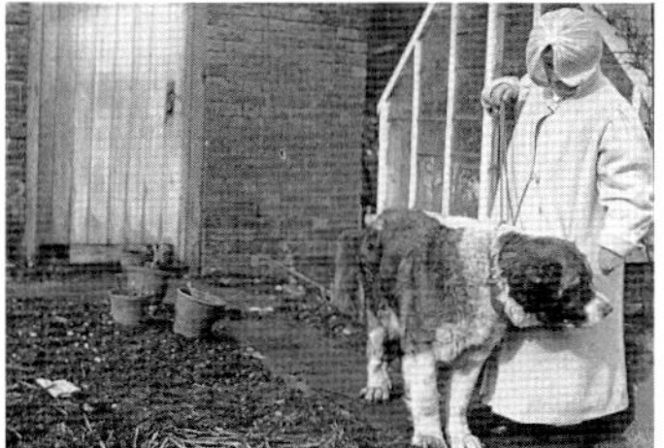

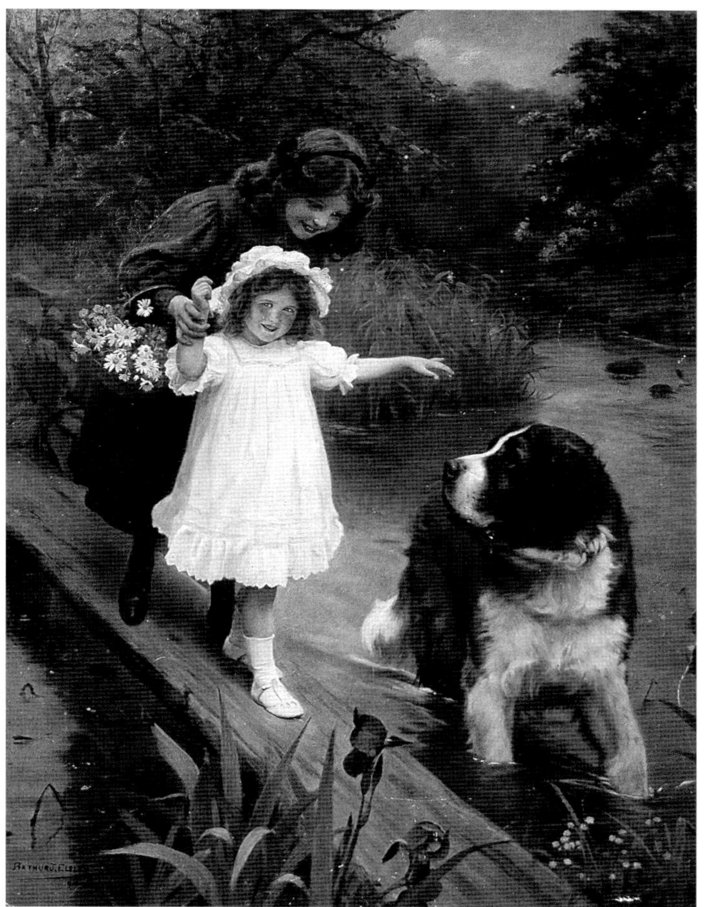

Little Sister

Her Morning Ride / [possibly Safe Across]

signed and dated 1911

Details of original painting unknown.

Two boys with a collie are guiding a handcart across a stream which is carrying the two girls featured in *Little Sister*. This is the third painting in 1910 and 1911 to feature rivers and streams. See also *Crossing The Stream*, signed and dated 1920. Elsley painted landscapes for pleasure and incorporated them in these works.

Maybe produced for the American market only, possibly called *Safe Across*, an American colour calendar manufactured by Thos. D. Murphy Co. 1929 and 1931.

Small colour photolithograph magazine page entitled *Her Morning Ride*, publication and date unknown, possibly *The Windsor Magazine*.

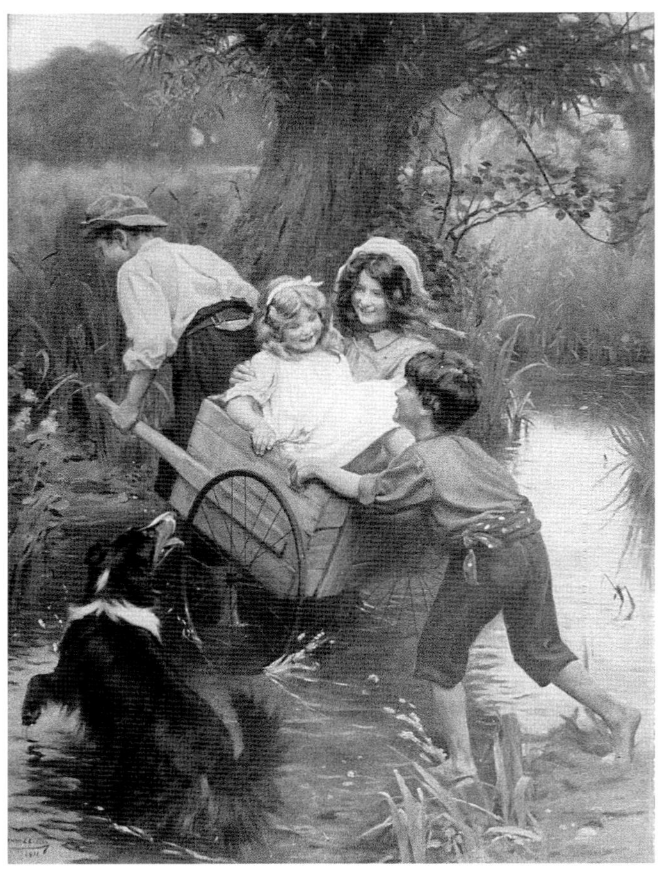

Her Morning Ride

Mother's Treasures *signed and dated 1911*

Details of original painting unknown.

This picture includes a print of Elsley's *Little Bo Peep*, 1900, hanging on the wall. A black and white photograph of the unfinished work shows the mother's dress has a different pattern and there is a rocking horse to her left.

Not to be confused with *Mother's Treasure*, 1908. Small colour page in *The Windsor Magazine*, c.1912.

Sepia photogravure, $20^{1}/_{4}$ins x $15^{1}/_{4}$ins (51.5cm x 39cm), presented with *The Queen Newspaper*, Christmas 1911, copyright C.W. Faulkner & Co. (the image on the print has been trimmed to exclude the rocking horse).

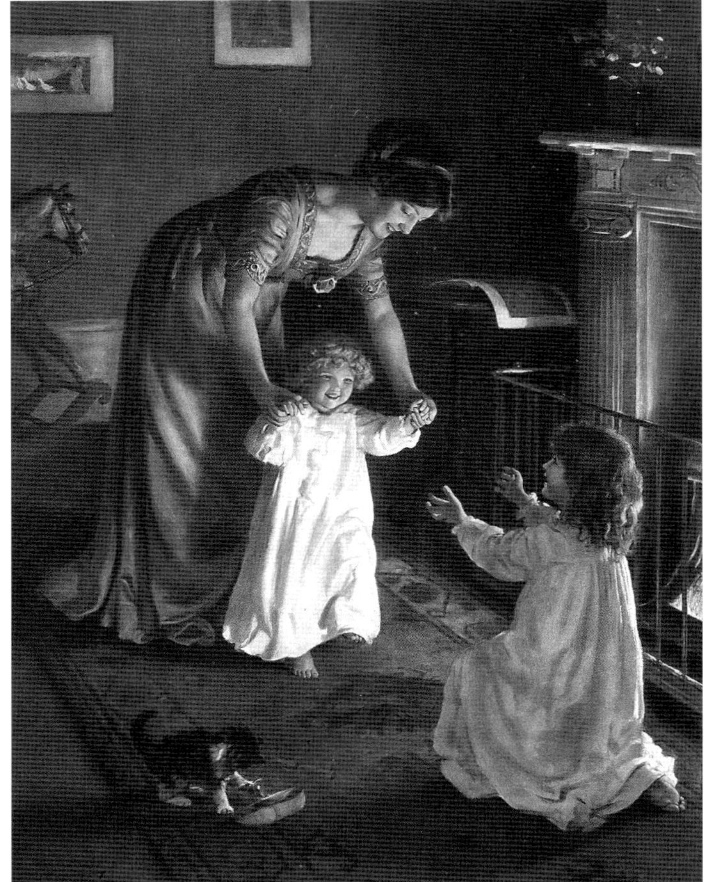

Mother's Treasures

Goodnight *signed and dated 1911*

Oil on canvas, 39ins x $28^{1}/_{2}$ins (99.5cm x 73cm). Auctioned in New York, 1992. Provenance: Thos. D. Murphy Company, Red Oak, Iowa (purchased directly from the artist for use as a calendar) (until 1913); Mr. R. T. Ballard, Helena, Montana (by 1913); Mr. and Mrs. Orton, Butte, Montana, bequeathed to Virginia O. Rickman (until 1991). Estate of Virginia O. Rickman, bequeathed to a friend (1991), who donated it as a gift to a Montana Foundation.

Extract from *The Antiques Trade Gazette*, 14 March 1992, p.32:

> "...none providing more excitement than Arthur John Elsley's *Goodnight*, a typical piece of high Victorian genre painting (even though painted in 1911), which shattered the previous auction best...the subject is the main attraction, the little girl in her night-gown being taken upstairs to bed, pausing at their foot to say goodnight to the family St. Bernard and two pups."

Not to be confused with the 1913 and 1914 works of the same title.

American colour calendar manufactured by Thos. D. Murphy Co. 1914, 1916, and 1927. **See page 81.**

Rescued *signed and dated 1911*

Details of original painting unknown.

Marjorie illustrates her article in *This England*, Winter 1981, with a photograph of this work. She calls it *Orphan from the Storm* and describes it as "a new-born lamb is brought by the shepherd to his cottage fireside and the loving welcome of his children".

The model for the shepherd was Mr. Gooderam of 19 Henstridge Place, London. Elsley again uses fire to light the work as in *Snapdragon* c.1895, *Mother's Treasures* 1911, and *Fireside Joys* c.1913. The previous work to feature lambs was *Motherly Care* 1895.

Colour chromolithograph, 23¾ins x 17½ins (61cm x 45cm), Frisby's Boot Co., 1915 calendar. The title *Rescued* is printed bottom left on the image. **See page 80.**

The Joy Of Spring *signed and dated 1911*

Oil on canvas, 37ins x 47ins (94.5cm x 120cm).

This work is a follow-up to *Rescued*, showing the orphaned lamb with the children the following Spring.

Sepia photogravure, 15ins x 20ins (38cm x 51cm), issued by Bovril in 1911, copyright C.W. Faulkner.

This Little Pig Went To Market *circa 1911*

Possibly the oil painting, 37½ins x 27ins (95.5cm x 69cm), sold at Christie's, London, on 1st August 1930. Uncertain whether this or c.1901 version.

This picture features Marjorie, aged eight or nine, with her governess, Miss Gomersall, and an unknown baby. Elsley photographed the baby sitting on her mother's lap in his studio. Not to be confused with the work of the same title, c.1901.

Sepia photogravure, 12¾ins x 9ins (32.5cm x 23cm), presented with *Mother and Home*, Christmas 1915.

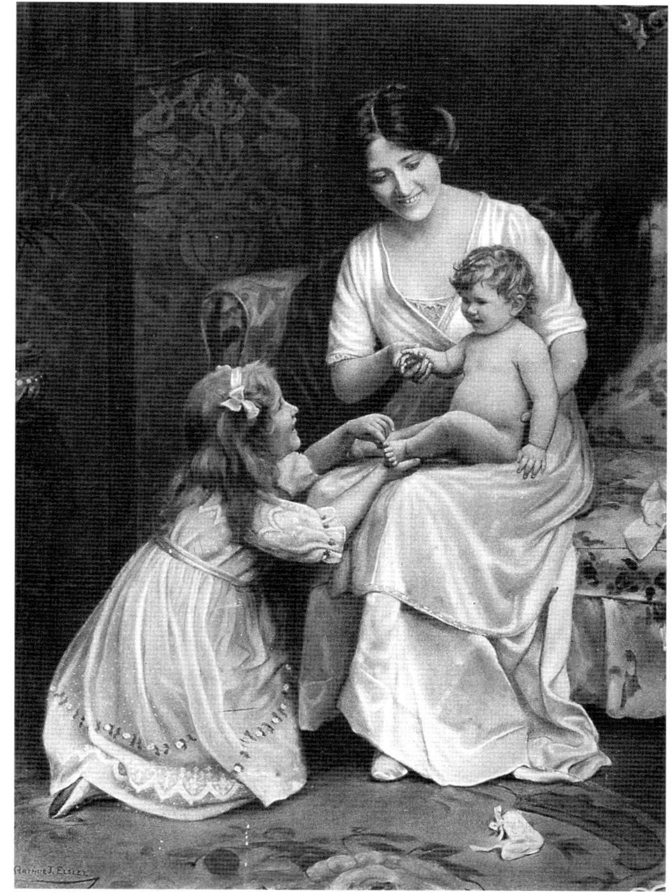

This Little Pig Went To Market

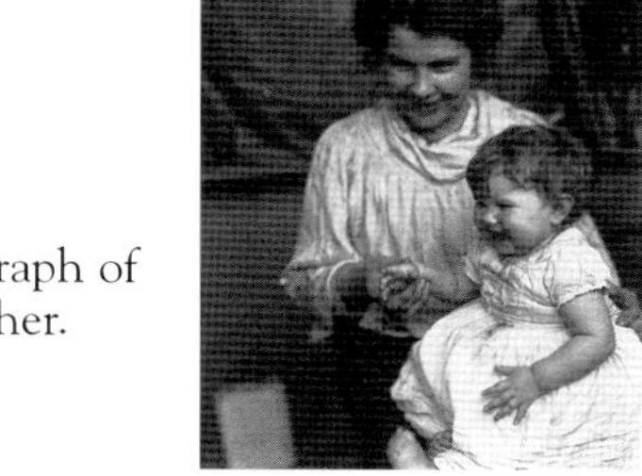

Source photograph of baby with mother.

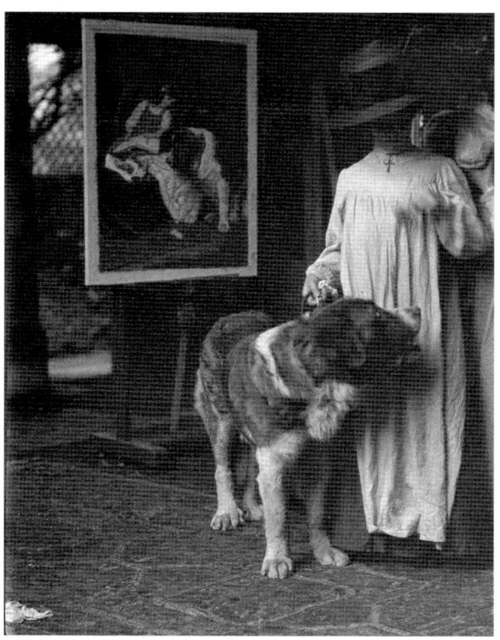

Source photograph of Miss Mumford and a St. Bernard for *Goodnight*. **See page 81**.

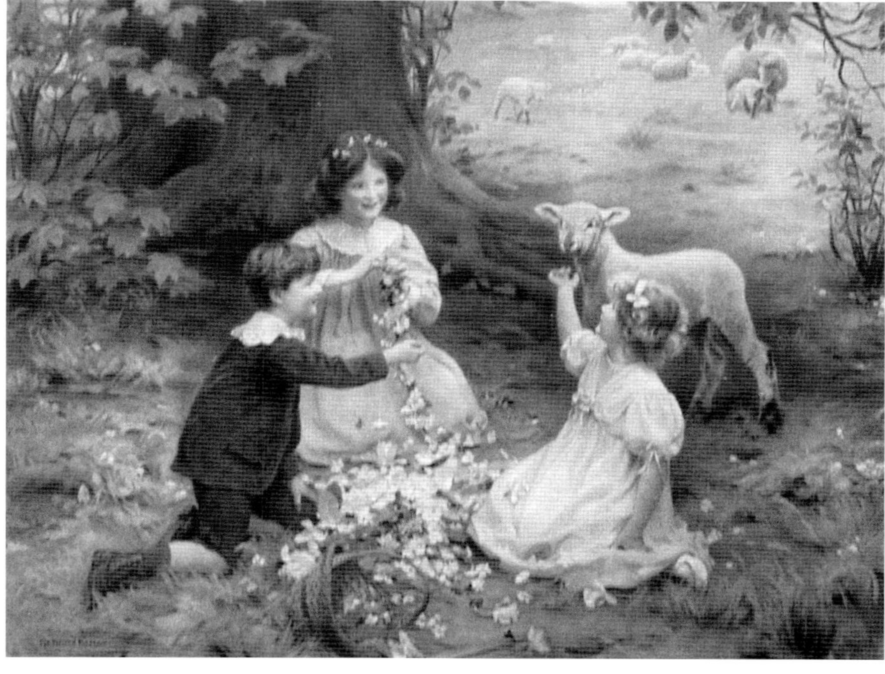

The Joy Of Spring

[The New Dress] *signed and dated 1912*

Details of original painting unknown. Recently owned by the John Noott Gallery.

A series of photographs was taken of Marjorie in another dress with a garland in her hands, and wearing the same floral crown. She was at this time attending The Elms, a small private school in the Finchley Road, run by Miss Dothie. She later went on to the Frances Holland School in Baker Street.

Modern colour print entitled *The New Dress*, published by Felix Rosenstiel's Widow & Son. Modern card printed by Camden Graphics called *The New Dress*.

Colour chromolithograph print, $27^{1}/_{2}$ins x 20ins (70.5cm x 51cm), probably a calendar, copyright unknown. **See page 82**.

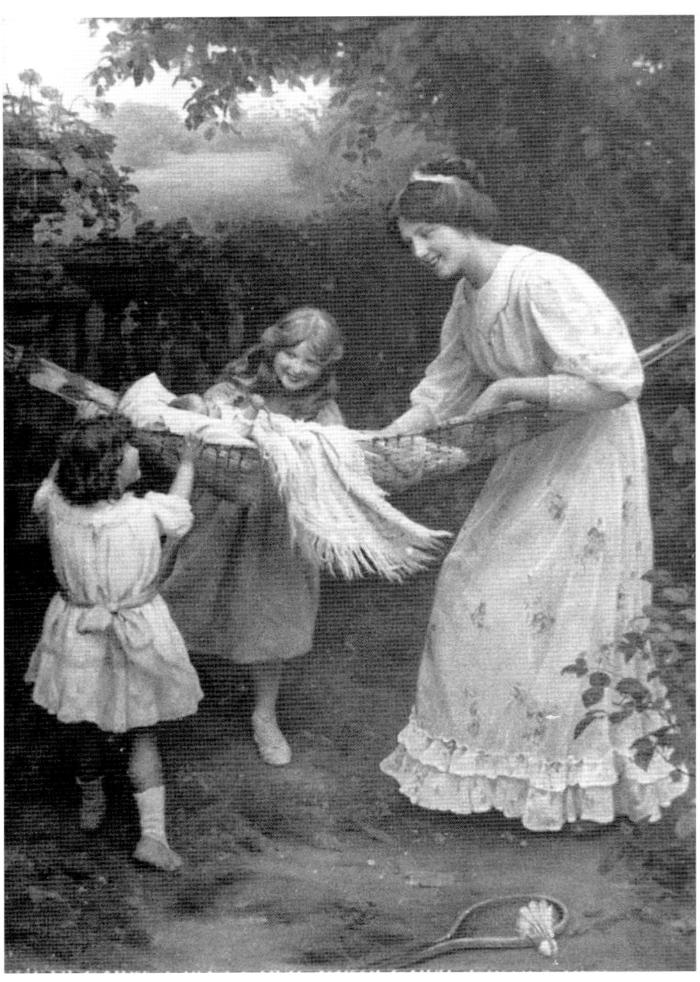

Swing, Swing

Swing, Swing *signed and dated 1912*

Details of original painting unknown.

Miss Gomersall and Marjorie in an imaginary garden. Elsley kept a hammock in the garden behind his studio.

Unrecorded as a print.

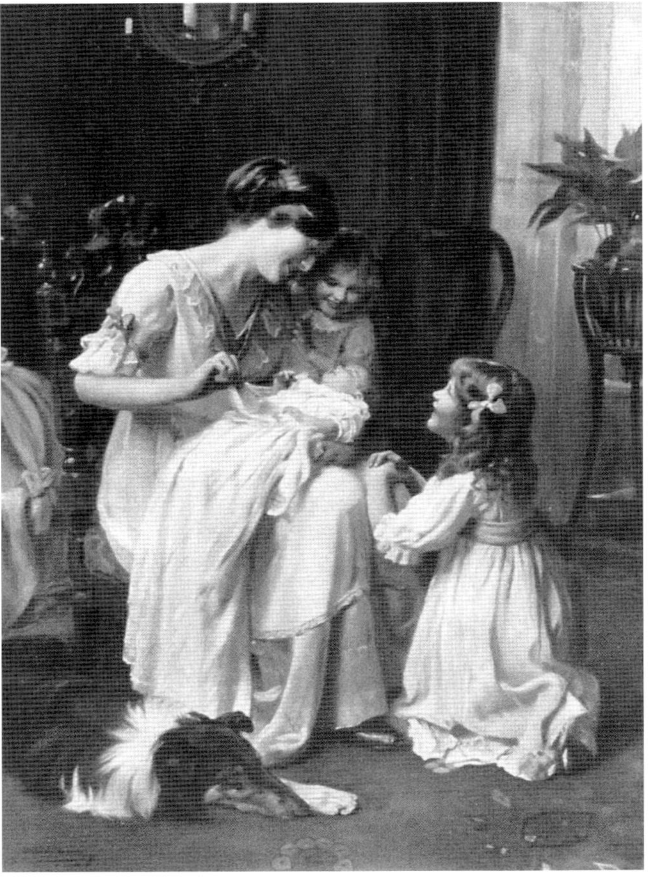

[Title Unknown]

[Title Unknown] *circa 1912*

Details of original painting unknown.

The metal jardiniere on the right of the picture was in Elsley's studio. Polishing it was very hard work so only the side facing outwards was cleaned for the benefit of those visiting the studio. Solomon J. Solomon the Royal Academician, founder of the Sphinx Art School, and Elsley's friend always told him "the clients think they are buying the studio not just the painting!"

Sepia photogravure, details unknown.

Do Be Careful *signed and dated 1912*

Details of original painting unknown.

Elsley's attention to detail, even included the worn toe on Marjorie's shoe. The garden tub appears again.

Colour photolithograph, $22^{1}/_{2}$ins x $16^{1}/_{2}$ins (57.5cm x 42cm), almost certainly a calendar, printed by Forman of Nottingham. **See page 88**.

As Good As Ever *signed and dated 1912*

Details of original painting unknown. Exhibited at the Royal Academy, 1912 (No.473) and was unsold.

A black and white photograph of the unfinished version shows the little girl without a hat, the dog with a short tail and there isn't a horse's bit hung on the wall.

Elsley was so busy in 1912, painting at least eight or nine works, that he took two canvases to finish on holiday.

Around September the family, along with their maid, went to stay for a month in a cottage at Barton-on-Sea, Hampshire. Elsley rented this cottage because it was advertised as having a studio. For his own pleasure Elsley also painted a landscape of Becton Bunny, a local beauty spot. One of his Royal Academy exhibits of 1915 was entitled *Becton Bunny, Near Barton, Hants,* (No.891) It was not reproduced and there is no record of its sale. A painting of this view, signed and dated 1912 was sold at the Studio Sale (part of Lot 13).

The model used for the blacksmith also sat for *The Punch And Judy Show*. The blacksmith, a very important person in the community, is mending a hoop which was a very popular children's toy. This work echoes Sir Edwin Landseer's *Shoeing the Bay Mare* which hung in the National Gallery and was reproduced as a Pears print in 1899.

Sepia photogravure, 20½ins x 15¾ins (52cm x 40cm), produced by Bovril in 1912, copyright C.W. Faulkner.

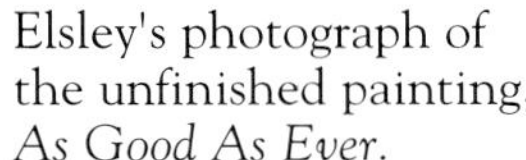

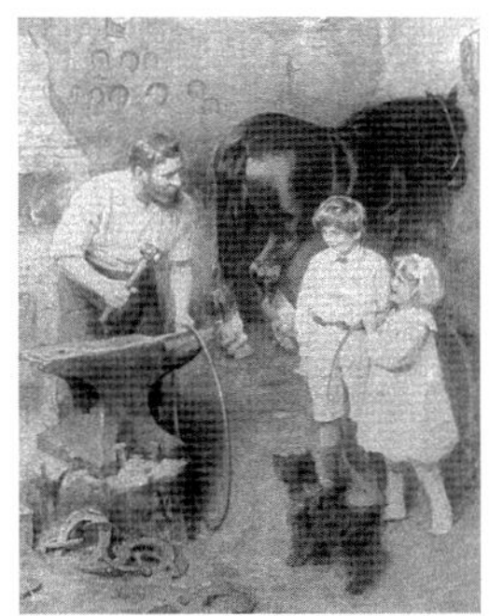

Elsley's photograph of the unfinished painting, *As Good As Ever.*

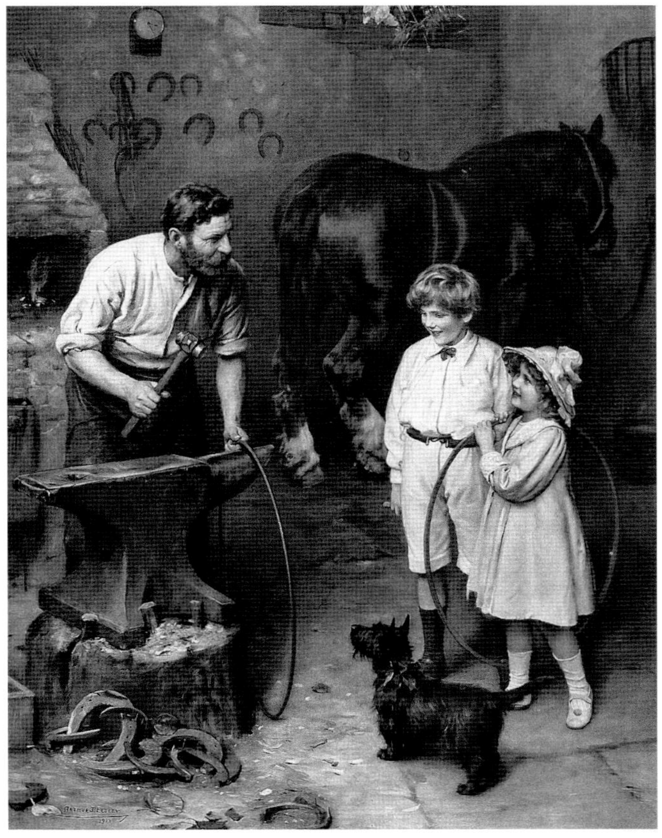

As Good As Ever

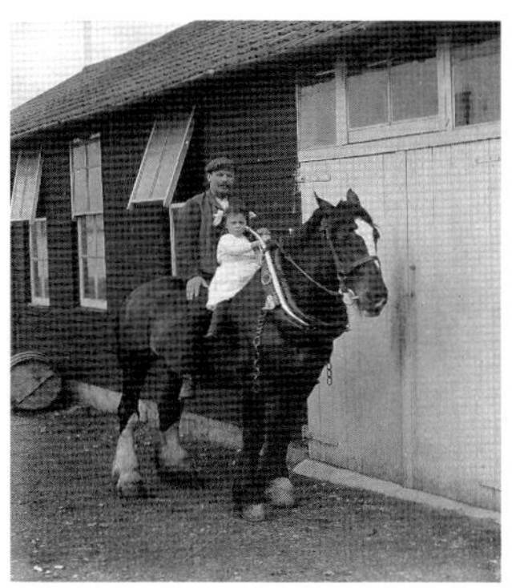

Source photograph for *Won't You Fix My Horse Too?*

Won't You Fix My Horse Too?

signed and dated 1912

Details of original painting unknown. Black and white photograph in Elsley collection, painting not signed or dated

Marjorie is the little girl holding her dee gee (toy horse) which also appears in *The Punch And Judy Show*, 1912, and the other girl is holding an early version of a roller skate. This composition combines his early equestrian works with his later speciality of children.

cf. *As Good As Ever*, R.A. 1912, and Sir Edwin Landseer's *Shoeing The Bay Mare*, R.A. 1844, and Pears print, 1899, hanging in the National Gallery at this time.

Painted for the American market and reproduced as a colour calendar by Thos. D. Murphy Co., 1915, entitled *Won't You Fix My Horse.* **See page 86.**

The Punch And Judy Show *signed and dated 1912*

Details of original painting unknown.

This work is Elsley's *tour de force*.The collie, called Old Scenter, was very well behaved. His owner lived opposite Clarence Gate, Regents Park. Marjorie remembers her father saying "Go on you old silly" to the dog who would follow without a lead. Elsley forgot to say it on one occasion and the dog refused to cross the road.

Elsley painted a small head and shoulders oil study of the central figure in this work, signed and dated 1908, which was sold at the Studio Sale (part of Lot 19). Either he had been working on the large painting since that date or had simply decided to include her in this position. The man wearing a policeman's outfit, borrowed from a relative, ran the W.H. Smith newspaper barrow at the end of the road. The drum man, wearing the bowler hat, was well known for "propping up the bar" at the local pub. The bearded man, holding a striped cane on the left of the crowd, was Mr. Cox a local character who lived at 112 Sixth Avenue, Queens Park. He was nick-named 'Slopper', and his job was to put down straw to deaden the noise of horses' hooves and help their grip on the cobbled street at the end of Queens Road, where Elsley lived. He also shovelled up mud and horse droppings and kept the street clean. For his labours, coachmen would toss him small change. The old man with an arm on his hip was Mr. Gooderam who appeared as the shepherd in *Rescued* 1911. The bearded man wearing a cap was the local carpenter

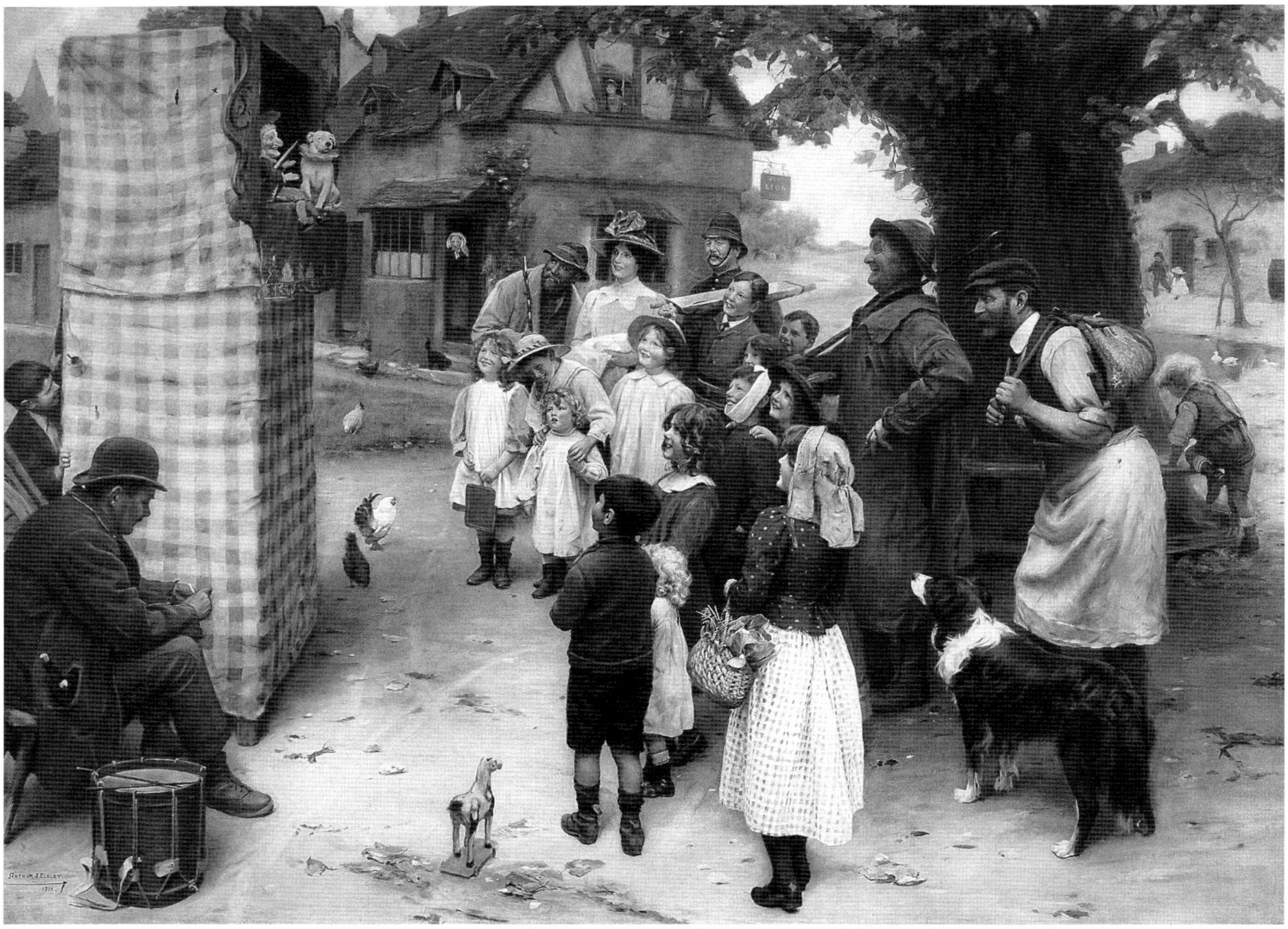

The Punch And Judy Show

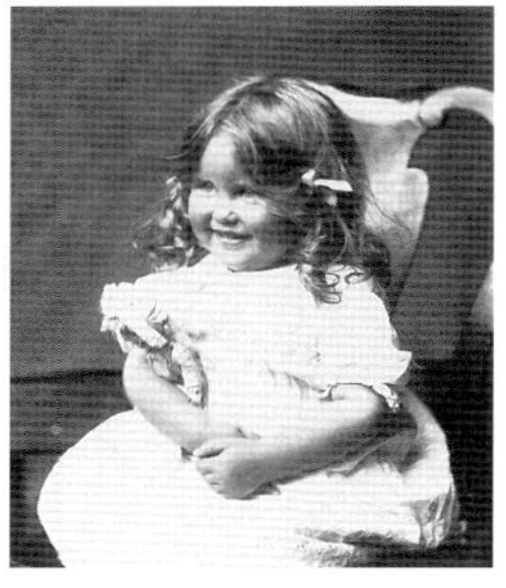

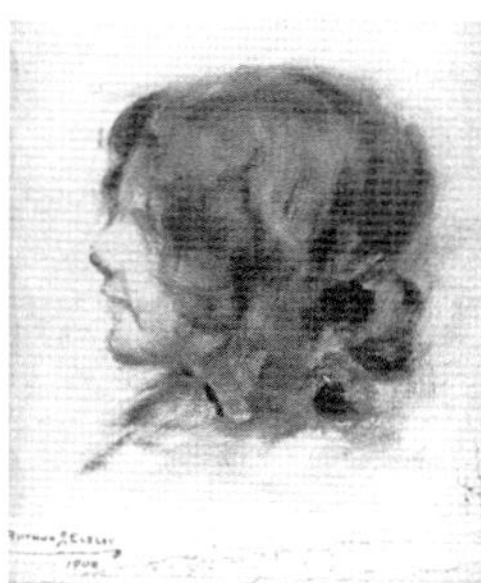

Far left, source photograph of Marjorie. Left, oil sketch of the central figure in *The Punch And Judy Show*.

who lived in the next street. (He also appears as the blacksmith in *As Good As Ever*, 1912).

The dee gee on the ground belonged to Marjorie and featured in *Won't You Fix My Horse Too?*, 1912. Marjorie's cousin, Frances Everett, is the girl, bottom left, holding the slate. This work was probably painted partly at Barton-on-Sea.

The Punch and Judy Show has been a popular subject with artists for a very long time. Elsley's version is the mirror image of a large engraving, after the painting by Thomas Webster, R.A., which had been published by the Art Union in 1859. Eugene de Blaas, a German artist residing in Venice whose works were exhibited and reproduced in Britain, twice painted this theme in the late nineteenth century.

Sepia photogravure, 20¾ins x 27¾ins (53cm x 71cm), published by Harrop & Co.

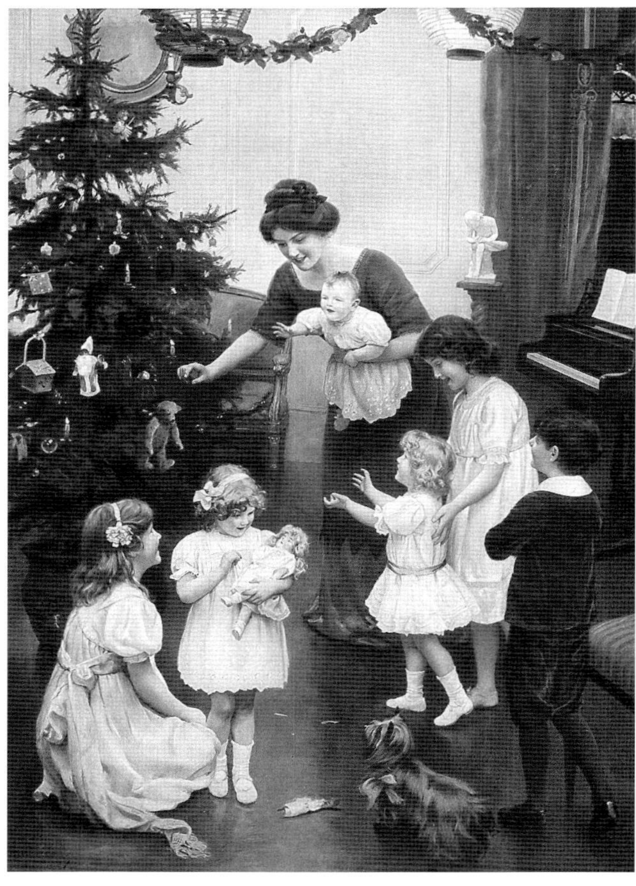

His First Christmas

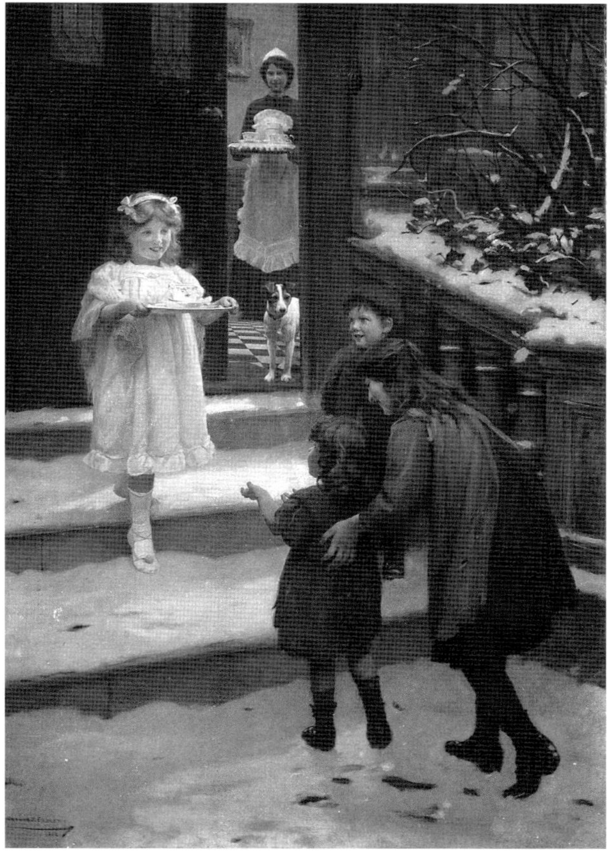

Charity

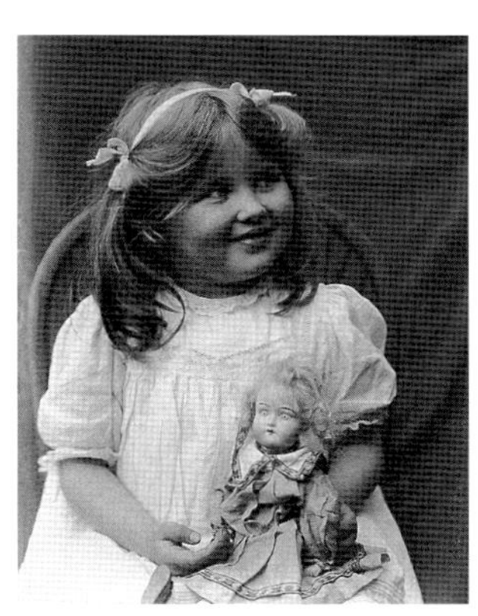

Photograph of Marjorie with her doll.

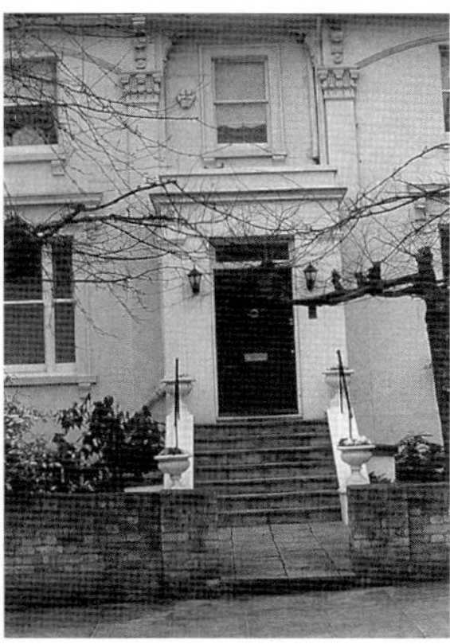

Queen's Road, St. John's Wood.

His First Christmas *signed and dated 1912*

Details of original painting unknown.

Elsley and Morgan both featured the phrase *His First* in a number of their works. Very few toys appear in Elsley's works, and this is only one of two to feature a doll – an expensive, German porcelain-headed one.

Sepia photogravure, 20½ins x 14¾ins (52cm x 37.5cm), presented with *The Queen, The Lady's Newspaper*, Christmas 1912. Small photogravure, 8ins x 6ins (20.5cm x 15cm), probably *The Windsor Magazine*.

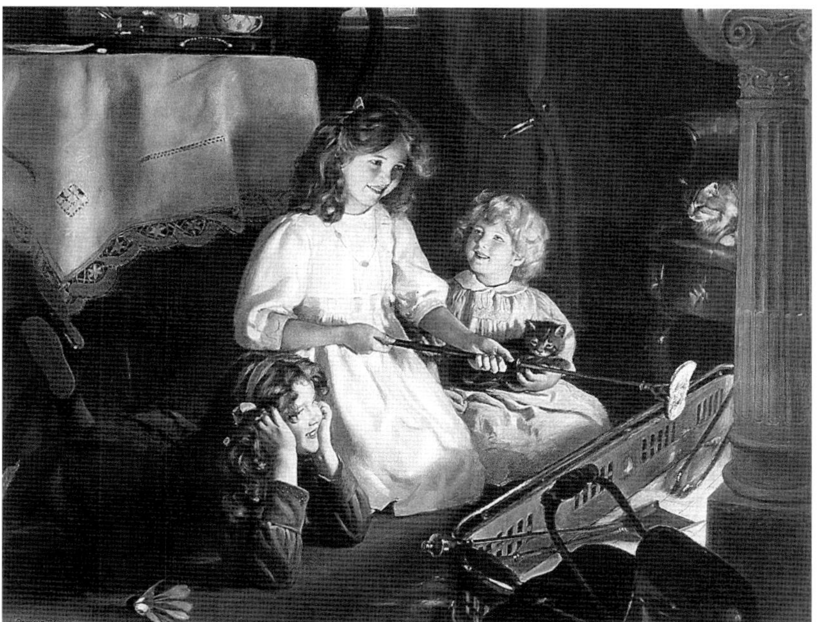

Fireside Joys

Charity *signed and dated 1912*

Details of original painting unknown. Exhibited at the Royal Academy, 1913 (No.95).

Sophie, the family's maid, is standing behind Marjorie. The stained-glass panels in the door were designed and made by Elsley and when the family moved to the house in Tunbridge Wells he made similar panels for that front door.

This work was inspired by Fred Morgan's painting *The Cheerful Giver* which was published as a sepia photogravure by Bovril in July 1904 and renamed *Little Lady Bountiful*.

Colour chromolithograph advertising show-card for Fry's Breakfast Cocoa and Chocolate.

Fireside Joys *circa 1913*

Details of original painting unknown.

Marjorie, aged nine, is the central figure toasting the bread and her cousin, Frances Everett, was the model for the girl leaning on her elbows. Her family came from Canada to stay in Slindon, West Sussex for two years (1911-1913), and were regular visitors to the Elsley household. The warmth of the oil lamp kept the cat still, and Elsley also used the lamp to fine effect in the glowing children's faces. Elsley again uses fire to light the work as in *Snapdragon*, c.1895 and *Rescued*, 1911.

Sepia photogravure, 16ins x 20¼ins (40.5cm x 51.5cm), produced for Bovril early 1913, copyright C.W. Faulkner.

Goodnight *signed and dated 1913*
Oil on canvas, 42ins x 30ins (107cm x 76.5cm). Exhibited at the Royal Academy, 1915 (No.554).

Miss Gomersall has an unknown baby on her back. Marjorie is in the pink dress in the foreground with her cousin, Frances Everett, holding a Mr. Punch rattle and teething stick. After this painting her family returned to Canada because Amy, Emm's younger sister became homesick. This is another painting with a Christmas theme and Elsley clearly tailored his work for use as Christmas presentation plates! Not to be confused with the 1911 and 1914 works of the same title.

Black and white photograph *Royal Academy Pictures*, 1915, p.123. Colour photolithograph page, 8ins x 6ins (20.5cm x 15cm), almost certainly *The Windsor Magazine*.

Sepia photogravure presented with *The Queen, The Lady's Newspaper*, Christmas 1913, copyright C.W. Faulkner & Co. Sepia photogravure, 8ins x 6ins (20.5cm x 15cm), publication unknown.

A Proud Mother *signed and dated 1913*
Details of original painting unknown.

The older girl's collar has a Liberty pattern. Like most artists Elsley kept a dressing up box with fragments of material and simply draped pieces over his models if they didn't have a complete outfit.

The background is taken from one of his landscape paintings. Produced as a crystoleum.

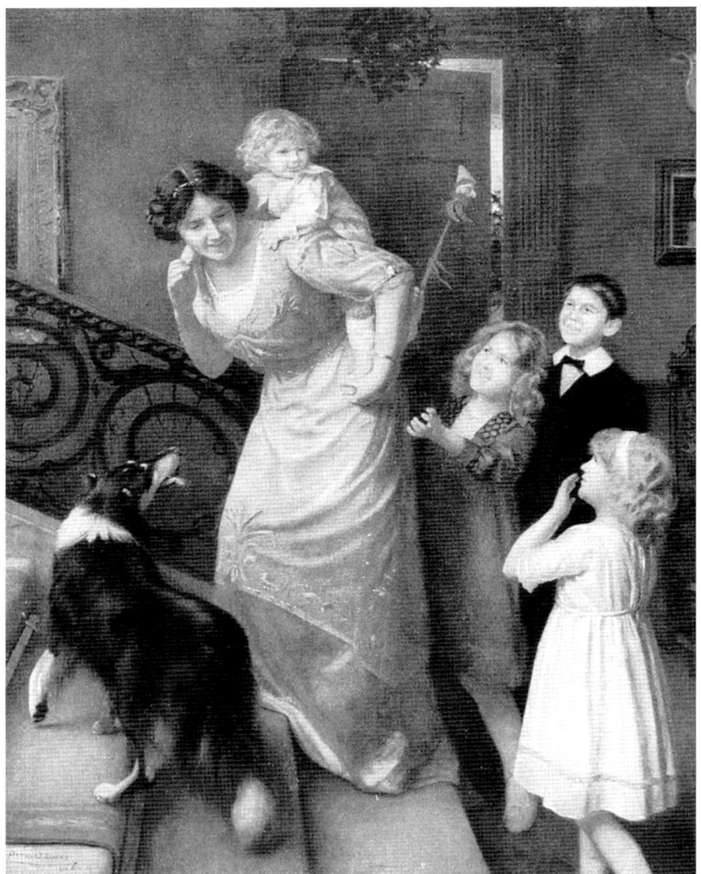

Goodnight

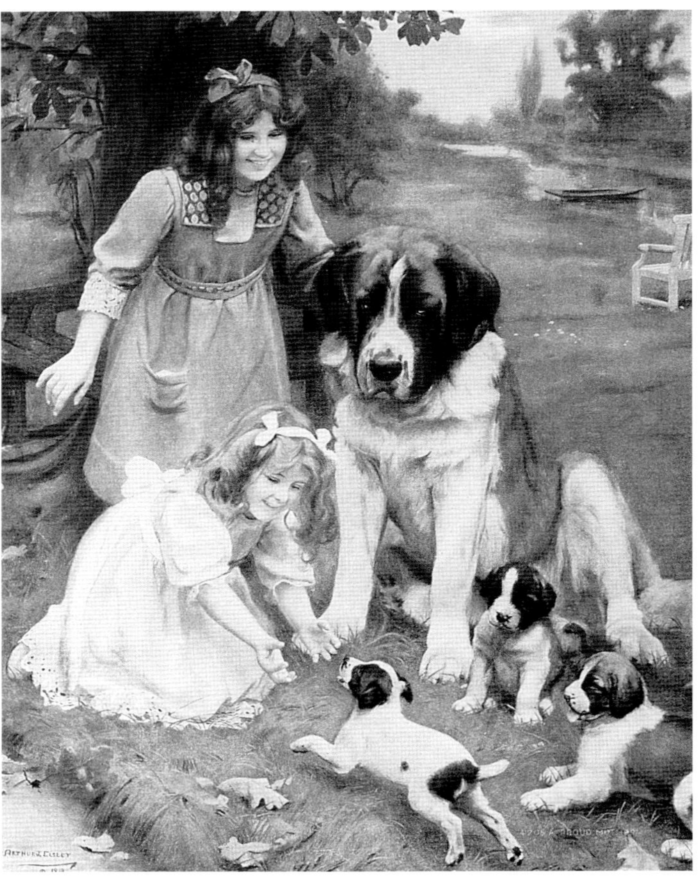

A Proud Mother

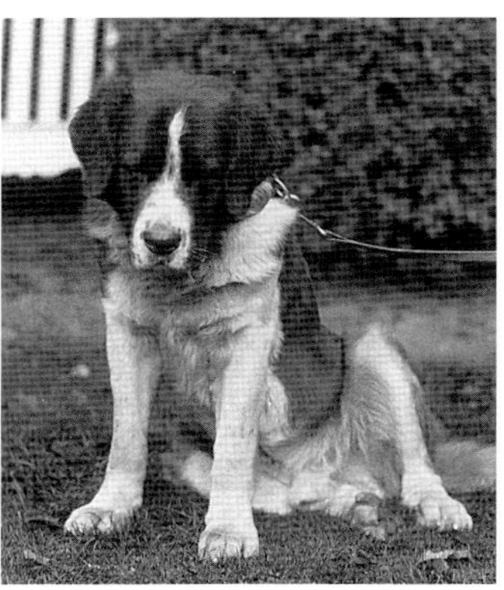

Source photograph for *A Proud Mother.*

A Helping Hand *signed and dated 1913*
Oil on canvas, 28ins x 36ins (71.5cm x 91.5cm). Possibly auctioned at Sotheby's, c.1920.

Elsley photographed the horse.

American colour calendar manufactured by Thos. D. Murphy Co., 1916. **See page 86**.

A Private Rehearsal *signed and dated 1914*
Details of original painting unknown.

This painting was inspired by a party held in Christmas 1913. Miss Gomersall is again the model for the mother holding the baby and this back view of her shows her lovely hair to great advantage. Marjorie also features twice – as the forward-leaning figure with an outstretched hand, and the dancer.

The pianist is Arthur Stacey, organist at the local

church. He lived at 18 Eaton Villas, Haverstock Hill, and worked in a bank. The tall girl at the back, or the girl with the black ribbon in her hair, is C.W. Faulkner's eldest daughter, Tess, who married the pianist Harold Crackston. Next to her is 'Queenie' in a similar pose to *Wake Up It's Christmas Morning*, 1909. The old lady in the chair appears to be Mrs. Knight, who was last featured by Elsley in c.1898.

Sepia photogravure, 19ins x 27ins (49cm x 69cm), produced by Bovril in 1914, copyright C.W. Faulkner & Co.

The War Horse *signed and dated 1914*

Details of original painting unknown.

The dog also features in *Here They Are*, c.1903, and *Goodnight*, 1914. It arrived at the studio with its hair tied in tapes which Emm had to undo before Elsley could paint it. The dancing dress with little roses belonged to Marjorie, but she was not the model for this work.

Colour chromolithograph, 9¾ins x 6¾ins (24.5cm x 17cm), presented with *Sunday Stories* magazine. **See page 88.**

[Guarding The Stile] *signed and dated 1914*

Oil on canvas, 39ins x 30ins (99.5cm x 76.5cm). Auctioned at Sotheby's, New York, on 12th October 1994 (Lot 201). Extract from Sotheby's Auction Catalogue, October 1994:

> "...Arthur John Elsley was beloved during his lifetime for his sentimental and playful depictions of children and animals. Groups of happy boys and girls accompanied by dogs in charming rural landscapes, as in the present work, were favoured compositions of the artist.
>
> Elsley, following in the Victorian tradition of Sir John Everett Millais, was a master of the 'story' picture. He secured his success by appealing to the sentimental attachment to woodlands and pasture of the burgeoning bourgeoisie, many of whom now resided in the suburbs of manufacturing towns. Elsley's works provide delightful escapism from everyday life by mirroring the playfulness and wonder of childhood."

Marjorie is the model for the girl sitting on the stile with the puppy on her lap. **See page 84.**

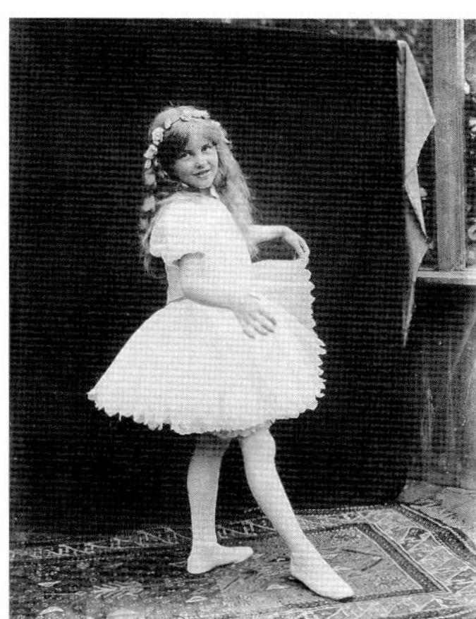

Photograph of Marjorie in her ballet dress.

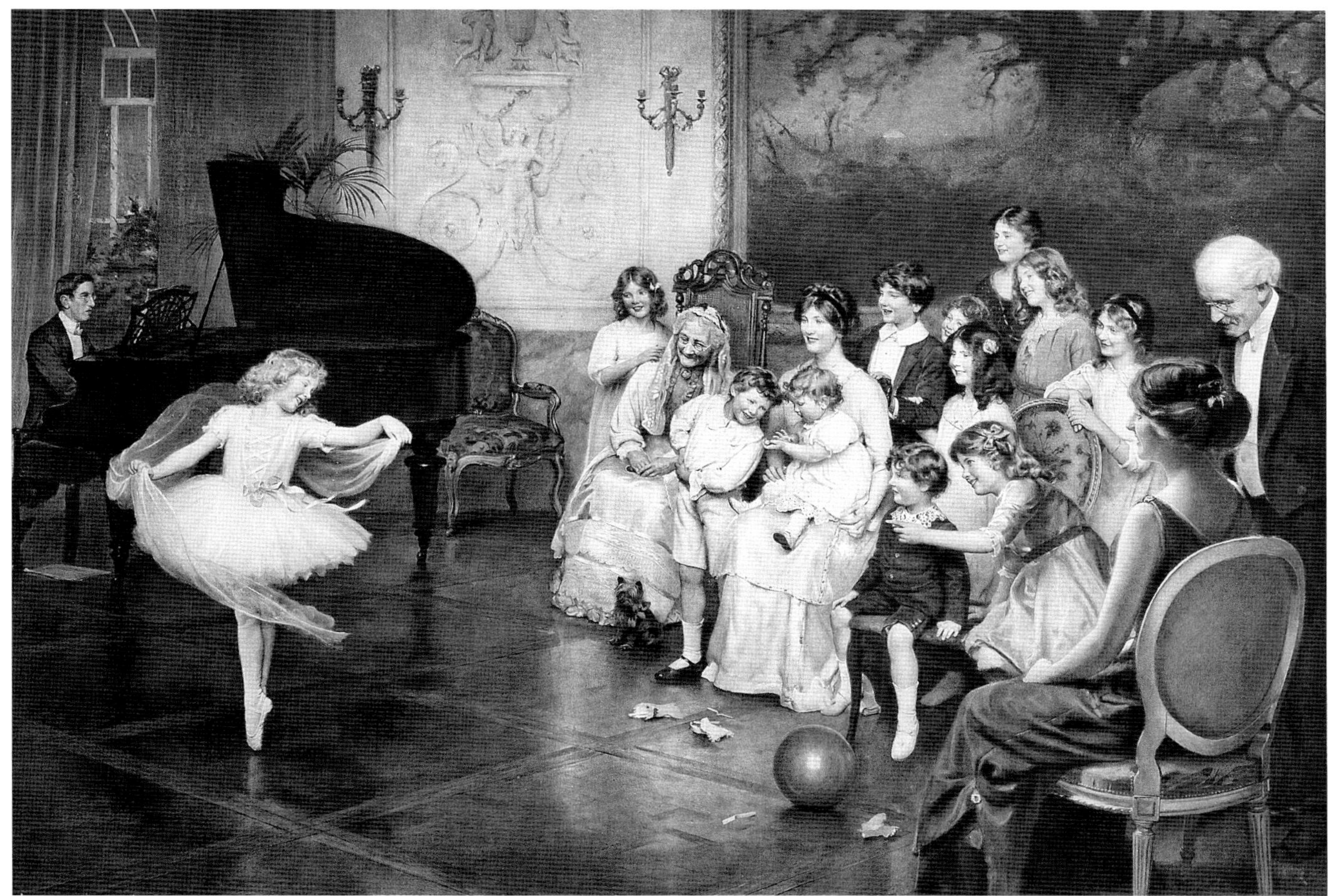

A Private Rehearsal

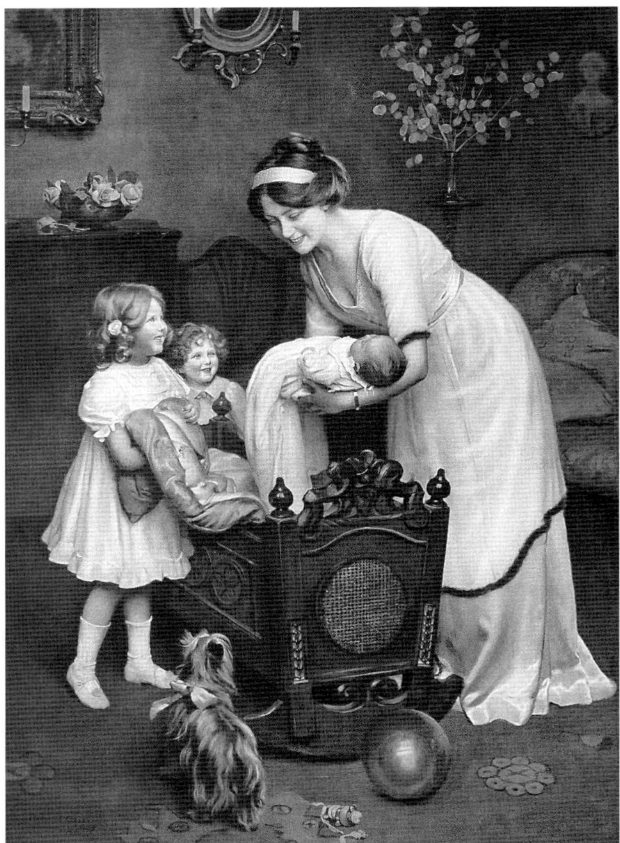

Bedtime / Goodnight

Bedtime / Goodnight *signed and dated 1914*

Oil on canvas, 43ins x 30ins (109.5cm x 76.5cm). Exhibited at the Royal Academy, 1914 (No 377), entitled *Bedtime*. In the 1980s-90s owned by Schillay & Rehs Galleries, New York.

This work features a much younger Marjorie in the same pose as used in *Private and Confidential*, 1906, and Miss Gomersall, c.1910. The little dog, Khaki, appeared as early as 1902 in *Baby's Birthday*. Not to be confused with the two works entitled *Goodnight* of 1911 and 1913. Modern colour print from the Stephen Selby Collection.

Sepia photogravure, 21ins x 15ins (54cm x 38cm), produced by Bovril in 1914, entitled *Goodnight*, copyright C.W. Faulkner & Co., 1914.

Bedtime Stories *signed and dated 1915*

Oil on canvas, 42¾ins x 29½ins, (109cm x 75.5cm). Auctioned in New York in 1996 for $220,000 establishing a world record for an Elsley.

Elsley made a shield-shaped mirror on a stand to reflect light onto Marjorie's piano music. For this painting he has turned it into a pole screen by replacing the mirror with a tapestry.

Sepia photogravure, 21¼ins x 14½ins (54.5cm x 37cm), produced by Bovril 1915, copyright C.W. Faulkner & Co.

A Chip Of The Old Block *signed and dated 1915*

Details of original painting unknown.

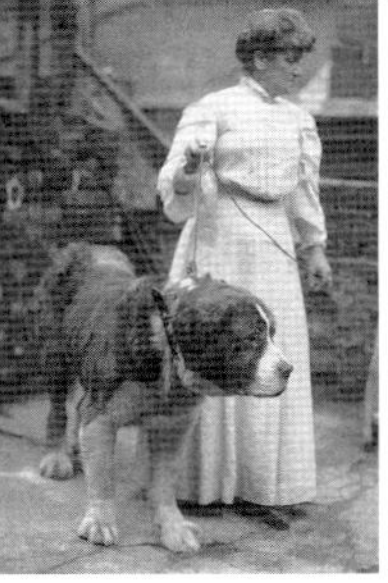

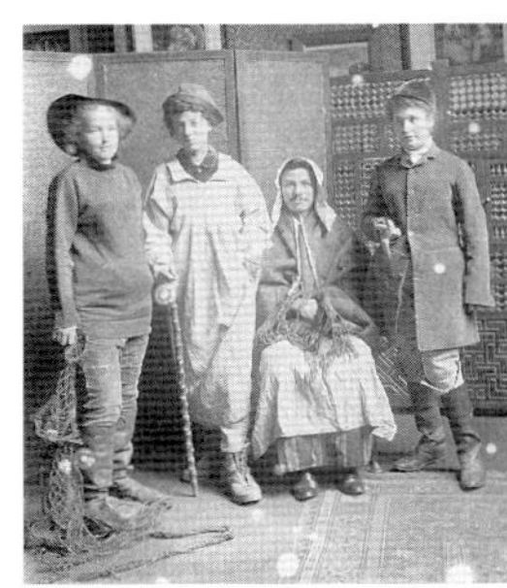

Far left, source photograph for *Who's Afraid*. Left, photograph in Elsley's studio with the model for the soldier in *A Chip Of The Old Block* seated centre, dressed as an old lady.

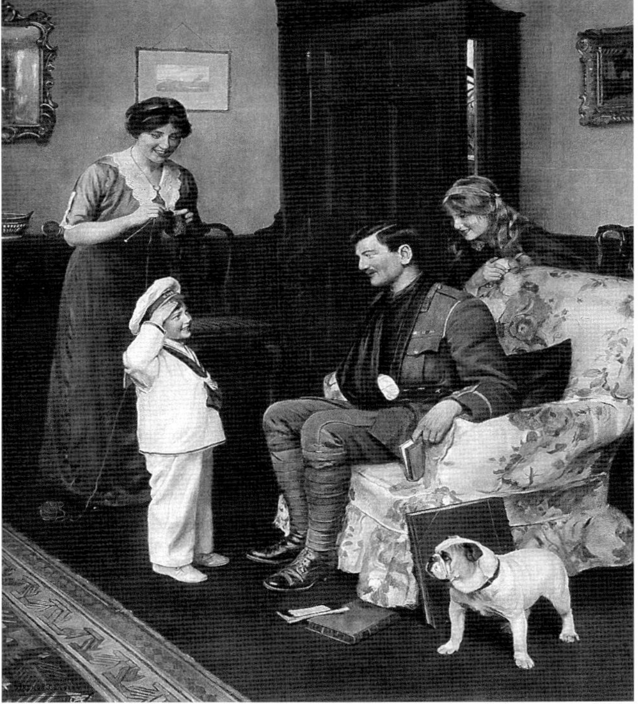

A Chip Of The Old Block

The models for this work are Marjorie, Miss Gomersall, an unknown man and, dressed as a sailor, Rosemary Coppock, the daughter of Marjorie's dance teacher. The bull-dog, a different breed to the usual, symbolised the British fighting spirit in the Great War. Elsley worked in a munitions factory during the war as he was too old to fight. His engineering skills were used to make a jig to test gun-sights and although his near-sightedness was ideal for this it put yet more strain on his eyes. He does not appear to have produced any works in 1916.

Sepia photogravure, 21ins x 15¾ins (54cm x 40cm), published by Bovril in 1915, copyright C.W. Faulkner & Co.

Who's Afraid? *signed and dated 1915*

Oil on canvas, 43ins x 34ins (109.5cm x 86.5).

The small girl is Marjorie. Extract from John Hadfield's *Every Picture Tells A Story*, p.92:

"Although hunting, shooting, and fishing remained prime recreations of the upper classes throughout the nineteenth century the rise of a prosperous middle class led to the promotion of domestic pets to membership of the family circle, as distinct from their normal habitat in

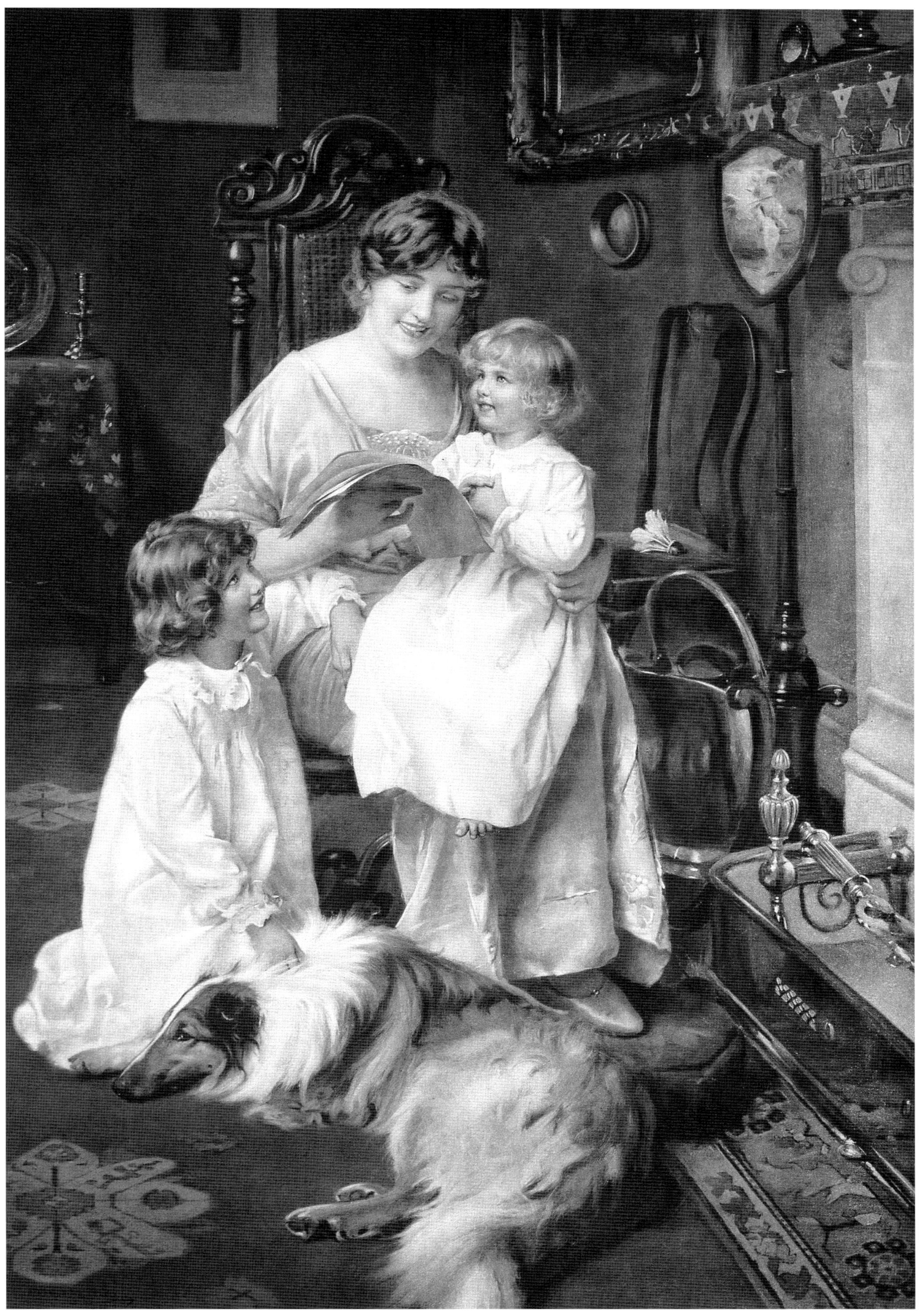

Bedtime Stories

kennel and stable. This particularly applied to the dog, who, to quote a biographer of Landseer, was elevated to 'something that closely approximates to human nature in its generous sympathies'".

American colour calendar manufactured by Thos. D. Murphy Co., 1917. **See page 83**.

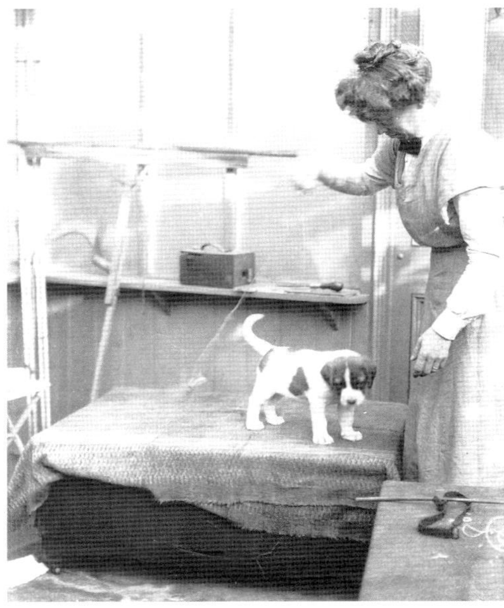

Source photograph for *Who's Afraid*.

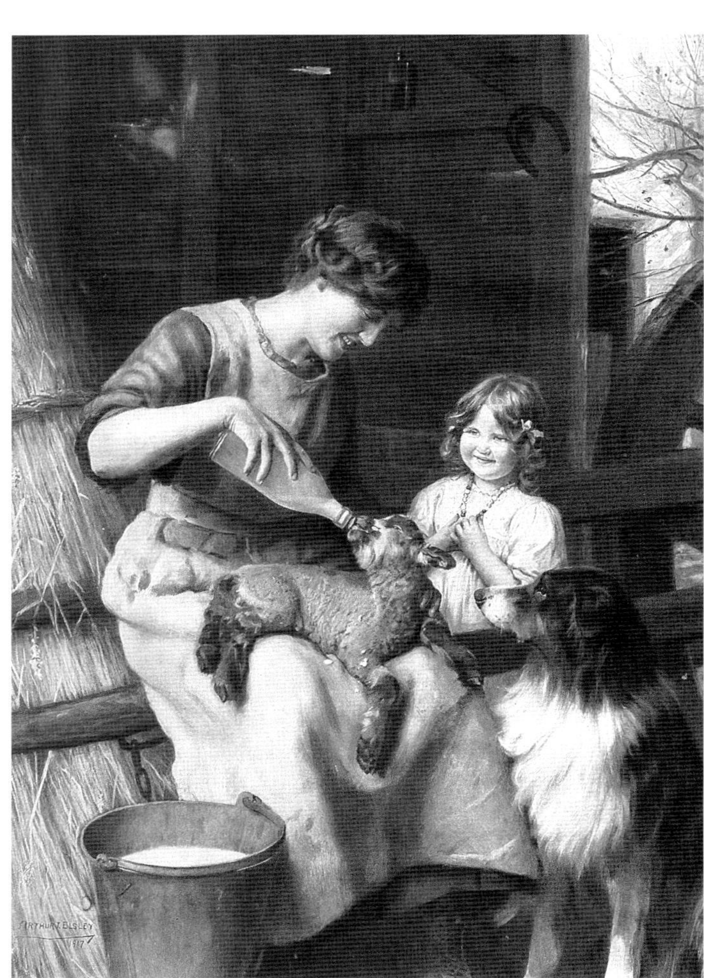

The New Shepherd

The New Shepherd *signed and dated 1917*

Details of original painting unknown.

This was the last known work to be bought by C.W. Faulkner & Co. Charles Faulkner had been Elsley's major patron and was a good friend whose children often appeared in the paintings. Faulkner died in extraordinary circumstances when his business hit bad times during the Great War. Disabled, he was given special permission to cross the railway track to save the longer walk at his home station at Hatch End, Pinner, Middlesex. On 18th November 1915, when using the crossing, he was hit by an express train.

Sepia photogravure, 20¾ins x 14¾ins (53cm x 37.5cm), produced by Bovril, 1917. This was also Elsley's last work to be reproduced for Bovril.

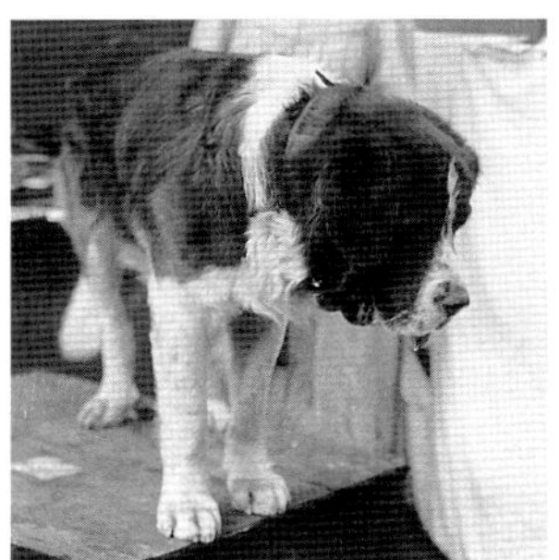

Source photograph for *Here He Comes*.

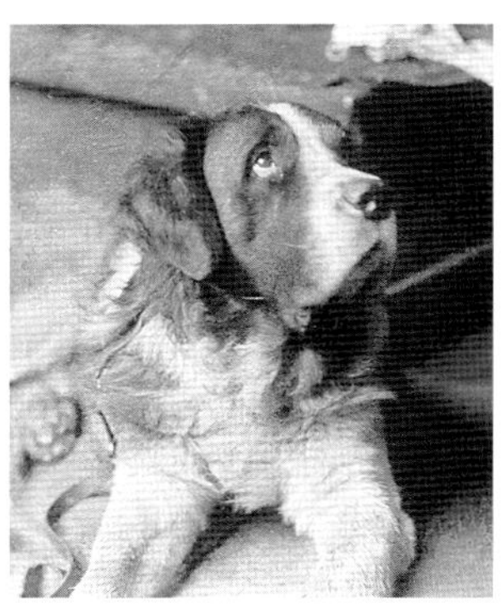

Source photograph for *No Thoroughfare*.

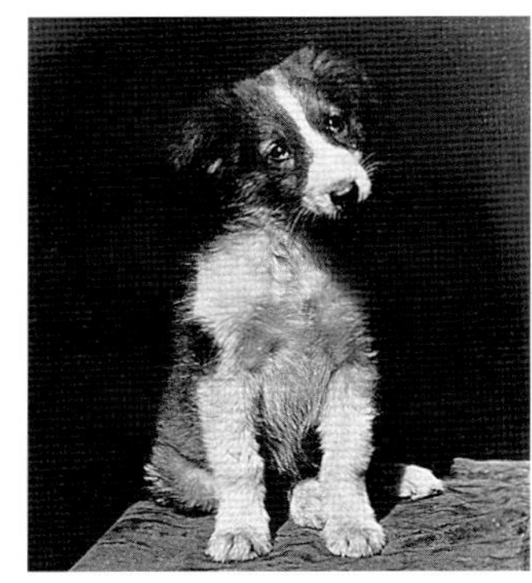

Source photograph for *Home At Last*.

Here He Comes *signed and dated 1917*

Details of original painting unknown.

Elsley painted this work incorporating an oil sketch of Marjorie from 1907, and a photograph of the St. Bernard standing on an up-turned drawer in the studio. This work was commissioned by Thos. D. Murphy Co., of America. The original version was dispatched by ship which was sunk by a German submarine. Fortunately Elsley had taken a photograph of it and re-painted it. Not to be confused with a 1901 painting of the same title.

In 1917, partly due to the shortage of work in Britain, and also as a favour to an old friend and patron, Elsley returned to canine portraiture. He painted Ellen Thomas-Stanford's dog Kylin, *Faithful and Fearless*, signed and dated 1917.

Modern greetings card, The Medici Society, now called *The Blue Ribbon*. American colour calendar manufactured by Thos. D. Murphy Co. 1921. **See page 87**.

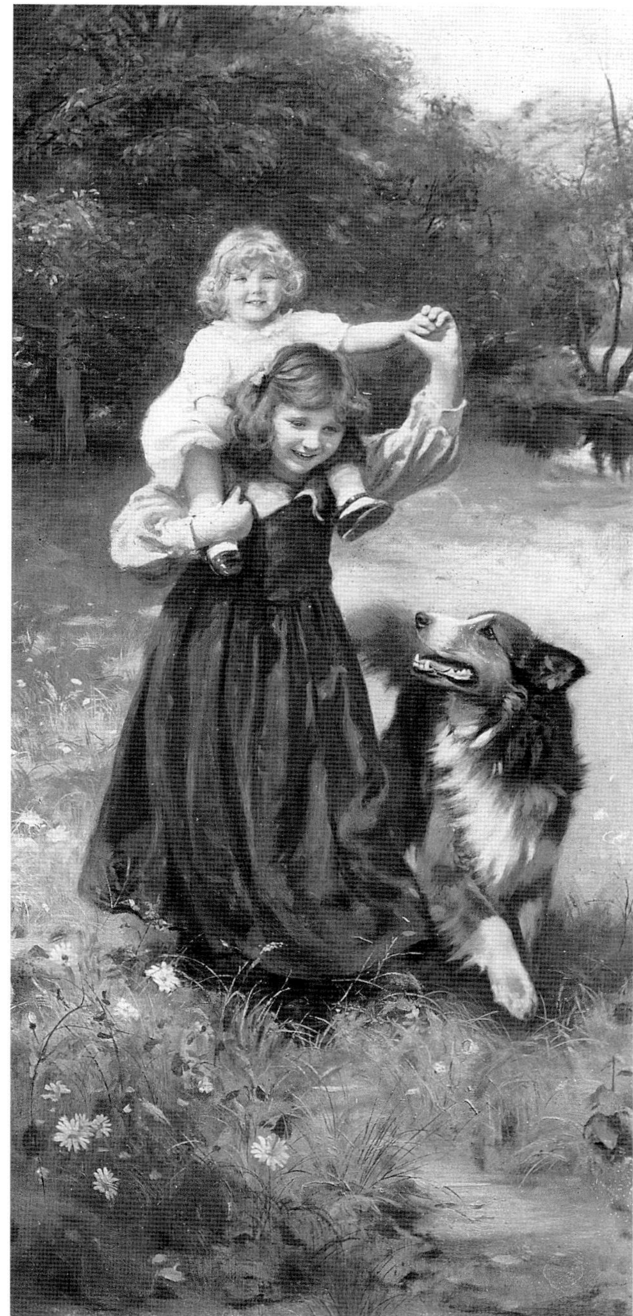

Pick-a-Back

No Thoroughfare *signed and dated 1917*

Details of original painting unknown. Not to be confused with the c.1902 painting.

It is not Marjorie in this work although the older girl has a similar hair style.

American colour calendar manufactured by Thos. D. Murphy Co., 1919, copyright 1917. **See page 86.**

[Home At Last] *circa 1918*

Oil on canvas, 36ins x 26½ins (91.5cm x 68cm).

Elsley photographed the collie pup Marjorie is holding. The painting is signed, and the date is possibly under the rebate of the frame. Similar composition to *Rescued*, 1911. Not to be confused with *Home Again* 1910. **See page 85.**

Pick-a-Back *circa 1919*

Details of original painting unknown.

Elsley took a photograph of the little girl, and another of the flowers bottom left, which were then incorporated into the painting. The older girl is Marjorie. Not to be confused with a 1907 work of the same title.

Black and white photograph of painting in Elsley collection.

Colour photolithograph page in *The Windsor Magazine*, date unknown.

An Uninvited Guest *circa 1919*

Details of original painting unknown.

Marjorie is the older girl holding the trowel. The toad was specially brought to the studio from a greenhouse in Farnborough, Kent, for inclusion in this painting. Not to be confused with the 1895 work of the same name.

Colour cover of *Ward Lock & Co's Wonder Book*, 1920 annual, not signed or dated. **See page 88.**

Secret Meetings *circa 1910 (or 1919)*

Details of original painting unknown. This is a reworking of *Time to Get Up*, 1898.

The Welsh terrier was probably Tatters who also featured in *Now Beg*, c.1913.

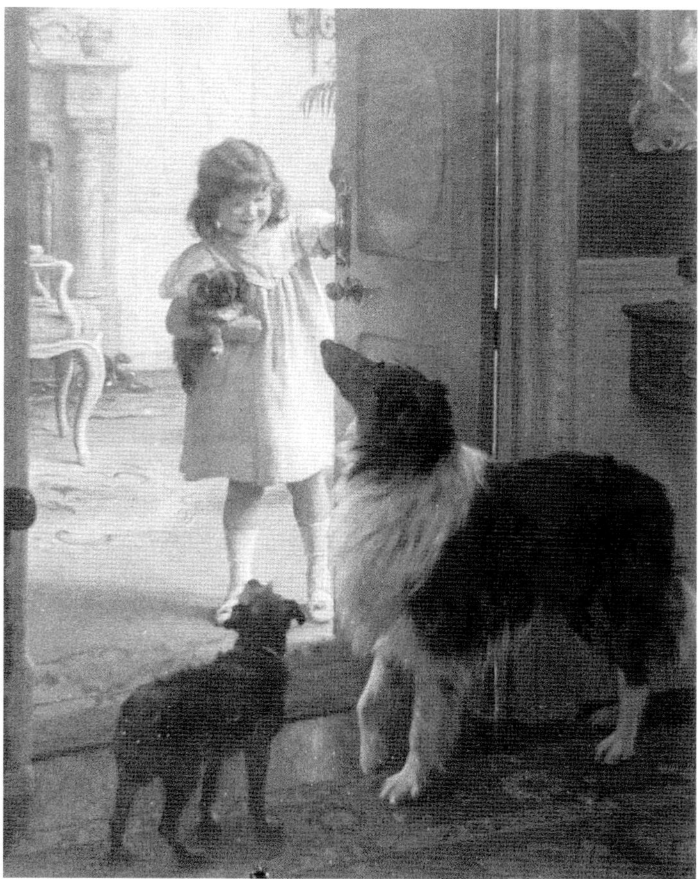

Secret Meetings

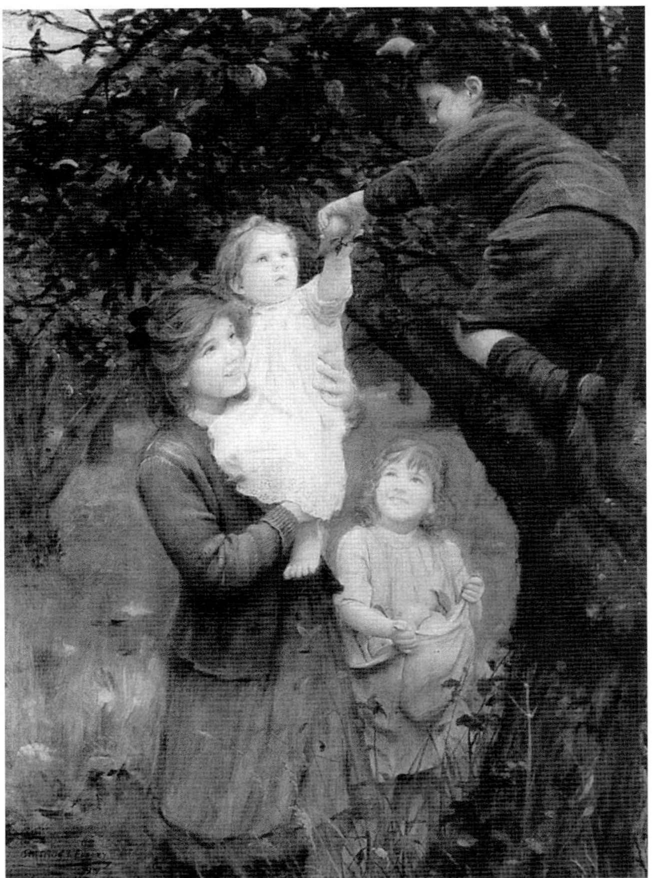

[Picking Apples]

[Picking Apples] *signed and dated 1919*

Oil on canvas, $37^{1/2}$ins x 27ins (95.5cm x 69cm).

Marjorie recalls that the apples were arranged in an apron and left in the studio overnight. When Elsley returned to the work he found some of the apples had been taken by the maid for her children.

Who Speaks First? *signed and dated 1919*

Details of original painting unknown.

The un-named child also features in *Fireside Joys*, c.1912. The woman is Marjorie's cousin, Evie, the daughter of one of Elsley's sisters. The Welsh terrier is Tatters who also appears in *Secret Meetings*, 1910 or 1919.

Not to be confused with the 1895 work of the same title.

American colour calendar manufactured by Thos. D. Murphy Co. 1922. **See page 87**.

'Twixt Love and Duty *signed and dated 1919*

Details of original painting unknown.

This painting is a combination of earlier images. Marjorie is painted from a photograph of her aged four, and the shepherd is reminiscent of *Here He Comes*, 1901. The collie is Old Scenter who appears in *The Punch And Judy Show*, 1912, and the puppy on the left is painted from the same photograph as the puppy in *Try Again*, 1906. Colour cover *Ward Lock & Co.'s Wonder Book*, 1922 annual, not signed and dated.

Small photogravure, copyright unknown. **See page 88**.

[Crossing the Stream] *signed and dated 1920*

Oil on canvas, 30ins x 22ins (76.5cm x 56.5cm).

Elsley photographed Marjorie in his studio with dummy legs on her shoulders. She was sixteen and attending the Francis Holland School. To get the feet positioned correctly she remembers having to stand in a photograph-developing tank of water. Her circulation stopped and her feet turned crimson!

Marjorie bequeathed this painting to Brighton Museum, and it now hangs at Preston Manor, Brighton, the home of the Benett-Stanford family, Elsley's early patron and friend. This house was left to Brighton by their late mayor and is home to a number of commissioned Elsley canine portraits together with a painting of *Ellen Benett-Stanford On Her Horse Congress*, 1885.

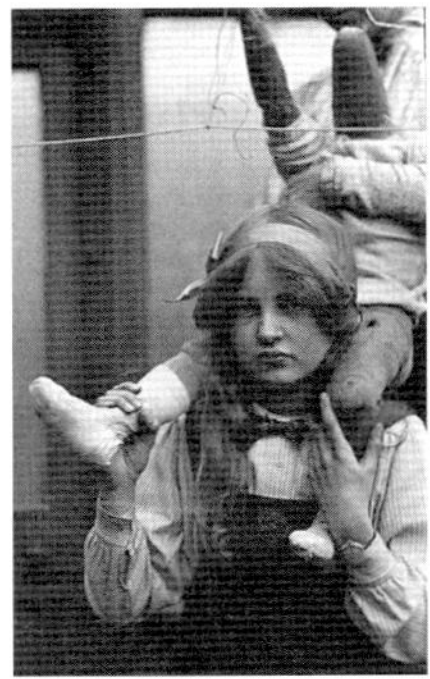

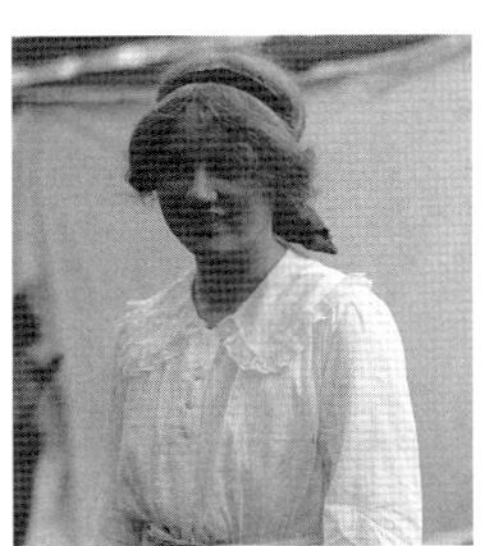

Source pictures for *Crossing The Stream*.

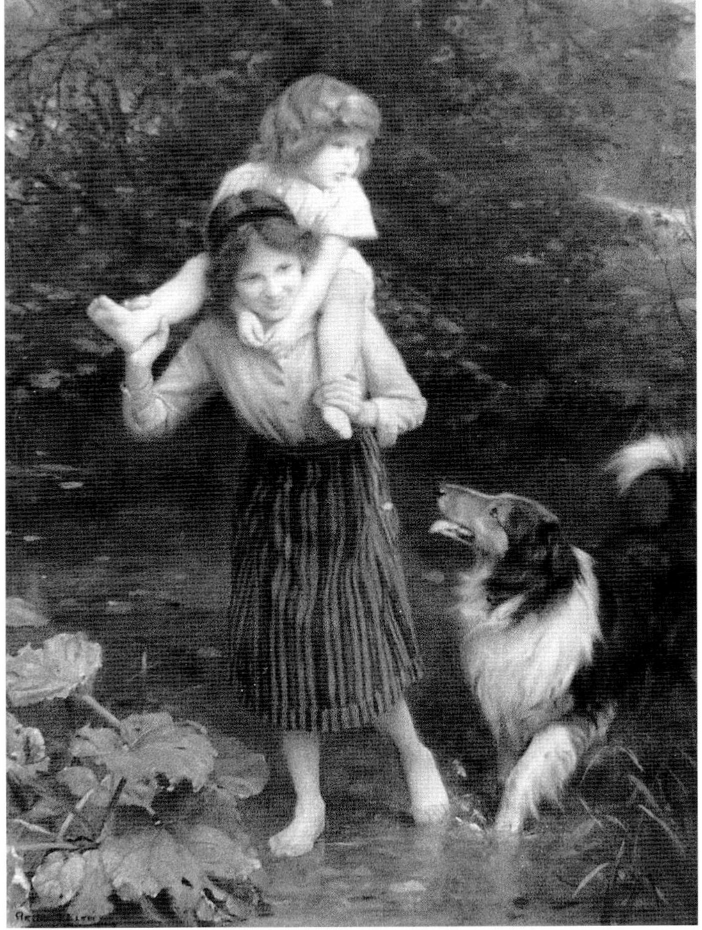

Crossing The Stream

There's Room For You
signed and dated 1920 (or 1922)
Details of original painting unknown.

Not to be confused with *Any Room For Me*, 1897, or *There's Room for You*, 1909, or *Room For One More*, 1910. American colour calendar *There's Room For You*, reproduced by Thos. D. Murphy Co., 1925 and 1930, and on a fan in 1926. **See page 87**.

You Dare *signed and dated 1921*
Details of original painting unknown.

A girl stands on stone steps playing with a St. Bernard while a boy sits on bottom step filling a spray pump from a watering can. Not to be confused with *You Dursn't*, 1905.

American colour calendar manufactured by Thos. D. Murphy Co., 1923 and 1926. **See page 87**.

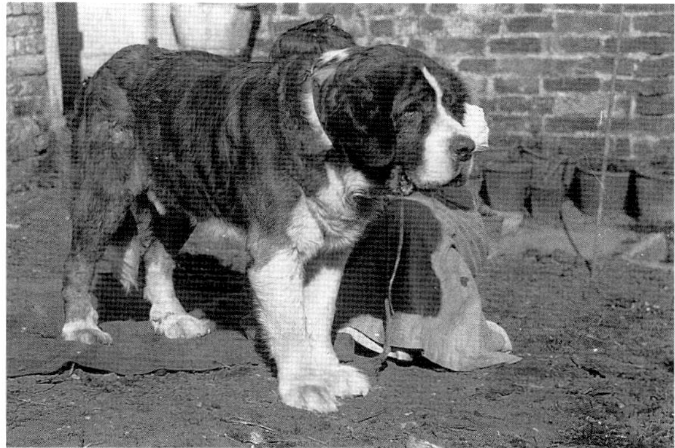

Source picture for *You Dare*.

A Trial Trip *signed and dated 1921 (or 1922)*
Details of original painting unknown.

American colour calendar manufactured by Thos. D. Murphy Co. 1924. **See page 87**.

A Loyal Guardian *signed and dated 1922*
Details of original painting unknown.

This work features cows from a much earlier painting.

American colour calendar manufactured by Thos. D. Murphy Co., 1927. **See page 86**.

Marjorie *signed and dated 1923*
Oil on canvas, 20¼ins x 16ins (51.5cm x 40.5cm), signed and dated 1923, sold at the Studio Sale (Lot 20) and now owned by the author. She is wearing an artificial silk dress which was cool to wear in the very hot summer especially in the studio at St. John's Wood Art School, where she was a student from 1921-1925. He also photographed her in this pose. An earlier painting of Marjorie was exhibited at the Royal Academy, 1917 (No.557), details unknown.

No print was made. **See frontispiece**.

Just For A Minute *circa 1920*
Details of original painting unknown.

Elsley features a colour print of his 1893 painting *A Dead Heat*. He also features the shuttlecock, a favourite prop. cf. *Do Be Careful*, 1912. Not to be confused with *Wait A Minute*, 1893.

American colour calendar manufactured by Thos. D. Murphy Co., 1926. **See page 87**.

[Portrait Of An American Family] *circa 1924*
Details of original painting unknown.

In 1924 Elsley was commissioned by an American oil mogul to paint a portrait of himself, his wife and their four children. The commission was almost lost because Arthur had put the letter aside but it was found much later when Emm was sorting out the family accounts.

The family were painted from photographs sent from America. Elsley sent a photograph of the unfinished canvas to America, which at this stage did not include the father who later arrived in England by ocean liner. Elsley then travelled to Liverpool to meet and photograph him. This work was not reproduced commercially.

Unfinished painting without the father.

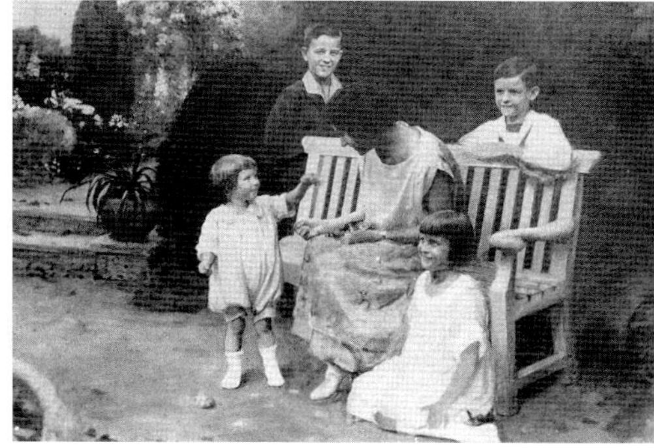

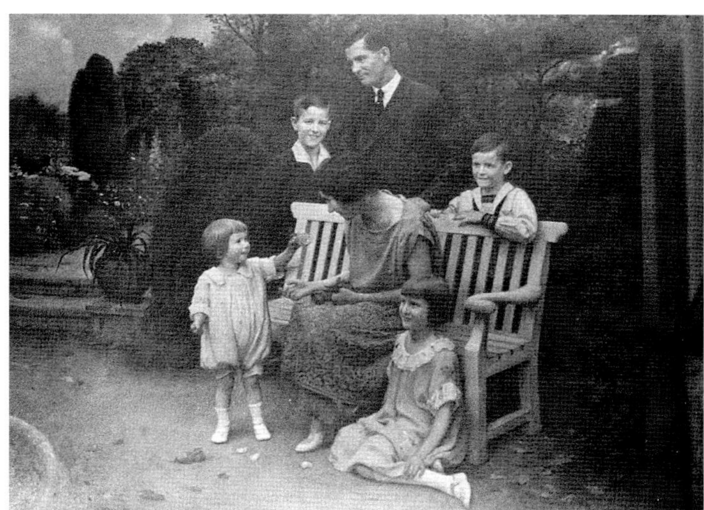

[Portrait Of An American Family]

BIBLIOGRAPHY

Anon "The Railway Invasion of the Artists' Quarter, St. John's Wood" (*The Sketch*, November 1894) p.195
Anon "The New Railway to London" (*Cassell's Family Magazine*, 1897) pp.492-500
Anon "Pictures of English Child-Life" (*Cassell's Family Magazine*, 1896) pp.461-8
Anon "How a Chromo-Lithograph is Printed" (*The Strand Magazine*, Vol.XXVII No.5, January 1904) pp.33-9
Barr, Robert "The Christmas Picture" (*The Idler Magazine*, Vol.V1, November 1894) pp.520-6
Bibby's Quarterly – Literary Supplement: Spring 1901, Christmas 1901, Spring 1902, Autumn 1902, Christmas 1902, Summer 1908
Blackburn, Henry *Academy Notes* (Chatto and Windus, London 1875-1907)
Blackburn, Henry *Royal Academy Sketches* (Chatto and Windus, London 1878-1906)
Bulletin of the Russell-Cotes Art Gallery & Museum, December 1936, p.48
Byatt, Anthony *Picture Postcards and Their Publishers 1894-1939* (Golden Age Books, Malvern 1978)
Collector's Mart No.24, September/October 1988
Daniels, Jeffrey *Solomon - A Family of Artists* (The Inner London Education Authority, 1985)
Dempsey, Mike *Bubbles Early Advertising from A. & F. Pears Ltd* (Fontana Paperbacks, 1978)
Dictionary of National Biography
Furniss, Harry *The Works of Charles Burton Barber* (Cassell and Co., 1896)
Gascoigne, Bamber *How to Identify Prints* (Thames & Hudson, 1986)
Gordon, Dr. Catherine *Index of Oil Paintings in Public Collections* (unpublished manuscript)
Graves, Algernon *Dictionary of Artists 1876-93* (George Bell & Sons, 1908)
Graves, Algernon *Royal Academy Exhibitors 1769-93* (George Bell & Sons, 1905)
Hadfield, John *Every Picture Tells a Story* (Herbert Press, 1985)
Hamilton, Clayton "Children in Paintings" (*Munsey's Magazine*, c.1909) pp.431-8
Hook, Philip & Poltimore, Mark *Popular 19th Century Painting* (Antique Collectors' Club, 1986)
Johnson J. & Greutzner, A *The Dictionary of British Artists 1880-1940* (Antique Collectors' Club 1890)
Kelly's Directory for London (various dates 1891-1914)
Knight, Frank & Rutley *Lever Sale at the Bungalow and Rivington Hall, Horwich, Lancs* (catalogue, November 1925)
MacKenzie, Ian *British Prints* (Antique Collectors' Club, 1987)
Mitchell, Ann "The Intrigue of a Child's Face" (*Victoria Magazine*, U.S.A. c.1993)
Morris, Edward *Victorian & Edwardian Paintings in the Lady Lever Art Gallery* (H.M.S.O. 1994)
Morris, Edward *Art and Business in Edwardian England: The Making of the Lady Lever Art Gallery* (Oxford University Press for National Museums & Art Galleries on Merseyside, 1992)
North, Lawrence "The Child and His Dumb Friends" (*The Windsor Magazine*, 1911/12) pp.175-80
Oldcastle, John "The Art of Mr. Fred Morgan" (*The Windsor Magazine*, June 1905) pp.3-18
Oldcastle, John "Christmas in Pictureland as Rendered by the Old Masters and the New" (*The Windsor Magazine*, December 1898) pp.3-14
Peak, Arthur T. "The Evolution of Christmas Annuals" (*The Windsor Magazine*, Vol.II, December 1895) pp.697-709
Pears, A. & F. *Pears' Soap? Pears the First 200 Years* (Pears booklet, 1900)
Pope, Jessie "The Children's Season" (*The Windsor Magazine*, December 1910) pp.121-30
Register *A. & F. Pears Limited, Works of Art* (now held by the Unilever Archive)
Royal Academy Pictures (supplement to *The Magazine of Art* 1888-1915)
Simon, Caroline & Bourne, Susan *The Age of Innocence? – Children in Art 1830-1930* (Museum Services of Blackburn Burnley and Lancashire County, 1989)
The Studio (issues 1.9.1898, 15.11.1898, and *Winters Special* 1898/9)
The Years' Art (various dates 1880-1919)
Who Was Who (Adam & Charles Black, various dates)
When We Were Young (exhibition catalogue City Art Centre, Edinburgh 1989)
Vincent, Adrian *A Companion to Victorian and Edwardian Artists* (David and Charles, 1991)
Ward Locke & Co.'s Wonder Book 1918, 1920 and 1922
Wheatley, Marjorie "Arthur J. Elsley the Children's Artist" (*This England*, Winter 1981) p.15
Wood, Christopher *The Dictionary of Victorian Painters* (Antique Collectors' Club, 1971, 2nd Ed. 1978)
Exhibition catalogues for the following:
    Nottingham, Castle Museum
    The Fine Art Society
    Institute of Painters in Oil Colours
Van Der Veer, Lenore "Models" (*Pearson's Magazine* Vol.XII, September 1901) pp.235-43
Van Der Veer, Lenore "A Man of Many Poses" (*The Royal Magazine*, December 1901) pp.162-5

EXHIBITIONS

Copyright reserved indicates the reproduction rights were sold separately, often prior to the exhibition.

The Royal Academy, Summer Exhibition

1878	(Exhibit 600)	*Portrait Of An Old Pony*	sold for 10 guineas
1880	(Exhibit 631)	*Spring* and *Autumn*	pair sold for £13.2s
1884	(Exhibit 48)	*Students*	unsold at 25 guineas
	(Exhibit 711)	*Bimba*	no price given/not for sale
1885	(Exhibit 892)	*Private And Confidential*	sold for 30 guineas
1886	(Exhibit 613)	*Vere Fane Benett-Stanford, Esq.,*	not for sale
	(Exhibit 765)	*Romps*	no price given
1887	(Exhibit 474)	*A Stitch In Time*	sold for 30 guineas
	(Exhibit 635)	*Contemplation*	sold for 15 guineas
1888	(Exhibit 51)	*Castles In The Air*	unsold at £50
	(Exhibit 415)	*A Challenge*	unsold at 40 guineas
1890	(Exhibit 563)	*The Baliff's (sic) Daughter of Islington*	unsold at £60
	(Exhibit 1043)	*An Unwilling Partner*	sold for £150, copyright reserved
1891	(Exhibit 657)	*Bob*	no price given
	(Exhibit 1156)	*Victims*	unsold at £250, copyright reserved
1892	(Exhibit 135)	*Don't Tell*	unsold at £120, copyright reserved
	(Exhibit 1008)	*I'se Biggest*	sold for £150, copyright reserved
1893	(Exhibit 516)	*A Dead Heat*	sold for £150, copyright reserved
1894	(Exhibit 911)	*Wait A Minute*	sold for £150, copyright reserved
1895	(Exhibit 325)	*Make Haste!*	sold for £150, copyright reserved
	(Exhibit 484)	*Snapdragon*	unsold at £180, copyright reserved
1896	(Exhibit 8)	*Soft Persuasion*	unsold at £150, copyright reserved
	(Exhibit 607)	*Motherly Care*	unsold at £150, copyright reserved
	(Exhibit 698)	*Pets*	unsold at £150, copyright reserved
1897	(Exhibit 705)	*Chicks*	unsold at £160, copyright reserved
	(Exhibit 1046)	*A Tempting Slide*	unsold at £160, copyright reserved
1898	(Exhibit 463)	*Hard Pressed*	no price given
	(Exhibit 891)	*Breakers Ahead*	unsold at £200, copyright reserved
1899	(Exhibit 579)	*At Bay*	sold for £120, copyright reserved
	(Exhibit 743)	*Divided Affection*	sold for £150, copyright reserved
	(Exhibit 880)	*Jackie and Herbie, Sons of Capt. J. Medlicott Vereker*	not for sale
1901	(Exhibit 890)	*Hold Up*	sold for £175
1902	(Exhibit 533)	*Spring Songs*	unsold/not for sale
	(Exhibit 712)	*I Sent A Letter To My Love*	sold for £200
1903	(Exhibit 286)	*Ladies First*	unsold/not for sale
	(Exhibit 391)	*Golden Hours*	unsold/not for sale
1905	(Exhibit 289)	*Good Night*	sold for 175 guineas
	(Exhibit 416)	*Baby's Turn*	unsold/not for sale
	(Exhibit 524)	*Won't You Try?*	unsold/not for sale
1906	(Exhibit 43)	*A Tempting Bait*	unsold/not for sale
1907	(Exhibit 832)	*Never Mind*	unsold/not for sale
1908	(Exhibit 832)	*The First Love Letter*	unsold/not for sale
1909	(Exhibit 271)	*There's Room For You*	unsold/not for sale
1910	(Exhibit 746)	*Blind Man's Buff*	unsold/not for sale
1912	(Exhibit 473)	*As Good As Ever*	unsold/not for sale
1913	(Exhibit 95)	*Charity*	unsold/not for sale
1914	(Exhibit 377)	*Bedtime*	unsold/not for sale
1915	(Exhibit 554)	*Good Night*	unsold/not for sale
	(Exhibit 891)	*Becton Bunny, Hants*	oil, not for sale
1917	(Exhibit 557)	*Marjorie*	not for sale
1927	(Exhibit 384)	*An Italian Garden, Casa Leoni, Bergamo*	not for sale

The Royal Society of British Artists, London

Winter 1881	(Exhibit 204)	*The Rule Of Three*	15 guineas
Spring 1882	(Exhibit 448)	*A Study*	10 guineas
Winter 1882	(Exhibit 235)	*Mother And Son*	10 guineas
Spring 1891	(Exhibit 348)	*The Lowing Herd Go Forth To Meet Their Young*	35 guineas
Spring 1897	(Exhibit 71)	*Homeward Bound*	no price given

The Walker Art Gallery, Liverpool, Autumn Exhibition

1885	(Exhibit 60)	*Students*	20 guineas
1887	(Exhibit 841)	*A Rest Day*	40 guineas
1888	(Exhibit 141)	*Castles In The Air*	40 guineas
1889	(Exhibit 1383)	*The Baliff's (sic) Daughter of Islington*	60 guineas
1892	(Exhibit 1047)	*The Christmas Goose*	£100
1893	(Exhibit 144)	*Who's That?*	£80
1894	(Exhibit 289)	*Which Hand Will You Have?*	£130, copyright reserved
1895	(Exhibit 40)	*First Favourite*	no price given
1900	(Exhibit 209)	*Little Bo Peep*	100 guineas
1903	(Exhibit 863)	*Golden Hours*	£250
1904	(Exhibit 831)	*A Tempting Bait*	no price given
1908	(Exhibit 1043)	*Pick Of The Litter*	£150, copyright reserved

The Institute of Painters in Oil Colours, London, Winter Exhibition

1884	(Exhibit 496)	*Mid-day Meal*
	(Exhibit 592)	*Students*
1886	(Exhibit 58)	*A Rest Day*
1887	(Exhibit 377)	*A Smithy*
1888	(Exhibit 555)	*On The Sick List*
1889	(Exhibit 164)	*A Good Samaritan*
	(Exhibit 515)	*A Siesta*
1890	(Exhibit 559)	*More Frightened Than Hurt*
	(Exhibit 661)	*Early Risers*
1892	(Exhibit 418)	*What's That?*
1893	(Exhibit 424)	*Peep Bo!*
1894	(Exhibit 224)	*Here's Father!*
1895	(Exhibit 355)	*A Tight Fit*

French Gallery, London, Winter Exhibition

1878	(Exhibit 116)	*A Homestead*	price unknown

Dudley Gallery, London, Winter Exhibition

1879	(Exhibit 277)	*A Rustic Study*	8 guineas

The Institute of Fine Art, Glasgow

1889	(Exhibit 231)	*Castles In The Air*	40 guineas
1894	(Exhibit 183)	*Which Hand Will You Have*	£130

Manchester City Art Gallery

1889	(Exhibit 99)	*Day Dream*	30 guineas
1890	(Exhibit 183)	*The Lowing Herd Go Forth To Meet Their Young*	22 guineas

The Royal Society of Artists, Birmingham

Autumn 1897	(Exhibit 194)	*Caught Napping*	£130
Spring 1903	(Exhibit 148)	*Spring Songs*	80 guineas
Autumn 1903	(Exhibit 100)	*The New Love*	£130, copyright reserved

Nottingham, Castle Museum

Autumn 1886	(Exhibit 503)	*Contemplation*	£21
	(Exhibit 539)	*Romps*	£10
Autumn 1887	(Exhibit 449)	*Chums*	£12.12s

Victoria Gallery, Bath, Opening Exhibition

Autumn 1900 (Exhibit 83) *Early Risers* [loaned by the founder of the Gallery, George Woodiwiss]

The Crystal Palace, London

1891 *The Baliff's (sic) Daughter of Islington* [Elsley was awarded a silver medal for this exhibit]

Cork International Exhibition

1902 (Exhibit 477) *Late For School* [watercolour loaned by *The Illustrated London News*, probably a copy]

ELSLEY PAINTINGS IN PUBLIC COLLECTIONS

Russell-Cotes Art Gallery and Museum, East Cliff, Bournemouth
A Tempting Bait, 1906

Hartlepool Museum Services, Sir William Gray House, Clarence Road, Hartlepool
So Tired, 1894

Lady Lever Art Gallery, Port Sunlight, Liverpool
Besieged, 1893

The Royal Liverpool Children's Hospital, Alderhey, Eaton Road, Liverpool
Here He Comes, 1901
Hold Tight, 1902

Royal Pavilion Art Gallery and Museum, Brighton
Picking Primroses, 1902
Crossing The Stream, 1920 (on loan to Preston Manor)
A Quiet Afternoon (pony and foal), 1928

Preston Manor, 194 Preston Road, Brighton
Jim, 1880
Ellen Benett-Stanford On Her Horse Congress, 1885
Pickle, 1893
Faithful And Fearless Kylin, 1917
Chu-Ki, 1927

MODERN PRINTS OF ELSLEY'S WORKS

Titles are those given by the companies and are not, necessarily, the titles given in this book.

The Medici Society, London
Baby's Birthday
Children Snowballing
The Favourite Of The Litter
Golden Hours
Love At First Sight
The Happy Pair
Pick Of The Litter
Never Mind
Rescue Party
A Tempting Bait

Felix Rosenstiel's Widow & Son Ltd., London
The Huntsman's Pet
Tea Time
High Expectations
The New Dress
Family Favourites
Love At First Sight
The Home Team

Thomas Ross & Co., London
Pick-a-Back

Stephen Selby Collection, London
Play Time
Goodnight
Wake Up It's Christmas

INDEX OF ILLUSTRATED PAINTINGS & PRINTS